Sociology on Culture

G000146442

Culture has become a touchstone of interdisciplinary conversation. For readers interested in sociology, the social sciences, and the humanities, this book maps major classical and contemporary analyses and controversies about culture in relation to social processes, everyday life, and forms of difference such as race, class, and gender. Hall, Neitz, and Battani discuss:

- self and identity
- stratification
- the Other
- the cultural histories of modernity and postmodernity
- culture and power
- production of culture
- the problem of the audience
- action, social movements, and change.

Sociology on Culture pays little respect to boundaries, drawing on diverse intellectual perspectives and a variety of topics about culture and the arts, from various historical time periods and regions of the world. The authors advocate cultivating the sociological imagination by engaging with the myriad of languages and perspectives in the social sciences and humanities, while cultivating cultural studies by developing the sociological imagination.

John R. Hall is Professor of Sociology at the University of California, Davis.

Mary Jo Neitz is Professor of Sociology at the University of Missouri-Columbia.

Marshall Battani is Assistant Professor of Sociology at Grand Valley State University, Michigan.

Sociology on Culture

John R. Hall, Mary Jo Neitz
and Marshall Battani

Routledge
Taylor & Francis Group

LONDON AND NEW YORK

First published 2003
by Routledge
11 New Fetter Lane, London EC4P 4EE

Simultaneously published in the USA and Canada
by Routledge
29 West 35th Street, New York, NY 10001

Routledge is an imprint of the Taylor & Francis Group

© 2003 John R. Hall, Mary Jo Neitz and Marshall Battani

Typeset in Times New Roman by Taylor & Francis Books Ltd
Printed and bound in Great Britain by TJ International Ltd,
Padstow, Cornwall

British Library Cataloguing in Publication Data
A catalogue record for this book is available from the British Library

Library of Congress Cataloging in Publication Data
A catalog record for this book has been requested

ISBN 0–415–28484–8 (hbk)
ISBN 0–415–28485–6 (pbk)

Contents

Preface and acknowledgements

Cultural analysis cannot be reduced to any single approach or discipline. Therefore, the present book is meant both to serve as a general introduction to the sociology of culture, mass media, and art, and to explore sociological approaches relevant to cultural studies and its various domains – for example, art history, mass communication, literary criticism, visual studies, and popular culture. In addition, people directly concerned with culture, and also those interested in journalism, market research, clothing and textiles, hotel management, business, and diverse other fields stand to gain from a sociological basis for understanding their own professional worlds and their personal experiences. Finally, the book offers a window on the sociological analysis of culture for graduate students and faculty in both sociology and the social sciences and humanities more broadly.

Three features of our approach deserve brief comment. First, we seek to provide an understanding of basic dynamics involving culture and the major controversies about them, but in our view any effort to consolidate a "comprehensive" introduction to the sociology of culture would do a disservice to the vitality of cultural studies, and probably signal its demise. Moreover, from a practical point of view, relevant research has mushroomed beyond what any introduction could consider in a meaningful way. In lieu of a comprehensive introduction, we instead explore an incomplete mosaic of specific topics that illustrate the sociological issues at stake. Second, we hope that readers will be provoked to pursue topics of special interest to them, and the suggested readings at the end of each chapter offer interesting points of departure, while extensive citations within each chapter direct readers to articles and books that examine specific issues. Third, the book is short enough that it may be used in courses as a core text, in conjunction with one of the several very good collections of readings on culture now available (for example Mukerji and Schudson 1991; Long 1997; Jameson and Miyoshi 1998; P. Smith 1998; T. Miller 2001; Spillman 2002; Friedland and Mohr 2003).

Sociology on Culture is based in part on an earlier book, *Culture: Sociological Perspectives* (J. Hall and Neitz 1993). For the present book, the three coauthors deeply appreciate the editorial support and encouragement of Mari Shullaw, our editor at Routledge, and the help of James McNally, also at Routledge. We also wish to thank Brad Wing for his assistance on Chapter 11, and Eiko Ikegami and Kyu Hyun Kim for their thoughtful and fascinating reflections on the cultural significance of Figure 5.2.

Finally, the authors gratefully acknowledge the permission of the University of Chicago Press for our inclusion in Chapter 3 of a revised version of sections from the essay by John R. Hall, "The capital(s) of culture," which first appeared in Michèle Lamont and Marcel Fournier, eds., *Cultivating Differences: Symbolic Boundaries and the Making of Inequality*, © 1992 by The University of Chicago, all rights reserved.

John R. Hall
Mary Jo Neitz
Marshall Battani

1   Introduction

> We say, "The wind is blowing," as if the wind were actually a thing at rest which, at a
> given point in time, begins to move and blow. We speak as if the wind were separate
> from the blowing, as if a wind could exist which did not blow.
>
> (Norbert Elias 1978, p. 112)

When you read the word "wind," think about "culture." Is it like the wind? Some cultural material – for example habits and gestures that are part of distinctive social repertoires – has its primary existence when people act it out. Other culture – a movie, for example – might seem different from the wind because there is a physical object called "the film." However, things are not so simple. Movies exist as very long strips of celluloid (or, increasingly, digital files), but when people talk about "the movie" they typically are not referring to the physical object at all. Indeed, films have very little significance unless people see them. This circumstance identifies a central puzzle about culture: the physical aspects of objects like films and paintings make culture seem like a thing in itself – a view that is reinforced insofar as we think of culture as external to us as individuals, and potentially capable of influencing the ways we act. Yet either people embody culture in daily life, or it lacks any social vitality and ends up gathering dust on a shelf in some warehouse. Culture is not the wind, but like the wind, it is difficult to describe with a language that treats it solely as though it were a material object.

When the sociologist Mustafa Emirbayer issued his "manifesto for a relational sociology" (1997), he quoted Norbert Elias about the wind to illustrate his argument that the "language" of sociology is sometimes not up to the task of analyzing the social world. Sociological descriptions, Emirbayer warned, too often focus on static things and conditions rather than dynamic, unfolding processes. To help redress this imbalance, in this book we explore a variety of languages that offer different ways to talk about culture in relation to social processes and everyday life.

The importance of being open to analysis through multiple languages becomes obvious when we consider a basic sociological point: a variety of issues call for consideration even in relation to a single overall set of events. In turn, diverse languages help explore diverse issues. Consider how things have changed in the wake of the terrorist attacks of September 11, 2001. These attacks, and other ones since, have had many different consequences – economic, political, psychological, and so forth – in diverse corners of the world. When we focus specifically on the cultural aspects, numerous questions emerge for people both in the U.S. and around the world. Some of the questions are controversial even as questions, leaving to one side how they might be answered:

- What sort of cultural milieu, and social processes of recruitment within it, would bring people to carry out acts that result in the deaths of large numbers of innocent people, and kill the perpetrators in the process?
- How do mass media in various parts of the world portray events in moments of social crisis, and how do their portrayals affect subsequent events?
- Are the West and the Islamic world undergoing a basic cultural "clash of civilizations," as Huntington (1996) calls it?
- Why is enormous world sympathy for the people of the United States as victims of the 9/11 attacks accompanied by resentment among significant numbers of people in Europe, the Middle East, and elsewhere of the United States government as a dominating global power, or even a terrorist state?
- What is considered terrorism by different peoples and states, and how are their definitions tied to issues of national identity? How, for example, have Palestinians and Israelis experienced 9/11?
- How do the destabilizing activities of relatively small groups of people – the Irish Republican Army or the Chechnian rebels in Russia, for example – affect wider social movements and the hearts and minds of people more broadly? Why do they sometimes amplify conflict, and under other conditions precipitate movement toward resolving conflicts?
- How, in the near term and over a longer period of time, are memories of terrorist events enshrined in people's minds, in public rituals, and at public memorials in various parts of the world? (See Figure 1.1.)
- What about relationships in various parts of the world between peoples of different ethnic identities: will they change on the basis of world-historical tensions? Will changes fuel further tensions?

These are serious questions, much more serious than ones that are often raised about culture. Which goes to show that, as Ann Swidler (1986) observed, culture becomes more important in unsettled times of social unrest, revolution, war, and the like. In unsettled times, core cultural meanings are destabilized; in effect, they may come up for grabs. It is not this book's purpose to address the above questions directly, but to show how the sociology of culture can provide people with the tools to explore these as well as diverse other cultural matters – high and low, ephemeral and august. To do so, we submit, requires the "sociological imagination."

C. Wright Mills (1959) is well known for his call for people to develop the sociological imagination in order to identify connections between our personal lives and the social and historical contexts in which we live. Not so widely noted, Mills made the following comment about cultural symbols: "their social relevance lies in their use to justify or to oppose the arrangement of power and the positions within this arrangement of the powerful" (1959, p. 37). Culture, in his view, is not a frivolous or derivative topic of study; it is central to any understanding of society. To see that Mills was right, one need only note the diversity of culturally focused public issues – for example, about "multiculturalism," efforts to ban fox hunting, teaching the "Western canon," the global spread of fast food, and the issues raised above about 9/11. Like Mills, we believe that making sense of the social world requires a sociological imagination, and we also believe that the fully developed sociological imagination requires a deep appreciation of culture. However, there is still the puzzle that we posed at the outset about finding the languages to talk about culture.

Figure 1.1 On September 11, 2002, a service was held at the cathedral in Copenhagen, Denmark – the Vor Frue Kirke – in memory of those who died in the 9/11 attacks a year earlier. Yet despite widespread sympathy about the attacks, many Danes are deeply suspicious of United States foreign policy in their wake.

Source: J.R. Hall photograph.

Culture, sociology, and cultural studies

How should culture be studied, and what specifically do sociologists have to contribute? After all, there are a number of scholarly approaches. During the twentieth century, anthropology as a discipline laid a central claim to the study of culture (although up until the 1960s, and to a somewhat lesser degree thereafter, anthropologists concentrated on less developed societies). Historians certainly studied culture before the 1970s, but earlier in the twentieth century they were primarily interested in intellectual history – the great ideas. Like these other fields, sociology has a long but uneven history of engagement with issues of culture.

From its origins in the nineteenth century, sociology has been defined by a tension between science and interpretation. This tension largely accounts for the unevenness. Early social theorists were centrally concerned with culture. Karl Marx gave an important place to ideology and consciousness in his theory of revolution; Emile Durkheim explored both normlessness (anomie) and the power of collective rituals; and Max Weber analyzed religious validation of self-denying asceticism in relation to an increasingly rationally organized capitalist social order (see Martin 2001). During the early twentieth century, some sociologists sought to theorize culture in "scientific" ways, for example as the stuff of transmission from one generation to the next (Park and Burgess 1921), as the effect of association (Cooley *et al.* 1933), or as societal adjustment to the environment. Others – such as Alfred Schutz (1967), George Herbert Mead (1934), and Karl Mannheim (1937) – focused on cultural meanings and their interplay with the creative activities of social selves that emerge from interaction.

Whether scientific or interpretive, from the 1930s onward cultural concerns got pushed aside, especially in the U.S. and Britain, where sociologists strongly embraced the idea of progress through science, and increasingly pursued quantitative research and general theoretical formulations. By the middle of the twentieth century, sociology in the United States was becoming established as a legitimate scientific discipline within the growing institutional field of the modern research university. In this context, Talcott Parsons famously described the frames of reference of action as three systems – culture, society, and personality. Culture, in this formulation, is an overarching system of meaning. This cultural system provides (or fails to provide) social norms of conduct that sustain society as a system by integrating personalities into it (Parsons 1951; Parsons and Shils 1951).

Yet, as Elizabeth Long (1997) points out, even in the brief historical period of the 1950s and 1960s when Parsons was at the peak of his significance, important sociologists chose cultural interpretation over grand theory. At the beginning of the 1950s, David Riesman and two colleagues wrote a widely read book, *The Lonely Crowd* (1950). In it, Riesman described a succession of American character types, from the tradition-directed person, to the inner-directed person oriented to self-perfection in the world of work, to the other-directed person who is less interested in achievement than in social acceptance – gained with a "glad hand." At the end of the 1960s (which didn't really happen until the 1970s) Riesman's theme surfaced once again, in Daniel Bell's *The Cultural Contradictions of Capitalism* (1976), which presciently argued that the emergence of postindustrial society was creating a disjuncture between the cultural identities appropriate to social worlds of leisure versus those of work.

Parsons's dominance came between these two bookends. By the end of the 1970s, his holistic view of culture as a totalized normative system was becoming displaced by sociologists who looked in more fine-grained ways at cultural processes in everyday life. Like their colleagues in other fields, many sociologists of culture in the 1970s and 1980s became engaged by French theories of language and discourse. Indeed, since the 1960s culture as a subject of inquiry has changed radically. For anthropologists, historians, literary critics, feminists, philosophers, and scholars in the emerging domain of cultural studies, as well as for a wide range of sociologists, investigations of culture now provide ways to link our understandings of history, texts, and social life. Culture has become a touchstone that draws the social sciences and the humanities into interdisciplinary conversation with one another.

Nowhere is the new interdisciplinary emphasis more obvious than in the domain of cultural studies. Yet the relations between cultural studies and more traditional academic disciplines have involved certain tensions over how to study culture. Granted, the tensions are to some extent fueled by stereotypes that academics sometimes construct about approaches with which they disagree. It is all too easy for advocates of cultural studies to portray sociology as an aspiring science that uses quantitative "number crunching" to unmask "laws," thereby denying the existential and cultural bases of social life. By the opposite token, some sociologists (along with other scholars) would like to dismiss cultural studies as based on the outlandish belief that the world is nothing but a set of texts, with no reality outside the meanings of those texts. It is thus important to consider the origins of cultural studies and its relation to sociology.

What are those origins? Clearly, in the early post-World War II era, culture became an increasingly central feature of social life in Western societies, notably in the explosion of popular culture marked by the advent of rock 'n' roll music in the 1950s and the emergence of strong countercultural movements during the 1960s. When scholars began to kindle a renewed interest in culture, some of them – including sociologists – began to gravitate toward interdisciplinary and avowedly political approaches. Specifically, in Britain Raymond Williams, E.P. Thompson, Richard Hoggart, and Stuart Hall and their followers sought to understand the culture of industrial working-class people while simultaneously encouraging social change (T. Miller 2001; Maxwell 2001). Their efforts led to the founding of the Centre for Contemporary Cultural Studies at the University of Birmingham in 1964 (discussed in Chapter 7).

British approaches to cultural studies are marked by a strong commitment to substantive analysis powered by interdisciplinary eclecticism. Through the 1970s, 1980s, and 1990s, practitioners of cultural studies in Britain drew on a variety of theoretical inspirations, from the early twentieth-century Marxist Antonio Gramsci to the famous French thinker Michel Foucault. The French scholars – not only Foucault, but also Roland Barthes, Jacques Derrida, and others – emphasized the analysis of texts and discourses, and their ideas were especially influential when cultural studies began to be taken up in the U.S. in the 1970s and 1980s. There, it became especially strongly established among scholars in the humanities who – also influenced by the emergence of feminist theory and postcolonial studies of cultural domination – were seeking to break out of the strictures of an elite-defined literary and artistic canon.

Despite the eclectic character of cultural studies, they almost always critique power and engage explicitly with politics. As Lawrence Grossberg describes the project, it both operates within academic disciplines and nevertheless critiques the (sometimes implicitly political) restrictions of those disciplines. As for the question of whether the world can be reduced to its textual representations, Grossberg is quite clear. Despite a focus on discourse, in the final analysis cultural studies "is not interested in the discourse *per se* but in the articulations between everyday life and the formations of power. Thus it ends with a different understanding of the context than that with which it began" (1997, p. 5). In essence Grossberg presents cultural studies as a politically inspired project that employs theories of representation to understand constraints on change that derive both from the power of culture and from the exercise of power by groups that use culture as a tool of domination. This project would certainly seem at odds with the tradition that conceives of sociology as an impartial, or value-neutral, scientific practice. Yet two points are worth making. First, Max Weber, the sociologist who proposed value-neutrality as an approach to sociology, did not argue that inquiry should be completely unmotivated by politics; indeed, he thought it very difficult to avoid political and other value interests. What he sought were circumstances where politics did not dictate how research was conducted or what answers would be acceptable (J.R. Hall 1999, ch. 2). Second, Grossberg acknowledges the important contributions that work within disciplines can make to cultural studies.

Defining the sociological contribution to cultural studies would be much simpler if we could say definitively what constitutes *the* sociological perspective on culture and what does not. But the truth is that the development of cultural studies since the 1960s and the resurgence of interest in culture among sociologists, along with a gradually increasing and uneven transdisciplinary dialogue, make simple pronouncements impossible. Important developments in poststructuralism, critical theory, feminism, subaltern studies, as well as the mutual poaching by conventional disciplines, have created circumstances where no single discipline can claim to monopolize the subject matter that falls within its domain. In our view, this is all to the good. The present book will be read by some in relation to the ongoing debate about how to study culture and in what venues. However, we regard this debate as a largely metaphysical one based on rather abstract issues about the boundaries of things called disciplines. Trying to resolve such a debate seems like a policing task that is not particularly helpful for analyzing and understanding culture. In particular, we do not think it useful to reproduce turf battles by staking out some territory that supposedly constitutes *the* sociological perspective on culture. Instead, the "sociology on culture" that we explore is multifaceted, and it pays little respect to boundaries, either ones that inoculate sociology from ideas that supposedly lie "outside" it or, conversely, other boundaries that would protect cultural studies, anthropology, history, or other domains from sociological poaching.

Given our view, then, why the *sociology* of culture? The reason is simple. We agree with Grossberg about the relevance of disciplines. They have been important sites in the development of methodological strategies, theories, substantive knowledge, and debates that can be very useful in cultural analysis. Precisely at the time when specific topics of cultural studies – from popular culture and mass communications to music history, literary criticism, art history, visual studies, and cultural history – are undergoing rapid change and development, it is useful to take stock of how sociological thinking can contribute to the analysis of culture. To build from Grossberg's comment about the connection between culture and everyday life, culture is always a social phenomenon, thus subject to analysis through various sociological lenses. Textual or discourse analysis will be insufficient as an approach to culture, and so would be a sociology that hoped to ignore texts and discourse (Grindstaff 2000). For this broad agenda, we think that cultivating the sociological imagination can best be facilitated by engaging myriad languages and perspectives of the social sciences and humanities, while cultivating cultural studies can be enhanced by developing the sociological imagination. It is this interchange that we advocate.

Thinking about culture sociologically

To begin with, there are some basic issues about how we might try to talk about culture that will benefit from some sociological attention. These have to do with defining culture, whether to distinguish between culture and society, and how to use clear concepts without stereotyping the things to which they refer. Let's consider each of these issues in turn.

Defining culture

On the surface, debating definitions may seem trivial. But those who write about "culture" sometimes mean very different things by the term, and they thereby fit culture into alternative theories that offer radically different understandings. Anthropologists at the beginning of the twentieth century defined culture as the way of life of a people, or as what an individual needed to know to survive in a society, or as what could be learned by an individual and passed down in a society. Sometimes social scientists have tried to narrow the concept in order to give it more analytic rigor. Yet narrower definitions lead to debates about what should be included, because they fail to include phenomena that on the face of it seem cultural. Though this book could not possibly treat culture in all its manifestations, we need an approach that is open to encompassing all kinds of culture, including, for instance, political culture, religious culture, and – a topic that compels the attention of corporations and other social groups – organizational culture. It is important to recognize, for example, the distinctive cultures of the shop, the enterprise, and the office (Harper 1987; Biggart 1989; C. Davis 2000).

The general ferment around the concept of culture today makes it impossible to pin down an ironclad definition. With a word that covers as much as "culture," we can never hope to capture reality simply through careful definition. In particular, as our opening puzzle suggests, it would be a mistake to offer a definition that makes culture into a "thing," thereby "reifying" culture and closing off possibilities of understanding the complex and subtle processes that are culturally inflected. Yet, paradoxically, considering how to define culture may help us move beyond mere issues of definition to understand the very complexities of the social world that make any definition controversial.

A number of approaches define culture in part by differentiating it from other sociological concepts. Thus, some sociologists speak of the difference between culture and society. Other approaches offer *internal* differentiations of culture: "high" culture versus "mass" or "popular" culture, for example, and "material" versus "symbolic" culture. We will revisit these distinctions throughout this book. In doing so, we are not interested in proclaiming some point of view as the "right" answer. Instead, we pursue the pragmatic idea that there may be alternative useful ways of analyzing culture. We want to explore both what limitations alternative approaches might have and how they can contribute to our understanding of culture.

At the outset, addressing one issue – the distinction between material versus ideal culture – can help affirm our inclusive approach. We propose as a very general *working* definition – subject to refinement on the basis of further analysis – that culture encompasses: (1) *ideas, knowledge* (correct, wrong, or unverifiable belief), and *recipes* for doing things; (2) humanly fabricated *tools* (such as shovels, sewing machines, cameras, and computers); and (3) the *products* of social action that may be drawn upon in the further conduct of social life (a dish of curry, a television set, a photograph, or a high-speed train, for example). It is worth remembering that "culture" comes from the Latin for "cultivating" or tilling the soil. Culture, in this sense, amounts to the ways of taking care of things.

With this definition we intentionally include both "material" as well as "symbolic" culture. Why might such a definition prove controversial? Some anthropologists (M. Harris 1979) give material culture its due, and archaeologists emphasize its importance, perhaps because material culture more often survives the ravages of time, while a song or a gesture will easily be lost. Tools, from the plow to robotics, seem central to how we conduct life. So material culture has obvious importance. Yet sociologists and most cultural anthropologists have tended to give pride of place to symbols and ideas, not tools and material objects. Clifford Geertz, for example, once defined culture as "an historically transmitted pattern of meanings embodied in symbols, a system of inherited conceptions expressed in symbolic forms by means of which men [*sic*][1] communicate, perpetuate, and develop their knowledge about and attitudes toward life" (1973, p. 89). The inspiration for this narrower, "idealist" (for its emphasis on ideas) delineation of culture seems to come from two directions: (1) from many cultural anthropologists and sociologists themselves, who see symbols and ideas as *the* theoretically important aspect of culture; and (2) from their theoretical opponents – "materialists" who regard the most significant social forces to be processes of economics and politics driven more by calculations of self-interest than by meanings. Apparently the "idealist" cultural sociologists and anthropologists would hope to establish their own distinctive realm of expertise, while the "materialists" may think that limiting culture to ideas and beliefs will make it easier to discount arguments about its importance.

Any strong distinction between material and ideal culture obscures more than it reveals. Yet we are stuck with the puzzle of language that we discussed at the outset. The study of culture is limited by culture! Following a longstanding sociological usage, this book will refer to all identifiable complexes of culture, from the very concrete (e.g. a painting) to the more nebulous (e.g. a way of life) as "cultural objects." But it is important to keep in mind what we mean. Griswold defines a cultural object as "shared significance embodied in form. Significance refers to the object's incorporation of one or more symbols, which suggest a set of denotations and connotations, emotions and memories" (1986, p. 5). In using this term, we certainly do not intend to "reify" the "object" as a *physical* thing. As Griswold makes clear, even seemingly very concrete objects – texts or paintings for example – may exist not only (and perhaps not most importantly) as physical objects. They also come to the surface as episodes of our socially shared but intimately subjective experiences. Are not obviously material cultural objects also ideal in some respects? Consider a play viewed by a theater audience. This cultural object has both material and ideal elements – speech and gestures, costumes and sets. Yet all of the material features have their rationales as practices because of the effects they can create in the minds of audience members. So it is with television, or with material products that become significant symbols, like clothing and Coca-Cola. In a world in which "oral tradition" has come to play a less and less significant role in the transmission of culture, even ideal culture is now typically passed along through use of technologies that depend on material process – the printing that makes this book possible as a medium for ideal culture, for example. Given the interdependence and interpenetration of material and ideal culture, it would be presumptuous to rule some kinds of culture out of bounds by fiat. Instead, it is important to consider the interplay of ideas and material things in cultural objects.

Culture and society

In turn, we expect to find myriad interpenetrating relationships between cultural objects and social life. Indeed, much culture is so deeply ingrained in people's habits and conduct that it may seem difficult to distinguish between, on the one hand, culture and, on the other hand, "the social" (social actors and their interrelationships or, in more objectifying terms, "society"). Certainly a distinction between culture and the social should not be imposed in any way that closes off inquiry, for example about the degree to which conduct of individuals is cultural versus how, and to what extent, it involves individual "agency" or what Parsons called "voluntary action." Yet for just this reason it is important to maintain an analytic distinction between society and culture. Why? Because there is no reason to assume an equivalence between the two, or some seamless transmission belt that connects one to the other. Indeed, the most important contribution of the recently deceased cultural sociologist Pierre Bourdieu was to show how much slippage there can be between the cultural structures of norms within a society and how people carry out practices in relation to them. As Bourdieu showed in *Outline of a Theory of Practice* (1977), people do not just follow cultural scripts when they give gifts or throw weddings. Rather, they use such scripts in innovative ways to accomplish particular ends of their own.

The same sort of distinction needs to be asserted at the level of group cultures and social groups. Here again, to collapse the distinction between culture and society would be to close off our understandings of relations between the two. This point has been developed by sociologist Herbert Gans in relation to matters of "taste." Some of us like poetry; others don't. One person may like folk music; that person's friends may loathe it. Gans says that there are "*taste cultures* which function to entertain, inform, and beautify life, among other things, and which express values and standards of taste and aesthetics." His conception includes material things such as automobiles and appliances, "insofar as ordinary consumer goods also express aesthetic values or functions" (1974, pp. 10–11). This approach should make it possible to identify a complex of cultural tastes that forms some sort of package – local skateboard culture or country-club culture, for example. Indeed, this usage reflects a growing tendency among sociologists to conceptualize culture in terms of situated meanings and "expressive symbols."

Yet Gans distinguishes culture from society: "Users [of a particular taste culture] who make similar choices of values and taste culture content will be described as publics of an individual taste culture, or *taste publics*, even though they are unorganized aggregates rather than organized publics" (1974, pp. 10–11). Gans underscores the difference between culture and society (where society is composed, in his terms, of "publics") in order to anticipate an empirical feature of the social world – namely, that there is no simple relationship between taste cultures and taste publics. The *same* culture may be used by *different* publics in ways that have little in common. Consider the country-and-western bar in a city of the American Midwest. The distinctive rockabilly and neo-bluegrass music, the cowboy/girl style of dressing, two-step dancing, and special forms of sociability and courtship offer badges of honor and a culturally saturated arena of action for a public attracted to a "country" taste sensibility. Other people (that is, participants in another taste public), say upper-middle-class urbanites, may visit a country-and-western bar not to *participate* in the spectacle (they would hardly know how), but simply to *view* it as some exotic anthropological excursion (see Figure 1.2).

Members of any given taste public don't necessarily congregate in a single place like the country-and-western bar: Gans's definition of the term "public" explicitly describes a diffuse social stratum. However, the same logic about diverse publics applies for both the diffuse and the face-to-face group. Consider "country" fashions: urbanites may wear cowboy/girl boots, hats, and belts, "duster" jackets, and the like, but the meanings they convey usually do not connect with the core meanings of country-and-western culture. Conversely, the hard core of the country-and-western bar crowd may connect with a quite different culture when they watch football games on television. People of *one* taste *public* may participate in a *variety* of taste *cultures*, perhaps maintaining their own distinctive way of doing so.

The country-and-western example shows that culture becomes "embedded" in our daily lives. To be sure, the specific embedding is different for the urbanites and the country-and-western taste public. But the embeddedness in each case serves as a reminder that even a sensible distinction between culture and society runs the danger of becoming reified. We all live in part by way of habits, manners, recipes, rules, mores, ethics, rituals, procedures, and other cognitive or symbolic devices. These kinds of "ideal" cultural objects can be distinguished analytically from structural features

Figure 1.2 The Texas two-step remains popular today, although other features of the culture
surrounding it have changed somewhat.

Source: Russell Lee Photograph Collection CN11405, The Center for American History, The University of
Texas at Austin.

(enduring patterns) of societies, but in the empirical world, "culture" and "structure"
may in some cases amount to mirror-image ways of describing the same thing. In
other words, culture often forms a seamless part of our worlds.

As an example, consider a hierarchical organization with definite positions of
authority, say a corporation that produces handheld computer equipment. It would be
possible to describe the factory floor in "structural" terms, based on its social-role
positions and their relationships, both formal and informal. Yet obedience to
authority is itself a cultural trait, as are respect, camaraderie, and an ethos of equality,
to say nothing of all the rules, policies, and rituals of the corporation. Thus, we must
recognize, in this example and in general, that "social structure" does not always exist
independently of "culture." Indeed, insofar as culture defines a patterned basis for a
group's structure, we may speak of such a pattern as a "cultural structure."[2]

The analytic distinction between taste culture and taste public and the problem of
culture and structure cut different ways in considering the relation between culture

and society. In the first case, the taste culture/taste public distinction absolutely requires that we maintain a firm distinction between culture and society, so that we can begin to examine the complex ways cultures are sustained, on the one hand, and, on the other, how people draw on culture in their everyday lives. Conversely, the embeddedness of culture in the structures of society suggests that maintaining a sharp distinction may sometimes prevent us from seeing the ways that structural aspects of society are culturally shaped. Rather than adopting any rigid theoretical position emphasizing a distinction between culture and society or their inherent unity, we therefore must explore the complicated relationships between aspects of things described in both theoretical languages.

Culture, classification, and typification

The fact that the distinction between society and culture is both problematic and important brings us to a related point, namely that cultural objects often are not always clearly fixed in their boundaries and their forms. When a cultural object is entirely and unambiguously contained within a category, we may speak of "classification." Thus, we know that the *Mona Lisa* as a painting is a particular cultural object, even if what the *Mona Lisa* "is" differs for its producer and its billions of (direct and mediated) viewers over the centuries. Similarly, one brand of cold refreshment beverage is not to be confused with another (at least not if their manufacturers have their way). True, in cases other than trademarked products there may be a question of where to draw the line that establishes the boundary of a class of cultural objects, but even in such circumstances of ambiguity social processes sometimes impose unambiguous choices. The choice between "pure" and "impure" does not leave much middle ground (M. Douglas 1966; cf. Zerubavel 1991).

   However, there is also a cultural logic that goes against the grain of clearcut classification: describing a cultural object often involves "typification," that is, the identification of a general pattern, even though the cultural objects themselves may "shade off," or differ to varying degrees, from the typical pattern. Thus, when we see a couch we usually do not run into trouble calling it by its name. Yet some pieces of furniture seem like couches, but not quite. The typification "couch" overlaps with typifications of other cultural objects, for example "loveseat," "daybed," "settee," and "sofa." Similarly, we may know a famous rendition of a song (the Beatles' "Yellow Submarine"), yet songs can be performed in many different ways, by both their originators and others. Folk songs that have been passed down through generations, for example, percolate through multiple channels, where they may be changed here and there, thus resulting in the proliferation of alternative versions, such that no one version is "correct." At a more general level of typification, categorizations of music can run into trouble, for example at the borderlands between calypso, reggae, ska, and Hip-Hop. Thus, it is important to keep in mind that *typifications* of culture do not always directly correspond to the cultural objects that they describe. Indeed, the contents of any given category or typification (rock 'n' roll music or Christian theology) may change over time.

   One well known example of "shading off" has to do with the cultural symbols of social interaction. As Clifford Geertz observed, "Contracting your eyelids on purpose when there exists a public code in which so doing counts as a conspiratorial signal *is* winking" (1973, p. 6). The definition of a wink seems straightforward. But the important thing to remember, Geertz goes on, is that a person can make this objective sign take on diverse meanings. A given wink can be an act of flirtation, a high sign, a parody of another's wink, or even a fake wink to make a third person think something clandestine is afoot between the winker and someone else. Geertz's example shows that the cultural materials we deal in are often especially important for the shades of meaning and nuances they take on in concrete situations, while, by the same token, the very capacity to recognize shades of meaning depends upon the cultural activity of typification.

"Typification" and "shading off" together represent an alternative approach that contrasts with "classification." In either approach we deal mentally with ranges of cultural objects which are themselves sometimes heterogeneous, but we deal with them in different ways. How culture works thus depends on both the particular culture and the cognitive ways that people attach significance to it.

The cultural possibilities of classification and typification that are part of social life also are problems for cultural analysis. This is so because the institutional patterns of culture identified by cultural analysts – such as "the Renaissance," "the Protestant work ethic," "jazz," and "reality television shows" – do not have the same empirical reality as, say, a chair, a painting, a person, the activity of singing, or a book. Such patterns are sociologists' (and literary critics' and historians', etc.) classifications and typifications. Cultural analysis thus is engaged in a process found in culture more generally – drawing lines of categories and defining patterns of typifications. Such analytic constructs do not completely describe reality, but they are useful nevertheless. Classifications give us ways of identifying what may be important aspects of a phenomenon, so that they can be examined in relation to comparable phenomena or other aspects of the same phenomenon. Typifications can be used as working hypotheses about how a complex of cultural material "fits together" as a set of meanings and, perhaps, how it works in social processes.

For example, what if we wanted to study the culture of a particular social group, say the middle class in the Netherlands? It probably would be possible to identify certain cultural traits of dress, diet, manners, childrearing practices, and so forth. A cluster of such traits might be proposed as a typification, "Dutch middle-class culture." Such a sociological typification is called an "ideal type" or sociohistorical model (Roth 1976); it is "ideal" not in the sense of "perfect," but in the sense of representing a hypothesized fundamental coherence of Dutch middle-class culture as a meaningful way of life. Importantly, such an ideal type or sociohistorical model is *not* the same as a "stereotype." That is, the ideal type specifically is *not* assumed to be a classification, a label, or a complete and adequate description of any given empirical reality. Instead, it is a concept hypothesizing what reality would be like under a given set of conditions (i.e. like a perfect vacuum in physics). Once formulated, a type or model (e.g. of middle-class Dutch culture) can then be compared with a variety of other types of culture as well as with social realities, asking such questions as: how has the culture changed over time, why and how do middle-class Dutch people invoke this culture (as opposed to other cultural possibilities), where do elements of the culture come from, how has the culture diffused into usage elsewhere, and how has it been modified in the process of diffusion? In sum, sociologists, like everyone else, use classifications and typifications to talk about the world. But this does not work unless we understand that words and the things they are about are not the same. As Louis Althusser once noted, quoting medieval philosophy, the concept "dog" doesn't bark.

Bringing culture into view sociologically

Offering a working definition of culture, distinguishing it from society, and emphasizing the problems of classification and typification are all preparatory moves. They
help to clear away misconceptions that might get in the way of the study of culture,
but they do not really provide the tools for getting on with it. What remains unanswered is a basic question: how to bring culture into view sociologically. Given that
most of us look at the world from our own points of view and see lots of things, it
seems worthwhile to ask what sociologists examine when they study culture?

There is, for better or worse, no single answer. Sociology as a discipline entertains a
variety of theoretical perspectives that are useful in analyzing or posing hypotheses
about culture and the social world. As we already have suggested, in the more or less
classic triumvirate of social theorists – Karl Marx, Emile Durkheim, and Max Weber
– each is a wellspring that continues to inform sociological work. Marx, famous for his
analysis of capitalist development, has been important both to scholars who want to
understand the political economy of culture and globalization and to critical theorists
and others, like Antonio Gramsci, who have been more interested in the relation
between culture and power. Durkheim, once a founding father of structural-function-
alist theory, has recently received renewed attention for his theories about cultural
boundaries and rituals. Weber remains important (for example as inspirational to
Geertz) because he spelled out a methodology that made room for cultural analysis,
and because he linked cultural meaning to social action in the everyday world. And
sociology as it developed in the twentieth century has yielded important innovative
lenses for cultural analysis. Most notably, because symbolic interactionists focus on
symbols and interaction, they, like the Weberians, are well equipped to take on empirical studies that can bring to light the complex processes by which culture comes into
play in social life. In a different way, the sociology of organizations and its latter-day
offspring, called the "new institutionalism," offer ways to examine how culture gets
produced, and the flip side, how culture shapes organized social activities. Finally, as
we have mentioned, sociology has not been isolated from recent interdisciplinary
developments, notably in the Birmingham School and among French and other theorists of discourse.

There is no point in detailing these theoretical currents in the abstract at the outset.
Their assertions and significance can best be considered through the topical analysis
of culture in the chapters that follow. These chapters are organized through "analytic
frames," which, like frames of photographs or paintings, define the focus and boundaries – in other words, the subject matter – of our discussions of culture. Surveying the
broad range of inquiry about culture, we can identify five especially important
analytic frames: (1) institutional structures, (2) cultural history and legacies, (3)
production and distribution, (4) audience reception and effects, and (5) meaning and
social action.

- *Institutional structures of culture.* This frame focuses on the overarching
  "patterns" of material and ideal culture that are represented in various social
  institutions such as language, personal identity, family, mass media, work, etc. In
  this frame – considered especially in Chapter 2 – culture is assumed to have the
  character of a "social fact," independent of individual consciousness. As an aspect
  of social processes, its tendencies cannot be reduced to the actions of individuals.

In modern societies, for example, we might be interested in a "culture of individualism" or in "the family" as an institutional pattern. In such considerations, it is important to recognize that not all culture is equally accessible to all individuals in a society. Instead, various cultural objects tend to end up among different social strata and groups, partly on the basis of socially organized production and distribution of culture (discussed below). As Chapter 3 argues, the stocks of culture of different social strata and groups are central conduits through which social differentiation and association occur on the basis of class, ethnic, gender, and other distinctions.

• *Cultural history and the persistence of cultural forms.* Historians, some cultural anthropologists, and historical sociologists take seriously the observation that cultural objects can spread from place to place and through time. Moreover, all societies may share certain basic kinds of cultural processes. Thus, contemporary cultural formations need to be understood in historical and comparative contexts. In Chapter 4 we take these possibilities seriously by asking about the significance of folk culture for cultural studies and for contemporary society. Chapters 5 and 6 pursue questions about the legacy of pre-industrial cultural forms and about the consolidation of mass culture associated with the rise of industrial society beginning in the nineteenth century. In a somewhat different way, Chapter 7 asks whether certain contemporary cultural developments can be described as "postmodern," how postmodern culture is tied to earlier cultural forms and industrial social organization, and to what degree the postmodern situation alters relationships between people, their cultural milieus, and their resources for participating in social life.

• *Production and the social distribution of culture.* The cultural materials available to people as they participate in social life are differentially distributed among individuals in diverse social locations. These differences are not simply "facts" of "human nature"; they are the consequences of how culture is produced and distributed, by whom and for whom. The ownership and control of cultural distribution – as well as the content of what is distributed – raise questions of the relation between culture and power, questions that are taken up in Chapter 8. The culture that is distributed does not come out of thin air either; it has to be produced by (often organized) social action. This frame therefore also explores the processes, resources, actors, roles, activities, organizations, genres, conventions, and recipes by which production and distribution of culture occur – a set of issues pursued in Chapter 9.

• *Reception and effects of culture.* The word "effect" is, in the narrow sense, debatable if it is taken to imply that social actors are passive receptacles of culture, but used more broadly it conveys concerns with the reception of cultural items by social actors, and whether (and how) any particular cultural object affects the beliefs, meaningful relation to life, and actions of an individual or social group. In Chapter 10 we will ask, for example, about the effects of television violence on children and of news coverage on public opinion. We will also want to consider how audiences draw meaning from culture, and with what consequences, when they view, for example, a painting.

• *Meaning and social action.* If, instead of analyzing the reception of a discrete cultural object by actors, we invert the focus – as we do in Chapter 11 – our frame becomes centered on actors and how they draw from among their enormous cultural inventories in actual conduct, and, in turn, how these processes reproduce or shift institutionalized culture. Here, it is important to consider not only individual actions, but also the occasions when culture shapes individual actions on a wide basis, in social movements and dramatic cultural transformations.

These five analytic frames inscribe a division of labor onto the sociological analysis of culture. Any particular frame generates boundaries of inquiry, by raising certain questions as central and treating others as worth addressing only insofar as they are relevant to the central frame. Yet, as we intend to show, these ways of understanding culture are neither mutually exclusive nor isolated from one another, a point that becomes evident when we launch into the sociological study of culture proper.

Notes

1 In the remainder of this book, any quotation of other authors who use gender-specific language to refer to persons in general will not be noted as such. Readers are asked to understand that, for the authors' part, non-gendered language for persons in the generic sense is in all cases implied.
2 For an early formulation of the term "cultural structure," used to describe institutionalized patterns in nineteenth-century U.S. communal groups, see Hall 1988.

Part 1
Culture and society

2 Culture, self, and society

How do good people create a good society? How does a good society create good people? These questions are bound up with understandings of whether and how cultures produce both the good society and the good person. Ancient though they be, these questions shift in their significance as the circumstances of people's lives change. Debates about the moral order were very much a part of early social science, but they fell out of favor with the growth of positivism and empiricism in the twentieth century. In recent decades, active public debate about moral issues has revived, both in the United States and in other countries. In the 1970s – labeled "the me decade" in the media – and the 1980s – labeled "the decade of greed" – politicians, intellectuals, religious leaders, and the media expressed concerns about the moral order. In the years since, serious debates have emerged about morality – both public and private – in issues as diverse as abortion, corporate scandals, former U.S. President Bill Clinton's sex life, and the sexual behavior of priests. At world courts, trials have been held of those accused of genocide in Rwanda, and of Serbian leader Slobodan Milosevic, accused of crimes committed in the context of war.

A number of social scientists have taken up questions about the good person and the good society, and they have addressed the issues in popular books reaching broad audiences. In the United States, understandings of American individualism are central to the debate. Dominating the critical discourse is a pessimistic evaluation that describes a "modern" culture as having reached its zenith. Leading American critics argue that the replacement of "traditional" (often religious) values by a "therapeutic culture" has created a culture that promotes "individual fulfillment" at the expense of community and society. These "internal" critics find odd bedfellows among writers from other cultures who critique "Western values" (see Chapter 4). There is an alternative to both the American and the external critiques, however, with a different view of the nature of the self and the connection between the self and society. This perspective sees the self in relation to others, and considers people's ongoing location in time and space to be a foundational issue.

In looking at alternative perspectives on self and society in the present chapter, we examine how social critics in one Western society – the United States – use the concept of culture to explore the moral order. This theoretical debate has been complicated by the emergence of "identity politics," in which any given person's community is no longer assumed simply to support and be supported by the dominant culture. Rather, identity politics locates the self in a community that exists in tension with the dominant culture.

One strand of the sociological tradition, stretching from Emile Durkheim to Talcott Parsons, theorized that culture works to tie together individuals and integrate a society. This tradition focused on the ways in which shared norms and values create social order. This formulation implies that culture is a kind of system for the social control of individuals, and that it integrates them into society, to the benefit of both individuals and the society. Yet this concise model may not apply very well today, since a major feature of modern society has been toward "freeing" individuals from constraining norms and rules. Precisely in the context of modernity, some scholars ask if a culture's rules might offer so little constraint that both the society and the individuals within it suffer. This, indeed, is Durkheim's (1951) explanation of anomic suicide, which he argued happens when normative regulations are relaxed to the point that they no longer offer sufficient guidance for human behavior. In the face of this threat, Durkheimian functionalists presumably take heart in the proliferation of normative popular culture, with the publication of books and magazine articles spelling out the rules on a wide range of topics, from dating to etiquette. A search for books through Amazon.com on "etiquette for children" in the fall of 2002 listed 130 titles, including *Be the Best You Can Be: A Guide to Etiquette and Self Improvement for Children and Teens*, by Robin Thompson; *365 Manners Kids Should Know: Games Activities, and Other Fun Ways to Help Children Learn Etiquette*, by Sheryle Eberly; and *How Rude! The Teenager's Guide to Good Manners, Proper Behavior, and not Grossing People Out*, by Alex J. Packer.

Despite the revival of etiquette in some quarters, for others attempts to sustain a general normative culture seem basically backward looking. In its place, they celebrate a proliferation of diverse communities, as well as new ways of making connections. There is a "moral discourse" here as well, about people looking for the meaning of life, and for ways to enhance life for themselves and others. When the local "Ultimate Phrizzbee" group signs on to pick up trash by the highway, they may not be making a political statement but they are engaging in a moral discourse, expressing a certain idea of the good person in the good society – one that is somewhat different from that which the rule books offer.

Alternative approaches have become the grist of a public debate on the nature of the good person and the good society. The writers considered in the present chapter – social scientists and public intellectuals – are concerned about how people think about the rules, what the rules are, how they are changing, and with what consequences. They also are concerned about who makes and disseminates the rules. Yet these writers do not simply stand outside the society observing it. They are (and for the most part see themselves as) engaged in the society and its culture. Their arguments are not only texts *about* a culture, their texts are *part of* that culture. No doubt this is true of all writings about the social, but because these writings have attracted a broad audience (a number of them have been best sellers in the U.S.) their impact on culture has been much more direct. Because the works of these scholars are not just interpretations of culture but a part of the culture on which they comment, the texts are of particular interest for a cultural analysis.

Individualism and therapeutic culture

In *Habits of the Heart* Robert Bellah and his coauthors (1985) questioned whether, and how, Americans sustain morally coherent lives. *Habits of the Heart* has generated lively debate about the nature of American culture. It is the best selling book written by sociologists since *The Lonely Crowd* (Riesman *et al.* 1950). Drawing from the nineteenth-century Frenchman Alexis de Tocqueville, Bellah and his coauthors described a fundamental tension between the individual's desires for self-fulfillment and the needs of the social order – in their terms, between individualism and commitment.

Alexis de Tocqueville was a young French aristocrat when he visited the United States in 1831. His observations of American politics, social relations, and cultural mores were published as *Democracy in America* (1945). Already early in the nineteenth century, Tocqueville saw Americans as having broken loose from the constraining forces that bound Europeans to traditional authorities. He admired the freedom, equality, and individualism of Americans, although he was concerned about the repercussions of the continuing existence of slavery in the southern states, and he did note a relative lack of freedom among married women (single women he found free in comparison to their European counterparts).

Yet Tocqueville also worried about the balance between American individualism and a collective social order. If Americans lacked sufficient commitment to common goals, he feared that they would not be able to govern themselves and the American experiment with democracy would fail. However, Tocqueville found evidence of two factors that could mitigate against the destructive aspects of individualism in American culture. First, he suggested that Americans saw a convergence between "self-interest rightly understood" and the collective interests of the society (1945, pp. 129–32). Second, he observed high levels of participation in voluntary associations. This participation, he asserted, both created ties between individuals and gave them the experience of participating in something larger than themselves. For Tocqueville, democracy depended on the development and maintenance of civic culture, and he found sustenance for the emerging civic culture in associations of volunteers as well as involvement in institutions such as churches, which, in America – unlike many European countries with established state churches – looked a lot like voluntary associations.

Individualism in American culture

One and a half centuries later, Robert Bellah and his coauthors worried that the negative effects of individualism had not been avoided. On the contrary, they argued that modern individualism is producing a way of life not personally or socially viable. They found that individualism has deep roots in American culture, and that it existed in several variations among the middle-class Americans whom they interviewed for *Habits of the Heart*.

When asked about the goals of a morally good life, these people spoke about success, freedom, and justice. Bellah and his associates described four different types of individualism, each type embodying particular strands of the American cultural heritage, each providing a different rhetoric for balancing the basic goals: first, "biblical individualism," represented by the Puritan John Winthrop, the first governor of the Massachusetts Bay Colony; second, "republican individualism," represented by Thomas Jefferson; third, "utilitarian individualism," represented by Benjamin Franklin; and, fourth, "expressive individualism," represented by Walt Whitman.

Biblical individualism and republican individualism are the older strands. The high regard for self-reliance and independence embedded in both traditions is moderated in biblical individualism by a connection between success and participation in an ethical community, and among republican individualists by a commitment to political equality (Bellah *et al.* 1985, pp. 28–32).

In turn, modern individualism encompasses "utilitarian" and "expressive" strands. The utilitarian strand echoes Tocqueville's "self-interest rightly understood." In its most general form utilitarianism holds that the rightness or wrongness of an action is judged by the goodness or badness of its consequences. Utilitarianism originated as a political philosophy in the eighteenth century with English reformer Jeremy Bentham, who believed that utilitarianism provides a rational basis for developing social policy. For utilitarians, the end goal that defines moral action is "the greatest good to the greatest number." Bellah and his coauthors, however, feared that contemporary utilitarian individualism provides an easy rationale for individuals to pursue their own wants and desires with little thought for the common good. As for expressive individualism, with its goal of the cultivation and expression of the self, Bellah and his colleagues argued that it provides few reasons for making commitments to a community, given that self-expression is the primary good (1985, pp. 33–5).

All four traditions of individualism emphasize self-reliance. In the past, the first three types were also tied to traditions that defined the common good and provided reasons for individuals to contribute to it. However, over time, Bellah and his colleagues argued, "a primary emphasis on self-reliance has led to the notion of pure undetermined choice, free of tradition, obligation, or commitment, as the essence of the self" (1985, p. 152). In turn, in the domain of love and marriage this notion fuels an ascendancy of the "therapeutic attitude," which has become much more widely diffused than the older notions of obligation and willingness to sacrifice oneself for others. In other words, the middle-class mainstream sees the authentic self as the source of their standards, and good relationships are based in self-knowledge, self-realization, and open and honest communication (1985, pp. 98–9). "For such expressive selves," Bellah and his colleagues maintained, "love means the full exchange of feelings between authentic selves, not enduring commitment based on binding obligation" (1985, p. 102).

The therapeutic attitude that takes one's own feelings as a starting point has profound implications for moral culture. Bellah and his colleagues described a "view of personal relationships centered on contractual exchange, enacted in communication and negotiation and grounded in each person's ultimate responsibility to himself or herself alone" (1985, p. 129). The healthy person follows a plan directed to the achievement of self-fulfillment. However, this emphasis on self-fulfillment means that joint decisions can be reached only through daunting negotiations:

> In theory, each person is supposed to decide what it is "important" to do in relation to the other and "judge the relative merits" of acts in relation to the other's reactions. Each must do so in the light of self-set values and accept that "you can only be responsible for your own actions."
>
> (Bellah *et al.* 1985, p. 129)

These assumptions in turn make politics impossible, both because the therapeutic attitude does not allow for moral consensus and because the ability to negotiate decisions breaks down with large numbers of people. Not surprisingly, then, many people interviewed by Bellah and his colleagues found interest-group politics repugnant.

The expressive individualism that Bellah and his colleagues found to be gaining dominance in American culture is based in a therapeutic culture derived from the practice of psychoanalysis pioneered by Sigmund Freud. Although Freud himself saw a need for individual submission to the social, psychoanalysis developed in the opposite direction. It undermined traditional moral authority and helped individuals break free from the inhibitions and repressions of bourgeois morality. In the rest of this section we review Freud's thesis and then look at the ideas of two social critics concerned about the modern destruction of moral authority. Like the writers of *Habits of the Heart*, these critics regard the individual as existing in conflict with the moral order.

The advent of therapeutic culture

In the late nineteenth and early twentieth centuries, many intellectuals, artists, and scientists identified with the modernist movements of the times, and saw themselves in rebellion against "traditional culture," which they regarded as dominated by arbitrary rules with little payoff for individuals. In their lives and writings, critical theorists such as Wilhelm Reich (1960) and Herbert Marcuse (1962) and artists like Henry Miller and Anaïs Nin (depicted in the movie *Henry and June*) championed sexual experimentation as a way to break down middle-class morality. The response of authorities suggests how threatening their writings seemed. Miller's *Tropic of Cancer*, originally published in Paris in 1931, was banned in the United States as pornography. Only in the 1950s did that book, along with *Lady Chatterley's Lover*, by D.H. Lawrence, become test cases in trials in Britain and the U.S. that resulted in the rolling back of censorship of materials deemed obscene. Anaïs Nin's most famous work, her diaries, was not published until the late 1960s.

Psychoanalysis contributed in important ways to the rebellion against the restrictiveness of nineteenth-century bourgeois culture. Freud, like many theorists of his day, defined culture as inherently restrictive. His ideas provided a theoretical rationale for the rebellion, and his "talking cure" laid the basis for the development of "therapeutic culture."

A member of Freud's circle of psychoanalysts and students, Gez Roheim, once commented: "In general we have no cause to deny the hostility of analysis to culture. Culture involves neurosis which we try to cure. Culture involves superego which we try to weaken" (quoted in Rieff 1991, p. 321). For some writers in the early part of the twentieth century, psychoanalysis was to personal life what Marxism was to economic life – a revolutionary way of thinking that could free people from the repressive order of the past. Psychoanalysis was intended to replace authoritarian moral culture with a therapeutic culture. Yet, starting with Freud, some psychoanalysts and interpreters of psychoanalysis retained a certain ambivalence about the permissiveness of the therapeutic culture that was replacing the restrictions imposed by the older moral order.

The psychoanalytically based critics acknowledged that their theory and practice participated in a (perhaps necessary) destruction of the old morality and the traditional authorities, but they worried about the "moral anarchy" that they saw as the consequence of destroying the authority of the father figure. For them, therapeutic culture presents its own dangers. Freud himself saw an inherent antagonism between the demands of civilization and instinctual desires. This view had its parallel in the sociological thought of Emile Durkheim, who, coming from a different angle, wrote in his

Moral Education about the "need for restraint" and the "limitations imposed by the discipline" of the social order (Durkheim 1989). For Freud, what was to be restrained shifted as his theory developed. Initially he framed instincts (or drives) primarily as sexual and attributed them to the id (the subconscious part of the psyche associated with demands for immediate satisfaction of primitive needs). Later, in *Civilization and Its Discontents* (1962), he developed the argument that humans must curb both sexuality and aggression for the survival of human society. In Freud's view, humans trade some of their possibilities for happiness for the security that civilization offers. As this metaphor suggests, the "trade" is not without cost. For Freud, the cost takes the form of guilt, inflicted by a punishing superego. In Freud's system, the superego acts as the conscience, judging the actions and intentions of the ego (the relatively conscious part of the psyche that works to balance the demands of id and superego).

Freud originally described the process for boys. The individual's superego is formed in the developmental process when external authority becomes internalized. This happens when the child renounces his desires for his mother and recognizes the authority of his father as internally valid. Because this account is based on male children giving up their mother in the process of identification with the father, Freud called it the Oedipus complex. His explanation of girls' ego formation process was less satisfactory. It included the claim that because girls did not have to break with their primary relationships to their mothers in order to achieve identification with the same-sex parent, their superegos never develop as fully, and therefore girls' capacity for justice is always less than boys' (Freud 1990).[1]

In *Civilization and Its Discontents* Freud posited an analogy between the development of the superego within the individual and civilization's development of cultural ideals and ethical codes. He argued that the two are interlocked, but that

> the mental processes concerned are actually more familiar to us and more accessible to consciousness in the group than they can be in the individual man. In him, when tension arises, it is only the noisiness of the superego which, in the form of reproaches, lets itself noisily be heard: its actual demands often remain unconscious in the background. If we bring them to conscious knowledge we find that they coincide with the precepts of the prevailing cultural superego.
>
> (Freud 1962, p. 89)

For Freud, then, individuals suffer conflict both within themselves and in relation to civilization. The need for society can be met only through restrictions imposed by culture.

The triumph of therapeutic culture

Philip Rieff, a major sociological interpreter, regarded Freud's description of ambivalence at the core of human nature as his major contribution. For, unlike previous conceptions of a divided self in Greek and Christian cultures, Freud did not judge the warring factions. He did not think that human nature is "fallen"; nor did he see the superego as "above" the id and ego. Among psychoanalysts, the "modern project" involved setting the individual free from guilt, free from punishment by the superego. For Rieff, the success of this project – that is, the "triumph of the therapeutic" – has meant "the defeat of culture," where culture stands for traditional moral authority that was the source of feelings of guilt. What does the concept of culture entail when used in this way?

The common use of the term "culture" to describe a people's whole way of life includes a range of behaviors and norms, as well as material objects. By contrast, culture in psychoanalytic theory is more narrowly construed as moral culture – the cultural proscriptions that restrict and inhibit the behavior of individuals. It distinguishes between "maximalist" cultures (those with many rules and proscriptions) and "minimalist" cultures (those that tolerate a wide range of behavior).

A maximalist culture is described by Lynn Davidman in her book about Jewish women returning to orthodoxy. A rabbi explaining to a group of women why they might want to observe the rules of a kosher kitchen tells them: "[T]he bottom line of Judaism is the sanctity of life. Keeping kosher is a way of beginning to *limit* the life you eat" (Davidman 1991, p. 138; emphasis added). Orthodox Judaism is a maximalist culture with rules that govern many aspects of daily behavior. Keeping a kosher kitchen is one example. The rabbi uses the word "limits" in the same way as Rieff does when he talks about the essence of culture being that it puts limits on what is permitted to us as humans, for whom all things seem possible.

Critics like Rieff regard the twentieth century as a period when Western cultures moved from maximalism to minimalism (see Figure 2.1). Traditional moral authorities such as the churches and parents no longer have (or, in many cases, want) the power to make rules and enforce them. There is a sense in which, compared to other eras, almost anything goes. Rieff argues that this new freedom has released the contemporary middle class from the excesses of guilt that were part of the Victorian bourgeois childhood of Freud's youth; but, in his view, the lack of restrictions has been pushed to the point that individuals and society now no longer have any direction.

For Freud and Rieff, culture provides the "limitations" that are necessary to give shape and direction to human activity. Yet culture is not just a set of rules; cultures also provide symbolic forms for expressing forbidden desires, for example rituals that invert the social order by exalting the deviant or mocking conformity, and art, which – through sublimation – is expressive and repressive at the same time. Culture, then, amounts to a set of controls and releases. Both Rieff and Freud studied the tension between them.

Rieff invoked the Greek and Christian philosophers who had argued that individual fulfillment comes through positive identification with cultural symbol systems and subordination of the self to the social order. In this view, the healthy person and the good citizen are the same, and the therapeutic and the moral are connected. However, in the emerging industrial order individuals were increasingly integrated through economic interdependencies rather than social ones. This new social order did not demand the classic sacrifices.

Rieff argued that the modern project destroyed *religious* culture based in *interdiction* (rules) and replaced it with a *therapeutic* culture based in *relations*. For Rieff, meaning and direction come from the ability to set limits, and the replacement of maximalist culture by a minimalist culture destroys this ability, and thus the possibilities of order, morality, and truth. Indeed, in a fascinating essay on the trial of Oscar Wilde, Rieff argued that "repression is truth." He explained:

> A culture in crisis favors the growth of individuality.... Hypothetically, if a culture could grow to full crisis then everything could be expressed and nothing

Figure 2.1 The Roman Catholic Church exemplifies the trends that Rieff describes. Between the
first Vatican Council in the 1870s, with its rejection of modernism and the
uncompromising position on the authority of the pope, and the Second Vatican
Council in the 1960s, with its endorsement of the authority of the People of God,
following the rules marked practicing Catholics as separate from other people. After
Vatican II, the Catholic Church both moved away from its emphasis on rules and
changed some of the remaining rules. Although maintaining the rule that women
cannot be ordained as priests, as we see in the above illustration of the two girls
assisting the priest, altar girls are now permitted.

Source: photo by Rita Reed, from *Growing Up Gay*, 1997, p. 33.

would be true. To prevent the expression of everything: that is the irreducible
function of culture.

(Rieff 1991, p. 279)

This understanding of culture is both elitist and public. It is public in its focus on the
expression of communally shared norms and values rather than private behavior. And
it is elitist in its focus on the rules rather than what people actually do. In turn, rules
require guardians who spring from a cultural elite. This cultural elite may be identical
with social and political elites, but it may also be separate from, or even opposed to,
these other elites. Whatever the cultural elite's relation to other elites, in a maximalist
culture it expresses, even embodies, moral demands (Rieff 1966, pp. 246–9).

As Rieff noted, one of the ways that guardians protect a culture is by maintaining a
separation between public and private worlds. For instance, consider the relatively
"maximalist" culture of fundamentalist Christians: the rule that "wives are submissive
to their husbands" shapes public culture, and it is regarded as appropriate that men

hold the leadership positions. However, in private women exercise power in many ways (Brasher 1998; Griffith 1997). For guardians of fundamentalist Christian culture, the prospect of checking to make sure that women are submissive in every context (and punishing those who are not) would be self-defeating: not only would it be a lot of trouble for the guardians, but it would probably result in a loss to the community of the creative energies of the women. As Rieff has stated, "the very life of every culture depends upon its powers to mask and transform private motive into something very different, even opposite, when it appears in public" (1991, p. 282). Thus, guardians similarly need to leave room for rituals and art – not only high culture but popular genres such as romance novels and horror films – for they translate between the public and private spheres, sometimes offering remissions that serve the culture by keeping the public zone normatively intact.

Ironically, as Rieff himself recognized, therapeutic culture – a minimalist culture – itself has been carried by a cultural elite. By the beginning of the twenty-first century, however, therapeutic culture has undergone a remarkable diffusion. No longer is it primarily situated in intimate relationships between therapists and patients. Instead, self-awareness movements and a complex of entrepreneurs and small companies reproduce the therapeutic culture through self-help books, workshops, seminars, tapes, and videos that they distribute to a mass audience. Some critics now wonder to what extent the therapeutic culture has eclipsed both a work ethic and ethical sentiments of responsibility for others.

The democratization of therapeutic culture

Christopher Lasch shared with Philip Rieff the view that Western cultures have substituted a minimalist culture of toleration for the punitive rules of the Victorian bourgeoisie. Lasch looked to psychoanalytic theory to explain, not the guilt of the Victorian bourgeois, but the narcissism of twentieth-century managers, artists, academics, and others. He saw the "devastation of personal life" as a fact of life in advanced capitalist society. His most popular book, *The Culture of Narcissism* (1979), can be read as a sequel to Rieff's *The Triumph of the Therapeutic* (1966). Here, Lasch addressed the democratization of therapeutic culture through the spread of the personal-growth and self-awareness movements. Unlike others who have critiqued the self-awareness movements, Lasch saw them as symptoms of the problem, not the problem itself. Why, he asked, do people have so much trouble sustaining relationships? Why is the divorce rate so high? Why do so many fathers fail to support their children? We might add, what kind of society produces a situation where school children take guns and kill teachers and other students in their schools?

Some have explained the therapeutic culture – and especially its democratization in the rise of the self-awareness movement – as a result of the post-World War II rise of affluence and leisure, which provided money and time for the pursuit of the self. Lasch resisted such an explanation. He suggested instead that the therapeutic attitude is a typical middle-class attempt to apply typical middle-class problem-solving techniques (education, self-help) to a significant problem – the collapse of personal life. This problem is a consequence of many factors, Lasch argued, among them the growth of bureaucracy and technology and the collapse of liberalism. But he suggested that a growth of the psychological condition of narcissism holds the key to understanding what he portrayed as moral crisis in the U.S.

In the narcissistic condition, the formation of the self is disrupted. The result, in psychoanalytic terms, is not the neurosis familiar in Freudian days (i.e. hysteria and obsessional neurosis), but rather character disorders. Despite illusions of omnipotence, the narcissistic person needs others to validate his or her grandiose self. This modern condition differs from that of the nineteenth-century individualist. In Lasch's view, "For the narcissist the world is a mirror, whereas the rugged individualist saw it as an empty wilderness to be shaped to his own design" (1979, p. 10).

Drawing heavily on psychoanalytic theories, Lasch (1979, pp. 37–40) put together the following catalog of characteristics of a narcissist: vagueness; diffuse dissatisfaction with life; feelings of futility and purposelessness; emptiness and depression; wild oscillations of self-esteem; an inability to maintain meaningful human relationships; heightened self-esteem coming only through attachment to a strong admired figure from whom acceptance is craved; the tendency to act out impulses rather than to repress or sublimate them; and the tendency to cultivate a protective shallowness in emotional relations and to be sexually promiscuous, even polymorphously perverse. The narcissist finds it difficult to play, to have close involvements, or to mourn. Although the narcissist can get along in the world (and may be a charming person), his or her devaluation of others and lack of curiosity reinforce feelings of emptiness and an impoverished inner life. The narcissist's self-esteem is dependent upon the constant approval of others. Yet fear of emotional dependence and fear of commitment, together with a manipulative and exploitative approach to personal relations, make these relations unsatisfying.

Lasch attributed such importance to the psychoanalytic personality disorder of narcissism for two main reasons. First, he thought that changes in the prevalent form of pathology reflect changes in society as a whole. For Lasch, narcissism is the psychological dimension of people's increasing dependence on bureaucracy, the state, and corporations. Just as people have grown dependent upon the society to meet various practical and organizational needs, narcissism represents dependence upon others for self-esteem (1979, p. 10). Second, Lasch suggested, a certain fit between the narcissist and the demands of the social order may give narcissists a certain market value:

> The narcissist rises to positions of prominence not only in awareness movements and other cults but in business corporations, political organizations, and government bureaucracies. For all his inner suffering, the narcissist has many traits that make for success in bureaucratic institutions which put a premium on the manipulation of interpersonal relations, discourage the formation of deep attachments and, at the same time, provide the narcissist with the approval he needs in order to validate his self-esteem.
>
> (Lasch 1979, pp. 43–4)

It is the apparent "success" of the narcissist that led Lasch to postulate a "culture of narcissism." Lasch thus moved from the discourse of individual pathology found within the psychiatric community to the argument that American culture supports and expresses narcissism. Just as Freud argued for a correspondence between the individual superego and the cultural superego, Lasch argued for a correspondence between individual narcissism and cultural narcissism.

Lasch criticized modern society as "over-organized," and he connected the growth of narcissism to the changing relation between workers and their work, embodied in the relocation of work from factories to offices. When people feel no personal responsibility for an end product and style is more important than what one actually does, doing good work ceases to be a source of self-esteem. What counts is recognition by others. Lasch saw the roots of contemporary narcissism in the deterioration of the work ethic, which, he argued, no longer makes sense: it does not offer the key to "success" in most people's work contexts. Furthermore, Lasch argued, the changing definition of success at work has repercussions for leisure, which becomes increasingly tied to consumption. These changes in the nature of work and play have undermined other institutions, particularly family life and education, which, Lasch maintained, used to provide some distance between the individual and the economy.

In a recent book, James Nolan (1998) has extended Lasch's argument, claiming that the therapeutic culture now dominates American public policy in many areas. He demonstrates how United States civil case law, criminal case law, public education, and welfare policy have all became aligned with a therapeutic ethos that celebrates an emotional and unencumbered self. In Nolan's account, a self closely resembling the narcissistic self that Lasch described is now taken as normative in the ordinary actions of the state.

Many parallels can be found among the various arguments of the social critics concerned about U.S. culture. Bellah and his coauthors, Rieff, and Lasch all theorize social life in terms of an essential antagonism between the desires of the individual and the demands of the culture. They all describe a contemporary moral crisis in the U.S. related to the growth of a therapeutic culture. In their views, this culture allows the expression of individual desires to such an extent that moral culture is undermined. Yet they do not see the main *source* of the problem in the motives and behaviors of individuals. Lasch explicitly refutes this common misinterpretation (1984, p. 19). Thus, they do not think that the problems of moral culture can be resolved by simply exhorting Americans to be better people – to be less selfish, for example. Rather, they suggest that people do not really have the degree of choice heralded by expressive individualism. Changes in the division of labor and the development of bureaucracy are among the causes of modernity, and it is modernity itself that fails to support commitment.

Overall, the writings we have considered here foster an understanding of the problems created by modernity, but offer few solutions. Part of the attraction of psychoanalysis is that it captures so well people's experiences of the internal tension between immediate wants and desires and their sense of what is socially beneficial or morally good. Freud departed from earlier religious formulations about this tension by arguing that the repression of desire could have harmful effects. He held that culture – defined as the rules of society – can be overly punitive. Yet by defining culture largely in terms of its rules and negative sanctions, psychoanalysis helped to promote the imbalance that critics like Freud and Lasch regarded as threatening.

What does the approach of Bellah and his colleagues add to the discussion? Early on they stated their main purpose: "to deepen our understanding of the resources our tradition provides – and fails to provide – to enable us to think about the moral problems we are currently facing as Americans" (Bellah *et al.* 1985, p. 21). By using the language of individualism rather than psychoanalysis, the very language of *Habits of the Heart* helps put readers in touch with particular American rhetorical traditions. In the act of analyzing the American discourse on moral action, Bellah and his coauthors also promoted a discourse that more seriously engages moral issues.

Is the contemporary situation, then, one of individuals pitted against society, striving for freedom against the constraints of social institutions and relationships with others? The understandings offered from Freud to Lasch may unnecessarily pose an opposition between character and culture, and between traditional communities and modern societies. There are other theoretical approaches to moral culture. One such approach, coming out of feminist theory, treats the person in relation to the culture and society rather than in opposition to them. Another approach eclipses rules and sanctions as the bases of moral culture. Instead, moral culture is defined by concrete practices – stories, rituals, expressions – that create ties between people in various kinds of communities. Rejecting Freudian theory and the critique of individualism, these approaches begin to recast the discussion of moral culture.

Narrative identity and moral culture

Sociologists often lament the individualism of modern society (and of people in the United States, where these cultural characteristics of modern life are most fully embodied). Yet, at the same time, most mainstream sociological theory has taken for granted an understanding of the modern person as an autonomous individual. In Chapter 5 we will examine the historical processes of rationalization accompanying the rise of modernity that produced conditions for a kind of individual existence radically different from what preceded it. Here we are concerned primarily with how the historical shift to the "modern man" was conceptualized by social theorists. The notion of the modern person as a separate and autonomous individual is central to the work of political theorists from Thomas Hobbes in seventeenth-century England to the contemporary philosopher John Rawls. Social contract theory – from Hobbes to Rawls – is based upon a set of premises about the actions of free and autonomous men. These premises are easily found in the economic modeling of rational-choice theory. However, critical theories, including Marxism and psychoanalytic theory, also posit a radically separate individual – either alienated from or in conflict with society.

One notable exception to the individualizing tendency in modern social theory is pragmatism, which developed a more social conception of the individual (Wiley 1994). More recently, feminist theories explore ideas of connected or relational selves. And, as we will explore below, poststructuralist theories of identity also challenge the modernist conception of identity as rooted in the conflict between individual actors and society, but from quite a different direction. They *de*construct the ideas of inner identity and outer society, and, indeed, the notion of an authentic self. In postmodernist writings, the image is thus of the self as fluid and transitory.

As Somers and Gibson have pointed out, ideas about the autonomous self and the conflict between actors and society are the legacy of nineteenth-century social theory. In the face of this legacy, they argue, there are now openings to new possibilities for understanding identity and social agency that incorporate the dimensions of time, space, and relationality. They seek to understand action as contextualized, occurring in particular times and places:

> Researchers outside of sociology are coming to grips with a new historically and empirically based narrativist understanding of social action and social agency – one that is temporal, relational, and cultural as well as institutional, material, and macro-structural.... Everything we know is the result of numerous crosscutting story-lines in which social actors locate themselves.
>
> (Somers and Gibson 1994, p. 41)

Following this line of thought here, we look at two examples of contemporary theorizing about the self and identity, both of which are grounded in the social movements of the 1960s. The first comes out of particularistic claims to identity by participants in the movements; the second, out of a critique of the essentialism of those claims. After considering these moments of identity politics, we will return to the narrativist understandings that Somers and Gibson invoke.

New social movements and identity politics

One impetus for the opening to new theories of action and identity has been the emergence of new kinds of social movements beginning in the 1960s. These movements for change will be considered in their cultural aspects in Chapter 11. At this point we want to explore the ramifications of these groups and their practices for theories about identity.

Hobbes's social-contract theory imagined self-interested individuals. The French Enlightenment went a step further, positing these self-interested individuals as driven to repel the forces of authority – the church, the family, and the state – in the name of freedom from domination. The movement into modern society imagined a move away from tradition and constraint and toward freedom. Social movements of the nineteenth and early twentieth centuries primarily organized people around the issues of class and nation, with the European labor movement being perhaps the prototypical social movement. These movements were never as strong in the United States as in Europe (Sombart 1976), but they did provide a paradigmatic set of cases for social-movement theorists, both in the U.S. and elsewhere.

The new social movements with their origins in the 1960s, in contrast, have incorporated a broad definition of politics, extending cultural issues into public arenas to an extent much greater than did the class politics at the heart of the Marxist left. They often organize around categorical features of individuals. Black, feminist, and gay liberation movements and the Greens have fought legal battles for rights, but they also have advocated and carried out various kinds of cultural politics. For example, the famous "Miss America protest" of 1970 was a media event, addressing a cultural issue – appearance norms for women – in a cultural mode. In the new social movements, groups of people who previously felt marginal to the system have joined together on the basis of shared identity to pursue goals that are often defined as "expressive" or "self-actualizing."

For African-Americans, the civil rights movement initially addressed issues such as voter registration and segregation. But Black Power, Black Nationalist, and Afrocentric movements fought battles on cultural terrains, and these struggles moved into the universities as well. Thus, the scholar Cornell West stated in an interview with bell hooks that "the intent of Black Studies is to redefine what it means to be human" (hooks and West 1991, p. 52). In other words, there would be a normative break with the dominant white society. A new politics of identity would be pursued through new practices. One example is the celebration of Kwanza. This week-long holiday at the end of December is an amalgam of several African festivals marking the first fruits of the harvest. Maulana Karenga, a Black Studies professor in California in the 1960s, created Kwanza to symbolically connect African-Americans to a common, imagined past. As we will show on other fronts in Chapter 4, such "invented traditions" create ties among participants: taking part in Kwanza makes a statement about both one's individual and collective identity.

Identity can be expressed in ways accessible to others through self-conscious adaptation of particular cultural contents, most significantly music, dress, and styles of banter. These sorts of expressions are often regarded as trivial, but they are vital for the sustenance of individual and group identities (see Figure 2.2). The body itself carries meaning, and participants in particular subcultures manipulate it in various ways to express various sorts of meaning (Sanders 1988).

Symbols, of course, are "multi-vocal" – they can carry more than one meaning. In an evocative essay, Andrea Benton Rushing (1988) writes of her life, and of her daughters and her mother, by talking about her hair. As the essay begins, she has landed in Ghana, accompanying her engineer husband to a job. She and her three daughters all had their hair styled in Afros, but found the heat uncomfortable: "One-third of your body's heat escapes through the scalp's pores. While it struggles to fight its way through six inches of hair, you just plain suffer" (1988, pp. 325–6). So they did the practical thing: they changed their hairstyle to the local closely braided cornrows. However, actions are rarely only practical. Six years later, back in the U.S. and still in cornrows, Rushing states, now "wherever my three daughters and I go…people stare at us" (1988, p. 326). The cornrows have different meanings for Rushing and the people who see her in various situations.

Figure 2.2 Appearances convey identity markers even as players from Senegal and Sweden compete in a sport that transcends national boundaries at the World Cup Soccer Finals, in Oita, Japan, in June 2002.

Source: Reuters/Kimimasa Mayama.

In Rushing's essay we learn of her "conversion" from the straightened hair that was the standard in her childhood. She recounts the embarrassment that she felt when as a child she once let her straightened bangs get wet – snow melted on them – and they suddenly curled. She recalls seeging the singer Odetta at a nightclub in the early 1960s: "I was mesmerized by her stunning face framed in its short kinky halo" (1988, p. 334), but it was ten years before she adopted "natural hair." She told her disapproving teachers that "the personal is political," and she tried to convert others to the natural style. As for her children, "long before they were born, back in the glory days of black being beautiful, I'd vowed that no daughter of mine would have her hair straightened as long as she lived with me" (1988, p. 328). Rushing's hair provides a way of instantly communicating her identification with Afro-American culture.

Yet Rushing also makes a confession: speaking of a daughter's pleading for "just a little Vigoral or Lustrasilk in her hair to make it easier to comb," she says, "I have kept faith with the nappy pride of black is beautiful. And, yet I've betrayed my heritage after all. I am, you see, a beautician's daughter" (1988, p. 328). In her narrative Rushing performs a "transformation" herself: for her daughters, who have lived in Ghana, she reinterprets the work of her mother, aunts, and grandmothers as ritual priestesses, symbols that her daughters recognize – but perhaps the women whose stories she tells would not. Using the symbolism of hair, Rushing locates herself within several traditions; she speaks of the "black is beautiful" brothers and of her hairdresser mother. Rushing's cornrows signify her identification with a multi-layered African-American culture.

As with Rushing's live identity politics, so identity politics more generally challenges the ideas of "universal man" integral to modern social theory based in the Enlightenment. Participants in the new social movements have refused the status of "outsiders" who deviate from the supposedly universal norm by making the argument that the supposed "generic man" was in fact a very particular man: white, male, middle class, Western, and heterosexual. They insist that what constitutes deviance in society often is only so when measured against some idea of what is "normal," and that what gets considered normal often reflects the ability of groups with power to set the definitions. As Somers and Gibson note,

> New theories of identity politics have shifted explanations from the notion of the universalistic social agent to particularistic categories of concrete persons. Based on the assumption that persons in similar social categories and similar life-experiences (based on gender, color, generation, sexual orientation, and so on) will act on the grounds of common attributes, theories of identity politics posit that "I act because of who I am," not because of a rational interest or a learned value.
>
> (Somers and Gibson 1994, p. 53)

These theories dispute claims by Freud and other theorists of socialization that identity is learned through a process in which the rules of society are internalized. To the contrary, in these accounts identity manifests itself from the inside out.

The relational self in feminist theory

The core idea of the women's liberation movement, that the personal is political, is emblematic of the enlarged scope of issues important within the new social movements. Many participants in the women's liberation movement feel that their collective action is based on a common identity they share as women. Out of that experience, some feminists have developed alternative ideas for talking about the self, community, and moral culture. Feminist writers, for example, have articulated an ethics based on practices of caring. The strand of contemporary feminist theory that we look at here posits a model of the self connected to others. This model differs from the model of the self as separate and autonomous. Indeed, it argues that any increasing autonomy for the individual in the modern shift from community to society reflects the experience of men more than women (Hartsock 1983).

Nancy Chodorow (1978) argued that the connected or relational self develops out of early childhood experiences. Males must develop their gender identity in households where "women mother" and fathers are largely absent. Boys therefore establish their gender identity by becoming "not female" in the presence of their mothers. Girls, by contrast, identify with their present mothers, with whom they remain in relation. They never separate in the decisive ways that boys do.

What are the consequences of differential structural conditions of socialization? Gilligan's (1982) work on moral development speaks to this issue. She has portrayed girls with "connected selves" as working through moral choices in ways markedly different from males. Subsequent work has emphasized that the observed differences in behavior are not due to some essential characteristic of women (even one that is based in nearly universal early childhood experiences), but rather come out of particular experiences of subordination. This strand of feminist work counters the premise in mainstream social thought since Hobbes that morality resides in the actions of free and autonomous men who agree to observe the social contract. By elaborating a kind of morality based in relation rather than autonomy, this approach contests the view of those who, because they assume nurturance by women to be "natural," fail to see it as "moral."

Psychological theories of moral development glorified separation as a mark of maturity, placing the achievement of autonomy at the top of their maturation scales. Freud is not the only one who found women less individuated and therefore less developed in their sense of justice. Gilligan's own work came out of her puzzlement about the studies by her teacher, Lawrence Kohlberg, in which males always seemed to come out "at a higher stage of development." Commenting on Kohlberg's studies, Gilligan noted a paradox: "the very traits that traditionally defined the 'goodness' of women: their care for and sensitivity to the needs of others, are those that mark them as deficient in moral development" (1982, p. 18). Gilligan went on to describe a different path to moral development based on what she calls an "ethic of care," as opposed to Kohlberg's "ethic of rights."

Both Kohlberg and Gilligan used a research methodology in which they presented people of various ages – most often adolescents – with a set of hypothetical dilemmas and then asked them what they would do. Kohlberg formulated the problem of "Heinz": his wife is dying and needs a drug that Heinz cannot afford to buy for her. Kohlberg asked the participants in the study if Heinz should steal the drug to save his wife. Males tended to weigh the rights of the pharmacist to receive money against the rights of the wife to life. On the other hand, Gilligan found, females were less likely to accept the terms of the problem. For example, Gilligan cited one participant who sees the problem as the pharmacist: if the pharmacist knew that Heinz's wife would die without the drug, he would surely give it to her (1982, pp. 26–9).

On the basis of tests like this one Gilligan came to argue for the "different moral voice" of the women she studied. She saw three ways that the ethic of care differs from moral development as described by Kohlberg. First, it emphasizes responsibility and relationship instead of rights and obligations. Second, it employs a form of moral reasoning that is concrete and contextual rather than formal and abstract. Third, it does not consist of a set of abstract principles, but rather of activities and daily practices. A mature person, according to the ethic of care, recognizes her connection to others and theirs to her, and at the same time can articulate her own wants and needs. In Gilligan's account, " Morality is seen by these women as arising from the experience of connection and conceived as a problem of inclusion rather than one of balancing claims" (1982, p. 160).

Gilligan's theory came out of a critique of Kohlberg's universalizing of a male construction of morality. In turn, a number of writers have questioned whether Gilligan's theory should be described as a female morality. Joan Tronto has argued for an "ethic of care" as an alternative form of moral reasoning, but not limited to women. She cautioned that the claim for the existence of a distinct "women's morality" could be dangerous insofar as it reifies differences between men and women. But Tronto also cautioned against simply seeing the ethic of care as "a complement to traditional moral theories based on justice reasoning" (1987, p. 663).

In reviewing previous research Tronto found evidence that members of other subordinate groups, including African-American and working-class people, behaved much like the females in Gilligan's study (Tronto 1987, pp. 649–51). She argued that the life experiences of people in subordinate groups frequently require attention to relations between people. Tronto cited Robert Coles's study of Chicano, Eskimo, and Indian children who criticized Anglos for their lack of attention to others and to the earth (1987, p. 450). She suggested that an ethic of care will necessarily be contextual, with moral decision-making based, not on abstract rules of justice, but on the needs of individuals in particular contexts. In the studies she reviewed, Tronto did not find the moral individual portrayed as the isolated person, separate and autonomous, released from the bonds of community and independent of society, doing his job and riding off into the sunset. The middle-class girls Gilligan studied, like the working-class men studied more recently by Lamont (2000), placed a high value on caring about others.

Gilligan's work and the controversies that have arisen around it have stimulated an alternative discourse about moral culture. Developmental psychologists, philosophers, sociologists, and others are talking about a form of moral reasoning that is contextual rather than universalistic, that is embedded in relationships rather than isolated in the actions of an autonomous individual. The different voice that Gilligan has made available for people to hear differs not only from the voices of Lawrence Kohlberg's subjects, but also from the "individualistic voices" that Bellah and his colleagues identified.

Gilligan, like Freud, developed her understanding of identity in the context of theories about human development. In neither case, however, do the ramifications of their understandings of culture hinge on accepting the particular details about developmental stages contained in their developmental models. Gilligan makes it possible to consider a model of culture in which the individual exists in relation, rather than opposition, to others. Her work also suggests that culture does not consist of rules, but rather of activities, practices, and contextualized interpretations. Implicit in this approach is a challenge to the emphasis on rules in theories of moral culture – from Durkheim and Parsons, as well as Freud and Bellah.

Essentialism and identity in cultural studies

In order to pursue further the ideas of relationality, context, and practice, it is first important to consider charges that the categorical identities associated with many of the new social movements have been susceptible to essentialism – the idea that identities are based on inherent characteristics. In the essentialist view, identities are "naturally" given, rather than socially constructed. There are two major problems with this approach. First, it is ahistorical and, second, it downplays differences among members of a category in favor of highlighting differences between categories.

For example, to return to the theory of Nancy Chodorow, the claim that women are more relational than men because women engage in mothering must be formulated carefully. For Chodorow, mothering is a *social* relationship, not something that is biologically given. However, others have used her theory with less care. Although she theorizes that when men engage extensively in mothering it alters the social dynamics of mothering, Chodorow herself pays little attention to how the social relation of mothering varies in different times and places.

The use of categorical identities suppresses difference. As the feminist movement emerged, for example, women of color, lesbian women, poor women, older women, and younger women began to see that they had different interests. African-American women found themselves allied with black men and white women, but it was a struggle to carve out recognition for themselves in either place. Participants within the overall feminist movement found themselves unable to define the distinctive characteristics that identified "women's experience." The category was useful for some purposes, but not for others.

This issue became central for how cultural-studies scholars thought about identity. Also influenced by the new social movements, these scholars largely responded negatively to the essentializing of identities. However, within cultural studies, the intellectual roots of the concept of identity draw, not from social psychology, but from poststructuralist philosophy. The nineteenth- and early twentieth-century philosophers who produced modern social theory had a conception of the individual, but it was a "universal individual." They gave little attention to the problem of differences among individuals. The issue of difference came to the fore in a compelling way with the critique of essentialism. The poststructuralists, especially those who build on the work of Derrida, take the problem of difference to be fundamental.

Eli Zaretsky offers the following review of poststructuralist thought in relation to the philosophical tradition:

> Identity in philosophy refers to at least two separable questions – first, what gives a thing or a person its essential nature, i.e., its *eidos* or form, and thus its continuity through time, and second what makes two persons or things the same. The notion of identity involves negation or difference – something is something, *not* something else. Poststructuralists such as Derrida problematized identity, for example by arguing that identity presupposes differences, that it involves the suppression of difference, or that it entailed an endless process of deferral of meaning. Poststructuralism, therefore, contributed to the complication of identity politics by introducing what is sometimes termed a politics of difference, a politics aimed less at establishing a viable identity for its constituency than at destabilizing identities, a politics that eschews such terms as groups, rights, value, and society,

in favor of such terms as places, spaces, alterity, and subject positions, a politics
that aims to decenter or subvert, rather than to conquer or assert.

(Zaretsky 1994, pp. 199–200)

In Zaretsky's view, the poststructuralist take yielded what he calls theories of "non-identity" (1994, p. 211).

Identity politics then, helped to produce theory in cultural studies that speaks not of persons and selves, but rather of locations and subject positions. Thus, for example, discourse theory posits that culture is composed of "subject positions," not individuals. It challenges the assumption, central to modernist thought, that in each of us there is an underlying person who is the same across different contexts. The implication of the modernist view is that the person is somehow independent from social life.

In the 1970s, the development known as the "linguistic turn" turned cultural and social theories toward the model of language (Bonnell and Hunt 1999). Again, Zaretsky provides a useful summary:

> [T]he famous distinction between *langue* and *parole* suggested a fruitful way of conceptualizing the distinction between the individual and society, according to which each individual carries the society (*langue*) around in his or her head, but also that each time we speak we do so on the basis of codes that have dissolved and been remade within us (*parole*). On this basis, gender, race, and other social factors could be understood as "codes" possessing a grammar and a semantics all their own, while these codes – i.e., "culture" – are constantly being remade in different discourses and so can interpellate different subjectivities.

(Zaretsky 1994, p. 209)

With this formulation, the opposition between the individual and society disappears.

The contribution of the French philosopher and sociohistorical analyst Michel Foucault to theoretical movements associated with the linguistic turn is very important. Foucault rejected the idea of modern individual autonomous selves in conflict with society. This meant that he also rejected ideas such as repression and alienation, which start from the premise of such a conflict. Foucault's ideas about power are discussed further later, especially in Chapters 5 and 8. Here we are concerned with his ideas about the processes through which human beings are made into subjects. He saw knowledge as intimately bound up with discipline, rather than with freedom or liberation, as the Enlightenment philosophers believed. Through studies of prisons, schools, and hospitals, Foucault examined how discursive practices work to produce "order" in modernity. In his studies of the confessional and psychoanalysis, he argued that even in the most intimate and personal aspects of our lives, in our sexuality, for example, we observe and discipline ourselves through our participation in discourses that organize our thought and action. Discipline works not through constraining individuals and their actions, but by producing them. For Foucault, there is no single power structure operating outside of individuals. Rather, he saw modern human beings as "self-observing subjects." In his understanding, the older distinction between a powerful external social order (society) and an autonomous, perhaps resisting, self does not hold. How, then, did Foucault conceptualize society? He regarded it as "separated into a plurality of power strategies, discourses, and practices, all of which intersect, succeed one another, and are distinguished by the type of discursive formation to which they pertain and by their degree of intensity, but not by their rela-tion to any totality" (quoted in Zaretsky 1994, p. 211). For Foucault, there is no essential self that can be liberated – either by therapy or by revolution.

The implications of poststructuralism for the study of identity are important and diverse. Some poststructuralists have taken on the project of deconstructing categories that themselves organize the social, for example the notion of the "homosexual" (Sedgewick 1990) or "woman" (Wittag 1992). Others have explored the idea that iden-tity is an enactment or a performance. Judith Butler's (1990) brilliant deconstruction of gender is an effort to make gender and the body unintelligible to any project of defining identity. Identity is enacted or performed, constantly renewed and asserted. Judith Halberstam (1998) asks the reader to contemplate what "masculinity" might be about if it becomes disconnected from maleness – that is, if a categorical space is created for "female" masculinity.

Consider the difference between these authors and Christopher Lasch. For Lasch, late capitalism is a period in which the possibility of attaining and sustaining personal identity is collapsing, and the narcissist has no core self. By contrast, the postmod-ernists celebrate fluid identities as a central characteristic of the postmodern condition (discussed in Chapter 7).

The idea of identity as something that is performed, thus something fluid and constantly shifting, may resonate with many experiences that people have, but most individuals also experience their own selfhood as having some core sameness that carries over from minute to minute, day to day, over a lifetime. The face validity of these two radically different experiences of identity and self raises a key question: how might it be possible to theorize about continuity without essentializing identity, and in a way that acknowledges the insights of the deconstructionists? One possible answer comes from considering how the self is constituted in practices of storytelling.

Constitutive narratives

Building on both the feminist work on relationality and the critique of essentialism, Somers and Gibson explore the potential of narratives to generate a different approach to understanding identity and moral culture. Narrativity offers a way of conceptualizing identity that is neither universal nor essentialist, but rather temporally and culturally specific. Somers and Gibson offer the following definition: "Narratives are constellations of relationships (connected parts) embedded in time and space, connected by causal emplotment" (1994, p. 59). Narratives are "constitutive": it is through them that we come to be who we are. Through narrative we make events understandable. However, though each story is different, in the account of Somers and Gibson, narratives are largely not of our own making. Instead, people weave their own narratives in part by appropriating cultural scripts that have broader social exis-tences, what Somers and Gibson term "social narrativity." What is the relation between individuals and social narratives? To address this question, let us return to the issue of American individualism.

One of the criticisms about American culture in *Habits of the Heart* is that when Americans talk, individualism is their "first language." Bellah and his colleagues contended that Americans lack resources for discussing moral issues because no meaningful concepts or rhetorical devices exist for conferring legitimacy on the making of commitments to others. Yet Americans do make commitments. Bellah and his coauthors therefore admitted that "second languages" exist – languages of "tradition and commitment." These languages can be found in "communities of memory":

> Communities, in the sense we are using the term, have a history – in an important sense they are constituted by their past – and for this reason we can speak of a real community as a "community of memory," one that does not forget its past. In order not to forget its past, a community is involved in retelling its story, its constitutive narrative.
>
> (Bellah *et al.* 1985, p. 153)

In *Habits of the Heart*, constitutive narratives include tales of exemplary individuals, as well as stories about a community's origin and its collective hopes and fears. In addition, community rituals commemorate the past and make it meaningful in the present. In the fullest enactment of community, members are "socially interdependent." They "participate together in discussion and decision making, and…share certain practices which both define the community and nurture it" (1985, p. 333).

Yet Bellah and his colleagues contended that this "strong form" of community is outside the experience of the mostly urban middle-class Protestant people whom they interviewed. These people, unencumbered by commitments, live in "lifestyle enclaves" with other people like themselves: upper-middle-class singles in upscale urban apartment buildings; married people with children in suburban "neighborhoods" segregated by class and race; retirees in "residential communities" of trailers or condos segregated by class. "Communities of memory" may exist, the authors suggest, but if so they would be found in ethnic and racial communities and among some religious groups. Other people – the majority – lack a community with a constitutive memory. *Habits of the Heart* thus recognized the importance of narrative as a resource for moral culture, but concluded that it is inaccessible to most Americans.

The philosopher Alasdair MacIntyre (1984) has argued persuasively that moral arguments only make sense to people when the claims are embedded in a narrative framework. Narratives link actor and community, intentions and acts. Moral culture is about making sense of life, but people engage in making sense, not by referring to abstract principles and rules, but rather in contextualized interpretations that take the form of narratives.

Sara Ruddick (1989) has considered how families develop their own constitutive narratives. Her analysis suggests that families can exhibit some of the characteristics of communities of memory, as described in *Habits of the Heart*. Through storytelling, strong families provide their members with resources for transcending their selves. In the process, individuals may come to see themselves as connected (even in debt) to previous generations and believe that this obligation can be met only by preserving their heritage for future generations.

Ironically, *Habits of the Heart* has little to say about relations between parents and children. Yet Ruddick suggested that mothers use narratives when they tell stories to their children as part of the process of "nurturing a child's developing spirit." Through such stories, according to Ruddick, "a mother creates for herself and her children the confidence that her children have a life that is very much their own and inextricably bound up with others." She posited three virtues of mothers' stories: realism, compassion, and delight. With realist stories children learn trust; with compassionate stories children learn sympathy; and when their mothers' stories show delighted admiration for their normal accomplishments, children learn generosity (1989, pp. 98–101). In Ruddick's account, good storytelling is something learned within communities of mothers. "Moral teaching" is accomplished through narrative. Bellah and his colleagues missed this because, even though they acknowledged the power of the local ("communities of memory"), they yearned for a cohesive American moral culture and a "national community" (1985, p. 153).

> For a long time our society was held together, even in periods of rapid change, by a largely Protestant cultural center that sought to reconcile the claims of community and individuality. Rejecting both chaotic openness and authoritarian closure, representatives of this cultural center defended tradition – some version of the civic republican and biblical traditions – but not traditionalism.... That task has become increasingly difficult.
>
> (Bellah *et al.* 1985, p. 155)

The hope of Bellah and his coauthors for a coherent American culture is at odds with their own argument regarding the thinness of cultural resources available to most Americans in relation to communities of memory. Moreover, their nostalgia for a "national culture" – an elite and largely Protestant cultural center (1985, p. 155) – also neglects an important thesis in Tocqueville's analysis of nineteenth-century America. For him, the destructive tendencies of individualism can be countered if people participate in institutions and voluntary associations (middle-range organizations that may span several communities but do not constitute a national culture).

Finally, in their opposition between communities of memory and lifestyle enclaves Bellah and his colleagues underestimated the degree to which other kinds of communities – communities of choice – provide resources that support Americans in their moral commitments and ethical stands. Communities of choice can also develop communities of memory. In the United States, for example, religious groups may offer venues for the development and elaboration of constitutive narratives by people who create communities of memory (see, for example, Neitz 1987; Davidman 1991). In a modern pluralist society, individuals who belong to such communities usually participate because of their own *choice*. In effect, they practice "elective parochialism," deciding to participate in a limited community (R.S. Warner 1988). The research of Neitz, Davidman, and Warner all suggests that a community is made through cultural practices – participating in the rituals, knowing the stories, and passing them on to others. Commitment to others emerges through particular activities in specific communities. Thus, what Bellah and his colleagues described as a "second language" of commitment may well amount to a local dialect, one that is not readily apparent to sociological researchers who study individuals or whole societies rather than concrete groups.

Conclusion

Bringing together narrative and identity provides a conceptualization that suggests identity is relational and processual. It "embeds the actor within relationships and stories that shift over time and space and preclude categorical stability in action" (Somers and Gibson 1994, p. 65). In contrast to the formulation of relationality in some feminist writings as a normative ideal, Somers and Gibson treat it is an analytic variable: everyone is always embedded in a relational setting – that is, "a pattern of relationships among institutions, public narratives, and social practices. As such it is a relational matrix, similar to a social network" (1994, p. 70). A narrative-identity approach posits that people are "guided to act by the relationships in which they are embedded and the stories with which they choose to identify" (1994, p. 67) Individuals find themselves in multiple, culturally constructed stories, and they formulate and enact stories, not purely as individuals, but rather in a way that is mediated by social and relational settings in which they find themselves, and by the emergent possibilities of appropriating constitutive narratives in those settings.

A thesis of narrative identity avoids the idea that individual identity is formed in conflict with society. Indeed, the very idea of "society" as a totalizing abstraction is abandoned. In its place, Somers and Gibson examine relational settings. There is an important consequence. When identity is no longer theorized as in conflict with society, the "authentic self" is no longer restricted to the emotionally expressive self of the therapeutic model. A narrative identity approach argues that the self is not separate and autonomous; rather, it is formed in relation with others.

Narrative identity also embraces the idea that people all have multiple and incomplete identities. In Craig Calhoun's words, "As lived, identity is always project, not settled accomplishment" (1994b, p. 27). In turn, the collective project of making meaning in these terms is an inherently moral project. Calhoun observes:

> Our identities are always rooted in part in ideals and moral aspirations that we cannot realize fully. There is therefore a tension within us which can be both the locus of personal struggle and the source of an identity politics that aims not simply at the legitimation of falsely essential categories but at living up to deeper social and moral values.
>
> (Calhoun 1994b, p. 29)

The idea of narrative identity thus provides a basis to supersede the modern theories of moral culture based in rules, which implied a conflict between "societies," which make rules, and "individuals," who obey or resist the rules. Instead, moral culture is to be located by way of stories and social relations. Once we begin to talk about narratives, however, we are forced to recognize that stories are constructed. Then, new critical questions arise. Whose story is being told? Who is constructing the texts? We begin to explore these questions in Chapter 3 by looking at the important issues of culture and stratification, issues of who defines the value of various cultural resources, how, and with what consequences.

Suggested readings

Amy Best's *Prom Night: Youth, Schools and Popular Culture* (2000) gives an account of the prom as a site where teens forge identities, with attention to conflicts between the more deeply invested girls and the boys they date. Best is also attentive to differences in the meaning of proms depending on students' race, class, and sexual orientation.

Stephen Carter, a law professor, in *The Culture of Disbelief: How American Law and Politics Trivialize Religious Devotion* (1993), argues that Americans concerned with maintaining the separation of church and state have unnecessarily minimized the role of religion in American culture and politics. Carter believes that public discourse would be enhanced by a greater presence of religion in the public square.

Amitava Kumar's *Passport Photos* (2000) is an innovative presentation of the complexities of immigrant identities. Kumar brings together photography, poetry, theory, and cultural criticism, organized through the categories of a passport.

Michael Warner's edited volume *Fear of a Queer Planet: Queer Politics and Social Theory* (1993) exemplifies the debates about identity politics through the writings of gay, lesbian, and queer scholars.

Robert Wuthnow's *Acts of Compassion* (1991) is an interesting empirical study of individualism in the United States. It uses both survey data and interviews to investigate people's volunteering activities.

Note

1   Freud's analysis of female socialization has been criticized by many, including female analysts of his own day and feminists such as Horney (1967), Klein (1984), Chodorow (1978), and Flax (1989).

3 Social stratification and culture

Even casual observation will confirm that the diversity of people's cultural practices is connected to social stratification – the pattern of social positions in a society and the relations of these positions to one another. Every person has a unique life. Yet on a daily basis individuals find themselves doing the culturally understandable thing, facing the dilemmas of youth in either conformity or rebellion, taking on roles – friend, sister, lover, father – and occupational positions – doctor, salesperson, mechanic, teacher – that exist independently of any individual. Each person's repertoire of cultural practices is distinctive, yet many practices are widely shared, and individual differences in repertoires are neither random nor the product of personal taste alone.

True, the cultural objects that people encounter in the course of everyday life do not usually have any readily apparent order. They are everywhere, diverse, often in a jumble. However, the disarray is only a surface one. Culture is constantly being subjected to organization – in collections, shows, stores, programs, series, and channels. The dazzling variety becomes surprisingly coherent when we view it through the lens of social stratification. Individuals all make cultural choices much narrower than the available possibilities. People prepare and consume food in distinctive ways, and some are quite concerned with becoming "culturally accomplished" – learning to dance, to weave, to play music, ride horses, or windsurf. Such orientations to culture differ systematically by social position and group.

What are the alternative approaches by which such relationships between stratification and culture can be understood? In this chapter, we are not yet concerned with the exercise of social power by which cultural objects are distributed among a population (considered in Chapter 8). The relation of culture to social stratification is a topic in its own right. To consider this relation, we can identify three basic approaches: (1) a model of cultural groups, especially *classes as cultural groups*; (2) a model of *cultural markets shaped by classes*; and (3) a model of *multiple cultural markets* shaped by *multiple cultural groups*.[1] By exploring each of these alternative models, we will be in a better position at the end of this chapter to offer a general account of how social processes connect stratification and culture.

The group theory: castes and classes

The classical theory that social groups have distinctive cultural boundaries was put forward by Emile Durkheim in his studies on the division of labor and on religion (1964, 1995). As Durkheim saw it, complex societies with highly differentiated divisions of labor do not typically have much common or "collective" consciousness that is shared by all members of the population. Nevertheless, for all societies, he regarded religion as establishing a distinction between what is considered "sacred" and what is considered "profane" (that is, beyond the interest of religion). This distinction, he argued, is not really concerned with God in some spiritual sense, but with a social group's moral boundaries. Any group will have some rankings of hierarchy and prestige, but, for Durkheim, a solidary social group that affirms strong bonds among its members exists only to the degree that culture is fundamentally shared by all those members. In a group with a high degree of solidarity, culture thus serves as an ingroup/outgroup marker, and as a marker of conformity or deviance. To take one example, people often wear clothing or adopt hairstyles (often gender-specific) identified with a particular group – dreadlocks for reggae or Hip-Hop, a chador for a Muslim woman, a yarmulke for a devout Jewish male, and so on. Such cultural choices mark individuals' relations to groups for anyone conversant in group symbols, and they thus emphasize group boundaries.

Durkheim was not the only classical sociologist to study the relation between culture and social groups. Early in the twentieth century, the German sociologist Georg Simmel proposed a thesis about the "lowest common level," namely that culture must be accessible enough in its content and form to reach virtually all members of a group (1950, p. 37). For Simmel, like Durkheim, a group can thrive only on the basis of shared culture.

During the same period, another German sociologist, Max Weber, described the "status group" as a group of persons in a larger society who claim either a "special social esteem" or "status monopolies." Such groups, Weber held, amount to "circles setting themselves apart by means of…characteristics and badges" (1978, pp. 305–7, 932–33). As for specifics, the sources of status are various (lifestyle, education, occupation, family) and open to the invention of status markers by actual social groups – sometimes, with implications of subversion for the dominant social order, as Dick Hebdige (1979) has documented for British mods, rockers, punks, and Rastafarians.

A group-culture model of the sort described by classical social theorists seems useful to describe societies of certain times and places, for example "estate" societies like medieval Europe, institutionally racist societies such as South Africa during the era of apartheid and the U.S. South before Jim Crow laws were abolished in the 1960s, or "caste" societies such as the traditional social order of India. As Murray Milner (1994) observes for India, even without legal sanctions, status power can maintain groups and boundaries by such devices as controlling who engages in the intimate activity of sharing meals, and regulating sexual coupling through arranged marriages. Cultural structurings of social relations in such situations work because diverse people adhere to widely recognized social norms, which have the quality of de facto rules.

However, can a group-culture model account for stratification and culture in societies where a social order lacks any basis of enforcement in norms? The best-known effort to use this sort of model to explain non-caste societies is Karl Marx's analysis of socioeconomic classes as groups. Marx defined class positions not as a *continuum* of ranked occupations and prestige but as memberships within social *groups* opposed to each other on the basis of conflicting economic interests (e.g. workers versus owners of capital). Although Marx theorized that class has an objective basis (class "in itself"), only in a class "for itself" do people who are self-conscious about their shared class position collectively pursue their common interests. Where does culture come into this picture? For Marx, class centrally shapes consciousness and ideology.

Marxists thus regard culture as important because it "mediates" how people participate in an economically structured world by offering them recipes for dealing with
their circumstances, by providing ideologies that legitimate the existing class order,
and by providing meaningful interpretations about the persistent problems and frustrations that people encounter because of their class situations (Raymond Williams
1982, p. 24). As the historian E.P. Thompson (1963) famously argued, classes are
involved in their own making, and cultural traditions and moral outlooks are important in how class is made. Recently, scholars have criticized Thompson's account, but
they have done so by emphasizing even more strongly the significance of culture for
class experience and action (Somers 1997; Biernacki 1997, 2000).

Max Weber also identified distinct cultures of classes as social groups, but he did
so in a different way from Marx. Weber applied his concept of status groups to, for
example, propertied classes whose participants affirm their prestige and monopolize
their resources through marriage and inheritance. Whatever the ways people in propertied classes obtain wealth, they perpetuate their status groups by maintaining
distinct boundaries marked by particular education and expressive behaviors (Weber
1978, p. 307).

An American sociologist of culture, Herbert Gans (1974), has pursued Weber's lead
by identifying five class-based taste publics that embrace five distinctive taste cultures:
(1) high culture, (2) upper-middle culture, (3) lower-middle culture, (4) low culture, and
(5) quasi-folk low culture. Gans was careful to note that he was describing broad categorical clusters of culture, not fixed cultures drawn upon by bounded status groups
such as those described by Weber. He also pointed out that much culture – from opera
to rock – gains an audience from more than one class, and noted that crosscutting
distinctions of stratified culture might derive from ethnicity, gender, religion, region,
and other bases of social differentiation.

Overall, by describing class-based taste cultures, Gans showed that the stratification
of culture is not simply a matter of individual whim or status gradations along a
continuum of prestige. Instead, he identified basic shifts in overall orientation and logic
that mark boundaries between the various taste cultures he identified. Yet Gans did not
argue that class-based social groups are tightly bounded by culture. Class boundary
maintenance cannot be very strict, since classes lack sufficient organization or power to
monopolize "their" culture. It would be difficult for a committee of the upper class to
stop a lottery ticket winner from buying up high-culture paintings or becoming a
patron of the opera (or, more likely, buying that Mercedes). The fact is that today most
cultural objects – from material objects like cars and stereos to "human capital" such as
education and social skills – can be acquired in the marketplace. How might a theory of
culture and stratification take account of this central fact?

The market/class group theory

In his book *Distinction*, first published in 1979, French sociologist Pierre Bourdieu
(1930–2002) showed for France what Gans had found in the U.S., namely that there
are coherent social-class differences in the consumption of culture. Bourdieu stated in
the preface to the English edition that he wanted "to rethink Max Weber's opposition
between class and *Stand* [status group]" (1984, p. xii), and he argued that people's class
positions and aspirations are closely connected to how they style their lives.
Fundamental life sensibilities – what Bourdieu termed "habitus" – he regarded as

formed largely in the subtle nuances of class-located household life, based partly on family culture, inherited both materially and through socialization (see Figure 3.1). Classes are marked by the unconscious unity of habitus (Bourdieu 1984, pp. 16, 77, 101, 327).

Bourdieu was a very effective synthesizer. Much of what he discussed had already been analyzed by others. Thus, Weber had treated social classes as status groups with special lifestyles, and Bourdieu was posturing a bit to imply otherwise. And Thorstein Veblen (1965) and Herbert Gans (1974) had offered incisive accounts of the relation between social classes and culture. Nevertheless, Bourdieu consolidated an important analysis, arguing that status groups are mapped upon a class-based grid, that the terms of status are dictated by the dominant class, and that people – individually and collectively – employ "strategies of distinction" to vie for acceptance of their own worth by others.

> Competitive struggle is the form of class struggle which the dominated classes allow to be imposed on them when they accept the stakes [of distinction] offered by the dominant classes. It is an integrative struggle and, by virtue of the initial

Figure 3.1 Habitus is transmitted in part through the social interaction of daily life, as with the Hercules Brown farm family at their Maine dinner table in 1944.

Source: Gordon Parks photo, Special Collections, Photographic Archives, University of Louisville.

handicaps, a reproductive struggle [i.e. approximately recreating existing distinctions], since those who enter this chase, in which they are beaten before they start, as the constancy of the gaps testifies, implicitly recognize the legitimacy of the goals pursued by those whom they pursue, by the mere fact of taking part.

(Bourdieu 1984, p. 165)

In other words, people participate in a class-defined struggle for social distinction that renders status differentials legitimate even though the terms of the contest are set by a dominant class.

Despite Bourdieu's self-proclaimed emphasis on the agency of people's practice, sociologist Jeffrey Alexander (1995) regards his approach as a reconfiguration of a deterministic version of Marxism that is reductionist in its tendency to treat people's culture as instrumentally derived from their class-based pursuit of interests. From this point of view, Bourdieu can seem like a cultural philistine who does not take people's enjoyment of music or art seriously in its own terms. The validity of Bourdieu's account is thus open to substantial critique, but to critique it we must understand it first.

Class, cultural capital, and the ongoing struggle for status

Bourdieu's most distinctive innovation over earlier sociologies of class-status stratification was to shift from a static description of class-based cultural practices toward theorizing the processes by which status distinctions get defined and reproduced in relation to cultural objects over time. He did this by designating the concept of "capital" to represent significant resources that can be drawn upon in the conduct of life, and then defining class-stratified social space in terms of capital. For Bourdieu, there are three aspects to capital – volume, composition, and trajectory. Volume is simply the amount of capital. "Composition" refers to the relative preponderance of "economic capital, cultural capital, and also social capital." Bourdieu did not develop in detail his concepts of economic capital (i.e. wealth) or social capital, which refers to networks – "who you know." By cultural capital, he meant the knowledge, taste, and sensibilities, and the material possessions that together give a person the ability to lay claim to one or another kind of esteem or honor – that is, what Weber called status. Cultural capital in Bourdieu's account has two major sources – first, the habitus of family life and, second, education, which can substitute somewhat for family life in helping the individual to acquire taste and manners that mark a certain status. But, Bourdieu argued, education works better for the more public displays of cultural refinement (such as music or art appreciation) than it does for arcane areas of free-lance cultural practice (such as polo-team banter or comportment at an exclusive party) (1984, pp. 13, 94, 114).

In Bourdieu's account, some people have such a small amount, or *volume*, of capital – cultural or economic – that the relative *composition* between the two is meaningless. At the other end of the scale, a great deal of cultural capital usually comes hand in hand with a great deal of economic capital, especially over several generations. Indeed, at the very top end of today's art market, the difference between cultural and economic capital is all but erased because wealthy buyers of famous paintings are paying such high prices (the record is $82.5 million paid for a Van Gogh by a Japanese corporate executive in 1990).

By contrast to the bottom and the top of status hierarchies, in the middling regions the composition of cultural and economic capital is more variable: at any given class level, various individuals may have considerably more of one form of capital than the other, and such differences maintain distinctions between people of different occupational worlds. Thus, members of the non-wealthy but cultured French intelligentsia prefer less expensive aesthetic activities such as cooking exotic foods, while wealthier individuals at the same class level of taste tend to engage in more expensive forms of aesthetic consumption, such as going to fashionable restaurants (Bourdieu 1974). Similarly, but at a lower overall class level, in the French petit bourgeoisie Bourdieu located junior administrative executives and small shopkeepers in a cultural realm where pop singer Petula Clark found a following, whereas the typical interests of primary-school teachers and people in sociomedical services were more likely to include flea markets, antique shops, and impressionist painters (1984, p. 340).

Finally, *trajectory* is important in Bourdieu's theory. We each have status careers of mobility, from social origins to present position, to subsequent status destinations. For people of a given set of origins, say workers in a small factory town, small business owners in a suburban community, or large landowners raising livestock, there exist typical channels of individual mobility – trajectories. At a given time, different people may hold similar positions, but differences in trajectory (origins and future destinations) make for distinctions among them. The recent business-school graduate doing a brief tour of duty as a loan officer to learn that side of the banking business has a different sense of status honor than someone who has performed the job for years without hope of advancement.

By connecting people's trajectories over time with their struggles to acquire and protect cultural and economic capital, Bourdieu's analysis "sets in motion" a model of culture and social stratification. His theory thus is not based on trying to chart class groups and their boundaries sociologically. Instead, he portrayed a social world where these boundaries are incessantly tested and renegotiated by people who deploy culture as a kind of capital – something, like money, that can be gained or lost, and used to obtain other things in one or another market.

When Bourdieu's approach is applied to the actual social world, things become considerably more complex. For one thing, the capital value of the culture that we invoke, consume, or display is not fixed. To the contrary, any calculus of cultural value is altered by people's uses of it. No doubt there are simple values such as personal enjoyment that play into our cultural choices. But the purposes of people's cultural practices also may include "properly" identifying themselves for others in terms of status symbols (by wearing the "right" clothes as a stockbroker, for example) and promoting the social chances of children (by sending a child to the "correct" school). The invocation of culture – from how we dress and groom to how we decorate our living spaces and what lifestyles we take on – offers a basis for others to "sort" our social positions and offer or refuse us their esteem (Goffman 1951).

For the newly wealthy, as Thorstein Veblen (1965) already argued at the end of the nineteenth century, wealth must be "conspicuous" in its consumption. Thus, in Veblen's time wearing white clothes demonstrated that a person did not come near dirt, while a suntan was the mark of a worker who was forced to be outside. The meaning of a suntan has undergone shifts since Veblen's time, but then, as now, visible leisure activities offer the definitive proof that a person is not working. However, money and what it can buy alone are not enough to affirm one's status position. For people with "old money," *how to live* is more important than *what to buy* in maintaining the boundary against "new money" (Aldrich 1988). This is where arcane cultural practices such as the polo locker-room banter become important.

More generally, the cultural-capital value of objects and practices remains in flux because of two mutually reinforcing processes. First, people of less esteemed status positions may seek to alter perceptions of their status by adopting more esteemed culture, and such imitation may deflate the capital value of culture. Anyone with the money can buy a fancy car, and other people besides the rich can visit exclusive resorts. Similarly, middle-class people have increasingly adopted home furnishings with an "international" style that was previously associated with upper-class and upper-middle-class tastes. Such practices of borrowing and imitation are reinforced by a second process, namely the mass marketing of goods that bear the trappings of high status. Oil of Olay, once a strictly high-culture beauty cream, now has been successfully mass marketed, apparently without drastically diluting its prestige. Other name brands may go through a deflation of their cultural capital, especially through imitation and mass marketing. Gucci knockoff items for sale in hypermarket stores like Migros or Target tend to undermine the prestige of real Gucci objects available only through exclusive department stores like Saks Fifth Avenue. Mass-marketing strategies similarly tend to devalue goods culturally, such that high-status users may feel their purchases have been "ruined" (to quote one shopper's response to the new product line and marketing of a high-end brand of recreational clothes – Patagonia).

Taking account of these sorts of processes, Bourdieu described a status scramble in which cultural capital figures prominently, yet what counts as cultural capital changes according to who uses it and how. Given the inflationary pressures set in motion by efforts at imitation, if positively esteemed groups are to maintain exclusivity they must either effectively monopolize their distinctive goods, practices, and sites of sociability or keep altering these cultural "badges" in order to distinguish themselves from pretenders who have appropriated their previous ones. Thus, economic elites may abandon restaurants once they are invaded by others. Similarly, the self-styled avant-garde of youth culture (punk and Hip-Hop, for example) seek new fashion codes and cultural practices when their old ones become the objects of imitation and mass marketing. Indeed, beauty and fashion represent something of a prototypical example. Colors, fabrics, cuts of cloth, and style of garments constitute a general "language" of fashion, but the value of a particular "look" or way of dressing in part depends on the successful promotion by a class or status group of their definitions of beauty and fashion as the standards by which beauty and fashion in general may be judged (Lurie 1981; Banner 1983; M. Webster and Driskell 1983; Hatfield and Sprecher 1986; F. Davis 1992; Craik 1994; Crane 2000).

Not all culture is so easy to take off and put on as clothes. Subtle cues often mark our cultural origins. People seeking social mobility can be burdened by effects of socialization that reveal their class upbringing (dinner-table manners or lack of knowledge of Renaissance art, for example). We may attempt mobility through education (which yields cultural capital), but it is not easy for us to shed family socialization. Moreover, in societies with strong class boundaries of distinction individual cultural mobility is likely to be limited. Significant mobility is more likely to be consolidated over several generations, because over the longer time span even arcane cultural capital can be gained by marriage and changes in neighborhood, by choices of voluntary associations, churches, and schools, and by gaining entrance to exclusive clubs.

However, even in hierarchical societies, class mobility does occur, and in societies with higher individual mobility class-distinctive culture may be more easy for the individual to take on. Thus, although barriers of access to cultural capital constrain mobility, they certainly do not eliminate it. The possibilities depend not only on the individual, but on the social structuration of cultural distinctions and economic avenues of occupational mobility.

Societal patterns of cultural capital

The exclusivity exercised by class-based status groups is not just the sum of individual practices. Rather, patterns of culture–status relations differ from society to society and over time. Two examples illustrate the varying structurations of cultural capital in societies as wholes. First, consider the emergence of modern architecture: this happened in Europe rather than America in the 1920s and 1930s, David Gartman (2000) argues, because in the United States the technical professionals who promoted the modernist aesthetic became absorbed into corporate capitalism, and in this corporate world imperatives of mass marketing undermined the aesthetic of modernism. By contrast, in Europe capitalist development was slower during the interwar period, and technocratic professionals became allied with the state, where they found an outlet for the realization of their modernist aesthetic in public building projects. In this comparative analysis, cultural aesthetics were conditioned by the social locations of the strata that sought to advance them.

A second range of cases evidences a quite different process – of hierarchies of status becoming reconfigured in the wake of dramatic social change. The collapse of communist regimes in Russia and Eastern Europe in 1989 offers a laboratory for examining status hierarchies under such conditions. After all, communist ruling elites – the *nomenklatura* – were strongly entrenched before 1989. In countries like Russia, Poland, and Hungary, were these elites able to reproduce themselves after 1989, or was there a circulation of elites? The answers, according to an international research team, are mixed. In some countries, old elites declined in influence, but in Russia the *nomenklatura* did not experience dramatic loss of status (Szelényi and Szelényi 1995). There, previously entrenched elites were able to trade political and cultural capital for economic capital (Wasilewski and Wnuk-Lipinski 1995). The old elites in effect reinvented themselves under new circumstances. These postcommunist transformations suggest a more general possibility – that the relationships between different types of capital can change, and that one kind of capital (political) can be parlayed into another (economic). Moreover, the transformations demonstrate that cultural capital has a different character from economic capital.

The emergence of "postindustrial" society in industrialized countries beginning during the 1960s provides another example of the complex relation between economic and cultural capital. Theories of postindustrial society, once highly contested, now seem prescient in their description of late-twentieth-century economic changes in which increasing proportions of individuals worked at jobs where services, rather than objects, are produced (see Chapter 7). This transformation has established whole new echelons of social ranking for positions in travel agencies, tourism, franchise-restaurant management, computer-network administration, and numerous other occupations. Yet the social mobility of people moving "up" into new occupational positions has not required higher status groups to abandon their status positions.

Thus, sports instructors at a posh resort may make very good salaries, but they still are likely to encounter a gap of distinction defined by their clients. In response, tourist-service workers sometimes develop their own disdain (bordering on resentment), distancing themselves from the very patrons who make their livelihood possible, by valuing status traits different from their employers', nevertheless sometimes secretly envying those patrons (cf. Scheler 1961).

Transformations of cultural capital in postindustrial societies suggest one reason why poorer social classes have not tended to develop radical political consciousness. So far, capitalism has avoided the "inevitable" crisis predicted by Karl Marx. One explanation may be that economies of scale in mass production and the increasing production of symbolic culture have produced goods and services more cheaply. Inexpensively produced goods and services still can represent advances in consumption for those who buy them. For the less well off, things previously beyond their reach – a television (and the connection to popular culture it offers), a vacation cruise – mark meaningful advancements in cultural capital, even if class position remains constant. In these terms, the legitimacy of capitalism is more readily sustained if the expansion of cultural capital is greater than the cost of producing it, and if distribution of cultural capital to politically active strata is widespread. So long as people are able to develop their own personal cultural capital through mass consumption, they are less likely to identify with economic classes as self-conscious groups that pursue shared interests. Thus, the distribution of cultural capital can undermine class consciousness while paradoxically maintaining distinctions among classes as groups.

In general, Bourdieu's theory of class groups and cultural-capital markets suggests that classes operate in relation to coherent boundaries defined partly on the basis of culture, rather than purely through collective pursuit of economic interests. How does this class-market theory speak to the question of whether classes exist as distinctive groups? This question can be addressed by looking at the recent borrowings of upper-middle-class motifs within middle-class culture in the U.S. As late as the 1950s, middle-class culture retained an aversion to the cosmopolitan sophistication of the upper-middle class. Today, things have changed substantially. Nationwide chain stores like Sears have made intense efforts to shed their dry, sober, respectable images, and the emergent discount chain store Target commissioned famous postmodern architect and designer Michael Graves to produce a line of teapots, lamps, clocks, and other utensils. In a sort of hybrid postmodern marketing strategy, they now offer affordable designer goods that blur the distinction between upper-middle-class and middle-class culture.

What do the changes in content and style of middle-class culture mean? Has a continuum replaced any sharp boundary that previously existed between it and upper-middle-class culture? The answer is subject to debate. Bourdieu (1984, e.g. p. 327), like Gans (1974, p. 85), thought not. By their analyses, upper-middle culture often plays on ambiguity – especially through the use of symbolism, abstraction, and analytic discourse. On the other hand, straight or pop, middle-class culture retains its emphasis on clear and concrete meanings and unambiguous truth (or sharply contrasted positions in controversies); it is centrally organized by the affirmation of core cultural values, and by the resolution of dramatic events in clearcut ways.

Middle-class culture is oriented to an enormous audience, and its character may be explained by this fact. As Simmel argued a century ago, the boundaries of a social group are defined by the lowest common denominator of its culture – which every member of the group must share in order to participate (1950, p. 37). Thus, middle-class culture is necessarily limited in its content by the need to connect to a large and diverse audience. The key to this culture is its very broad accessibility: in middle-class entertainment, the audience can enter into the drama in a direct way, "identifying with the characters' joys and sufferings, worrying about their fate, espousing their hopes and ideals, living their life," without anxieties about whether they are missing "deeper" meanings (Bourdieu 1984, p. 33). Film, novels, and television action series, talk shows, and situation comedies must have unambiguous drama, and news is to be reported in ways that treat resolution of events in terms of established morality and public values, packaged in a coherent story (Gans 1974, p. 86).

A cultural boundary exists between the middle class and higher-status classes, Bourdieu suggested, because in the middle class what people actually know of culture falls short of what they themselves recognize as culturally important to know (it is important to choose a fine wine, but how do you know which one to choose?). The result of the middle-class shortfall in higher-class situations is either indifference or "pretension" – the display of culture in a way that exceeds self-assured familiarity. A parallel boundary exists for the working class, where both distinction and pretensions of being "cultured" are disdained in favor of utilitarian adaptation to circumstance – "making do" (Bourdieu 1976). Working-class culture often emphasizes suspicion of Culture with a capital C, along with respectability, intellectuals, manners, and elitist noblesse oblige. Rejecting these badges of cultivation allows working-class people to invoke a meaningful world in which people are "real," uncontrived, and straightforward in their likes and dislikes, where they may fart among friends rather than engage in presentations of self that deny the basic bodily processes (cf. Goffman 1971, ch. 2).

Just as Gans zeroed in on class-based tastes, Bourdieu argued that people differentially formulate distinctions (e.g. "refined" versus "common," "shallow" versus "deep") that map class boundaries. Yet, despite the parallels between Gans's and Bourdieu's approaches, Bourdieu's theory treats culture as a particular kind of capital, akin to monetary capital, that can be accumulated and used in the attainment of status in a class-based marketplace of distinction. This shift to a market concept has an important consequence: the coherence of class aesthetic boundaries is undermined by individuals' efforts in the cultural marketplace to acquire badges of distinction. They move upward and downward on scales of value that are redefined by the very motion of individuals on them. This flux in turn suggests two important directions for the critique and development of Bourdieu's approach: (1) examining the dynamics of class cultural-capital structuration (i.e. within the market/class group theory) and (2) extending the model to non-class-based status-group processes (i.e. by considering a market/status group theory.

Critiques of Bourdieu within the domain of class

Bourdieu developed his analysis of class and culture in a particular society, France. He argued vehemently against isolated grand theory, but advocated comparative investigation of parallel processes. For example, he pointed to the significance of political capital in the communist-era Democratic Republic of Germany (East Germany), and in considering Japan he warned against emphasizing surface differences (such as Samurai culture) that would mask parallel processes of distinction across nation-states (Bourdieu 1991, pp. 628, 630, 640).

A number of scholars have undertaken similar comparative analyses, but they have drawn into question Bourdieu's general thesis that an elite social class dominates the struggles over cultural capital. Thus, in a comparative analysis of France and the United States, Michèle Lamont (1992) focuses on the role of the *upper-middle* class rather than the *upper* class in setting the general terms of struggle. Other researchers have questioned Bourdieu's entire thesis of class-based distinction. Thus, David Halle compared the art that people had in their homes in affluent versus blue-collar households in urban and suburban neighborhoods of metropolitan New York. Time and again, Halle found Bourdieu's model overly simplistic. Of course wealthier people could afford more expensive art in their homes, but Halle did not find their tastes to differ radically from the less well off. Abstract paintings, for example, were likely to be appreciated for their decorative function – how well they match the home décor – rather than for sophisticated aesthetic reasons of the sort anticipated by Bourdieu's theory of cultural capital (Halle 1993, pp. 128–32). Family aesthetic choices are rooted in people's current lives and experiences as much as in differences of education and family background (Halle 1993, p. 84).

Are class differences in culture, then, really based on elite snobbery? Recent research in North America suggests a different answer – that higher class positions are more likely to be occupied by what Richard Peterson and his coauthors (Peterson and Simkus 1992; Peterson and Kern 1996) call *omnivores* – people with eclectic tastes who are willing to engage cultural materials across a variety of genres. Elite eclecticism is an important phenomenon, but it is manifested in complex ways. Bethany Bryson (1996, 1997) shows that eclecticism has its limits. Even the most tolerant, highly educated individuals are still likely to reject the music of the least educated – rap, country, gospel, and heavy metal. On the other hand, as Peterson and his colleagues expect, people in lower status positions are much more likely to be exclusive *univores* who embrace a single genre, often mapped on the basis of their race or ethnicity, geographic region, and other exclusive badges of identity. Bryson concludes that these findings do not so much discredit Bourdieu's account as transpose it toward understanding that elites can use multicultural capital as a basis for cultural exclusion (Bryson 1996, p. 897).

Some elites may base exclusion on snobbish boundaries, but, as Alexis de Tocqueville (1945) already noted in the early nineteenth century, they have tended to do so more in France (on which Bourdieu's *Distinction* is based) and other European countries than in more egalitarian North America. Moreover, snobbishness seems widely to have declined. It is true that in the latter half of the nineteenth century upper-class Americans tried to replicate Victorian culture in order to affirm their elite position, as Veblen so brilliantly showed. But from the waning years of the nineteenth century onward, and especially during the last quarter of the twentieth century, snobbishness probably has declined on both sides of the Atlantic. In France, for example, cultural elites have embraced jazz and, more recently, gospel music, even if they do so in ways that maintain status boundaries (in that this taste is less likely to be shared among the French popular classes). Here, as Bryson suggests, multicultural capital still functions to maintain distinctions.

The explanation for the elite shift to multicultural (omnivore) capital in the U.S. and other developed societies is not hard to find. Peterson and Kern suggest that the answer has to do with shifts in social structure, values, and the dramatic increase in mass-distributed culture (1996, pp. 904–6). Over the course of modernity, elite culture has changed dramatically in developed societies. At the beginning of the twentieth century, true aristocratic elites and pseudo-aristocratic business elites staked their distinction on conducting a refined life of social exclusivity. But already at that time, socially privileged American families were abandoning Victorian exclusivity and drawing on the aesthetic of Teddy Roosevelt's rough riders to teach their children to hold their own with many different kinds of people (Belasco 1979). This tendency only increased. Almost a century later, studying a workplace in Toronto, Canada, Bonnie Erickson (1996) found that managers' effective coordination of workers depended on their own ability to participate in culture shared *across* class lines, for example by taking part in sports discussions. Peterson and Kern neatly summarize the shift (1996, p. 906): as highbrow snobbishness fit the needs of the earlier entrepreneurial upper-middle class, in today's most developed societies there is a similar elective affinity between a new business-administrative class and omnivore tastes.

Elsewhere in the world, the relationship between elite and popular culture may be completely different. For example, political leaders and the elites they represent some-times have embraced a strong nationalistic culture in order to ally themselves with workers and peasants, as did Huey Long in Louisiana in the late 1920s, Adolf Hitler in Germany in the 1930s, Juan Perón in Argentina in the 1940s and 1950s, and Joseph Mobutu in the Congo (which he renamed Zaire) in the 1970s through the 1990s. This range of cases in which elite political cultures appropriate popular symbols suggests that the omnivore–univore relation to class cultures will be an important subject for further historical and comparative investigation.

Overall, the research on cultural capital and class initiated by Bourdieu builds on Gans's delineation of classes as culturally stratified taste publics by revealing not just static distinctions, but a dynamic complex of practices by which people give value to diverse cultural practices and objects, thus placing aesthetics and boundaries in contestation. However, Bourdieu's model of cultural capital has itself been subject to revision based on empirical research. These analyses do not deny the struggle for distinction; rather, they show that (1) the bases for distinction vary across national settings and (2) the class dominating any given societal calculus of distinction is not always the most privileged one. In turn, recent work also raises a question about whether Bourdieu's model needs more fundamental revision. Bryson (1996) shows that lower-status culture is often marked by *ethnic* exclusivity, while Erickson (1996) points out that sports discourse not only enhances class domination but tends to sustain *gender* boundaries. We are left to consider the relation of class to other cultural bases of distinction.

The market/status-group theory

Stepping back, two questions arise about Bourdieu's market/class group theory of cultural capital. First, is class the only important basis of such capital? At least theo-retically, it seems that other kinds of groups – religious or ethnic groups or motorcycle gangs – could establish and distribute various kinds of cultural capital. Do such status groups create solidarity among people across *different* social classes? Alternatively, are they simply a further differentiation of status *within* a particular class?

Second, we should ask whether the relation of non-class groups to culture might require a more complex approach than a class/market theory of cultural capital. If boundaries exist between dominant and subordinated non-class groups, what is the specific character of subordinated culture? Does it help members of the subordinated group survive in the wider world, or does it encapsulate them in a limited world?

In short, Bourdieu's project needs to be evaluated in relation to, for example, gender and ethnicity. We must ask questions such as whether gendered cultures simply represent two sides of class culture at a given level, or do men and women, gays and straights, live in the world in ways that fundamentally differ?

Bourdieu acknowledged that not all culture is economically determined:

> As the objective distance from necessity grows, lifestyle increasingly becomes the product of what Weber calls a "stylization of life," a systematic commitment that orients and organizes the most diverse practices – the choice of a vintage or a cheese or the decoration of a holiday home in the country.
>
> (Bourdieu 1984, pp. 55–6)

This suggests the possibility of other criteria besides class coming into play in distinctions of pure leisure and consumption. Of course, much leisure consumption can be located in class practices – of visiting an amusement park versus fox hunting, or horseshoes versus croquet. Yet class cultures certainly do not subsume all distinctions.

Let us consider people whose lives are *most* likely to be dictated by economic "necessity" – poor people. One way of looking at their culture is to treat it as a barrier to mobility. Thus, in the 1950s anthropologist Oscar Lewis claimed to identify a "culture of poverty" – a remarkably consistent pattern that "cuts across regional, rural–urban, and even national boundaries." This pattern, Lewis argued, could be "found in lower-class settlements in London…, in Puerto Rico…, in Mexico City slums and Mexican villages…, and among lower class Negroes in the United States." Lewis's ethnographic accounts did not portray culture as an absolute trap; nevertheless, he argued, "One can speak of the culture of the poor, for it has its own modalities and distinctive social and psychological consequences for its members" (1959, p. 2). This analysis was and is controversial. It has met concerted critique from social scientists as well as intellectuals on the Left who take it to "blame the victims" for their own predicament (e.g. Leacock 1971; Gresham and Wilkerson 1989).

However the culture-of-poverty thesis is assessed, there is considerable room for debate about whether the cultural-capital model adequately explains poor people's cultures. On the one hand, the poor find themselves exposed to the cheapest of petty commercial culture – "dive" restaurants and cafeterias, secondhand stores, tabloids, and cheap movie theaters. Moreover, they are the targets of state and religiously organized welfare and charity programs that provide, not only food and shelter, but distinctive cultural visions of moral community – both among the poor themselves, and by better-off people in relation to them (Allahyari 2000). These circumstances would suggest that the poor partake of what Bourdieu calls a "dominated" cultural aesthetic – one defined from the outside.

Conversely, as Michael Harrington made clear in his famous book *The Other America* (1962), conditions of poverty are diverse, and the poor are often cut off from the worlds of the more fortunate. They do not engage in commercial consumption to the same extent that more moneyed classes do, and this implies that they are less easily reached by mass popular culture and that their culture is more likely to be considered "deviant." They thus represent an extreme of what Michel de Certeau (1984) argued more generally, that the complexity of everyday life eludes social or sociological efforts to compartmentalize people on the basis of categorical distinctions. Paradoxically, the distance of the poor from class-defined commercial mass culture leaves room for the importance of "quasi-folk" cultures composed through the ongoing practices of people who live socially marginal lives (Gans 1974).

Cultures of the poor have been described in essays like George Orwell's *Down and Out in Paris and London* (1933), autobiographies by hoboes Jack Black (1988) and Boxcar Bertha (Reitman 1988), and ethnographies such as *Tally's Corner* (H. Lewis 1967), *Carnival Strippers* (Meiselas 1976), *Gender and Slum Culture in Urban Asia* (Thorbeck 1994), and *Sidewalk* (Duneier 1999). The ethnographic accounts underscore Gans's point, that people mediate their distinctive senses of honor in relation to other socially constructed boundaries besides class, for example ethnicity, gender, and geographic locale. Writing during the Great Depression of the 1930s, George Orwell described men on the road in France and Britain who inhabited a different social world from people who had a more settled existence – in a city, suburb, town, or farm community. Boxcar Bertha told her story of making it as a woman in a predominantly male world of hoboes. Thorbeck describes the complex life strategies of women who live in urban slums in Sri Lanka and Thailand. Tally's corner was a hangout for black men who formed a status group with its own moral code about their relations with the women who live beyond their group boundary. Duneier's *Sidewalk* residents in New York City develop rationales of their life choices that are not simply the product of external "domination" of their culture. And carnival strippers live outside conventional women's roles, at a high cost to their social status and to their interactions with men, but with their own distinctive sense of honor even as relative social outcasts.

Of course, as cultural studies have emphasized in recent years, while no one's social identity can be reduced to a theorized central dimension of stratification, nevertheless class, ethnicity, and gender remain important socially structured bases of inequality (Omi and Winant 1994). People's situations inevitably involve multiple axes of identity, typically in flux because of changing social circumstances. Joanna Bourke (1994) shows, for instance, that among the working class in Britain, class is mapped and remapped over time in relation to aspects of gender and ethnicity, with women struggling over domestic, occupational, and sexual issues while members of different ethnic groups contend over occupations and neighborhoods. In a different way, Kimberly Grimes (1998) explores how constructed understandings of ethnicity and gender undergo shifts for people from Putla, Mexico, when they migrate to the United States. And, as Lamont (2000) argues, both black and white working men in the U.S. evaluate other people more on the basis of their own moral standards than by using the standards of their supposed superiors.

Because people's social circumstances seem ever changing, a key question concerns the conditions under which people will try to organize collectively on the basis of any particular axis of social stratification – class, gender, or ethnicity. If they try to do so, they are confronted with how to handle other distinctions in relation to whichever one they seek to affirm as axial. Thus, there is a continuum in the ways that non-class bases of culture can be articulated with class and culture. At one extreme, gender or ethnicity or status-group culture may provide a wholly *alternative* basis of cultural solidarity that cuts *across* (and reduces the importance of) class distinctions. At the other extreme, non-class bases of culture may be structured wholly *within* classes. These alternatives can be explored briefly for gender and ethnicity as examples of social criteria that give rise to status groups.

Gender

If biological differences in sex determined gender roles of men and women, then we would expect similar patterns of gendered culture to exist across different social classes. In this vein, the early-twentieth-century German sociologist Georg Simmel described feminine culture as tied to the specific form of "female nature," and he argued that, "with the exception of a very few areas, our objective [i.e. public] culture is thoroughly male" (1984, p. 67). Feminists point to the many public cultural accomplishments of women artists, novelists, musicians, and others whose work has not been incorporated into the historically male-defined canon of legitimate cultural accomplishment. All the same, feminist theories of patriarchal society share Simmel's view that the dominant societal cultures – religion, art, music, legal institutions, and so on – are cultures dominated by men. Feminists also have applied a theory of patriarchy to the sexual division of labor in the household, arguing that male power defines a situation in which not only sexual reproduction but parenting and housework are predominantly ascribed as female tasks. Such cultural patterns of gender relations are explained as the consequence of social differentials of power between males and females that cannot be reduced to class (O'Brien 1981; Polatnick 1983).

Patterns of male-dominated gender culture can be found in otherwise diverse societies around the world, from China and Japan, to India, the Arab world, Africa, Europe, and North and South America. Nevertheless, the meanings of "female" and "male" (and other gender categories such as lesbian, queer, and transsexual) differ considerably across societies, and they change over time. Some societies have three genders – men, women, and men-as-social-women or "manly hearted women"; in other societies, gender roles may be so narrowly prescribed that for a woman to perform certain actions she has to be reclassified as an "honorary man." These gender differentiations can prove very durable within societies; as Judith Lorber has observed, efforts to "bend" or otherwise transgress gender boundaries may have the opposite effect: transgression as deviance reinforces definitions of "normality" (1994; cf. Foucault 1978–86; Herdt 1994; Fradenburg and Freccero 1996; D'Emilio and Freedman 1997).

Despite cross-cultural differences, the social construction of gender is frequently connected to other dimensions of stratification. Since industrialization took hold during the nineteenth century, the relation to social class has become reconfigured. The very concept "feminine" may be associated with the delicacy and sentimentality of a leisured life, sensibilities quite different from the "maternal" attributes of strength, nurture, and generosity that are more likely to be associated with a woman who works as a homemaker. The dominant women's gender identity can shift between these (and other) possibilities, mirrored by changing men's gender identities. Thus, for the U.S. during the nineteenth century, Ann Douglas (1977) has argued, a strong identity as matron of household production was displaced by a *less* powerful – and highly sentimentalized – *feminine* gender role for women. During the same period, middle-class male gender identities shifted from pioneer virility toward feminized constructions – exemplified in the outlook of (male) novelists and Protestant ministers. In Douglas's thesis, the nineteenth-century feminization of American culture had uneven consequences: middle-class wives, for example, became the moral leaders of families, but they also were reduced from producers to consumers. With the emergence of an industrial society, civility, commerce, and the display of a lifestyle came to count more among the middle classes than physical strength, endurance, and stern moral fiber.

Other analysts have pointed to the opposite tendency, still tied to class dynamics: as industrialization and postindustrialization have proceeded, increasing numbers of women have acted in ways that fly in the face of Victorian notions about "the fairer sex." In London of the 1880s, some bourgeois women took to the streets, shopping, engaging in charity work, sometimes being mistaken for streetwalkers (Walkowitz 1992, ch. 2). Women in New York at the dawn of the twentieth century faced the problem of how to construct cultural definitions of gender that would allow freer contacts between the sexes among strangers without women taking on the label of "whore" (Peiss 1986). In smaller communities in the U.S., the mass diffusion of the automobile during the 1920s created a new freedom for youth, who could meet at "roadhouses" beyond the purview of the town square (Lynn and Lynn, cited in D. Bell 1976, p. 67).

In the wake of industrialization, changing gender roles and reactions to feminism as a political movement led some people to a sexual "nostalgia" – a longing for the supposed good old days (Doane and Hodges 1987). To be sure, as women have moved increasingly into wage and salary occupations, progressive male sensibilities about gender have emerged. Yet cultural rites of passage from boyhood to manhood persist, for example in adult-organized little-league baseball, with its motto of "character, courage, loyalty" (Fine 1987). And research by Christine Williams (1989) shows that even when women and men enter occupational roles traditionally filled by members of the opposite sex – women into the Marines, men into nursing – they maintain and reinforce their own gender identities in social worlds dominated by the opposite gender. In these and many other emergent gender situations, men and women are exposed to a variety of cultural models, for example the stereotyped role models displayed in advertising (Goffman 1979). Yet how people arrive at their senses of gendered identity is not well understood. Probably both mass-media gender scripts and direct social interaction in gendered life circumstances are influential. The result of shifting roles and contested new role models is a set of gender contradictions – between social realities and cultural tools, and between competing cultural definitions of situation. These contradictions are the likely source of sexual nostalgia for some, and gender-role reconstruction for others.

Sexual nostalgia, however, does not seem to claim an equal audience across social strata. Rather, gender cultures differ from class to class, so that, as Bourdieu argued, "there are as many ways of realizing femininity [sic] as there are classes and class fractions" (1984, pp. 107–8). The working class, for instance, tends to define strong boundaries between men and women, such that many genres of entertainment – action dramas, "confidential" gossip magazines, sports – are distinct in their gender appeals (Gans 1974, p. 90).

Yet how are we to explain the distinctiveness of male versus female culture, where it occurs? Bourdieu's model implies that individuals possess different resources and sensibilities (in the case of gender: auto mechanics, sewing, nurturing, beauty, authority), and that these give them the cultural capital for maintaining social position within an overall class system of distinction. For a dominated cultural group – women in a patriarchal society – cultural resources would offer the basis for survival in a "man's world." On these grounds, the distinctiveness of women's culture would largely function *within* one or another class situation.

A contrasting view suggests that women's culture offers a basis of solidarity and power *alternative* to the world dominated by men. Thus, Smith-Rosenberg has argued, "Women who had little status or power in the larger world of male concerns, possessed status and power in the lives and worlds of other women" in the eighteenth- and nineteenth-century U.S.:

> Women helped each other with domestic chores and in times of sickness, sorrow, or trouble. Entire days, even weeks, might be spent almost exclusively with other women. Urban and town women could devote virtually every day to visits, teas, or shopping trips with other women. Rural women developed a pattern of more extended visits that lasted weeks and sometimes months, at times even dislodging husbands from their beds and bedrooms so that dear friends might spend every hour of every day together.
>
> (Smith-Rosenberg 1975, p. 10)

Today, with increasing numbers of women in the wage and professional labor force, most women do not live in worlds so separate from men. Consider an occupation once completely dominated by men – investment banking. In London, things have completely changed. Gender is still important, but now there is a variety of (hetero-sexual) gendered identities and performances that can credibly sustain a person's effective impression management in high-level banking. Indeed, "femininity, conventionally assumed to be part of the reason for the disadvantaged position of women, may become a positive advantage" (McDowell 1997, p. 207).

Yet the emergence of new gendered performance possibilities for women working in previously male-dominated settings does not necessarily imply either that the women's worlds described by Smith-Rosenberg have disappeared or that women's culture today solely functions to position women within class status cultures dominated by men. A study of contemporary women and the popular culture of romance novels by Janice Radway (1984) suggests considerably more complexity. Like other genres that construct realistic plots, romance narratives about women and their love lives unfold with the twists and turns based on protagonists' dilemmas and choices. Reading romances thus suggests that women have power to shape their lives. Yet the diverse plots are "formulaic," in that they follow prescriptions about "the essential ingredients to be included in each new version of the form." In this respect, "each romance is, in fact a mythic account of how women *must* achieve fulfillment in patriarchal society" (Radway 1984, pp. 29, 17). Given the romances' dualism of choice and mythic prescription, they maintain an ideology of women's roles that perpetuates male dominance by focusing the exercise of power within constraints of a patriarchally organized society. All the same, Radway's romance readers often experienced empowerment. The novels helped establish their own personal realms – separate from their worlds of work, children, and husbands. Moreover, sorting through the issues confronted by heroines in the romances sharpened readers' skills at negotiating the trials of a patriarchal world.

As the studies by Williams and McDowell demonstrate, significant gender reconstructions take place within work worlds shared by men and women. On the other hand, as Smith-Rosenberg and Radway both suggest, women's culture has value (capital, if you will) because it sustains either an alternative domain altogether or a power in the world of men that cannot be reduced to the cultural values of that world. In these accounts, even if we use the language of Bourdieu's theory, some cultural capital of women is in a currency that is valued in a different market than one completely defined by class – one shaped by the specific interests of women in their relations with each other and men.

Ethnicity

Like gender, ethnicity (sometimes defined culturally in terms of biological, hence "racial," characteristics) is typically assumed to be an "ascribed" identity – that is, one based on socially unchangeable characteristics of the individual. However, as with gender, despite the biological substrate of physical features that is sometimes invoked, the variety of ethnic identities held by genetically similar people, along with the genetic diversity of peoples clumped together as a "race," demonstrate that both race and ethnicity are social constructions. Thus, the specific label and content of individuals' ethnic identities depend on social circumstance. Whatever their ethnic identities in Mexico, for example, emigrants become "Chicanos" or "Mexican-Americans" simply by taking up residence in the U.S.

As with gender, at two extremes, ethnic identity can either encompass different economic classes or an ethnic group may include predominantly members of only one class. Each of these circumstances will yield quite different cultural practices of distinction in relation to group boundaries. Paralleling gender, the key question concerns the existence of what may be called ethnic cultural capital, and its relevance to other axes of distinction (J.R. Hall 1992; Connolly 1997).

At one extreme, we find slavery, "legal" segregation of blacks in the U.S. South before the civil-rights reforms of the mid-twentieth century, and apartheid in South Africa before it was brought to an end in the 1990s. In such cases, an ethnic group is almost completely class contained and out-marriage is prohibited. An ethnic group becomes, in effect, a caste akin to those found in India. What, under these circumstances, is the culture of ethnicity? A classic study undertaken in the southern U.S. during the Great Depression – *Caste and Class in a Southern Town* (Dollard 1957) – describes an elaborate racist ideology and strict mores of public behavior. The completely white-dominated public culture maintained white solidarity concerning segregation by branding any white who deviated as a "nigger lover." As for blacks,

> The tendency among students of culture to consider such acts as tipping the hat, shaking hands, or using "Mr." as empty formalisms is rebuked by experience in the South. When we see how severely Negroes may be punished for omitting these signs of deference, we realize that they are anything but petrified customs.
>
> (Dollard 1957, pp. 178–9)

Dollard found some blacks emphasizing class distinctions toward other blacks to try to distance themselves from the stigmatized racial ethnicity. Members of the black middle class often went to great lengths to avoid invoking whites' cultural stereotypes about poor blacks – the "mammy" image, sexual promiscuity, and emotionalistic religion, for example. Poorer blacks enacted two roles. Publicly they tended to conform to mores ultimately enforced by white violence; beyond the public world, they maintained a subcultural space where they could assert other identities. Despite the potential of this "hidden" world as an arena for resistance, the basic posture of blacks in the town Dollard studied was to accommodate themselves to their inferior position, as defined and maintained by the white caste (1957, p. 255).

Dollard may have missed the "inside" of U.S. southern black culture because he was an outsider. Other researchers have argued that blacks in the South maintained solidarity against white domination, and that the black church as a social institution was essential to this solidarity. The civil-rights movement that emerged in the South during the 1950s had diffuse origins in a network of black religious and other social organizations (J.C. Jenkins and Eckert 1986; Lincoln and Mamiya 1990; Robnett 1997), and this implies that southern blacks had a significant preexisting covert culture of resistance.

As with the case of gender, a dominated ethnic group may use one kind of cultural capital with a currency in the wider world, while a separate kind of cultural capital establishes status within the group itself. Thus, ethnic cultural capital does not always reduce to class cultural capital by any straightforward "currency exchange."

Yet when an ethnic group is not simply contained within a single caste-like class, distinctions within the ethnic group may reinscribe class lines. This suggests that the question of whether ethnic cultural capital persists or declines may be explained in class terms. Thus, in *The Declining Significance of Race* William J. Wilson argued that the expansion of the black middle class in the U.S. after the civil-rights movement resulted in a "deepening economic schism…with the black poor falling further and further behind middle- and upper-income blacks" (1980, pp. 151–2).

These changes are reflected in contemporary similarities and differences between middle-class and lower-income blacks, and between black and white middle-class families. Pursuing comparison of blacks in different class situations, Woodard (1988) describes distinctive leisure pursuits of middle-class blacks, who are likely to engage in activities economically inaccessible to the poor. Another study – of class differences in how families interact with their children's schools – shows that both black and white middle-class parents tend to be more interventionist than working-class and poor parents. However, compared to white middle-class parents, black parents of the same class put extra interventionist efforts into insuring that their children do not fall prey to racial discrimination or insensitivity (Lareau 2003). The issues of cultural capital for middle-class blacks, then, have to do with letting go of some practices that have a basis in ethnicity, and simultaneously remaining sensitive to actions by others that may discriminate based on ethnicity. This dual approach seems to confirm arguments about the omnivore–univore continuum discussed above. Recall that in Bryson's (1996) analysis elites are cultural omnivores who ironically use their *multi*cultural capital as a basis for exclusion. By contrast, univore cultures are more likely to be found in lower-status groups such as ethnic groups that base their identity on exclusive cultural badges. In this circumstance, ethnic boundaries are more consistently maintained among lower-status groups, whereas upward mobility requires dampening of the ethnic aspects of one's identity.

How are univore–omnivore differences to be explained? A thesis of cultural hegemony following Gramsci (1971) would posit a ruling elite's interest in promoting univore ethnic boundaries in lower strata in order to "divide and conquer" and thus maintain their own dominant position. However, Gramsci also recognized that dominated groups may establish their own autonomous cultures to promote empowerment. In *There Ain't No Black in the Union Jack*, Paul Gilroy (1991) has explored just this possibility. Concentrating mainly on Great Britain, Gilroy shows that even when race is treated as a cultural construction, this "de-naturalizing" move can maintain racism by reinforcing *national* distinctions between the English, Scots, and Welsh, to say nothing of blacks, Arabs, Hindus, and others. Modernity and its nationalist constructions of society thus confront blacks with challenges centered on the need to recover and validate black culture and reincarnate the sense of belonging that had been erased by slavery (Gilroy 1991, p. 219). Bauman (1996) describes a similar problem for a wider set of groups. In the multi-ethnic town he studied, Southall (just west of London), ethnicity and culture become aligned in reified constructions of communities – Sikh, Hindu, Muslim, Afro-Caribbean, and white. Either people remain locked into these pre-given categories or they have to reconstruct their identities in relation to new cultural meanings and new bases of community.

Under such circumstances, Gilroy argues, black music – from rhythm and blues to reggae and Hip-Hop – has given black youth an alternative to external definitions of identity. Moreover, when such music has become popular among youth of diverse ethnic origins it has provided an opening to the possibility that black and white young people might discover common or parallel meanings in their blighted, postindustrial predicament (1991, p. 171). Here, to use the language (but not the theory) of Bourdieu, black music such as Hip-Hop establishes cultural capital of its own that goes against conventional hierarchies of distinction (see Figure 3.2). In the process, it may empower social movements that crosscut the conventionally bounded ethnic cultures maintained by lower-status groups. Ironically, ethnically based culture holds the potential to break down inter-ethnic antipathy in ways that may enhance cross-ethnic class solidarity. Cultural distinctions based on ethnicity are not inherently divisive, for the consequences of imitation or diffusion remain open.

Figure 3.2 Individual rappers from different ethnic backgrounds participate in Wales in an event
called a "freestyle cypher" (sometimes just called "freestyling"). Such an event
involves a friendly competition trading spontaneous rap improvisations, what might
be called a "battle of rhymes." Cultural capital is thus on display in the participants'
abilities, but the basis of status transcends conventional class and ethnic divisions,
even though the cultural form has decidedly U.S., urban black and Puerto Rican
ethnic origins.

Source: James McNally photo.

Culture and stratification in social process

Neither gender nor ethnicity can be disentangled from class, yet their mutual structurings break down any simple class-hierarchical model of culture and stratification. Moreover, there are other axes along which both sociologists and people in general map cultural distinctions – age, religion, sexual orientation, community, social-club memberships, and diffuse social collectivities such as cowboys, soccer fans, and environmentalists. Thus, Bourdieu's theory is incomplete. Class cannot be disentangled from the "multicultural" situations of actual social life. A female corporate manager and her male office administrator enact a social relationship that is simultaneously infused with cultural meanings about both class and gender (and ethnicity and a host of other identity traits as well). Though class, ethnicity, gender, and so on can be analyzed separately, in life they are intertwined. Bourdieu's theory of cultural capital thus needs to be extended beyond class to recognize a wider range of groups employing their own forms of cultural capital, sometimes in ways not open to direct exchange or commensurability.

Perhaps because Bourdieu wrote primarily about France and at a time when immigration had not yet become so significant, he gave little attention to religious and ethnic diversity. Today, both France and many other societies are more heterogeneous. Even when he wrote, Bourdieu recognized the importance of distinctions other than class, and he understood that cultural distinctions often are produced and applied in relation to particular groups. However, he mostly tried to subsume other kinds of distinctions (avant-garde versus bourgeoisie, men versus women) within a class-as-status-group framework.

Two amendments should be brought to Bourdieu's analysis. First, even for class-based cultural capital there is a question about the source of value. Bourdieu recognized that the aesthetics used to evaluate cultural choices are contested. Nevertheless, he concluded that the working class is subject to a "dominated 'aesthetic'." The double standard of high culture demands that members of the popular classes defer to an aesthetic defined from the outside, even if that aesthetic contradicts personal preferences: "Yes, it's beautiful, but you have to like it, it's not my cup of tea" (Bourdieu 1984, p. 41; cf. Gans 1974, p. 78). Yet, as we have seen, the source of any external aesthetic is open to debate. Moreover, aesthetic value may not be defined solely from the outside, even in classes that lack dominant power. Workers tend to respect craft abilities – being able to do things with one's hands and work collectively in physical ways. By these standards, many middle- and upper-class people will seem bumbling and inept.

A second issue is equally important. The social mapping of status by way of cultural capital does not proceed solely through the affirmation of class sensibilities. Cultural capital related to other kinds of status groups (e.g. religious communities) as well as other dimensions of stratification (e.g. age) may operate in ways that cannot be reduced to class. Both subcultures (cultures accommodated to the existing social order) and countercultures (cultures formed in opposition to the established order) establish "currencies" of cultural capital that do not necessarily align with the hierarchy of class distinctions described by Bourdieu. Sometimes these currencies elaborate more specialized distinctions within a class (Arab workers in France versus others) and sometimes they offer a basis of solidarity that cuts across classes (Smith-Rosenberg's nineteenth-century American women, for example). Yet cultural distinctions that go beyond class cannot be understood simply as surviving ethnic practices of immigrants or the gendered choices of people who are all seeking distinction within a single class-based status hierarchy.

Instead, as Michael Hechter (1978) has demonstrated, even in economic markets there is a "cultural" division of labor. When Hechter examined data from the 1970 U.S. Census, he found that ethnic subcultures (and, we can infer by extension, religion, gender, and other subcultural status groups) may offer bases for attempting to monopolize resources (jobs), sometimes within a class level, sometimes cutting across class levels in an economic sector (e.g. construction or banking). A status group with a distinctive culture provides a sense of identity different from class, and status groups may be able to control significant economic resources. When they do, individuals will find solidarity with the group an attractive proposition. This may be true no matter what the absolute value of the resources. Even if the group only controls "poor" resources (lower-level government jobs, for example), these resources may be valuable to group members if they themselves are poor. Whatever their basis, status groups may offer an alternative to the labor market for access to occupational positions, in which case the individual's access will be based upon displaying the status group's specific cultural capital (cf. Bonacich 1972).

Bourdieu described classes as defined through the struggles of individuals and occupational groups to establish themselves favorably within the overall social order. There is an important implication: the occupational division of labor has no inherent class divisions. Janitors truly may become sanitation engineers if the management of waste becomes socially valued because of its complexity as a technical problem; conversely, stockbrokers would lose distinction if their professional decision-making were taken over by computer-based "expert systems." Thus, class divisions are located through ongoing struggles for distinction that are always redefining the boundaries of classes-as-status-groups within an overall social order. But other possibilities exist, and they can be elaborated by adjusting Bourdieu's theory to incorporate the interplay of multiple forms of cultural capital and multiple kinds of group identification (see, for example, Bentley 1987).

In the first place, Max Weber famously argued that status groups may pursue their interests in the political realm, and he also pointed out that status groups may engage in collective economic action (1978, pp. 926–39). Classes-as-status-groups fit this formulation well since they are so closely tied to economic life. Collective economic and political actions by classes-as-status-groups can dramatically alter the value of various kinds of cultural capital. At the extreme, revolutionary upheavals may change class cultures altogether (L. Hunt 1984; Swidler 1986; Szelényi and Szelényi 1995). Bourdieu described the status order in political isolation and under conditions of relative normalcy, not in times of conflict or upheaval, or in relation to political mobilization of social classes. But there is no inherent reason why a refined version of his research program could not be extended in these directions.

Second, classes are not the only kinds of status groups that may be understood in terms of cultural capital. Self-conscious ethnic groups, people with a regional identity, women's groups, graduates of a particular school, members of clubs and religions, gay men, used-car sales personnel, soldiers in a unit that has seen combat, informal status groups based on leisure activities such as surfing, skateboarding – this list merely scratches the surface of the diverse groups that may value highly specific cultural meanings and practices. As we have seen, status groups sometimes blur class distinctions, and the value of culture for a status group can be something other than just status distinction: it may offer a basis of social survival and power.

Bourdieu recognized that cultural distinctions do not represent some generalized currency of "legal tender" among all individuals and status groups (1984, p. 113). Even money, which might be regarded as economic capital in its concrete form, is not simply a universal medium of exchange based on equivalence. As Viviana Zelizer (1989) has shown, people do not treat all money in their lives as "the same." This incomplete interchangeability of "capital" is even more pronounced for culture than for money. A corporate executive cannot expect his or her art collection to impress a butcher, any more than a factory worker wears clothes to gain distinction with people beyond his or her social circle. Wearing diamonds will take on a different significance at a debutante's ball than a truckstop cafe. Cultural capital, after all, is only good in the social worlds where one lives and acts, and the value that it has depends on the distinctions of currency in those particular social worlds. This means that Bourdieu's approach to cultural capital needs to be revised in the direction of theorizing status groups in general. Sometimes status groups are based on class, sometimes on other cultural criteria or a mix of them. A given kind of cultural capital sometimes interpenetrates, sometimes conflicts with, sometimes subsumes other standards of distinction. Given these possibilities, future research should explore the conditions under which various class versus other status-group identifications predominate (and for whom) and the conditions under which the exercise of cultural distinctions reproduces the status order or transforms it.

Conclusion

In this chapter we have found time and again that class and culture are closely connected. Bourdieu's theory of cultural capital shows that this is not a one-way causal relationship and that it cannot be understood solely by treating classes as groups. Instead, individuals and groups are actively employing cultural capital in their competitive "market" pursuits of distinction that reinforce, cross, or redefine class-group boundaries. Critiquing Bourdieu, we have argued that the stratification of culture and the uses of culture to affirm individual distinction go considerably beyond class. Ethnicity, gender, and other status groups can establish cultural currencies of distinction. In turn, individuals can employ these cultural distinctions in ways that affect their locations in a stratified society. Culture is not just a hierarchy of distinctions whose relative values get defined by a dominant class. Instead, individuals draw upon various sources of distinction in their negotiations toward multiple, overlapping, and competing bases of solidarity, identity, and social position. In all this, they may take on culture, not only as part of a struggle for status, but for diverse other reasons, including aesthetic pleasure.

In the previous chapter we explored the relation of the self and identity to culture. The present chapter has described the significance of culture as a sorting device and life pathway within stratified societies. These discussions reveal a rich texture of relationships between individuals, culture, and society. The following two parts of the book deepen this analysis, first, in Part 2, by examining the historical and contemporary developments of overall societal organization in relation to cultural formations, and then, in Part 3, by considering the questions of how culture is produced, consumed, and employed, with what connections to the social exercise of power, and what possibilities of agency.

Suggested readings

The work, and now the legacy, of Pierre Bourdieu are the subject of numerous studies. Fowler (1997) provides a useful introduction to his ideas, and a thoughtful demonstration of their salience to specific cultural and art movements and social strata. For a general survey of his work and its significance, see Swartz (1997). A special issue of *Poetics* edited by Richard Peterson (1997a) offers empirical evidence relevant to Bourdieu's theory of distinction.

The literature on class, ethnicity, and gender is by now enormous, but several studies stand out. Essays in *The Cultural Territories of Race* (1999), edited by Michèle Lamont, examine a variety of issues about racial and ethnic relations in the U.S., informed by cultural perspectives. As for gender, one of the best ways to explore its cultural character is through comparison. Puri (1999) uses in-depth interviews with twenty-two women to produce a fine-grained sociological analysis of women's construction of their sexuality in contemporary India. *Intimate Frontiers: Sex, Gender, and Culture in Old California* (Hurtado 1999) describes gendered life in the missions and the gold camps of frontier California. A variety of essays on "gender and culture in everyday life" can be found in Lamphere *et al.* (1997). Finally, in *A Question of Color* (1993), producer and director Kathe Sandler examines how African-American women and men confront the cultural and social manifestations of a caste system of color biased in favor of European standards of beauty.

Note

1   These three models can be understood in relation to Mary Douglas's (1982) typology of high versus low *market regulation* (a specific case of what Douglas calls "grid") and high versus low *group* allegiance (see J.R. Hall and Neitz 1993, p. 113).

Part 2

Cultural structurations and modernity

4 Cultural constructions of "the Other"

A fundamental assumption of our approach to the sociology of culture is that ideas matter, not only to people in general but to scholars and students of culture: *how* we think about things has an effect on *what* we think about things. We begin Part 2 of this book in this chapter by discussing early social theorists' ideas about original human societies, the "original" conditions of society, and the cultures of non-Western "others." The following chapters of Part 2 then consider modern and postmodern ways of thinking about the preindustrial deep past, the modern and industrial recent past and continuing present, and the trajectories of the present as future. These chapters explore how theorists, researchers, and critics have struggled with enduring questions, and sometimes posed new ones, regarding how to think about culture(s) in relation to time and place.

It's all about "us": the universal West

Western European intellectuals' understandings of what it means to analyze culture have been strongly shaped by attempts to study the cultures of smaller, more homogenous societies of other times and places. Yet their very conceptions of those societies have been influenced by Western experiences of modernity. The nineteenth-century social scientists who introduced the term *culture* into English usage approached their subject in ways influenced by their own society and culture. Dramatic social changes wrought by industrialization and urbanization led to new attempts to understand both the past and the present.

In one nineteenth-century development, the romantic movement looked backward with nostalgia for a "simpler past" and nurtured an intense interest in folk life and the cultural traditions of nations.[1] On the other hand, social Darwinists of the nineteenth century applied Charles Darwin's theory of biological evolution to societies, proposing an evolutionary hierarchy with primitive culture at the bottom and Western civilization at the top. Within a broader milieu of social scientists, the notion of "traditional" or "folk" culture – like the idea of *Gemeinschaft* (community) to which it was intimately related – was developed as an ideal type to be paired with (and contrasted to) the "modern" culture of *Gesellschaft* (society).

For anthropologists, who used the concept earlier than sociologists, to speak of a "culture" implied a whole way of life. In a lecture that Robert Redfield gave at the University of Chicago in 1939, he talked about how, returning from fieldwork among isolated primitive people, he found it odd to hear sociologists refer to different neighborhoods of Chicago as different "culture areas." Redfield's remarks are telling:

> [Anthropologists] commonly use the terms "community," "society," and "culture" interchangeably; while the distinctions among the concepts may be of significance in dealing with the modern urbanized and industrialized societies, in using them with reference to primitive societies there is often no need felt to make them, for the reason that there the group of people who live physically together are the same people who share those common understandings we call culture, and they are very nearly the same people who produce and consume their own goods.
>
> (Redfield 1940, p. 739)

For the many anthropologists of Redfield's generation who came to their conclusions by studying traditional ways of life in small, often remote, societies, "culture" is how society is organized.

In the same essay Redfield noted the implications of this understanding of culture for social science methodology: he explained that in a stable folk society sampling from the population is unnecessary. Given that anthropologists understood a group's culture to be ubiquitous and social roles to be undifferentiated, one informant could reveal whatever information the anthropologist needed: "What one adult male knows is enough like what the others know to make it possible to learn much about the whole society from no more than a single case" (1940, p. 740). This assumption of uniformity explains why social scientists did not think it necessary to differentiate between society and culture.

Scholars today who are aware of the biases in the original anthropological formulations of the concept of culture may still want to talk about the ways that cultures of certain tribal groups are meaningfully different from cultures of modern industrialized societies. For example, how is it that cultures may differ depending on the size of the population? What happens when a cultural group is small enough so that social norms are enforced almost entirely through face-to-face interaction? What if the society is homogenous? How are cultural forms different if they are not subject to commodity exchanges in economic markets? These are important questions for detailed research. Yet there is an overriding question central to the sociology of culture: whether it is legitimate to continue to use the concept of "traditional" or "folk culture" as a comparative benchmark for understanding how culture works in some generic sense.

In this chapter, common understandings of "traditional" (what came before modern) and "Culture" (as the whole way of life of a people) are problematized. This agenda reflects our interest in a tension between two sorts of knowledge. Scholars have researched the empirical shifts in daily life activities and people's worldviews that have taken place with the emergence of the modern world economy and the advent of industrialization. Yet this knowledge coexists with a growing current of thought about the inadequacy of the concepts that scholars have most often used to talk about those shifts. We now know that traditional societies were not uniform, any more than modern ones are. Ask yourself whether India today has more in common with "traditional" India or with "modern" England. The attempt to answer this question points to the difficulties with the terms themselves.

This chapter offers fundamental criticisms of the traditional/modern dichotomy. We begin with a brief review of how social scientists developed and used this dichotomy. We examine how concepts of "modern" and "Western" were conflated, and how non-Western cultures were constructed as "Other." We then trace in detail how assumptions about religion, meaning, and community solidarity are reflected in the use of the concept of ritual, as applied to "primitive" societies and as applied to "modern" societies. In turn, we explore recent work that challenges these assumptions.

Conceptualizing the past as a mirror of the present

The concept of "traditional" or "folk" culture is one half of a dichotomy, typically contrasted with its opposite, "modernity." Thus, in the emergence of modern social theory, the characteristics that particular theorists attributed to traditional culture became specified as the inverses of their concerns about their own societies. Ferdinand Toennies and Emile Durkheim were primarily interested in community solidarity and the problem of how, with the decline of traditional community, individuals were (or were not) integrated into a common moral order. Max Weber, on the other hand, focused more on the development of rationality and the routinization of social life in bureaucracy, and parallel transformations of religion.

In contrast to the sociologists who assumed that "primitive society" came before "traditional society," many nineteenth-century anthropologists – including Henry Maine, Louis Henry Morgan, E.B. Tylor, and James G. Frazer – took it as their task to theorize about the original characteristics of human society. But, again, much like Europeans imagining the new world three centuries earlier (see Figure 4.1), what the anthropologists described as the original state of nature was an inversion of their own society:

> For them modern society was defined above all by the territorial state, the monogamous family, and private property. Primitive society therefore must have been nomadic, ordered by blood ties, sexually promiscuous, and communist.... The pioneer anthropologists believed that their own was an age of massive transition. They looked back in order to understand the nature of the present, on the assumption that modern society had evolved out of its antithesis.
>
> (Kuper 1988, p. 5)

Early societies were seen as tightly bounded communities, maintaining individuals' commitments to the social order. In comparison with modern cities, earlier forms of community did not seem to exhibit much "social disorganization," and social control appeared to be "spontaneous."[2]

When anthropologists moved from the armchair to the field, it became clear that the primitive society as an ideal type did not describe what they were observing. Truly primitive societies were hard to come by: fewer and fewer had escaped some encounter with the West, and even when relatively isolated groups could be found they did not match the theory. In response to this theoretical shortfall, in the 1930s anthropologist Robert Redfield puzzled about "intermediate societies" where religion and family are strong, crime rates are low, and yet members participate in a money economy and may see themselves as part of larger political and economic structures. This intermediate type more closely approximated what Redfield had observed in the Mexican village he studied. For these intermediate groups – where local culture had adjusted to the civilization of the cities – he offered the term "folk" society (1940, p. 735).

Figure 4.1 The artist who made this early woodcut, circa 1505, never visited the Americas but
based this image on a description by Vespucci. He features his subjects practicing
cannibalism and open sexuality, dresses them in feathers, and gives them beards.

Source: anonymous artist, The New York Public Library Picture Collection.

For Redfield, making a contrast between folk and modern societies accomplished a
number of goals. It provided theoretical grounds for extending the scope of anthropology. "If all the 'vanishing peoples' of the earth should indeed vanish," he
maintained, "we would still have to study the acculturated people, the folk people
changing under the impact of urban growth" (1940, p. 742). Thus, Redfield pushed for
more than just a change in subject. He urged anthropologists to move from refining
theoretical typologies to studying actual social processes, often opposed to one
another in their tendencies, in concrete situations of social change.

However, the notion of finding a pure conceptual contrast to modern society
continued to be alluring. After World War II, the French anthropologist Claude Lévi-
Strauss proposed two forms of knowledge – the savage and the domesticated
(mythical and magical versus scientific thought) – that parallel the dichotomy between
primitive and modern culture. Lévi-Strauss postulated these as two "strategic levels at
which nature is accessible to scientific enquiry: one roughly adapted to that of perception and the imagination, the other at a remove from it" (cited in Goody 1977, p. 7).
Modern thought Lévi-Strauss characterized as scientific, abstract, and historical – as
opposed to primitive thought, which he described as concrete, magical, intuitive, atem-
poral, and mythic.

Sociologists after World War II tended to work within a shorter time frame than the anthropologists, looking at the relatively recent, and in some places ongoing, transition to industrial society. Talcott Parsons (1951) influenced many students of modernization with his formulation of "pattern variables." He argued that a set of five interrelated variables, taken together, distinguished between the value orientations of modern society and those of traditional cultures. How closely Parsons associated modernity with Weber's ideas about rationalization and bureaucracy is evident in his choice of variables contrasting modernity with tradition: status by achievement versus socially ascribed or designated status; rational neutrality of judgments versus (emotionally biased) affectivity; orientation to self versus orientation to collectivity; specificity versus diffuseness of role task sets; and egalitarian universalism versus the particularism of siding with favorites (Parsons 1951, pp. 101–12). Although such dichotomies were based on differences that Western observers noted between Western industrial and other societies, theorists using the dichotomies too often reified the observed differences, making them into explanations of development. Thus, Parsons and his followers assumed that if they could describe modernization as it occurred in the West, then they could both explain why some societies remained "undeveloped" and predict how modernization would happen in developing countries (Rostow 1960; McClelland 1961).

By providing the basis for an abstract model, these dichotomies contributed to the theory-building efforts of several generations of sociologists and anthropologists. But, beginning in the 1950s, the sweeping generalizations of the dichotomies have been challenged by important empirical and theoretical work of social scientists that asks whether standard concepts of traditional and modern accurately portray either modern or traditional cultures. The switch from talking about traditional culture to traditional cultures – in the plural – is emblematic of this interest in understanding the specific character of particular groups instead of trying to develop a grand theory about primordial society or about modernization in general. The challengers have discovered self-interested rational peasants living in folk cultures (Popkin 1979) and bureaucrats in modernizing nation-states who maintain affective and particularistic commitments (Taub 1969). They have found that particularistic and ascriptive factors are important in the bureaucracies of modern societies (P. Blau 1955; Granovetter 1974).

Yet, in the face of such studies, intuition and observation still suggest that there are meaningful differences between those cultures that might be described as "modern" and those described as "traditional," even if the differences are not captured by the generalizations of the theories. One response to this puzzle is to shift from merely describing differences by using typological contrasts to trying to identify particular determining mechanisms that give rise to a more variable range of differences. Forms of communication constitute one such dimension of variation. Focusing on this dimension, some anthropologists are moving toward using as categories "oral" (or, sometimes, "unlettered") cultures and "literate" cultures. Goody (1977, pp. 146–62) provides a rationale for doing so. He argues that this conceptualization avoids a dichotomy, because cultures can be literate to different degrees, and, furthermore, that the distinction is based in direct observation and therefore is less Eurocentric than earlier ones.

The presence (and degree of diffusion of) writing has tremendous implications for any given culture, and literate cultures differ in important and systematic ways from oral ones. Not only does writing greatly increase the possibilities for the storage of culture, it also alters the nature of language. As Goody explains, writing "shifts language from the aural to the visual domain and makes possible a different kind of inspection, the reordering and refining not only of sentences but of individual words" (1977, p. 78). Thus writing facilitates not only the recording of oral traditions but the development and elaboration of other forms of thought. Lists of various kinds – inventories of persons, objects, or events, guides to future action, integrated sets of concepts – permit higher degrees of abstraction and ordering. A telling sign of how writing was used to increase organizational power is that three-quarters of the cuneiform inscriptions surviving from the ancient Middle East are administrative and bureaucratic records (Goody 1977, p. 79).

Another possible way to measure differences between various degrees of develop-ment among societies is to describe their relations to markets and trade. In early societies it is likely that the work of artists and poets was oriented to rituals connected to religious and political institutions (themselves closely tied together in some settings). The social locations of these cultural activities could change yet remain isolated from the market – and its more substantial effects – for a long time. For example, Raymond Williams has traced how the functions of the ancient Celtic poets called bards became increasingly specialized as social organization and the mode of production changed. After the Christianization of Ireland in the fifth century, the priestly function and the bardic function separated. The priests became associated with writing while the bards remained tied to the oral tradition for a longer period of time. For centuries bards and other artists established relations with patrons who protected and supported them. This patronage was quite different from a situation that emerged in later stages (and which continued to overlap in time with some forms of patronage), in which artists offer their works as commodities for sale to a general public on a market. Of course, there are historically specific forms of patronage as well as different kinds of market relations (Raymond Williams 1982, pp. 33–54). The general point remains, however: the culture of the bard who lived in the castle of a local lord differed from that of the modern poet who sells works to publishers who print and distribute them to an anonymous public.

Social science and popular contrasts between traditional or folk culture and modern culture have relied upon idealized dichotomies based on the specific modern-izing experience of the West. These dichotomies have been an important basis for the development of scholarly ideas commonly in use for understanding both contempo-rary cultures and their predecessors. Critics now challenge these idealized contrasts, not only when they are made across time periods, as between traditional cultures of the past and modern cultures of the present, or across regions, but also when they are used to differentiate between traditional cultures outside the West and modern cultures in the West. We now turn to the latter usage.

Conceptualizing "the Other"

Watching countries in Asia, Africa, and the Middle East become industrialized and urbanized as they move into global markets makes it very clear that modernization has more than one face: it appears different in different cultural contexts. Japan long served as a model of an "alternative modernity" for an Arab world that experienced Western modernity as what Iranian revolutionary writers label "westoxification." From the Middle East, Japan was viewed as an Eastern country "that successfully borrowed technology and science from the West while preserving its own traditions" (Abu-Lughod 1998, pp. 14–15). But the relation of Islam to modernization is complicated, for it also has promoted alternative forms of change.

In Singapore, for instance, the Malay population, at 14 percent, is a minority, and one that is historically identified as Muslim. In the past, the commitments to Islam of Malay people living in Singapore coexisted with indigenous Malay religious practices – of dress, folk medicine, and traditional arts, including a form of martial art (*silat*) and traditional dance – all of which were associated with magical beliefs. However, since 1970 these indigenous practices have been declining, especially among the younger and more educated Malays in Singapore (Zainul Abiden 2002). Yet there is no decline of religion in favor of nonreligious institutions and practices. Rather, the traditional Malay practices are fading because they are regarded as violating Islamic beliefs. The Malay process involves a reinvigorated embrace of an Islamic heritage similar to the "internal conversion" that Clifford Geertz (1973) described in Bali. In both places, broader social changes are associated with an intensification of a drive to acquire religious knowledge, rationalization at the level of dogma and creed, and religious bureaucratization. In Singapore, there were local factors – notably increasing rates of literacy among Malays and changing methods of instruction within a state-sponsored religious education program – that interacted with the wider Islamic movement to inspire Malays to articulate a specifically Islamic modernity. Thus, as they have become more "modern," people have been less likely to follow traditional folk practices, but more likely to adopt Islamic dress and practices rather than Western ones.

Social scientists are now seeing the necessity of unlinking theories about modernization from the specific form that the process took in Western Europe, the United States, Canada, Australia, and New Zealand. In a provocative book, *The Clash of Civilizations and the Remaking of World Order* (1996), Samuel P. Huntington revives the concept of "civilization" to discuss important cultural differences among contemporary modern and modernizing societies. In the cold-war era after World War II, political differences between capitalist societies and societies with communist economic systems seemed very important. But as countries of the Eastern bloc increasingly began to experiment with capitalism, and especially after the collapse of the Soviet Union in 1991, a capitalist economic system began to be taken to be an essential feature of modern society. In this context, some political analysts predicted a harmonious "new world order" under global capitalism. Others, however, began to give renewed importance to cultural differences among societies.

For Huntington, a civilization is the broadest cultural entity – the way of life for a people, "the biggest 'we' within which we feel culturally at home as distinguished from all the other 'thems' out there" (1996, p. 43). Unlike societies or nations, civilizations do not have clearcut boundaries. Although Japan is an exception, most civilizations bridge more than one state. Huntington identifies the following major contemporary civilizations: Chinese, Japanese, Hindu, Islamic, Western, Orthodox, Latin American, and African (1996, p. 47). He argues that the West is one coherent civilization, and that what is distinctive about the West predates modernity. For Huntington, a number of characteristics together constitute Western civilization: a classical legacy from Greece and Rome, Western Christianity (Catholicism and Protestantism), European languages, separation of religious and secular authority, rule of law, social pluralism, representative bodies, and individualism (1996, pp. 69–72). Any such list is bound to be controversial, but the basis on which it is formulated is important to note. Huntington's analysis exemplifies how the collapse of Soviet communism and the increasing diversity of modernisms have undercut any classification of societies along a traditional/modern dimension and made cultural distinctions increasingly important to political analysts. There is evidence of something similar in popular thinking. The them/us thinking that emerged in the United States after 9/11 was cast, in significant ways, in cultural terms.

Westerners such as Huntington are increasingly self-conscious about the very sense of Western identity that many people once took for granted under a tacit assumption that the West represents the pinnacle of social and economic development, to which other societies might well aspire. The implications of a more self-conscious Westernism are still up for grabs. Huntington, for example, argues that Western culture is a unique historical constellation, not a universal endpoint, and that countries like the United States should emphasize the Western aspects of their cultural heritage. He therefore opposes policies and practices that would enhance cultural diversity. Others in the United States who might agree about the uniqueness of the West nevertheless argue for policies that encourage multiculturalism. Despite their differences, however, both Huntington and the multiculturalists agree that "modern" does not presume "Western."

Overall, changing understandings of civilization and culture are breaking down an implicit association that undergirded much Western writing about non-Western societies, especially societies of "the East." Just as Western social theorists constructed dichotomous categories that contrasted traditional cultures to their own Western experiences of modernity, they also tended to cast the non-Christian Eastern civilizations as "the other" – exotic, mysterious, unchanging, and inferior – in ways that ultimately would provide the intellectual rationale for Western pursuit of colonial empires. Edward Said's masterful *Orientalism* (1994) examines this discourse produced by Western writers and scholars in the post-Enlightenment era about Eastern – especially Muslim – cultures. English, French, and – in the twentieth century – American scholars typically wrote about "the Orient" in terms of its significance for the West. In Western "Orientalist" writing, spatial relations between "the East" and "the West" became a starting point for designating Orientals as inherently different from "us" – exotic "others" who would benefit from the imperialist ventures of Western nation-states. European cultures gained strength and identity in part through the construction of a cultural discourse that distinguished the West from these cultural "others."

Strikingly, nineteenth-century European writings about Muslim cultures rarely distinguished among different Muslim peoples, and "Arab" civilizations were described as though they existed outside of history, in a permanent premodern condition strongly shaped by life in the desert. In these writings, Said notes, "'the Arab' or 'Arabs' have an aura of apartness, definitiveness, and collective self-consistency such as to wipe out any traces of individual Arabs with narratable life histories" (1994, p. 229). This sort of Western discourse of Orientalism did not accurately reflect the cultures it purported to describe, but it produced an Orientalist representation that could be put to use, by defining cultural others for Westerners in their relations with the East. Said is careful to show that Orientalism as a discourse has not been static; he describes it instead as an ongoing conversation representing the Other, a depiction that changes in response to unfolding knowledge and events, but which continues to serve the purposes of the Western powers.

Overall, the deconstruction of sometimes romantic and nostalgic but also self-serving and imperialistic conceptions both of the past and of the non-Western world has led scholars to try to move past stereotypes and grand theory, by developing new approaches for locating cultural expressions contextually, in relation to native understandings and local knowledges (Geertz 1983). We will turn our attention to these approaches at the end of this chapter. But before doing so it is important to consider the problem of tradition a bit further, in one of the most strongly theorized of "traditional" cultural processes – ritual.

Ritual and the traditional/modern dichotomy

Ritual – defined as standardized, repetitive activities, oriented toward the sacred – was often taken by early social scientists to be an essential characteristic of religious practice in premodern societies. These scholars postulated that through ritual individuals in primitive and traditional cultures established and affirmed their common bond. Similarly, more recent scholars see religious ritual as the place where "cultural ideas (thought) and social dispositions (action) are integrated" and can be observed in such a manner as to inform our understanding of a culture (C. Bell 1997, p. 80). The concept of ritual has been used to divide traditional and modern societies. Yet, we want to suggest, this understanding is based on misleading assumptions.

Religion and ritual: the legacy of Durkheim

In *The Elementary Forms of Religious Life* (1915), Emile Durkheim laid the groundwork for a functionalist understanding of religion. He was concerned with explaining how religious rituals integrate a society, rather than tracing historic developments and causes or understanding the personal experiences of individuals. Durkheim postulated that when premodern peoples worshiped their deities they were in fact worshiping society, the powerful social reality that is greater than any individual.

Durkheim argued that cultures divide the world into two categories, the sacred and the profane, and that rituals tell people how to behave in the presence of the sacred. In his view, rituals are structured in such a way that when people gather together and perform the required acts as a group the result is an intense emotional experience. He maintained that, although participants describe their experiences in terms of the power of God, in fact God is the power of the group. For Durkheim, the idea of God in a ritual is a symbol for society.

Durkheim thus was interested in rituals as social acts that have benefits for the society. He believed that the intense individual emotional experience called "effervescence" is only possible within the group context, and individual experiences were only of concern to him insofar as they help or hinder production of the group's experience. In his view, involvement in rituals requires that individuals submit themselves to a particular collective discipline of the group, and the collective activity then serves to reaffirm the cohesiveness of the group. So long as the particular expressive forms of rituals are passed down through time, the continuity of the social values of the society is affirmed.

Given this basic functionalist model, Durkheim worried that, although ritual might fulfill its functions effectively in primitive, traditional, or folk cultures, it would work less well in modern societies. In his early work, Durkheim argued that integration in modern societies is based predominantly on the division of labor, through people's economic interdependence. However, the presence of alienation (individual separation from society) and anomie (generalized normlessness) in modern societies implies failures of integration: economic interdependence does not necessarily *feel* like social integration. In his later work Durkheim looked for "functional equivalents" of religion – secular organizations and rituals that could fulfill the functions of integration.

An English scholar, anthropologist E.E. Evans-Pritchard (1974), later agreed with Durkheim that religions are social creations, but disagreed with Durkheim's position that religions are nothing more than "symbolic representations of the social order." Whereas Durkheim's theoretical work emphasized a collective emotional experience, Evans-Pritchard's field studies among the Nuer in Africa showed that individuals at religious rituals vary in their behaviors, degree of attention to the ritual activity, and feelings. He argued that what matters at a ritual is not how individual participants feel, but rather that the essential acts are carried out. Although Evans-Pritchard's work is still centered in social functions of religion, by recognizing individual variability it moves away from a reification of ritual in so-called "primitive societies" and advances the idea that rituals can only be understood within a society's own conceptual categories.

Durkheim made the important sociological point that rituals reflect the social order, but his work oversimplified religion, neglecting to ask what specific cultural work rituals do. This gap is addressed by an important current theoretical approach, practice theory. Drawing on scholars such as Pierre Bourdieu, Marshall Sahlins, and Sherry Ortner, practice theorists see religious rituals, like other human activities, as creative strategies by which people in groups continually reproduce and change their social and cultural environments. According to Catherine Bell,

> Many practice theorists are concerned with analyzing large processes of historical and cultural change, often developing more nuanced versions of Geertz's model of the interaction of human action, needs, and experiences, on the one hand, with traditional cultural structures, organizational patterns, and symbolic systems, on the other. In addition, practice theorists are particularly attuned to the political dimension of social relationships, especially with regard to how positions of domination and subordination are variously constituted, manipulated, or resisted.
>
> (C. Bell 1997, p. 76)

Practice theorists see ritual as a resource and a site where groups negotiate their way forward, aligning current situations with enduring cultural structures. Although the theorists Bell cites have studied mainly non-Western tribal peoples, a similar shift away from the oversimplifications of the dichotomous typification can be found in recent studies of rituals in modern Western societies.

Ritual as habit

A key part of defining ritual – across times and places – has been to assert that they are standardized, repetitive activities. In modern secular society, removed from the cultural contexts that gave traditional rituals meaning, rituals have been seen not only as standardized and repetitive, but as empty, and social scientists using the term have moved further and further away from asserting the centrality of the experience of the sacred that was part of the original formulations. Robert Merton, for example, used the term "ritualist" to describe someone who performs the outer gestures of an act without any commitment to the ideas and values that might be expressed through it (1957, p. 131).

Symbolic interactionists made this shift as well. Early advocates of dramaturgical analysis used the word "ritual" according to the older meaning – publicly established ceremonial activities. They mainly saw rituals as ways of communicating and maintaining group traditions (e.g. K. Burke 1950, pp. 272–3; Duncan 1968, pp. 185–91). Erving Goffman, however, treated rituals (much as Sigmund Freud had) in an ironic tone: he took the term out of its customary usage in order to emphasize habitual behaviors in everyday life. In *Interaction Ritual* (1968), Goffman examined everyday social interaction as a kind of ritual composed from "the ultimate behavioral material" – the "glances, gestures, positionings and verbal statements that people continuously feed into the situation, whether intended or not." In order to identify the "countless patterns and natural sequences of behavior occurring whenever persons come into one another's immediate presence," he advocated an ethnographic method (1968, pp. 1–2). In *Relations in Public* (1971), Goffman went further and argued that the older kinds of rituals ("rituals performed to stand in for supernatural deities" and "extensive ceremonies involving long strings of obligatory rites") have little place in modern society. "What remains are brief rituals one individual performs for and to another," what Goffman called "interpersonal rituals" (1971, p. 63). The rituals that he analyzed thus consisted of the presentation and reception of small units of behavior in face-to-face interaction. His brilliant work shaped how many sociologists have thought about ritual since.

Perhaps because of Goffman's influence, anthropologist Mary Douglas complained of the "anti-ritualist" bias among contemporary sociologists, whom she saw as part of a "revolt against ritual." She sought to reclaim the concept of ritual for the description of meaningful activities, in part by questioning the premise that meaningful ritual occurs in primitive societies whereas ritual in modern society will necessarily signify empty conformity. Douglas argued that

> to use the word ritual to mean empty symbols of conformity, leaving us with no word to stand for symbols of genuine conformity, is seriously disabling to the sociology of religion. For the problem of empty symbols is still a problem about the relation of symbols and social life, and one which needs an unprejudiced vocabulary.
>
> (M. Douglas 1973, p. 21)

Putting aside the usual evolutionary framework that has dominated so much theory about ritual in traditional and modern societies, Douglas specified the conditions under which ritualism will be highly developed. One condition is the belief that symbolic action is effective in accomplishing the desired results. A second condition is that the culture be sensitive to condensed symbols – rich symbols that have different meanings at different levels, which become integrated in subconscious mental life and thus connect inner and outer aspects of experience (1973, pp. 26–9). Exploring the ethnographic record, Douglas argued that ritualism will be strong when a group is characterized by tight social bonds, and she found examples of high and low degrees of ritualism in both primitive and modern cultures.

The sociology of culture benefits from the diversity of theoretical approaches reflected in the debates over ritual because the diversity facilitates exploration of the multiple ways that rituals mediate between everyday life and social and cultural structures. Rituals, it seems, can help to maintain a community, but they can also provide an important mechanism for incorporating changes into an established tradition. For example, a study of Catholic Charismatics found that rituals such as testimonies and healings were performed in public and the established meanings were generally available to group members, yet the rituals were also the context in which changes of meaning were negotiated (Neitz 1987, pp. 30–8). The degree of negotiation that occurs in any organizational setting will vary (P. Hall and Spencer-Hall 1982). Certainly, a developing sect like the Catholic Charismatics may be more open to negotiation than other more established groups, for new members both receive socialization into a tradition and must appropriate it as their own. Sometimes doing so means changing that tradition.

Yet negotiation is present in more venerable traditions as well. In a study of orthodox Jews in contemporary urban America, Samuel Heilman has argued that if a religious tradition is to survive it must be able to "make the new holy" and "make the holy new" (1981, pp. 144–5). New aspects of the present (some of them at least) have to be brought into the tradition's world of meaning, and the tradition has to be understood as applying to new members and their world. Heilman shows that maintenance of the group is accomplished, not only through preserving its traditions, but also through continually redefining them.

Any tradition that cannot incorporate the new is a dead tradition. A story illustrating this point comes from Kuba in the colonial Belgian Congo: young tribe members excitedly brought motorcycles to show to their king, but he was unimpressed by the noisy and uncomfortable vehicles. He was fascinated, however, by the tracks that motorcycle tires made, and he had his artists incorporate the patterns into the designs that marked his reign. Modern people tend to be romantic about "tradition" and view "innovations" as corruptions – especially when the source of innovation lies outside what is defined as the tradition. This, however, is fundamentally to misunderstand the nature of culture as living practice (see Figure 4.2).[3]

Indeed, it is important to ask where traditions come from in the first place. Once traditions are established, people often take for granted – as we are intended to – the assertion of their authority and legitimacy. One or another person will be surprised to learn that the image of "Africa" orally transmitted in Haitian *vodu* (popularly known as "voodoo") is a cultural construct (Larose 1977), or to discover that the colorful kilts and tartans associated with the highland clans of Scotland originated in the nineteenth century. As nineteenth-century "traditions," they owe much to the formation of the highland regiments within the British military, the romantic movement's fascination with the cult of the noble savage, and resourceful woolen manufacturers who saw a new market for their plaids (Trevor-Roper 1983, pp. 25–30). In "the invention of tradition" that Eric Hobsbawm (1983) has described within modern societies, "tradition" is not static at all, but rather fabricated to meet various needs – emotional needs of ordinary individuals, political needs of those in power, economic needs of enterprising capitalists.

Innovation and conformity in rituals

The process we are calling making the holy new and the new holy is examined in Barbara Myerhoff's remarkable book *Number Our Days* (1978), a study of elderly

Figure 4.2 At first glance, this necklace from Kenya seems like a "traditional" tribal craft piece. Closer inspection shows that it is a *bricolage* that uses non-indigenous materials, including half a zipper, a plastic-insulated piece of copper wire, several buttons, and a piece of aluminum.

Source: J.R. Hall photograph.

Jews who had migrated to the United States as children or young adults early in the twentieth century. Myerhoff recounts how the subjects of her book gathered around the Aliyah Center in Venice, California. There they tried to make sense of being Jewish and American, old and deserted by their children. They were survivors, but without heirs to their culture or witnesses to their past. The book is organized around four crises that occur at the Center and the resolution of each crisis through an improvised, but elaborately staged, ritual. The crises – two of social relations, two of beliefs – all threaten the fragile collective life of the group. The rituals reassert some aspect of the community's common Jewish heritage, yet each ritual also reflects the fact that in America the community's members have not retained the old ways and their lives are now constrained by old age.

Myerhoff seeks to tease out how innovative rituals achieve the desired effect – reintegrating the group. For example, some substitutions can be made in a ritual as long as enough standard items are included (1978, pp. 104–5). The power of rituals inheres in the repetition of specific acts. Yet for rituals to work the repetitive acts must be personally meaningful to the individuals, invoking a sense of belonging to a community outside themselves, and a continuity with a past and future existence. These meanings have to be constructed in the wake of the dissolution of stable family life and departure from the *shtetl* (the small segregated Jewish towns in Eastern Europe), and if they are to work they must bridge diverse experiences in the United States. As Myerhoff notes: "For this personal coherence, this sense of psychological integration to take place, the individual must be capable of finding and reliving familiar parts of his/her past history" (1978, p. 108).

Myerhoff is most interested in the achievement of continuity in the face of discontinuity. Discontinuity can occur when repetitious acts no longer strike resonant chords in those who practice them. Or, as is the case for the people at the Center, people may lack the cultural or material resources for performing the standard rituals in standard ways. For instance, standard practice demands lighting *Shabbat* candles at dusk, but by then the old people are at home, as they do not feel safe on the streets of their urban neighborhood after dark. So at the Center candles have to be lit at noon, when all members of the community are gathered for the main meal provided there.

Continuity is not necessarily created simply by the repetition of standard acts, however: the new must be made holy. The old people at the Aliyah Center are thrust into creating rituals because, even though their social conflicts threaten the dissolution of the group, they are psychologically dependent upon one another. Myerhoff, the modern anthropologist, judges that innovative rituals succeed because they do what rituals are supposed to do. Her critic from the community, Schmuel, is not so sure. He remembers the traditions of the Yiddish community where he grew up; to him the innovations are lies that people tell themselves. Speaking of the others who participate in the Center's activities, Schmuel tells Myerhoff at one point that they are "trying to get back what they saw in others but themselves never really had" (1978, p. 112). He thus acknowledges the importance of an elite steeped in learning – the shamans, priests, and rabbis who carry cultural traditions, oral and written. Schmuel's comment raises questions about the existence of a truly "common culture" even in the supposed folk societies of the old people's Eastern European childhoods: he suggests that even there people had very different degrees of access to "common symbols" of Jewish culture and that symbols may have had different meanings for different people.

Myerhoff's two loosely connected worlds of Eastern Europe and California can be illuminated by a notion that some anthropologists have come to espouse – of ritual as process. The influential work of Victor Turner (1967) suggests that rituals create a special space and time outside of ordinary interaction. Within this space, innovation, as well as the maintenance of tradition, can occur. Turner calls such a space "liminal" after the Greek word for threshold. In Myerhoff's book, the folk culture of the old people's Eastern European childhoods is contrasted with the heterogenous and pluralistic urban world they have come to inhabit. In these two settings different rituals are performed, but in neither case can the rituals appropriately be described as "empty." Indeed, in the terms of Turner's theory, Myerhoff focuses on the power of rituals to constitute a liminal space/time in which meanings can be reborn.

Secular rituals

Anthropologists such as Mary Douglas, Turner, and Myerhoff share with Goffman the notion that daily life is routine. Yet they differ from Goffman in appreciating ritual as a break in daily routines. For them, the possibility of meaningful ritual is not associated solely with folk culture, or with repetitious, or even overtly religious, acts. Instead, ritual is a symbolic and expressive act, a structured means of creating a special time and place in which individuals experience themselves as part of the community. This understanding of ritual is continuous with the views of the founding social theorists insofar as it associates rituals with integration into a community. However, whereas the founding fathers assumed that such integration into a community was most characteristic of folk societies, Douglas observes that ritualism is not always present among indigenous peoples (1973, pp. 37–9), and she, like Turner and Myerhoff, sees effective ritual – civil and political as well as religious – occurring under certain conditions in modern societies.

Indeed, social solidarity is an important issue for secular nation-states as well as for religiously bonded communities, and symbols and rituals can be important bases for maintaining and reinforcing a sense of social belonging. In the U.S., secular holidays such as Thanksgiving, Memorial Day, and the Fourth of July, like Cinco de Mayo in Mexico, commemorate important "events" in the history of the nation and offer opportunities for the retelling of stories and making connections between past and present.[4] Lyn Spillman's (1997) study of centennial and bicentennial celebrations in the United States and Australia shows the complexity of articulating what cultures share. She suggests that national identity is not singular, but rather that nations develop symbolic repertoires from which successful commemorations can draw.

Jeffrey Alexander (1988) argues that Durkheim's analysis of ritual in archaic religion in fact provides a good model for understanding how symbolic processes work in modern societies. In *The Elementary Forms of Religious Life* (1915), Durkheim had claimed an independent causal importance for symbolic classification through the elaboration of the distinction between the sacred and the profane, and he demonstrated the close relationship between ritual processes and the formation of social solidarity within groups. For Alexander, the value of this work is that it lays out a model – "the religious form of transcendent experiences" – that can be used to analyze "certain universal processes" (1988, p. 191).

Applied today, the model suggests that even secular power in modern societies has a certain numinous or sacred quality: it cannot simply be reduced to legitimated authority role obligations of office. Furthermore, values are created and maintained through rituals that allow members of groups and citizens of nations to experience this "sacred" or non-mundane power. In Alexander's view, what is of use in Durkheim's sociology of religion is not the notion of rituals as standardized and repetitious acts, but rituals as institutionalized ways of achieving social solidarity by putting individuals in touch with the sacred that transcends everyday routine. These aspects of secular rituals in modern nation-states are exemplified, for example, in ceremonies of public ritual surrounding the British monarchy. Analyzing these rituals, Cannadine (1983) has argued that the pageantry, rather than amounting to surviving remnants of the glories of an imperial past, actually has increased over the last century and a half to serve modern appetites, in particular giving an impression of stability in the face of change. Commenting on Queen Elizabeth's Silver Jubilee in 1977, Cannadine writes: "The jubilee ceremonial was an expression of national and imperial decline, an attempt to persuade, by pomp and circumstance that no such decline had really taken place, or to argue that, even if it had, it did not really matter" (1983, p. 160). The contradictions between what is unchanged and what is changing are perhaps even more striking in the elaborate observance of Queen Elizabeth's 2002 Golden Jubilee. Despite well-known changes in the royal family, including the traumas of royal divorces and the death of Princess Diana, crowds in the hundreds of thousands honored their Queen in the elaborate public (and now televised) ceremonies that we have come to expect of the British monarchy (Amis 2002).

As important as rituals are for producing and reproducing legitimacy for sacred and secular powers within an established order, groups outside that dominant order may also use rituals – to express resistance and rebellion. The political scientist David Kertzer (1988) has suggested that political rituals have a conservative bias, but also the potential for innovation, precisely because invention and tradition are so intimately connected. Gay and lesbian commitment ceremonies demonstrate this complicated dynamic. Because most countries outlaw marriages between same-sex couples (the Netherlands is one exception), gay and lesbian weddings have a contradictory significance. On the one hand, the fact of gay and lesbian weddings attests to the meaningfulness of rituals of commitment for the couples who go through them even without the possibility of legal marriage. Some interpreters see the embracing of the wedding tradition as a sign that gays and lesbians are conforming to the dominant heterosexual traditions. Others claim that the ceremonies constitute a challenge to legal systems that refuse to recognize committed partnerships among non-heterosexual couples. Lewin's (1998) study of commitment ceremonies in the United States in the 1990s documents the multiple and sometimes contradictory meanings to everyone present at these gay and lesbian weddings.

Once the concept of ritual is removed from the evolutionary (and hierarchical) frame of social science's founders, its theoretical place need no longer be limited to serving as the defining characteristic of unchanging primitive or folk culture. The consequence, however, is that the standard contrast between modern and primitive or traditional culture becomes undermined. If, as we have argued, the concept of folk culture derives from the contrast between traditional and modern, then the concept of folk culture is undermined as well. A similar difficulty about folk culture emerges in relation to the construct of autonomy.

Theorizing autonomy and contact

Like Myerhoff's protagonist, Schmuel, we may wonder about the nature of the "community" that is evoked in conceptions of folk culture. As this chapter already has shown, the early social theorists saw folk societies as autonomous, economically independent groups where members shared values. Social control could be accomplished through face-to-face interaction and informal mechanisms, especially rituals. The early theorists regarded folk communities as less differentiated than their own, with less elaborate hierarchies, fewer social roles, and little variation in personality types. They described folk communities in contrast to modern societies as homogeneous entities having little contact with outsiders, preserving the "traditional" ways.

However, the assumption that the premodern *Gemeinschaft* (community) was autonomous and isolated can be shown to be flawed. Migration has been a fact of human existence from the earliest times. Adjustments in the often fragile balance between populations and food supplies, conflicts between nomads and cultivators, and the search for trade all provided reasons for individuals and whole groups to move, thereby encountering other groups. The notion of undiscovered or pre-contact cultures may have some relevance in describing the expansion of the West and the particular consequences of cross-societal contact, but it would be foolish to think that most groups of indigenous peoples had no contact with others outside of their own group. Yet that very notion is embedded in the concept of traditional culture.

An alternative approach is offered by Eric Wolfe, who argues that we must understand human history as "bundles of relationships." In a review of the contacts and encounters experienced by "peoples without history" before 1400, Wolfe traces extensive patterns of trade, conquest, and settlement that occurred independently of Europeans (1982, pp. 24–72). He suggests the importance of looking for connections between peoples rather than treating each society as an "integrated and bounded system set off against equally bounded systems."

In fact, it is possible that cultures become most strongly defined not in *isolation* from other cultures but in *interaction* with them. Groups create boundaries in order to differentiate themselves from those outside, and the boundaries continue to exist despite movements of people across them. Fredrick Barth has argued in his work defining ethnic groups that, contrary to the common assumption about the importance of isolation for the maintenance of distinct cultures, "categorical ethnic distinctions do not depend on an absence of mobility, contact, and information, but do entail social processes of exclusion and incorporation" (1970, pp. 9–10). Barth further argues that ethnic groups often maintain stable relations across boundaries, with other groups, and that cultural distinctions can be maintained even in the context of long-term interaction and interdependence.

Rather than seeing traditional and modern cultures as opposing types, theoretical developments outside of the sociology of culture suggest, it is more appropriate to look at relations between groups. Contacts of various kinds – including trade and warfare – have cultural as well as economic and political ramifications for the people involved. This relational approach raises issues of power that were hidden by the earlier formulations. "Contact" has not usually been neutral, even for various social strata within the more powerful of two societies in contact. This point is made by world-systems theory, which analyzes the patterns of relations between "core" capitalist countries of a particular "world economy," societies on the periphery, countries between the two extremes, and "external" arenas outside the world economy (Wallerstein 1974, 1979). The theory seeks to explain the character of any given world economy by examining how traders and manufacturers in core societies profit from an unequal exchange with economically and politically subordinated peoples in other societies.

Consider the trade in luxury goods, and its implications for relations between peoples – both within and between regions. Long before Marco Polo's journey to China in the 1270s, the demand for silk and other luxury goods in Europe spurred contact between the East and the West: traders traveled over land along the "silk road" between the Mediterranean and China. The goods themselves were purchased by elites, who typically paid for them with money raised by taxes and other resource transfers from their subjects, or through warfare and plunder. Trade – both ancient and in the modern capitalist world economy that began to emerge in the 1500s – connects people in diverse social relationships, both within and across regions.

To recognize connectedness and power is not necessarily to privilege structural categories over subjective and cultural ones, although world-systems theorists tend to do so. Local societies have often responded to contact with external forces on the basis of their own cultural meaning systems, shaping the transformations of their social orders that occurred through encounter with Western societies (Sahlins 1985). We are not left just with structural categories to explain such interactions.

Beyond dichotomies

Modern European and American social scientists sought to explain the world and their place in it through a series of related dichotomies: primitive or traditional or folk as opposed to modern; past as opposed to present; non-Western as opposed to Western. In considering these dichotomies, we have argued that the division of the modern Western societies of the writers from their own past and from the non-Western world distorted both sides of the dichotomy. In the service of a general theory, a grand narrative, it overlooked diversity within the modern West and designated those outside the West as symbolic Others.[5]

There are several further questions raised by this analysis. First, how are these dichotomous distortions connected with the larger "crisis in representation" that emerged toward the end of the twentieth century? Second, how has the project of deconstructing concepts of "the Other" produced new approaches and questions? As we have argued, traditional cultures were by no means isolated, autonomous, or static before contact with the West. Nor, then, should they be isolated in our analysis either. In part that means cultural analysis should take account of economic and political relations within and between social groups, but it also means that analysis should explore how those forces play out within local contexts in relation to crosscutting issues of nationalism, ethnicity, gender, and religion.

Folk culture and the crisis of representation

This chapter has presented considerable evidence that nineteenth- and twentieth-century social theorists developed the concept of folk culture as an idealized mirror-image of their own idealized societies. They "created" images of the past that they believed could explain the things that they were seeing in the present. To assert this in turn raises questions about what happens when any of us – scholars, students, or people in general – talks or writes about the social world, our memories, and history. Is any one of us less culturally bound than the modern social theorists? How is the account anyone gives shaped by who we are and where we are located? What is the status of the accounts we generate?

These questions are especially important for anthropologists, historians, and sociologists, who have a professional obligation to try to get things right, or at least be honest about the difficulties of doing so. In an essay titled "Partial truths" (1986), James Clifford speaks for the new epistemological critique of earlier philosophies of knowledge based on the assumption that ethnographers and historians "represent" or capture reality when they create textual descriptions of people in other times and places. "Culture [is] composed of seriously contested codes and representations," he argues, adding, "the poetic and the political are inseparable, and...science is in, not above, historical and linguistic processes" (1986, p. 2). In effect, Clifford is suggesting that social scientists invent rather than represent reality. His account is intentionally provocative, but the issues examined in this chapter help us to see why he might make such a claim. In trying to understand the dislocations of their own time, early social theorists "invented the past." The dichotomies that they developed to contrast their own times with the past were driven by particular theoretical and practical concerns.

To say that social scientists "invent" rather than "represent" reality implies that there is no one single truth out there to be discovered (by scientists or anyone else), and that the writing process is as important a part of research as the data-gathering process. Social scientists are engaged in interpreting what they have learned. For instance, ethnographers today are less and less likely to experience research as a triangle made up of three separate points: an objective *observer* who writes about some exotic *others* for an *audience* distant from those studied. Instead, ethnographers today are increasingly likely to find members of their subject group among their audiences (Neitz 2002). Facing up to this condition, George Marcus has explored the specific problems involved in the writing of anthropological texts "once the line between the local worlds of subjects and the global world of systems becomes radically blurred" (1986, p. 171). If "everyone is connected to everyone else," what reasonable boundaries can be drawn in writing an ethnography of a particular group? Marcus discusses two possibilities: the multi-local ethnography and the strategically situated ethnography. He also suggests the possibility of mixed-genre writing by social scientists, in hopes of more self-conscious reflection about the choice of site and subject.

Our considerations about folk culture have identified two related considerations. One has to do with content. If societies no longer can be treated as isolated and autonomous, how can social scientists acknowledge the connectedness of social groups without moving to a level of abstraction that misses the rich character and significance of local cultures? The other is a concern about the authority and legitimacy of the writer and the written representation: how should social scientists and historians represent themselves and their subjects? The remainder of this chapter explores some of the new directions being taken by scholars addressing these issues.

New approaches: colonial and postcolonial studies

Several recent approaches at the borders of history, anthropology, and cultural studies look for new ways of examining the relations between indigenous groups and the West. Coming out of a sense of disillusionment, not only with liberal theories of modernization, but with the grand narrative of Marxism as well, and influenced by a growing awareness of how knowledge – scientific, ethnographic, and colonial – is produced, the new approaches share the belief that culture is an important component in their studies. They are attentive to who is telling the story, with what data. They also are concerned with local societies, but not as isolated entities. Rather, they see what happens in local sites and their particular contexts through a perspective that is relational. The new work is often identified with various regional and area studies, and with postcolonial, colonial, and subaltern studies. Recent work of scholars in these approaches moves beyond the dichotomies inherited from nineteenth-century Western thought.

Subaltern studies developed in India in the 1970s, following internal conflicts within the nation-state that centered on the repressive measures put in place by the government of Indira Gandhi and the failure of the modern capitalist government to represent the people and to solve problems of social and political inequality. According to Gyan Prakash, "The term 'subaltern,' drawn from Antonio Gramsci's writings, refers to subordination in terms of class, caste, gender, race, language, and culture and was used to signify the centrality of dominant/dominated relationships in history" (1994, p. 1,477). There is considerable tension within subaltern studies, however, between the recovery of the subject and analyzing how subalternity was constituted by dominant discourses.

Subaltern studies does not presume to recover the subjectivity of "real subalterns" as subordinated individuals or groups. Rather, its project is to locate an unspoken presence of subalterns inside the very elite discourses that suppressed and fragmented the subaltern presence. While, of necessity, subaltern scholars rely in large part on the records of colonialists, they read those records "against the grain" so as to recover the agency of subjects, at least as they were reflected in the actions and reactions of elites.

Discussions of the cultural practice of *sati*, where Hindu widows burned to death, throwing themselves on the funeral pyres of their husbands, illustrates some of the challenges for subaltern studies. In our time, debates about the practice are informed primarily through the nineteenth-century sources, namely elite indigenous patriarchs who supported *sati* and the British modernizers who wanted to abolish it in the name of the emancipation of women. In the construction of the debate, however, the women's voices are absent, not simply because there are no sources, but, as Spivak (1988) has pointed out, because the debate was constructed in such a way that there was no subject position from which the widow could speak. In this case the attempt to retrieve the voices of subject populations poses an impossible contradiction: to recover a subaltern "presence" is to posit a "voice" that never existed.

Subaltern studies joins with other forms of postcolonial critique in a project of, in the words of Dipesh Chakrabarty (1992), "provincializing Europe." The grand historical narratives of Western thought always had Europe as their reference point. As Chakrabarty observes:

> Europe remains the sovereign, theoretical subject of all histories, including the ones we call "Indian," "Chinese," "Kenyan," and so on. There is a peculiar way in which all these histories tend to become variations on a master narrative which could be called "history of Europe."
>
> (Chakrabarty 1992, p. 1)

In such theoretical metanarratives, Europe, or the West, came to stand for modernity. Non-Westerners who speak of modernity do so with categories already created by Europe, but Europeans have had the privilege of being oblivious to other cultures, except insofar as the exotic Others were useful to them for their own purposes. Postcolonial critics oppose these binary oppositions. Prakash explains: "the aim of using a strategy is not to unmask dominant discourses but to explore their fault lines in order to provide different accounts" (1992, p. 1,486).

Another group of critical scholars questions even the term "postcolonial." They suggest that it, too, summons a dichotomous image – of before/after – when in fact in many ways "the culture of the imperial power still sets the standards" (Cooper and Stoler 1997, p. 33). They further suggest that the idea of the "postcolonial" essentializes the nature of the colonial experience. While not dismissing the power of states or the world economy, those who gather under the flag of colonial studies begin with the premise that relations between the colonizers and the colonized go both ways. In other words, the actions of colonizers have been, and continue to be, shaped by the particular circumstances they encounter among the indigenous populations and subject societies they colonize. This approach breaks down the conceptual process of *othering* by bringing the colonized and the colonizer into the same frame. Cooper and Stoler propose directions for colonial studies as follows:

First toward a recognition that systems of production did not just arise out of the impersonal workings of a world economy, but out of shifting conceptual apparatuses that made certain kinds of action seem possible, logical, and even inevitable to state officials, entrepreneurs, missionaries, and other agents of colonization while others were excluded from the realm of possibility; second, toward a recognition that what was imaginable in terms of social policy reflected histories of distant metropoles as well as the immediate opportunities; and constraints of conquest while the colonial experience shaped what it meant to be "metropolitan" and "European" as much as the other way around; third, toward a focus on the way colonial states sought knowledge and influence over the ways in which individuals, families, and institutions were reproduced.

(Cooper and Stoler 1997, p. vii)

Here, "Europeans" and "others" are not bifurcated; they are connected, and multiple and hybrid in their identities. Thus, colonial-studies scholars seek to understand "competing versions of whiteness" (1997, p. 16) among colonizers of different classes, and how members of the indigenous populations – women, peasants, laborers, religious leaders – may have different interests as well. These scholars also show how the "otherness" of the colonized was not stable, but rather a matter of ongoing contestation in contexts where boundaries were permeable. They investigate questions such as how specific regimes decided how "French" colonial subjects could be; or when the laws governing French citizens apply to the children of French fathers and Vietnamese mothers (Cooper 1996; Stoler 1997).

For all the significance of the new work in colonial studies, however, it hardly offers a new basis for totalizing history; nor should it. The history of the Middle East is a case in point. Scholars observe that the "colonial" history of the region is complicated by the Ottoman Empire and Iran, which were never colonized. These societies, like others, modernized in the context of an emergently dominant Europe, but with a greater autonomy of alternative traditions. As these examples suggest, encounters between the West and the East were not always technically "postcolonial." Still, the metaphors of postcolonial studies – such as translation, hybridization, and dislocation – seem better to describe relations between more and less modern nations than older ones such as imitation, assimilation, and rejection. In short, creative new ways of thinking from postcolonial studies have a wider relevance (see Abu-Lughod 1998, p. 18).

To illustrate the possibilities, consider how gender politics has played out in the symbolism of the veil in Iran. As Sullivan (1998) argues, women have become the symbols of Iranian national identity through a protracted historical process:

In Iran's conflicted efforts to construct national, revolutionary, and Islamic modernities, the figure of the "woman" has repeatedly constituted the overdetermined sign of an essentialized totality, as a metaphor for a besieged nation, an embattled self, a delicate interiority, the uncontrollable other, the "unpierced pearl" to be bought and protected, or the sacred interior.

(Sullivan 1998, p. 228)

In 1934, Reza Shah visited Turkey and decided to follow Atatürk's policy of disengaging secular politics from religion. He banned the wearing of the veil in Iran, a form of "modernization from above." During the Iranian revolution of 1979 that ousted

Shah Mohammed Reza Pahlavi, the wearing of the veil became a symbol of protest by women who marched against his regime. Yet many of these same women were astounded when the revolutionary government passed laws requiring women to wear the veil outside their homes. Women again marched in protest. Sullivan notes: "Thus the *chador* is used by opposing camps for opposite reasons: the veil as a symbol of liberation from a dictatorial state and as an instrument for hegemonizing a revolution by those whose only aim was political power" (1998, p. 224).

The new approaches of subaltern studies and colonial theory offer a powerful critique of the dichotomous thinking that has informed so much of Western thought. These approaches have produced new understandings that indeed move historical, social, and cultural analysis toward "provincializing" Europe. But what of ethnography?

Cultural specificity, global and local cross talk

In discussing the crisis in representation above, we posed the question of how social analysts can write about local cultures in ways that emphasize connections rather than autonomy, but without moving to a level of abstraction that loses the rich description of local cultures. We also discussed concerns about the scholarly authority of researchers, who, as the critics of the ethnographic tradition argue, can at best hope to provide "partial knowledge" of the societies they describe. Anna Tsing's (1993) study of the Meratus Dayaks in the Meratus mountains of Indonesia is one attempt to reconceive how ethnography can be done in light of such critiques.

Tsing puts forward a conception of "marginality" as a way of exploring "the local" and "out of the way places," not as isolated Others or some remnants of an ancestral past, but as sites of discursive contestation. The local here involves, not so much a place, but rather "acts of positioning" (1993, p. 31). She is interested in the ways that the women and men whom she encountered explain local cultural politics in relation to regional issues. Her analysis of the local Meratus and their nativist beliefs explores their relations with institutions based on different beliefs and interests that come into their world: those of their Muslim Behar neighbors; the Indonesian central government, with its projects for development, building, and resettlement; and global capitalism, with agendas for extracting the resources of the rainforests (with male employees who sometimes contract for services from female Meratus). Tsing places gender at the center of her analysis in order to illuminate the connections between internal cultural issues and issues of region, colonialism, and development. This emphasis on gender helps to show the importance, even among the Meratus, of both heterogeneity and of trans-communal links through which communities are forged.

Rather than explain the responses of the Meratus in terms of Western anthropological categories, Tsing uses the actions and stories of the Meratus to unsettle Western understandings. The model that Tsing employs is not one of "the expert" explaining "the Other" for the benefit of a group of Western modern scholars, but rather of a conversation. Tsing argues that her approach entails a change in scholars' understanding of theory: it too becomes decentered. In this ethnography Tsing shows how theory can come from many sources, including the wisdom of the Meratus and the visionary prophecies of their male and female shamans. She shows the reader one way an account might look if the writer took seriously the idea that theory is co-

constructed between the writer and her subjects and is not just the privileged product of Western elite thought.[6]

Conclusion

Although the concept of traditional culture – and, behind that, of primitive culture – was integral to the theoretical enterprises of the founding fathers of social science, these concepts are now extremely problematic. The concept of primitive culture, with its Eurocentric base, is no longer acceptable. In current academic work the idea of "traditional culture" also has mostly lost its meaning. While scholars will want to talk about the radical changes that occurred with modernization, and about times and places in which those changes had not yet occurred, somewhat less grandiose conceptualizations and new methodological approaches now seem more appropriate to these purposes. Some researchers may still want to speak of "traditional cultures," but they are more likely to use a term that designates a more specific place and time, for example talking about the culture of sixteenth-century rural France. For other purposes it may be useful to use a term that designates specific technologies or production processes. The degree of integration into a market economy may also be important. And, as was noted earlier, among cultural anthropologists it has become common to talk about oral or preliterate cultures, and Eric Wolfe (1982) uses the phrase "peoples without history."

Rejecting the dichotomy between premodern and modern societies, with its associations of modernity and Westernization, also has ramifications for analyzing modern society. Where previous theoretical constructions pointed primarily to discontinuities, now scholars see the possibilities of finding continuities. In this chapter we have examined how the concept of ritual – developed in relation to primitive societies – can be used by sociologists of culture to understand fundamental human experiences and actions that can be found (structured in various ways, to be sure) in all kinds of societies.

Finally, what of the concept of folk culture: where does it stand? In a pluralistic world where every corner has been subjected to the gaze of the mass media and everything has its price, folk culture acquires a narrow meaning. In Europe, folk culture refers to the traditions of local peoples, including dress, food, dialect, religious practices, dance, all remnants of distinct local cultures – all now connected to the ongoing struggle between proponents of national and ethnic identities and seekers of European unity.

Folk culture in the U.S. often refers to specific cultural artifacts transmitted orally from one generation to another. In its most common contemporary sense it is almost a genre of arts and crafts, defined by cultural transmission and learning outside of schools or books. Such a definition, of course, can easily reify "tradition" and fail to recognize the normal processes of innovation. Is a carving of a traditional subject by a traditionally trained carver from an indigenous population using traditional methods and subjects but nontraditional materials authentic folk culture? What if the innovation is partly a response to market demand (Graburn 1967, 1976)? Two identical objects – for example stools or masks – are produced, one for use in a traditional ritual and one for an American dealer in primitive art; are both authentic to the same degree? Is folk culture produced for a market still folk culture? These questions speak to a set of important cultural shifts that took place before the industrial revolution beginning in the late eighteenth century, but long after the most settled parts of the world had become increasingly interconnected.

Suggested readings

For a study of Buddhism among the Sherpas of Nepal carried out from the emerging "practice perspective," see *High Religion* by Sherry Ortner (1989). Ortner combines historical and anthropological analysis to account for the development of celibate monasteries in Nepal in the early twentieth century, and shows the establishment of religious rituals in a process that is motivated by human intentions and embedded in social structures. Her more recent book on the Sherpas, *Life and Death on Mt. Everest: Sherpas and Himalayan Mountaineering* (2001), is an interesting discussion of the encounter between the indigenous culture of the Sherpas with the climbing industry, including its ramifications for gender relations.

The debate concerning whether Western scholars can write about non-Western cultures without perpetuating the myths of European imperialism has been especially vociferous in anthropology. An interesting point for entering the debate is Marshall Sahlins's controversial work on the death and deification of Captain Cook in Hawaii in 1779. *How "Natives" Think: About Captain Cook, for Example* (1995) seeks to tell the story from a native point of view.

For a look at some of the many meanings of "development" in countries from Chili, Japan, South Africa, Germany, Turkey, Hungary, Taiwan, and Indian to the United States, see *Many Globalizations: Cultural Diversity in the Contemporary World* (2002), edited by the scholars Peter L. Berger and Samuel Huntington. The authors explore the idea of an emerging global culture, but show that it has many variations, and also that it is changing the West as much as the developing world.

Notes

1   E.B. Tylor is usually credited with being the first to introduce the word "culture" into English usage, in his work *Primitive Society* (1871). The idea, however was familiar to those who knew German, for in Germany the celebration of the "*Volk*" was very much a part of the romantic movement to reclaim a traditional agrarian past, deemed "purer" spiritually because uncontaminated by the customs (and genes) of other ethnic groups.

2   The word "spontaneous" comes from Redfield (1940, p. 737).

3   For a more extended discussion of this point with regard to early modern Europe, see P. Burke 1978, pp. 23–64.

4   Bellah (1970) analyzed these and other "national symbols" and suggested that a "civil religion" tying citizenship and public duty to religious behavior in a set of national symbols surfaced in the United States in the nineteenth century after the disestablishment of the churches.

5   Grand narratives also distorted critical aspects of the modern West. On this point, see, for example, Latour 1993.

6   For a similar argument in a different context, see P. Collins 2000.

5   Preindustrial sources of contemporary culture

We might find a few pristine examples, but what are conventionally called "traditional cultures" have changed: they survive, if at all, disconnected from their origins, within an encompassing, alien social order, marginalized by the increasing predominance of other kinds of culture. Much of what people call "folk" culture today consists of remnants, reworked and distributed through the mass media. Thus, the "folk song" has become a genre – a conventionalized form of music, and it is produced and distributed in a manner similar to other genres of music, for example "classical music" or Hip-Hop. Similarly, "folk festivals" are produced using more widely available techniques of concert promotion.

While "traditional" culture has become transformed into "folk," actual culture contents of traditions have diffused into contemporary culture by way of motifs, melodies, myths, and other elements. The routes are diverse. Music of West Africans was carried by them when they were captured, forced into slavery, and brought to the Americas, and the motifs of this music have found their way into contemporary samba, jazz, rhythm and blues, and soul music (R.F. Thompson 1959). Modern artists – for example Paul Gauguin, Henri Matisse, and Pablo Picasso – took inspiration, "borrowing," as Kubler (1962) calls it, from the visual motifs of indigenous cultures (Gardner 1959). And modern architects were asked to appreciate buildings built "without architects" (Rudofsky 1964). But these importations of motifs and styles presume modern culture is already established. How did this come about?

Answering that question depends on analyzing the relationship between society and culture: does culture have independent causal importance, or do the emergence of new technologies and rising social classes (notably the middle class) explain changes in cultural form and content? An initial issue concerns the degree to which contemporary cultural forms and patterns of content have changed from those of earlier, non-market societies that were based on simpler technologies. It seems reasonable to think that some significant parallels exist between culture today and earlier cultures, for example in the ways rituals and myths work. Still, most contemporary culture, including rituals and myths, is profoundly different from earlier culture, and we must therefore suspect that culture is subject to some new processes that have changed its character.

Many of the differences between earlier cultures and modern culture can be tied to three factors: (1) the industrial revolution that began in the late eighteenth century, powered by harnessing non-human, non-animal energy – first, coal-generated steam from the engine developed by James Watt and others, then electricity, gasoline, and nuclear fission; (2) the related emergence of a "consumer society" in which most people satisfy most of their needs and wants by using money to make purchases; and

(3) the parallel development of mass media – mass-distributed newspapers and magazines beginning in the nineteenth century, and twentieth-century developments of radio, television, communications, and computer networks. These are all important factors, to be considered in Chapter 6. Yet accepting them as a sufficient explanation of modernity would obscure other important developments. What about sources of modern culture that *preceded* the industrial revolution?

This chapter sketches earlier developments that are particularly important by identifying key preindustrial shifts toward contemporary cultural dynamics. We ask whether the ways in which culture works today depend in part on processes that already were established before the advent of modern mass media. In addition, given the importance of the modern mass media, we explore an early case – printing – that shows how technology can manifest itself in cultural change. To consider these issues, we look comparatively at various "civilizing" regions of the world prior to the nineteenth century.

Of course it would be possible to go back further in history, for example to ancient Mesopotamia, India, China, Egypt, Greece, and the Roman Empire. But we need not do this to identify the key preindustrial patterns that shaped the character of modern cultures. In India, China, Japan, the region of Islamic culture centered in the Middle East, and in old Europe beginning at least as early as the eleventh century there were important consolidations of court life, pursuit of knowledge, patronage of arts by religions and the wealthy, and the gradual development of new economic and organizational forms.

In part, the development of modern social forms depended on innovations that originated in one region of the world or another and diffused to other regions. Thus, by the thirteenth century trade in textiles was a bridge that linked the various corners of the old world, from China, through the "silk road," to the Middle East and Europe (Allsen 1997). Similarly, contacts developed between Arabs and Europeans across the Mediterranean, via Spain, Italy, and the routes of the Christian crusaders to the Holy Land. These interactions brought the diffusion of all kinds of culture. For example, Europe was influenced by important elements of Arabic culture – scholarship, architecture, the decorative arts, textiles, ceramics, music, and language. To note one important development, European ideas of romantic love have their origins in Arab sentiments spread by troubadours – musician-poets who moved up through southern Europe beginning in the eleventh century. Overall, a wide swath of the old world was already becoming well connected through migration and trade long before modern society emerged.

Today, the origins of modernity are hotly debated. Following a longstanding analysis, some scholars identify distinctive economic and cultural developments in Europe prior to the nineteenth century that they argue account for the initial occurrence of the industrial revolution there rather than elsewhere. Other scholars argue that even by the late eighteenth century Europe was no more advanced than other civilizational regions, and that the breakthrough in Europe can be explained by a conjuncture – the invention of the steam engine in a region (England) possessing exceptionally high-quality deposits of coal that could be used to fuel industrial machines (Goldstone 2000; on the debate, see Stokes 2001).

How the controversy about world history will be resolved depends in part on understanding preindustrial culture and its relation to social and economic changes. Two linked sets of developments were of the greatest significance. First, processes of "routinization" and "rationalization" changed cultures, forms of social organization, and the economics of production and distribution. Second, as towns became increasingly central in a growing market economy, the forms of culture, as well as support for it, became tied to new social groups. We explore each of these broad developments in turn.

Routinization, rationalization, and capitalism

One of the classic debates in sociology concerns whether cultural phenomena (often too narrowly described as "ideas") have causal significance in their own right. In the crudest version of a so-called "idealist" position, an idea such as "freedom" represents a "spirit" that has causal force. More sophisticated arguments establish linkages between culture and the interests and practices of individual people and social groups. In the latter view, reality is in part "socially constructed" through the ideas that give meaning to action and shape to social organization (P.L. Berger and Luckmann 1966). As Clifford Geertz asserted in a quotation famous among social scientists, "man is an animal suspended in webs of significance he himself has spun" (1973, p. 5). Here, the crucial question is whether cultural forms, meanings, and practices can be deduced from the personal and group situations and interests of the people who advance them. If culture can simply be "read off" individuals and groups, it can be treated as derivative. If this cannot be done, on the other hand, even if culture is not somehow "autonomous," it has to be considered causally important.

One way to address the issue of culture's significance for modernity is to consider two processes that Max Weber (1978) described as key to the emergence of the modern world – rationalization and routinization. *Rationalization* may be defined as a process in which a particular activity is increasingly overtaken by "rational" ways of doing things: goals are met in ways that are considered to be as efficient and effective as possible.[1] When aspects of the world become reorganized according to dictates of efficiency and effectiveness, we may speak of rationalization. Thus, the changes in how fast-food restaurants operate are a process of rationalization, designed to ever more quickly produce and serve (hopefully!) better tasting and more nutritious hamburgers, at lower and lower costs and increased profits.

Often associated with rationalization is a parallel development – *routinization*. When activity is organized in order to systematize sequences of action so that the same activity can be repeated over and over again, we may speak of the development of routines, or routinization. For example, the old-style waitress at a cafe typically performed a variety of tasks but lacked an overall routine, and she took the prerogative of stopping to joke with delivery men and talk with customers. By comparison, the job of the contemporary worker at McDonald's or Burger King around the world has been narrowed to a set of clearly circumscribed routines: one person takes orders, another flips burgers, and so on. With routinization, the predictability of social action increases, and large numbers of people become systematically organized into closely coordinated activities.

Weber thought that rationalization and routinization gradually became important in transforming the organization of social life in parts of Europe during the Middle Ages, and especially with the spread of Protestant Christianity after the Reformation beginning in the sixteenth century. Yet he did not advocate the idealist position that rationalization increased as the manifestation of some "spirit" of history: his own studies suggest that multiple currents of rationalization took hold in spheres as diverse as personal life, work, and the distribution of culture. Other researchers have shown that similar rationalization and routinization occurred elsewhere than old Europe, for instance in late-medieval Japan. In the West, the rationalizing developments converged with a gradual but profound reorganization of economic life that accompanied the emergence – beginning in earnest in the sixteenth century – of a globalizing economy of production and trade centered in northwest Europe. Diverse though the sources of rationalization, and as complex as their connections with world-economic changes were, the consequences added up to more than the sum of the independent developments.

Rationalization and personal life

By the sixteenth century, isolated developments toward rationalization were under way in various corners of the world, but many basic aspects of people's lives remained untouched. To understand this kind of world, let us consider the problem of social identity that is raised by a true story told in a film, *The Return of Martin Guerre*. One day in 1556 in a village in the south of France, a man appeared and announced that he was the husband of a woman who lived there, Bertrande. Martin Guerre had disappeared years earlier, leaving behind his wife of nine years and a newborn child. The man recounted the reason for his disappearance – he had gone off to war – and the village people welcomed his return. Bertrande took him into her arms. But eventually the Martin Guerre who shared a bed with Bertrande lost favor, and came to be confronted in court with the return of the real Martin Guerre.

The story of Martin Guerre generated a heated debate among historians (N.Z. Davis 1983; Finlay 1988; N.Z. Davis 1988). Could Bertrande really have been duped by the imposter sharing her bed, or did she play along in order to regain her respect and a husband? Beyond these questions is a more basic one: what kind of world could sustain such a situation? In a word, it was a world in which personal identity had not become rationalized. Perhaps the deceit would not have worked in more cosmopolitan areas of sixteenth-century France, and perhaps even today a similar charade might be pulled off. Still, the imposter's deceit would be much more difficult in our era of rationalized identity. Today newborn babies may become confused in a hospital, but the confusion can be settled by DNA tests, which also can be used on adults. People may adopt aliases and move to new places to start new lives, but if they try to assume someone else's identity they have to obtain a fake social security number, driver's license, and other organizationally produced badges of identity. By contrast, all Martin's imposter had to do was get people to accept him in the *social role* of Martin Guerre. What is taken for granted today as a concrete reality – officially recorded personal identity – barely existed in the sixteenth century, at least in areas like Martin Guerre's village.

Rationalization has far more intimate consequences for the person than the exterior signs of identity. The inner being of humans – personality – is also affected. This is apparent in the distinction between "madness" and "sanity," described by Michel Foucault (1965). Although these categories may seem like "natural" descriptions of human possibilities, Foucault showed that the distinction is a cultural one, and that it emerged historically. In his account, madness as a social construct can exist only in opposition to the construct of the disciplined, organized mind based on reason. Thus,

Foucault theorized that there must have been an era when neither madness nor the rational person in any modern sense yet existed – a time when the average person lacked a self-disciplined personality subjected to the dictates of modern reason, just as communities lacked the standards, labels, and facilities of "confinement" by which to establish a separate identity of "madness." In a sense, "madness" was invented through rationalization. Defining mental disorder required confronting difficult questions. How was a classification system for different types of madness and their relation to other categories to be established? Was madness rooted in animal passions, was it a product of idleness and poverty, or was it to be regarded as a moral failing of the individual? Were the insane to be imprisoned, segregated from society at large, or treated for diseases? Foucault showed how rationales of classification concerned with madness changed over the centuries according to its meaningful construction.

But it is not just the mad who have become subject to rationalization. The rationalization of social conduct among people deemed sane is equally important. In part, that rationalization has involved the development of a "culture of civility" (Elias 1982). In the twelfth century even the elite classes of territorial lords and warring knights in Europe were still a rough crowd. On the other side of the world, in Japan, the Tokagawa state that ruled the country from the late sixteenth century to the middle of the nineteenth century confronted a similar problem. How was the class of Samurai warriors to be constrained?

The pacification of warrior identity took different directions in Japan and Europe. In Japan, the Samurai warriors emphasized an individualistic ethic of honor based on the principle that a man (and it was men!) wronged by another man could salvage his prestige by resolving the matter through his own action, for example by killing a man who committed adultery with his wife. But the Tokagawa regime gradually redirected the Samurais' individualist culture of honor into bureaucratic arenas. There, the Samurai were to be judged as honorable according to their official rank, and on the basis of their performance of obligations toward superiors and inferiors. The Samurai culture of "honorific individualism" was "tamed" (Ikegami 1995).

In Europe, the rechanneling of honor centered, not on bureaucracy, but on the courts – royal settings in which the social and political life of the elite transpired as though on a stage. Using the language of Freudian psychology to describe medieval European society, the sociological historian Norbert Elias painted an image of a feudal elite whose members lacked "drive-control" and failed to channel their "elementary urges" into "refined pleasure"; instead, they lived by the sword and acted out impulses of gratification and aggression in plunder and rape (1982, pp. 72–3).

In the long, slow rebuilding from the "dark ages" that followed the collapse of the Roman Empire in the fifth century M.E., courtly society gradually became established in Europe. As early as the eleventh century, it could be found in domains of the wealthier feudal landlords. The courts offered venues for the display of wealth through patronage of the arts and entertainment, and they became settings for performances by minstrels, poets, and wandering troubadours. This milieu gave greater importance to refined behavior – manners. The courtly person no longer could depend solely on physical strength; instead, self-control became important. By the seventeenth century, La Bruyère could say:

> A man who knows the court is master of his gestures, of his eyes and his expression; he is deep, impenetrable. He dissimulates the bad turns he does, smiles at his

enemies, suppresses his ill-temper, disguises his passions, disavows his heart, acts against his feelings.

(quoted in Elias 1982, p. 272)

In a word, courtly action became calculating; life became something of a performance: acting out social roles emphasized a "presentation of self" to impress others – a feature that sociologist Erving Goffman (1959) has shown is central to modern life.

The "inner" rationalization of personal thought and conduct can take diverse directions. For the West, the development of courtly manners persists today in high-society etiquette and in modern Western ideas of romantic love. In Japan, Samurai culture helped sustain a different sort of individuality, more directly connected to official conduct. Yet the personal self only amounts to half the equation of modern identity, for such identities are based on a dichotomy between personal life and work.

Rationalization of work

In medieval Europe, rationalization of work emerged first, not on the feudal estates that depended on the labor of peasant farmers, for the lords of such manors could rarely gain direct control over peasants' activities. Instead, it developed in the medieval monasteries of the Roman Catholic Church, which could claim absolute obedience to religious authority. By the eleventh century, monastic authorities were using this power to organize agricultural and other kinds of production rationally (Duby 1968, pp. 175–81). This "outer" rationalization of organized activity was accompanied by demands upon the monks for devoted and dutiful work.

Such "asceticism" – individuals' self-sacrifice as a sign of devotion to God – has taken various forms historically, and those forms have had consequences beyond their religious origins. Medieval European monasticism was designed to be an "otherworldly" retreat from "this" world, a kind of heaven on earth. Yet monasteries achieved a rationalized organization of work that was nearly impossible in the wider agrarian world of feudalism. The feudal lord could demand rent and labor from peasants, but the feudal manor was rarely organized as an integrated unit of production. Monasteries' administrators, by contrast, had to provide for the needs of all the members of their communities, and they engaged in rational planning and strict organization of work.

However, the ascetic rationalism of monastic life was not unique to the West. In late-medieval Japan, Buddhist monasteries operated in similar ways, organizing work for production of commodities such as *sake* for the market, and providing the organizational form on which subsequent non-monastic production was based. Clearly the West was not alone in the rationalization of work. Yet the consequences of rationalization were different in the two parts of the world. Japanese monasteries provided a template for subsequent institutionalization of capitalism in Japan, but the full significance of these changes only took hold after an irreversible shift toward modern industrial capitalism occurred in the West. In Europe, by contrast, the monasteries' innovative systematic organization of productive activity became directly important in the rationalization of work processes in European capitalist manufacturing that began slowly to emerge beginning in the sixteenth century, and with greater force during the industrial revolution (J.R. Hall 1978, pp. 40–1; R. Collins 1986, pp. 52–4; R. Collins 1997).

With the Protestant Reformation that began in Europe in the early sixteenth century, the work asceticism that had been enforced *externally* in the monasteries became psychologically *internalized* by Protestant believers, who treated work in "this" world as a "vocation," or "calling" by God. In the famous analysis of Max Weber, Protestant religion had important consequences for economic life: under a regimen of "inner-worldly asceticism," Protestants with anxieties about their own salvation were told by ministers to quell their anxieties by working hard, avoiding either indolence or the pursuit of personal pleasure. Rank-and-file Protestant ascetics engaged in self-disciplined work that reinforced a modern, rational form of capitalism by supplying workers who were predictable and reliable. In effect, workers subjected themselves to "inner" rationalization of their habits and conduct – not only in relation to religious duties, but also in matters of work. Adopting what is often called the "work ethic," they became almost human machines, or "workaholics."

The advent of the inwardly disciplined Protestant type of worker reinforced more rapid economic growth in Protestant regions of Europe than in Catholic ones, Weber argued (1958a). Religion also became an important basis for certifying the integrity and honesty of people engaged in business. Eventually, members of a religious group might screen potential members concerning their economic practices, and having done so, they could vouch for the honesty of one another (Weber 1946, p. 302ff.). In these ways, religion contributed to the rationalization and predictability of economic life. As a form of culture, religion altered people's ethics of everyday life in ways that contributed to a revolutionary transformation of society as a whole.

Rationalized distribution of culture: the cases of music and text

Weber did not argue that religion caused modern capitalism, even if he showed the significance of rationalization of work organization and conduct for how capitalism developed. Nor did he limit his consideration of rationalization to the economic sphere. In *The Rational and Social Foundations of Music* (1958b), Weber showed that the development of complex harmony in music depended upon the invention of a rational system for notating music on paper, based on a standardization of musical time and pitch. Traditional music is seldom reproduced exactly, and it is reproduced from memory rather than from musical scores. Slippage, or "drift," therefore occurs between successive performances, especially when music passes from one person or group to another (Kubler 1962). It thus can be difficult to determine any "definitive" version of a folk song (P. Burke 1978, p. 114). By comparison, "a somewhat complicated modern work of music...is neither producible nor transmittable nor reproducible without the use of notation" (Weber 1958b, p. 84). The modern Western system of notation originally developed in the medieval Roman Catholic Church. A great systematizer of religion, the Church sought to impose a uniform liturgy, or specified form, for its services across Christendom. With careful copying of liturgies by monks, what counted as the "same" mass could be performed simultaneously in all the cathedrals and churches of Europe, beginning as early as the sixth century, and attaining increasing complexity as monks continued to refine their systems of notation (Seay 1965, pp. 40–1; Weber 1958b, p. 86). The medieval Christian mass thus represents an early case of "mass production" that did not depend upon machines or technology, even printing.

What written scores accomplished for music, writing had already accomplished much earlier for the spoken word, where pitch and timing did not require such explicit notation. However, in both cases, so long as copying of documents remained the province of scribes and monks, the distribution of these cultural materials remained largely confined to social elites, and the distribution of culture reinforced an existing social order rather than encouraging a new one. But the letter alphabet, itself a rationalized "notating" of oral words by their combinations of sounds, ultimately made possible the invention of movable type so that multiple copies of the same text could easily be printed.

As Elizabeth Eisenstein (1979) has shown, the technological innovation of modern printing fueled a revolution that altered the social equation momentously. Three changes stand out. First, printing broke the church's monopoly on religious texts; Protestant reformers depended heavily on printing for the dissemination of their ideas, and the Bible became widely available to an increasingly literate population. The consequences for religious organization and authority were tremendous. Second, printing transformed the conditions of cultural work. Before printing, labor-intensive processes of cultural production inhibited wide distribution of texts. Scholars had their hands full with the laborious tasks of copying and interpreting classical and religious works, rather than producing new ideas. Printing based on movable type freed up mental labor, and gradually intellectuals began to pursue questions beyond the frame of religious theology, through secular humanistic and empirical scientific inquiry (Wuthnow 1989). Not only philosophical books were published, but also practical ones about construction engineering, swamp drainage, and agriculture. Third, printing became an important occupation in the growing towns. Printers supported and reinforced the new religious and intellectual developments that were good for the printing business. Partly on the basis of the revolution in printing, the European medieval social order previously centered on feudal and religious authority weakened, and new social classes began to emerge and assert their power.

Indeed, the consequences of modern printing were as important for politics as religion. Multiple avenues of political communication existed prior to the invention of printing, such as proclamations, political sermons, rumors, private correspondence, and petitions. But as David Zaret (2000) shows, all these forms were constrained by norms of secrecy and privilege that tended to inhibit public discussion of political controversies. The invention of printing did not directly "cause" more open political discussion in what Jürgen Habermas has termed a "public sphere." However, it did enhance and ultimately alter traditional forms of political discourse – notably the "petition" to an authority concerning individual or group grievances. Printed petitions could be widely distributed, and thus they had greater potential for mobilizing public opinion than handwritten ones. A new technology did not "determine" political culture, but it created opportunities for discourse to spill out beyond its traditional forms and engage ever larger numbers of people in a common political conversation.

Rationalization of symbolic culture through material innovation such as musical notation and printing was not uniform in its effects. Rather, these changes set in motion a variety of new possibilities of distributing culture. As we have seen, the consequences depended on what social groups took advantage of the possibilities, and how these groups were empowered as a result.

Rationalization, the world economy, and the cultures of consumption

Given that rationalization and routinization occurred in concrete instances of personality, work, and cultural forms, there is a broader question: how did rationalization affect the overall centuries-long social and economic transformation toward modern industrial capitalism? Concluding his study of the Protestant ethic, Max Weber famously wrote, "it is, of course, not my aim to substitute for a one-sided materialistic an equally one-sided spiritualistic causal interpretation of culture and of history" (1958a, p. 183). Weber did not limit his analysis of rationalization to the systematiza-tion of religion, personal thought and conduct, and symbolic and material culture. In the economic sphere, he argued that rationalization has touched the most diverse activities, from the production of iron to the consumption of household goods.

An important precondition was the gradual emergence in Europe of "absolutist" states as organizations that claimed a monopoly on the use of force in their territories. This process might seem to have everything to do with power, not culture. But, as Chandra Mukerji (1997) provocatively argues for France, state-building was not divorced from culture. Instead, the palaces and gardens of the courts themselves were increasingly designed on the basis of rational engineering plans, and the same engi-neering technologies came to be applied to the consolidation of states' territories (for a different cultural analysis, of England, see Corrigan and Sayer 1985).

Any attempt to date the beginning of state absolutism in Europe would be arbi-trary, but from the fourteenth and fifteenth centuries onward, and especially by the seventeenth and eighteenth centuries, absolutist states also rationalized the conditions of commerce, by moving toward universally applicable laws. Business entrepreneurs were thereby increasingly able to anticipate their profits and losses in rational ways (Weber 1981; R. Collins 1986; Schluchter 1989). Of course, the explanation of modern capitalism is hotly debated, for the West was hardly unique in these features. China, for instance, had a centralized state bureaucracy from 1100 M.E. Some important differences seem to be that China was an empire, whereas Europe had: (1) competing states, (2) social classes with increasing independence from the state in the aftermath of feudalism, and (3) a relatively autonomous sphere of religion (Wong 1997, p. 79; Stokes 2001, p. 37).

In Europe, the emergence of state forms conducive to modern social and economic transactions was coupled with an economic transformation that eventually would encompass the entire world. By the sixteenth century there was a European-centered globalizing economy (Wallerstein 1974). Its fundamental engines were capitalist agri-culture and the gradual development of long-distance trade with colonies that offered opportunities for raw materials, profit, and investment in new enterprises. Mercantile capitalism reinforced the growth of towns, and the power struggle between the feudal lords of the countryside and the towns' craft producers and entrepreneurs was resolved by the absolutist states that established centralized governments and uniform laws. Thus, although rationalization and routinization of trade relationships occurred in many parts of the world and over a very long time, the states in Europe that domi-nated the process during the centuries just before the final breakthrough to modernity at the end of the eighteenth and beginning of the nineteenth century were the ones that in turn dominated the world during the modern era.

Capitalist trade, of course, involved material objects, and, as our definition of culture in Chapter 1 suggests, such objects need to be considered in their cultural aspects. Much material culture before the modern era was based on longstanding practices of agriculture, engineering, and technology. Craft and trades production changed only gradually until around 1800 (Braudel 1973). However, changes that did occur took place in part because culture shaped the nature of goods. By the opposite token, goods newly traded across long distances – like sugar, tobacco, and tea – transformed culture.

Consider the question of why for centuries clothing in Europe was dominated by the use of black cloth rather than cloth made with color dyes. According to Schneider (1978), Europe could obtain the fancy dyestuffs for polychrome cloth production only via the luxury trade from Asia. Thus, brightly colored clothing was a sign of wealth in Europe, while black cloth was less expensive because it could easily be produced using locally available dyestuffs. For both medieval monks and sixteenth-century Calvinist Protestants, black symbolized asceticism, and for the European population as a whole black had a non-elitist, egalitarian significance. Favoring black promoted (especially northern) European strength in cloth production as early as the twelfth century, and avoided siphoning off capital toward Asia.

Cultural tastes in textiles figured in economic development in later centuries as well, but in different ways. By the seventeenth century, with spreading consumerism among the popular classes, the demand for inexpensive, brightly colored calico cotton cloth imported from India was becoming unshakable in England. Unsuccessful in taming the cultural taste by banning calico imports, English entrepreneurs developed innovations in cloth production and dyeing that made possible a nationally produced alternative, thereby undermining the unfavorable trade. The nineteenth-century industrial revolution that was centered in English textile production thus had its origins partly in English capitalist responses to cultural tastes previously satisfied through long-distance trade (Mukerji 1983).

The studies by Schneider and Mukerji only scratch the surface of connections between culture and trade in the centuries leading up to the modern era. Different but equally important histories could be charted for commodities such as sugar, tobacco, and tea. The differences notwithstanding, these histories demonstrate that economic development toward the modern world economy was not a one-sided material process driven by the emergence of Europe. To the contrary, new cultural tastes and practices in various parts of the world created demand for material goods that contributed to the routinization of markets and trade relationships. Thus, from the sixteenth to the eighteenth century in England, an older and intense prejudice against the importation of "fripperies" – such as felt hats or gloves of Spanish leather – gave way to a situation where, as Thrisk observes, "it was becoming possible to indulge in a few luxuries to delight the eye" (1978, p. 15). Culture influenced the locations of economic growth and the character of technological innovation, and it altered the styles of life of the people who developed new practices of consumption.

We have seen rationalization and routinization to be vehicles of social change that operate on a variety of fronts, shaping the production and distribution of symbolic and material culture, the efficiency of organization, and even the personalities and habits of individuals. Yet rationalization and routinization are not abstract forces, and they are not inevitable developments. Rather, processes of rationalization are spatially, socially, and temporally uneven, and always subject to reversals based, if nothing else, on the resistance of people to regimentation (Roth 1987). Concrete individuals and social groups act in rationalizing ways for a variety of reasons, and those who rationalize their conduct and organization sometimes gain power in ways that cannot be anticipated on the basis of their initial social positions.

Nor are rationalization and routinization caused by technology or economic interest alone. Quite to the contrary: the invention of musical notation for mass distribution of culture came *before* the technological invention of printing; the consequences of printing for political debate depended on its interaction with *previous* political practices; and the development of work discipline as routinized conduct *preceded* industrialization. In short, rationalization of social processes sometimes developed prior to, and independently of, the changes in economic conditions that would make the processes so significant. Indeed, rationalization was central to the very conditions of economic predictability that made the modern world economy possible. The origins of rationalization are diverse, as are the connections to other social changes. But together the consequences have been enormous: the technical, economic, cultural, and organizational advantages of rationalization to those individuals and groups who pursue it have accumulated to the point at which rationalization is a basic institutionalized cultural feature of society today that shapes our entire mode of life.

The urban-based economy and emergent forms of culture

So far, we have traced the significance of culture for the emergence of modern society, economy, and personality. In turn we want to ask: what were the consequences for culture of changes during the time just prior to the modern era? To address this question, it is useful to distinguish between alternative types of culture. Sociologists sometimes follow the anthropologist Robert Redfield (1956), who identified two separate but interdependent cultures – the "great tradition" of an elite and the "little tradition" of common folk. The great tradition is one of serious music, arts, and a literature that claims to capture the greatness of a civilization. The culture of the little tradition, on the other hand, is passed along without the benefit of formal academies, through the telling of tales, craft production of daily needs, and the singing of songs passed from generation to generation. This distinction suggests a basic, widespread stratification of culture that has existed since ancient times. How were these traditions affected by the changes in the centuries prior to the modern era?

For all the significance of the globalizing economy over the past 500 years, the spread of market society – in which people increasingly satisfy their needs and wants through purchases – has affected people differently depending on their class situations, religion, gender, ethnicity, region, and whether they live in cities or rural areas. All the world is not equally transformed even by dramatic changes. Nor have rationalization and routinization been the only cultural vehicles of transformation. The kinds and forms of culture themselves shifted too. These changes can be traced by exploring how the great and little traditions intersected with a growing urban society. For the so-called early modern period preceding 1800, it is important to trace three related developments: (1) the diffusion by which the little tradition spread among social groups in urban space; (2) the emergence of a market economy that transformed elite culture and forged a distinctive basis of popular culture; and (3) innovations in genres of cultural production tied to new kinds of audiences.

Popular culture from traditional cultures: the case of the guilds

Trade, the towns, and craft production for market grew in fits and starts in Europe during the late-medieval period and the subsequent expansion of the Europe-centered globalizing economy. As a result, the "little" tradition was transformed, even if the older cultural forms did not entirely disappear. Consider the account of Peter Burke (1978), who has shown that in the late eighteenth century members of the elite who became fascinated with what they called "folk" culture could go out and collect fairy-tales, songs, popular poems, and rhymes. The same could be done in the twentieth century (Randolph 1976), and no doubt even today – with different "traditional" stories, to be sure. In the countryside, many people maintain lifestyles of the peasantry, yeoman farmers, and the rural aristocracy, clinging to a diverse range of (shifting) old ways. But even rural culture has changed dramatically, because rural people appro-priate new culture emerging in the social worlds around them. Historically, when European towns grew with economic expansion, elements of the "little tradition" were incorporated into – and eventually eclipsed by – an emergent urban popular culture.

In part, urban popular culture in Europe simply drew on various traditional cultures brought to town, improvised in their forms, adapted by town dwellers to their new situations. Thus, the festival and trade-fair culture – long part of the little tradi-tion – found its way into the towns, but with a difference. Folk badges of traditional cultures became mapped on to urban patterns of social stratification, and the popular classes among town dwellers participated in new cultural practices. The craft guilds represent an interesting example that shows this remapping of little traditions on to urban culture.

In the medieval period guilds in Europe were relatively egalitarian associations of craftsmen who sought to monopolize economically productive activities such as weaving. As trade spurred production in the late middle ages, the guilds increasingly opposed the rationalized specialization of tasks within crafts. In the long run, however, they could not stop specialization, and from the fourteenth to the eighteenth century they gradually lost their monopolies to more rationalized production orga-nized through entrepreneurship. The greatest challenge came from the "putting-out" system: as early as the thirteenth century, and increasingly thereafter, entrepreneurs began to subcontract with separate workers, guild members or not, to perform discrete tasks such as washing, spinning, and weaving of wool cloth (Weber 1981, p. 136ff.).

How did the guilds try to maintain solidarity in the face of this competition? Partly they redeployed longstanding traditional cultural practices. The solidarity in the guilds so important to an egalitarian organization was nurtured by distinctive craft cultures. Just as small communities often possess distinctive cultural "badges" of identity that distinguish their people from those of another community, guilds too developed distinctive cultures. As Peter Burke observes, "[g]uilds had their own patron saints, their own traditions, and their own rituals, and they organized the leisure as well as the working lives of their members." Religious festivals like Corpus Christi, Burke goes on, "often were organized on a guild basis," and the guilds were true fraternities, "particular about who they admitted to the craft" (1978, p. 36). A craft, then, was not simply based upon a set of skills. In addition, craft guilds created distinctive informal cultures of dances and work songs and sagas of craft life that might tell, for example, the story of a shoemaker as a hero. Such practices could help a craft guild sustain what Max Weber called a "status group" – a group of individuals who "successfully claim a special social esteem, and possibly also status monopolies" (Weber 1978, p. 306). Status groups occur in many different situations – religious, political, social. What interests us here about the guilds as status groups is that they often created their distinctive identities by replicating traditional kinds of culture in urban, occupation-ally stratified societies.

In the long run, guilds as status groups could not maintain either the solidarity of their members or their monopolization of craft activities. The capitalist quest for profit through rationalization – initially pursued by way of the putting-out system – won out over inefficient guild monopolizations of craft work. Eventually, in the eighteenth and nineteenth centuries, the factory came to dominate production (Weber 1981). Yet, even today, particular occupational groups seek, sometimes successfully, to monopolize their skills through enforcement of cultural boundaries (R. Collins 1979), and occupational groups such as travel agents, restaurant workers, and website developers develop their distinctive sense of social esteem and their own cultures. The examples of the guilds and their occupational descendants show that sometimes the little traditions of urban popular culture improvise on and adapt older traditions to the needs of particular social groups who seek to enhance occupational identity under historically new circumstances.

Popular and elite culture: money and consumption

Just as the European guilds mixed older traditions into urban popular culture well before the industrial revolution, people more generally – especially in the towns – witnessed a complex and interconnected flowering of high and popular cultures. The major force probably was the increasing importance of money, however obtained. Capitalist trade yielded profit, and this profit placed wealth in the hands of entrepreneurs and the state. As capitalist activity spread, more money found its way into the hands of common people. These changes altered the economic or "material" basis of support for cultural production. Exactly how this occurred remains an open question. Conventional historical accounts describe the economy of Western Europe pulling ahead of the rest of the world beginning in the sixteenth century, fueled in part by territorial expansion and in part by changes in culture connected to work, consumption, and science. But some historians recently have argued that the West, China, and Japan were roughly on a par economically even through the late eighteenth century. Earlier in this chapter we considered different cultures of work; here we focus on consumption.

Prior to the breakthrough to modern industrialism, societies that had developed sufficient material surplus tended to generate warring elites, sometimes pacified by empire or kingship and religion. Such elites generated cultures quite distinct from the little traditions. Thus, South Asia has an ancient tradition of sculpture, architecture, and, later, painting, tied to Hindu and Buddhist religious sects. In China, well before 1000 M.E., there were beautiful tomb sculptures, religious illustrations, and landscape paintings – all figuring in the life of the elite. Egypt, Greece, and Rome had their great public works of architecture. In Europe during the so-called dark ages after the collapse of the Roman Empire, the "great tradition" of the elite's high culture was maintained by the patronage of the church and, to a lesser extent, at the feudal courts. Much of what is exhibited today as medieval European "art" really consists of surviving paintings and carvings that served as visual stimuli in religious rituals, along with practical items such as tapestries and knightly armor that supported the medieval elite's way of life. Such objects typically were produced communally by highly skilled artisans who combined functionality with aesthetics to create fine craft objects (cf. Becker 1982, ch. 9).

The key question historically is how and why culture shifted in the great transition to modern societies. Kenneth Pomeranz (2000, pp. 128–9) addresses this question by focusing on cultural capital in relation to a topic we considered in Chapter 3 – social stratification. How, Pomeranz asks, does consumption of goods become historically linked with the cultural maintenance and enhancement of social status? To answer this question, he follows the distinction of anthropologist Arjun Appadurai between "coupon" status systems, "sumptuary" systems, and "fashion" systems. In *coupon* systems, found in less economically dynamic societies, there is a relatively finite supply of desired objects, and only certain individuals have the right to possess them. *Sumptuary* systems, by contrast, can be found where the availability of consumable goods is rapidly expanding. In this circumstance, found in China, India, and Europe before modernity, efforts are made to regulate extravagant or excessive consumption. Finally, in the *fashion* systems that are widely prevalent today, commodities are easily available and ever shifting in style and character. As Pierre Bourdieu argued, elite groups under the latter circumstances try to create barriers limiting access to the high culture necessary for refined display of status. Thus, Pomeranz asks: how and where did a high-consumption fashion system emerge in the premodern period?

Many parallels in patterns of consumption can be found among China, Japan, and Europe from the sixteenth to the eighteenth centuries. Most important initially, elites began to link social status with cultural refinement demonstrated through consumption. Once elites in Europe felt more secure from the threat of war, they began to shed their personal retinues of knights, servants, and tenants, and started building estate houses rather than militarily defensible castles. As Pomeranz observes, these new houses could hardly display status if they were empty: "Mirrors, clocks, furniture, framed pictures, china, silverware, linen, books, jewelry, and silk clothing, to name just a few items, all became increasingly 'necessary' signs of status for well-off western Europeans" (2000, p. 130). Nor was consumption of such goods restricted to social elites. In an emerging money economy, goods could be had for a price, without inspection of the social credentials of the purchaser. New commercial and occupational classes were emerging in Europe, and, with them, novel patterns of consumption.

Among newly wealthy entrepreneurs of the emerging bourgeoisie, high culture underwent changes. Religious themes in "art" were supplanted by other kinds of subject matter, and the notion of "art for art's sake" gradually became established as a basis for criticizing and collecting. In time, artists became free to explore their aesthetic visions on canvas destined for the art markets rather than for individual patrons (Hauser 1982, pp. 280–2). To be sure, the newly wealthy wanted to affirm their own status and self-esteem. They therefore continued the institution of religious patronage, and they improvised on patterns of court patronage by commissioning paintings of themselves and their families. But newly wealthy people also developed secular and urbane tastes that countered those of religious and courtly life, and by the sixteenth century themes ranging from Greek mythology to landscape and scenes of social life began to be treated in oil paintings.

A new culture of material consumption also emerged beyond the arts. Whether this shift in Europe was more tied to luxury or popular consumption remains open to debate. As Pomeranz notes, the classic argument of the German scholar Werner Sombart holds that luxury consumption promoted the initial growth of artisanal classes in Europe, and thus the "trickle-down" growth of capitalism. On the other hand, Max Weber's analysis of the Protestant ethic (1958a) charted the growth of European capitalism in relation to the *abandonment* of luxury consumption tied to sumptuous display of social status. Probably both elite *and* regulated popular consumption were occurring, and each in its own way spurred new economic activity. Whether one or the other was the key to long-term economic growth is an argument that remains to be settled.

One way to get at the question is to look at the objects themselves. Material goods, after all, were the stock in trade of capitalism, and as the new economic pattern took hold, goods became increasingly available through commerce to ever broader classes of people – whether through "trickle-down economics" or rational self-regulation of consumption. On this issue, Chandra Mukerji (1983) has demonstrated the significance of material culture for the expansion of capitalism. However sober and ascetic the Protestants may have been – wearing black or not – they did consume, and other people of means reveled in material culture, buying books, clothing, furniture, and tableware (see Figure 5.1).

Material consumption in the money economy of the towns had long extended beyond the upper classes, and this tendency increased as towns grew, especially from the fourteenth century onward. With the sixteenth-century expansion of the Europe-centered world economy, production of consumer goods became more specialized by

Figure 5.1 The material culture in this seventeenth-century painting by the German artist Wolfgang Heimbach suggests the increasing material abundance of the period, while the other people's postures toward the well-heeled man seem to represent deference and, perhaps, an ambivalence about the inequalities connected with such abundance.

Source: © Alinari/Art Resource.

region, and regions where particular goods were no longer produced became more dependent on trade. This meant that goods were increasingly standardized "products." In England between 1550 and 1750, for example, entrepreneurs initiated a variety of projects producing goods for local and national consumption. They employed significant numbers of the poor in part-time work as "artificers," making pins and nails, buttons, salt, and starch, knives and tools, pots and ovens, ribbons and laces, knitting stockings and so on (Thrisk 1978, pp. 6–7). In turn, women and children engaged in part-time work, or by-employment, supplemented the incomes of their households, and bought felt hats and iron cooking pots, sword blades and glass bottles, nails, gloves, and knitted woolen stockings. By the late sixteenth century, a fairly well-off farmer could have

> a fair garnish of pewter in his cupboard…three or four feather beds, so many coverlets and carpets of tapestry, a silver salt, a bowl for wine (if not a whole nest), and a dozen spoons to furnish up the suit.
>
> (quoted in P. Burke 1978, pp. 246–7)

Although there is considerable debate about when things changed for whom, McCracken (1988, pp. 11–16) posits two major phases in the development of modern consumption in the West that preceded industrialization: (1) the consumer boom in sixteenth-century England, when nobles began to consume "with new enthusiasm on a new scale," and novelty and fashion started to appear as indicators of status; and (2) the eighteenth century, when consumption spread beyond the nobility to people in other classes who started to use consumption as a form of self-expression. An important shift in the meaning of consumption accompanied its overall increase: what had been considered a vice began to be seen as a virtue. Prior to 1700 the dominant mercantilist views held that demand for goods was inelastic. A newer formulation found an early statement in Mandeville's controversial poem "The Fable of the Bees," first published in 1705. Invoking the slogan "private vices, public benefits," Mandeville argued that the very characteristics that the moralists cautioned against – such as luxury, pride, avarice, vanity, and envy – could benefit the economic system.

Yet the question remains: how different were these English from, say, the Chinese? One way to address this question is to look with Pomeranz at the consumption of "ordinary luxuries" like sugar and tea (and tobacco and coffee). Here, consumption started from a very small base in Europe, but it increased dramatically. By 1800 most of Europe looked very similar to China. The outlier was Britain, which had relatively higher levels of average consumption (Pomeranz 2000, p. 127). We should not conclude that Britain broke through to an industrial revolution because people started to drink tea with sugar in large quantities! And it is important to recognize that not everyone could afford either the "ordinary luxuries" or the tableware and pottery or china with which to serve them. Overall, consumer culture was regionally and nationally uneven, and rather limited until the early nineteenth century. Nevertheless, it could be found well beyond an elite social stratum.

Clearly, the expansion of consumer culture was also happening in other parts of the world – notably China, Japan, and India. Did a specific pattern of consumption in Western Europe contribute to the consolidation of self-sustaining economic growth – something that did not occur elsewhere? Certainly other factors were highly significant, such as the "discovery" of the western hemisphere and the transfer of precious metals from there to Europe. But even these economic changes had their cultural manifestations. As Pomeranz writes, Europeans used the silver to buy prestige goods from Asia, and this flood of goods to Europe "made the wheel of fashion spin faster here than elsewhere" (2000, p. 161). The connections among cultural and economic processes remain open to further research. However, as is already evident, consumer society began to expand both in elite and popular classes well before the industrial revolution, and with this expansion came a thirst for material goods that could only be satisfied by ever more efficient production. The overall development changed the very institutions through which economic exchange occurred. In medieval society "the market" designated a special arena for commerce, clearly set apart in time and space from daily life and regulated by custom and law. However, as production and consumption grew from the sixteenth to the eighteenth century, this concrete market gave way to the modern sense of the market as an abstract entity (Agnew 1986). Cultural changes in consumption and the emergence of the modern market probably did not directly "cause" the industrial revolution, but they gave entrepreneurs incentives to produce and distribute more goods more efficiently.

Popular and elite culture: money and patronage

Despite continuities with the "little traditions" of small communities, popular and high culture both differ in key ways from traditional culture. Partly this difference concerns "patronage" – that is, support for cultural workers by other individuals and groups. Sometimes patronage occurs through direct aid to cultural workers (i.e. outside of market relations, by providing materials, facilities, and even food and shelter). Sometimes, too, patronage is mediated by marketplace consumption, as when patrons pay money for works of art or buy tickets to attend a concert. Of course even small communities will have some specialization of cultural work; for example, village musicians performing outside a market economy may receive certain benefits as a result of their performances. But, historically, the terms and conduits of patronage changed dramatically as highly differentiated forms of popular and elite culture developed.

Indeed, beyond small communities, the gradually increasing availability of goods and art for purchase during the centuries immediately before the industrial revolution raises an important question. Can the "great" and "little" traditions still be distinguished from each other with the rise of commercial cultural distribution? Amassed wealth no doubt continued to be important for patronage of art, for only substantial assets could support its most elaborate productions. But who were the groups with such assets and how did they act as patrons?

Consider Florence, Italy, where medieval patronage was based largely on support of the church, and art remained heavily religious after other regions had shifted to more secular themes. Over the centuries, the sources of Florentine church patronage shifted as the political economy of Italy changed. In the thirteenth and fourteen centuries the trade guilds controlled artistic production. However, by the fifteenth century the guilds lost out to less monopolistic organization of craft production; it was then the wealthy merchants, such as the famous Medici family, who took on patronage. Finally, as the merchant class became politically powerful, their patronage was supplanted by the city's ruling princes, the Medici Grand Dukes, who used their powers of taxation to finance patronage that enhanced their public image (Pillsbury 1971; Goldberg 1983).

The shift toward state patronage had numerous parallels elsewhere in Europe, and the emergent approach was not simply a matter of promoting the general public welfare:

> [A]t the time of the Renaissance, the princely courts took over both the cities and the Church. Therewith they took over both the production and the direction of art, and made it serve their propaganda and their prestige. Art was pressed into service for evanescent outward shows, in the public spectacles, the triumphal processions, the "Joyous Entries" of princes; it was made permanent in great princely collections, the continuation, in a new age and a new form, of the medieval princely treasure-houses.
>
> (Trevor-Roper 1976, p. 8)

Elite patronage involved more than collecting or charity; it served ends of state- and self-aggrandizement.

How distinct was this European elite culture from popular culture? Sometimes the subject matter was worlds apart, as with paintings depicting the pomp and circumstance of the courts and the lofty status of elite family members. Yet social analysts from Redfield to Peter Burke have emphasized longstanding continuities between popular and elite culture, as well as parallel connections embedded in the structure of social life. Thus, a good deal of poaching infused the great tradition with the culture of the little tradition. The elite in 1500 participated along with everyone else in popular culture, for instance in the great festivals. More generally, cultural producers for the elite would often rework popular themes. And Robert Darnton shows that seventeenth- and eighteenth-century servants and wet nurses could bring popular stories like Little Red Riding Hood and Sleeping Beauty into the homes of the rich and directly into the mental life of their young (1984, p. 63).

Cultural access was not exactly a two-way street, however. As Burke argues, the popular classes lacked regular access to the princely collections in palaces and the private performances of music and plays. Yet those in the popular classes interested in mobility could try to imitate the culture of higher-status groups, and their efforts were facilitated in part by the increasing market orientations of artists. At the beginning of the sixteenth century, for instance, Dürer produced paintings, woodcuts, and engravings – works by the same hand that went to people of different economic means (Mukerji 1983, p. 64). In turn, mass-produced pictorial prints of art like Dürer's offered affordable images accessible to broad classes of people. Thus, Mukerji argues, "the increased production and use of consumer commodities was helping to join rich and poor into similar market relations and gathering together buyers throughout Europe into common patterns of taste" (1983, p. 77). The result was a cosmopolitan artistic aesthetic.

Over time, clear continuities developed between high and popular culture – in production techniques, marketplace relationships, and content. By the late eighteenth century, both popular culture and elite culture were becoming cultural alloys subjected to ever shifting mixtures. Despite, or perhaps because of, these emerging hybrid forms, elite taste publics often have been at pains to distinguish their culture from popular culture. Thus, Peter Burke described two significant movements: (1) the attempts to "reform" popular culture on the part of "the educated, usually the clergy," and (2) by 1800, the effective withdrawal of the elite from participating in popular culture, marked by divergences between classes in how they viewed the world (1978, pp. 207,

270). This divergence can be addressed by considering a final issue about preindustrial culture – performance.

Cultural performance and audiences

Questions about the nature of performance, and, more specifically, the theater, have attracted fascinating speculative efforts at historical reconstruction. The late-nineteenth-century cataloguer of myths Sir James Frazer sought to connect Greek mythology with the cycle of the seasons; from this argument comes the more general thesis that theater emerged from seasonal festivals, carnivals, and pageants. An alternative view holds that performance originated in traditional religious rituals of healing and magic performed by shamans (conventionally called medicine men). In this account, the performances of rituals and trance magic that shamans used was meant to intervene in the "other" world of spirit forces – sometimes codified in mythology and personified with deities. Dance-drama ritual in more formalized religions such as Hinduism – and in highly conventionalized secular dramas in China and Noh theater in Japan – may amount to codified versions of shamanistic ceremonies (Kirby 1975; cf. Weiss 1973). Whatever its origins, theater developed in diverse directions, and in complex relations to society, as Figure 5.2 suggests for Japanese kabuki theater.

Earlier practices are quite distant from modern Western theater, and they thereby remind us that cultural performances are socially constructed and organized in conventionalized ways. The specifically modern dramatic performance of a *story* is an invention that has continuities with radically different precursors. One thread of this complicated development can be explored by looking at the medieval European conventions of performance and their audiences, and tracing their connections to modern performance.

Medieval European entertainers often did double duty, not only performing at the feudal courts, but also wandering through villages and towns, gathering audiences on the spot, traveling to the great and small markets and trade fairs, where they offered sideshows to the main business of buying and selling goods. It is precisely this continuity of practice across venues that suggests to Peter Burke the accessibility of popular culture to the social elite in Europe. Yet two connected developments alter the equation. First, a new conventionalization of dramatic form eventually all but eclipsed the kinds of medieval performances held at the courts and the fairs. Second, both the audiences for performances and the themes of drama shifted along class lines. It does not seem unreasonable to assert that a new secular and modern relationship between performance, cultural meaning, and socially stratified audiences already became established well before the advent of the mass media, on the stage of the theater.

Whence this European form of theater? There seems to have been no single source. One influence, religious drama in the Christian church, probably represents an elaboration of the medieval mass liturgy, which was sometimes embellished with theatrical devices such as someone riding an ass to church on Palm Sunday. In addition, the Christian church may have promoted morality-play dramatizations as a competitive response to the emerging secular theater against which the church railed (Kirby 1975, p. 152; Tydeman 1978; Kuritz 1988, pp. 124–7).

Beyond the church, the cultural life of medieval Europe had long revolved around seasonal festivals such as elaborate pre-Lenten celebrations of Carnival. Festivals were communal, and often religiously organized despite their public character. However, at

Figure 5.2 This Osaka School woodcut by Utagawa Kunisada (1785–1864) portrays the ethics of Samurai culture by representing the actor Ichikawa Kuzo playing the Samurai Sanzo in the kabuki theater, a Japanese form of drama that originated in all-women acting troupes during the sixteenth century, displaced by all-male troupes in the seventeenth century. Sanzo is dancing in honor of the god Daikoku in the play *Maimopsu Iro no Tanemaki*. By the time this 1841 woodcut was made, the Samurai as a warrior class had long since been "tamed," but they continued to hold a fabled place in Japanese theater, art, and culture more broadly, where they sometimes served as surrogates in the discussion of contemporary political issues.

Source: © Werner Forman/Art Resource, New York.

the fairs and markets there was an increasingly commercial side of what was becoming entertainment in a modern sense. Cultural production was becoming a business. Buying and selling the necessities of life took place amidst a jumble of diverse acts – jugglers, musicians, lay preachers, and a host of other figures who might try to drum up an audience and ask for donations after a performance. The genre of the folk mummer's play falls within this tradition, and it is another important antecedent of modern performance. In a typical medieval staging, in the clearing of a space amidst a gathered audience, often at a market, two performers brag about their exploits and then fall into mock combat. One of them dies, a doctor enters and claims miraculous healing abilities, and brings the slain combatant back to life. "The performance ends with a collection of money from the audience and with a song" (Kirby 1975, p. 142). The mummer's play amalgamates medicine, music, and the hawking of "cures" – a sort of acted-out advertisement. It represents the commercialization of shamanism, ritual, and entertainment, a form of popular culture that survives today in diffuse ways – in circuses, television shows, fairs and conventions, and advertising.

The mummer's play is not modern theater. Nevertheless, the distance between the two is not far. "All the world's a stage," William Shakespeare (1564–1616) had the character Jacques proclaim in *As You Like It*. This assertion could attain easy acceptance because Shakespeare and his contemporaries established a new form of drama. Shakespeare was "acutely aware of the fabricated nature of conduct both on and off the stage" (Burns 1972, p. 10).

With Foucault and Elias, we already have explored how the self became rationalized prior to the industrial revolution in a way that created a gap between private inward feelings and what sociologist Erving Goffman (1959) called "the presentation of self" as public performance. In the England of Shakespeare's time, dramas on the stage became a basis for exploring the tension between the self and acting as the presentation of self in the wider world. This self-conscious exploration was revolutionary as a cultural development. According to Steven Mullaney (1988), the revolution was a popular one, and it offered an alternative to the previous dramatic genres favored by the elite.

In Mullaney's account, the entire city of London in the sixteenth century was used as a sort of public stage for royal pageants and hangings at the scaffolds – forms of public spectacle promoted by the elite for popular consumption. But the popular theater of Shakespeare and his contemporaries was not located in the public spectacle space. It took root in the zone known as the Liberties, at the suburban boundaries of London. There, the lazar-houses filled with lepers, the brothels, the bear-baiting rings, open-air marketplaces with their circus-like sideshows – these established a cultural template of "marginal spectacle" that set the stage for the radical and licentious popular stage. To the authorities in London, Mullaney suggests, the popular theater itself was a social plague that replaced leprosy – like leprosy, to be contained at the margins. There, it drew together into a conventionalized dramatic format much of the preexisting spectacle of jugglers, musicians, fools and jesters, actors and hawkers who operated in the Liberties precisely where the new London theater scene became established. Shakespeare's plays, then, were popular entertainment of the time. Yet their treatment of some elite-oriented themes – political drama, for example – reinforces Burke's thesis that the social elite of the early modern era also participated in popular culture. At the least, there was much they would find of interest.

Elsewhere in London, in so-called private playhouses, other variations on popular theater – "city comedies" – were beginning to serve a more specialized clientele. As a genre, city comedy hardly suggests the importance of enduring values of civilization in the "great" tradition. Nevertheless, these farces often gained wide popularity with an elite audience, especially younger sons of noble origin, who, if they lacked inheritances, sought their fortunes in London. English Puritans of the late sixteenth and early seventeenth centuries took a dim view of city comedies, and the reason for their antipathy probably can be found in the attraction that these plays held for their primary audience. As Wendy Griswold has described it:

> City comedy presents wily, ambitious characters pursuing fortune, status, and love. The genre celebrates the adventures of urban and urbane rascals operating in the wide-open economic milieu of Renaissance London. Its characters demonstrate skills appropriate to an age of expanding opportunities, as they unblushingly lie, scheme, take risks, ignore propriety, flout conventional morality, fleece the gullible, and enjoy themselves hugely all the while.
>
> (Griswold 1986, p. 14)

Hardly the sort of cultural material that Puritans would embrace.

Worse, from the Puritan viewpoint, the city comedies can be read as more than just humorous entertainment. Drawn from stock theater types such as the trickster of folklore and Vice of the medieval morality plays, the central characters in city comedies – the "gallants" – offered obvious role models to the young private playhouse patrons.

> In city comedy the smart and aggressive, be they younger sons, servants, or con men, achieved wealth, forgiveness, and sometimes even respectability.... This portrait of the reconciliation of economic activism with elite social status was obviously appealing to the young gentlemen in the private theater audience, for it made a cultural virtue of their economic necessity.
>
> (Griswold 1986, p. 52)

In effect, city comedies countered that sober model of rational industry favored by Puritans with a comic promotion of an alternative ethic embodied in the capitalist entrepreneur as wheeler-dealer. Theater made a virtue of living by one's wits.

The emergence of concerns with status, money, and property in a market economy mark the consolidation of a modern bourgeois class of entrepreneurs prior to the industrial revolution (Raymond Williams 1982, p. 161). Of course today city comedies are rarely presented on the stage, and they are of little vital interest to the bourgeois classes. Yet major elements of the genre live on in popular entertainment directed to other social strata facing anxieties about social location that parallel those of the early bourgeois. Today, Hollywood is the world's primary producer of popular movies and television programs, so it makes sense to look to its products for continuities with city comedies in the past.

Consider two Hollywood movies. *Ferris Bueller's Day Off* (1986) follows the adventures of a high-school student who cuts school for a day by faking an illness to his loving parents and then gets into a series of outrageous difficulties. His friends are nervous but Ferris somehow manages to talk, walk, or drive his way out of trouble, masterfully manipulating circumstances at an elite restaurant, a modern art museum, a baseball game, and a street parade. By the time his parents arrive home at 6 p.m., Ferris has shown his audience that there is a school of life beyond the classroom, and that a cultural omnivore like himself can triumph over adversities by operating effectively in a variety of cultural settings.

Another "city comedy" aimed at the middle class, *Legally Blonde* (2001), similarly deals with the tensions that youth experience in finding themselves, but with a different twist – one that challenges taken-for-granted cultural hierarchies. In this movie, star Reese Witherspoon plays Elle Woods, a seemingly clueless, resolutely middle-brow, blonde, southern Californian college-sorority president. When Elle's career-oriented boyfriend jilts her on his way to Harvard Law School, she becomes obsessed with getting him back, and uses highly unusual means to get into – and succeed at – Harvard Law School. But in the end, she finds that her old boyfriend is not really worth getting back and she has found more important things – success at a real career and a new love.

Modern European theater depended on a radical innovation relative to its immediate medieval predecessors – the performance of stories with plots on stage. On the basis of that innovation, the plot structures of theater in Shakespeare's – and other – historical times have provided inspiration for many popular movies today. The continuities in the genre of city comedy thus suggest a more general point. Dramatic entertainment "works" for audiences when it somehow resonates with their interests. But this effect of drama was established centuries before the advent of the mass media. The question of what transpires in the "reception" of culture by individuals is pursued in Chapter 10. For the moment, it will suffice to consider the ancient Greek philosopher Aristotle's theory of tragedy. Basically Aristotle suggested that the audience becomes engaged in the struggles of protagonists by identifying their own hopes, fears, and anxieties with struggles portrayed theatrically. "Catharsis" is the emotional release that the audience experiences through this process. A similar thing happens with comedy: we laugh at things about which we have hopes and anxieties. The city comedy thus connects best with an audience that shares the narrative space of its plot. The social strata that are targeted as the audience for a genre of drama may change: the "city comedies" of today most often seem directed at middle-class youth coming of age. The settings and situations and props are changed to fit the sensibilities of the times. However, the fundamental theatrical devices used to offer up recipes and meanings of life predate by centuries the mass media that now serve as the central conduits of cultural distribution.

Conclusion

The industrial revolution is often regarded as the decisive basis for modern consumer-oriented ways of life within societies that are highly stratified. Scholars today also sometimes suggest that the sheer volume of mass-mediated experience signals the onset of "postmodern" society. The next two chapters explore these industrial and postmodern developments. Yet, as we have seen, rationalization and routinization – two processes reorganizing thought, activity, and cultural products – have their origins *prior* to the industrialization that reinforced their impact. Thus, any assertions about the significance of the industrial revolution and the mass media must be balanced by comparison with the benchmark of preindustrial culture.

Although popular culture is sometimes treated (for example by Burke) as synonymous with traditional culture, commercialization of economic activity before the industrial revolution created a central tension between, on the one hand, popular culture as the culture of and by the people and, on the other hand, the commercial urban popular culture that took hold with the consolidation of mercantile capitalism – beginning in force in the sixteenth century in Europe and at other times in other parts of the world. Especially in Europe, China, and Japan, well before the industrial revolution, culture became organized and distributed in a differentiation of styles and genres increasingly geared to different social strata of consumers. On an ever widening mass basis, these audiences loosened their ties to traditions of indigenous and elite cultures handed down from generation to generation, and began to participate in and consume culture in self-conscious ways.

These developments were only rudimentary and tentative compared to today. Yet their occurrence at all suggests some important points relevant to sociological explanations of culture. First, technological change is not a sufficient basis on which to explain cultural change. True, the technology of printing had tremendous consequences. Yet the innovations of printing were anticipated by procedures of mass distributing culture that predated movable type. Moreover, as Michael Schudson (1978) has argued (for a later time period, the nineteenth-century U.S.), technological innovations themselves may be driven by changing patterns of social organization. Innovations in technology, in other words, are not autonomous "prime movers" of cultural change. In particular, rationalization and routinization represent transformations of social interaction and social organization that do not always depend upon technological innovation.

Second, some aspects of how culture "works" do not depend on any particular technology or medium. It is important to consider in what sense a digital recording is or is not "the same" as a live performance of music, and whether a film or TV drama is "the same" as live theater (see Chapter 6). However, whatever differences can be attributed to technology, there is a solid "cognitive" or symbolic core aspect of culture – the meaningful communication of aesthetics and ideas – that "works" in similar ways across a variety of technological contexts and in traditional, elite, and popular culture. Thus, it is important to distinguish between (1) the effects that *media* of trans- mission have, and (2) consequences of people's interaction with the symbolic *form* and *content* of cultural objects that parallel one another across different media.

Finally, thinking about the period before industrialization shows that culture is not simply a "natural" byproduct of societies. Instead, within a given social situation various social groups try to control the content and character of culture, how it is distributed, and by whom. The cultures of religious groups, the elite, and the popular classes differ from one another, as we have seen especially in the example of theater. Thus, it is a basic sociological thesis that there is no "pure" culture: all cultural objects – symbolic and material – have to be understood in the contexts of their social origins and their significance for their audiences and users. To say this, though, does not reduce culture to its material conditions, for symbolic content is important whatever the material conditions of production. Ideas and cultural tastes cannot simply be reduced to their material origins, and, by the opposite token, material developments of economic structure and change often generate the distinctive cultural problems, mean- ings, and products that different social groups take up. Given the diversity of factors we have considered, no reductionist sociological theory about culture – idealist, mate- rialist, or other – can be adequate to explanation.

Suggested readings

Fernand Braudel's book *Capitalism and Material Life* (1973) surveys the preindustrial world to identify widely shared ways of life having to do with food, shelter, drink, and clothing, as well as the character of towns and the growth of technology and a money economy. Though other authors have challenged his arguments, no one has provided a better panorama of preindustrial material culture.

Michel Foucault, in *Madness and Civilization* (1965), raised the fundamental ques- tion of how cultural distinctions develop and are applied at different moments of history. By choosing to explore "madness," "insanity," and "reason," he shows how even cultural categories that might be thought "timeless" or even biologically given are historically constructed.

Peter Burke's *Popular Culture in Early Modern Europe* (1978) covers a wide range of topics, from the actors who spread popular culture, to the forms and genres, their cultural codes, and the relation of different social strata to the cultural worlds in which they were immersed.

Kenneth Pomeranz, *The Great Divergence* (2000), especially Chapters 3 and 4, develops a comparison of Europe and China in the preindustrial period that helps bring to light the relationship between the rise of modern capitalism and the growth of consumer culture.

For Japan, Eiko Ikegami has written eloquently, in *The Taming of the Samurai* (1995), about a warrior class of people that was key to the society, and how basic features of honor, harmony, conflict, and collaboration in Japanese culture can be traced to the historical trajectory of this social group.

In "Cosmologies of capitalism" (1994), the anthropologist Marshall Sahlins provides a fascinating comparative account of how the global expansion of capitalism produced interlocked but alien cultural interpretations between explorers and traders from the West and three societies of "Others" with whom they came in contact – the Chinese, Hawaiians, and the Kwakiutl of North America's Pacific Northwest.

"Cultural history is dead: (long live the Hydra)," by John R. Hall (2003), provides a wide survey of recent work in cultural history, much of it concerned with times prior to industrialization.

Note

1   Weber did not think that goals could be rationally determined, except in relation to other goals (in which case they are means). The use of rational *means* indicates nothing, in his definition, about the value of the *ends*. The ultimate demonstration of this came after Weber's death, in the Nazi concentration-camp organization of genocide, which depended on "rational" techniques of bureaucracy (see Rubenstein 1978).

6 Industrialism and mass culture

Well before industrialization began to take hold in the latter part of the eighteenth century, the relation of culture to the social was altered by other developments: a growth of rationality, increasing routinization of daily life, and the development of market society and individualism. It is nonetheless the case that industrialization has vastly increased the scale of those changes and brought even more widespread and dramatic changes in how people live their lives. As the cities grew, there were changes in where and how people lived. There were changes in the kind of work people did and the degree to which they had control over their work. There were changes in their pursuits during leisure time and in the choices available to them for consumption. The shift to a society increasingly organized around the mass production of material culture was felt most deeply in the West, and in other parts of the world according to how they were incorporated into a globalizing industrial economy initially centered in northwest Europe. This chapter focuses on the emergence of cultural forms tied to industrial mass society and its globalization.

As we explore debates about mass culture, we will examine how consumption patterns changed with industrialization, and how these changes have been viewed by intellectuals. We will consider new commercial practices – such as department stores – and new forms of persuasion – such as advertising and the rise of purchasing on credit – that made consumption possible for ever wider strata of people. We will also look at how participation in the culture of consumption varied by class, gender, and place. Finally, we will explore modern consumption patterns in Asia and pursue the implications of subaltern studies.

Patterns of consumption changed at different times for different people. In Chapter 5 we described the broad development of modern consumption prior to the industrial revolution. As goods and money became more available the meanings of consumption also changed. Long before industrialization, people began to use goods to express their status (or the status they desired), and novelty and fashion began to be valued for what they indicated about a person's wealth and status. In turn, with the industrial revolution people began to buy things in the market that they had previously produced for themselves or done without. As industrialization gathered steam in the nineteenth century, people embraced ever more diverse styles of consumption to express a variety of things about themselves, including their stances toward the dominant bourgeois culture.

Questions about the implications of these changes were very much a part of nineteenth-century social thought. But the scope of the questions shifted as the changes unfolded. Initially, the concerns about the nature and meaning of modern society surfaced in connection with issues of citizenship and universal suffrage. Precapitalist European states, governed by aristocracies, had recognized various status groups, and the status of individuals was "ascribed" on the basis of their group identities. Modernizing societies fostered the growth of individualism both psychologically – in the development of personality – and legally – in the gradual (and still incomplete) extension of rights to all legitimate adult members of the society.

Many nineteenth-century writers hoped that industrialization would release the laboring masses from the unending toil that had previously characterized their existence, freeing them to pursue the higher things in life. They would become active and informed citizens. They would cultivate an interest in the arts and participate in the cultural life of the society. Some of the hopefulness can be seen in a later description of "mass society" by a defender of the modern social order, the twentieth-century social theorist Edward Shils:

> The new society is a mass society precisely in the sense that the mass of the population has become incorporated *into* society. The center of society – the central institutions and the central value systems which guide and legitimate these institutions – has extended its boundaries....
>
> Modern industrial techniques, through the creation of an elaborate network of transportation and communication, bring the various parts of mass society into frequent contact. Modern technology has liberated man from the burden of physically exhausting labor, and has given him the resources through which new experiences of sensation, conviviality and introspection have become possible....
>
> Mass society has aroused and enhanced individuality. Individuality is characterized by an openness to experience, an efflorescence of sensation and sensibility.... People make choices more freely in many spheres of life, and these choices are not necessarily made for them by tradition, authority or scarcity.
>
> (Shils 1967, pp. 1–3)

Even in the nineteenth century, some thinkers – for example Jacob Burckhardt and Friedrich Nietzsche – saw dangers in the growth of mass society. On the political side they feared that the masses would be vulnerable to manipulation by demagogues. On the cultural side they feared that high culture would be overwhelmed by the imposition of the commonplace. As Ortega y Gasset later put it, "The mass crushes beneath it everything that is different, everything that is excellent, individual, qualified, and select" (1932, p. 19).

In the twentieth century, two developments shaped concerns about mass society. First, there was the spread of new forms of mass communication. Initially photography, then moving pictures, radio, and television, and now the internet all have created new possibilities for the consumption of mass-produced culture as a passive practice. Critics feared that the population would become homogenous, and that individuals would be increasingly susceptible to fascist appeals. Second, the twentieth-century critics of mass culture increasingly included radicals who held no nostalgia for a golden agrarian past. Rather, they thought that industrialization's promise of freedom for the masses had been lost to modern society. In the twentieth century, radicals as well as conservatives regarded mass culture as vulgar and exploitative.

Critical theory

In the first half of the twentieth century, social critics began to ask whether mass production enhanced the average person's quality of life, how it served society, and what hidden costs it might have. For critical theorists involved in what became known as the Frankfurt School, one of the costs of mass production was a loss of "authenticity." Although their arguments center on music and painting, they also apply to fast food and other cultural forms and practices. As we will see, similar arguments also came to be applied to identity and the self.

In the 1920s a group of young German intellectuals committed themselves to reexamining the foundations of Marxist theory, and for a time they worked to bring about a conjunction of Marxism and psychoanalysis. They were deeply influenced by the rising tide of fascism in Europe, and their critique of mass culture incorporated a psychoanalytically inspired exploration of conscious and unconscious openings for fascism in mass culture. The Frankfurt School critics established the interdisciplinary Institute for Social Research, which they dedicated to a radical examination of bourgeois society through both philosophical and empirical investigation. Due to their radical political stands and the fact that many were of Jewish descent Institute members were physically threatened by the Nazis, and the Institute relocated to New York City from 1936 to 1949.

Among the important contributions of the first generation of Frankfurt School researchers was their analysis of the crisis of modern culture. They judged the grand Enlightenment project to be a failure: the attempt to control social life through the exercise of reason and science had produced only imitation in culture and manipulation, such as Taylorism in industry. Unlike other Marxists of the period, the critical theorists saw culture as something more than simply a superstructure reflecting the base of economic structure. However, they also repudiated the notion of "art for art's sake" because such a view neglected the political importance of art. Although they looked for "general social tendencies" reflected in particular forms of art, they did not perform reductionist analyses that would seek to tie such tendencies to particular social groups. They considered the relation between art and social structure to be mediated and "dialectical" – that is, subject to complex mutual influences between various interacting elements. Even the most reified artifacts of "affirmative culture" – that is, culture affirming dominant bourgeois values – were interpreted as more than derivative reflections of a supposedly more fundamental economic reality.

Like sociologists today who study the production of culture (see Chapter 9), the Frankfurt theorists had little interest in seeing art as an expression of individual creativity. They did, however, argue that art has a "negative function" in relation to the affirmative culture of bourgeois capitalism. Theodore Adorno, who had trained with the composer Arnold Schoenberg in Vienna, wrote that art "is a force of protest of the humane against the pressure of domineering institutions, religious and otherwise, no less than it reflects their objective stance" (1945, p. 678). The modern mass culture created by capitalism, however, did not fulfill the possibility of the negative function.

Nor did the Frankfurt theorists find much to their liking in the art of communist countries. Their critiques of mass culture mostly focused on capitalist societies, but members of the Frankfurt School described the socialist realism of the then Soviet Union as offering only a "sterile orthodoxy." Adorno was also highly critical of the music of the Soviet Union. Commenting on Adorno's *"Gegängelte Musik,"* written in

1948, Martin Jay pointed out that "*gängeln* roughly means being fettered or led around by the nose," and described Adorno as attacking "the promotion of 'healthy' art by advocates of socialist realism" (Jay 1973, p. 196).

The critical theorists depicted modern culture as dominated by exchange values rather than use values. Adorno argued that, compared to the modern possibilities, precapitalist music allowed for a certain degree of autonomy and the expression of an authentic subjectivity. The composer was less separated from the performance, and the performers less constrained by the text. Cultures in premodern societies existed in direct relation to their societies, the critical theorists argued, whereas modern popular culture is imposed from above. As for the listeners, prefiguring later criticisms aimed at the original piped-in music – muzak – Adorno argued that through radio, music becomes a depersonalized "ornament" of everyday life, serving to reconcile the masses to the status quo.

The issue of reproduction received concerted attention from another of the earliest associates of the Frankfurt School, Walter Benjamin. In his best-known essay, "The work of art in an age of mechanical reproduction," Benjamin argued that, although something was gained with the ability to reproduce works of art and distribute them widely, something was also lost. Uniqueness and permanence are exchanged for transitoriness and reproducibility. Reproduction allows the work of art to "meet the beholder half way," in that it permits a wide audience to view a normally inaccessible original work. But what is lost is the uniqueness of a work of art, what Benjamin referred to as its "aura" (1969, p. 211). He maintained that original works of art have qualities of "hereness and nowness" that cannot be reproduced. Parallel analyses could be made for various art forms. Thus, for music, Adorno (1945) argued that radio could reproduce the nowness but not the hereness: listening at home to a broadcast of a live concert, a person hears the music at the same time as those physically present, but without sharing the sense of "being at the event."

Benjamin argued that reproduction changes the value of the original work. Part of a work's authenticity stems from its history – its (changing) relation to a specific place over time. As Benjamin observed, at one time many works of art had cult value because they were used for particular purposes in religious rituals. Yet with reproduction a work instead has what Benjamin called exhibition value (1969, p. 225). Viewing such a work of art is enhanced by the viewer's sense that it is an important work. With a widely reproduced work, anyone who views the original sees the original of the reproduction – that is, "the real *Mona Lisa*." As Benjamin argued, the authority of the work is gone, detached from tradition.

Given art's loss of authenticity, it might seem that Benjamin would prefer looking at photographs or going to the movies over visiting a museum. However, photography as an art form created a conceptual problem for Benjamin: since reproducibility is built into the form there can be no criterion of authenticity. As Benjamin observed, "to ask for an authentic print makes no sense" (1969, p. 224). This inherent reproducibility altered the basis of art: "the semblance of its autonomy disappeared forever" (1969, p. 226). When we look at photographs, and especially films, we see through the lens of the camera. Replacing the subjective "I" with the "eye" of the camera has radically changed perspective in a distinctly modern way.

All artistic attempts to reproduce reality produce illusions, distortions, and manipulations. But for Benjamin there are important differences. With theater and painting we are aware of the illusions we witness; we can sense the artists' activities in the production of the work. But the camera "penetrates reality," apparently giving us images without interpretation. When we see a photograph (or a news documentary) we tend to assume we are getting an "objective view" of what is "really there." The response to a film is important as well. Because a film is designed to be viewed in a collective setting, Benjamin held, "individual reactions are predetermined by the mass audience response they are about to produce" (1969, p. 234). For Benjamin, then, mass culture means that authenticity, true subjectivity, and autonomy are all lost. Both the product and the audience are debased.

Benjamin found the "negative" (critical) possibility of art in Dada[1] and the poetry and theater of Brecht, while Adorno identified it with the music of Schonberg. Neither of them liked the German expressionism of their youth, and they were not defenders of classical high-culture forms. Benjamin claimed that when aficionados treated high culture as "prized goods" they made fetishes of it, rendering it lifeless. But both men displayed interesting limits to their ability to understand certain cultural forms. To Adorno's amazement, Benjamin once said that he did not think that music could have the negative moment – expressing opposition to the dominant culture – unless it used words. And Adorno himself had no understanding of non-Western music, and revealed this bias in several articles critical of jazz.

The Frankfurt School studies of mass culture are grounded in Marxist critique, but they include a strong psychoanalytic component. They posit that cultural objects always have a multilayered structure, and that analysis must therefore address unconscious as well as conscious effects.

The dialogue between social theory and psychoanalysis was to be continued by a later generation of social critics. As we saw in Chapter 2, writers in the late 1970s and 1980s argued that a society based in mass consumption erodes authenticity, not of art, but of the self. However, there is a difference. Some of the more recent critics embraced a nostalgic vision that affirmed the virtues of the past. But the Frankfurt School theorists were not looking backwards toward a lost traditional community. The edge for critical theory instead comes from the argument that industrialization failed to fulfill its promise of making possible the good society. Over the course of the twentieth century, the critical theorists saw the growing predominance of a society of consumers partaking in mass culture. How did these changes come about?

Mass industrial distribution

Distribution is a highly variable and often complex link between manufacturing and consumption. With industrialization new ways of distributing goods came about. Thus, shopping as we think of it today emerged historically in the nineteenth century as a new pattern. Traditional open markets had offered common people the basic necessities – food, baskets, pots, locally produced cloth, and such. Itinerant peddlers brought goods as well as news from far-off places. In urban areas merchants catered to the wealthy. Their exclusive shops often had signs boasting of the noble families they supplied, but they did not display their wares to the public. Entering a shop implied an intention to buy. Making a purchase involved an elaborate negotiation between the buyer and seller.

With the industrial revolution, social institutions of distribution changed. Modern innovations such as the department store eclipsed the traditional ways of selling goods. But department stores – like other new merchandising innovations such as the mail-order catalog – amounted to more than just new ways of distributing goods. They both reflected a new ethic of consumption, and they helped create it, in part through advertising – one of the most pervasive aspects of modern society. In turn, by advertising, department stores provided the financial base for the growth of newspapers. As one New York reporter and editor said, "at the end of the nineteenth century the newspaper became 'an appendage of the department store' " (quoted in Schudson 1984, p. 152). The department store and advertising are thus two marketing innovations central to establishing the modern culture of consumption.

The department store

In Europe and the U.S. between 1840 and 1860, stores of a new kind began to appear in major cities, stores with different spaces for different kinds of goods. These "department" stores were an embodiment of efforts to routinize and rationalize selling. They sold a large variety of goods, displayed in such a way that customers could view them without the aid of a clerk. In another major innovation, stores set fixed prices and marked them on the goods. This pricing approach eliminated the time-consuming process of bargaining, and, together with increased sales volume, it meant department stores could charge less for items and still make profits.

Department stores also could gain from making distribution more efficient. Store owners and managers therefore worked to rationalize, not only the selling process, but their relationships to suppliers as well. Because department stores bought such large quantities of items, they had a bargaining advantage in their relations with suppliers. They also bought goods on credit, "thereby shifting onto the manufacturer the initial financing of supplies," and they required deliveries to be staggered, "so that in still another way the operating costs – this time the costs of warehousing – were largely shouldered by the supplier" (M.B. Miller 1981, pp. 54–5).

The rationalization of distribution also made possible another marketing innovation of the department stores, the reduced-price sale. Obviously such "reductions" could not be offered before the era when stores began to mark goods with fixed prices. At first department stores advertised special sales when they were able to get particularly good prices from suppliers who were having a difficult time selling excess inventories because they had overestimated demand. Soon enough, however, the sale became an important promotional device in itself. At the Bon Marché, one of the largest and earliest Paris department stores, the week of the midwinter white sale was, in Michael Miller's view, "the most important sales week of the year." This event symbolized the rationalization of distribution that occurred with the development of the department store: "Begun…as a mere merchandising gimmick," Miller recounted, "the *blanc* soon came to be the most organized week at the store, a model of the sophisticated sort of planning that Bon Marché directors and administrators were capable of producing" (1981, pp. 70–1).

The largest department stores competed in size with the largest factories – both in terms of physical space and number of employees. Already in 1898, Benson reports, Macy's had 3,000 employees; in 1900 Jordan March "was the fourth largest employer in New England, surpassed only by the Amoskeag Mills, General Electric's Lynn plant, and the Pacific Mills of Lawrence" (Benson 1986, p. 34). Department store managers felt considerable pressure to exert control over their enterprises, and Benson has documented their continuing efforts at rationalizing the selling process. In support of these efforts, they adopted new conventions for organizing goods, from the introduction of coat hangers to new store layouts that placed bargain goods in the basement; showcased cosmetics, jewelry, and other impulse items on the first floor; and segregated men's clothing from the rest of the merchandise. In the early twentieth century, rationalization also brought "systematic management," and accounting departments developed increasingly elaborate – though not entirely effective – methods for monitoring the productivity of their employees, from buyers to saleswomen (Benson 1986, pp. 40–7, 54–67).

The early department stores also provided services such as telephones, restaurants, restrooms, and meeting areas, and they used the services as a tool in competition. Store owners pledged not to misrepresent their goods, and promised refunds if customers were dissatisfied. Delivery services – often in the form of boys in uniform arriving in vehicles marked with a distinctive company symbol – brought packages to the customer's door. Each store hoped that the provision of services would induce loyalty among their customers (Benson 1986, pp. 84–91).

With the bourgeois matron as the ideal customer, the department stores provided public spaces for women in city centers that previously had been dominated by men. Consumption, described by Thorstein Veblen early in the twentieth century as the obligation of the bourgeois woman, became a respectable occupation for women. They could shop in department stores modeled as a hybrid of the home and the men's downtown club. As Hortense Odlum, president of Bonwit Teller, said, she "tried to have the policy of the store reflect…those standards of comfort and grace which are apparent in a lovely home" (cited in Benson 1986, p. 83). The stores provided places for women to meet as well as to shop; they thus gave women ways of participating in urban society (cf. Walkowitz 1992).

Shoppers, of course, were not the only women in the department stores. In the United States, women were over-represented among sales clerks as early as 1880. In the department stores, they made up from half to nine-tenths of the total employees (Benson 1986, pp. 179–80). As employees, these women felt far more ambivalent about the department store environment than their patrons. For women who wanted full-time jobs, sales work was steadier than manufacturing employment, and it paid better, although not as well as clerical work (which required more education). There was also some prospect of advancement in sales, but it was limited, and the long hours spent on one's feet attending to the needs of demanding customers made for a physically exhausting job. To try to make saleswomen conform to standards of bourgeois gentility, managers offered carrots and sticks. Store discounts for employees enabled saleswomen to buy as well as sell (although their wages sometimes put severe limits on the value of this benefit). On the other side of the equation, extensive penalties enforced regulations regarding dress and behavior.

The manager's ideal was a saleswoman who could share expert knowledge about the goods – respectfully – with the customer. The saleswoman's position thus entailed class contradictions. Managers wanted working-class women to represent the middle-class ethos of the store, by selling goods priced beyond their own means to middle-class women. In the face of such contradictions, saleswomen experienced ambiguous class status. As Benson notes, they were "driven by the social relations of the workplace to see themselves as members of the working class, [and] cajoled by the rewards of mass consumption to see themselves as middle-class" (1986, p. 271).

Nor did employees benefit from a fully modern situation. As Michael Miller wrote, at the Bon Marché, vestiges of more traditional relationships between employers and employees accompanied uneven efforts toward rationalization. The store's founders, the Boucicauts, took care of loyal employees by dispensing pensions and other benefits. They were especially effective at using the tradition of the family firm to promote the image of Bon Marché workers as constituting a "family." Miller notes that in strikes as late as 1919, many years after the death of the founding family, both sides claimed in their rhetoric that the other side violated the traditional practices established by the founders (1981, pp. 148–9).

In the United States, various forms of paternalism coexisted with Taylorism and scientific management as strategies for mitigating potential labor unrest. Still, department store workers sometimes demanded better working conditions. And on this front they attracted support from customers, some of whom were involved with reform movements of the progressive era and shocked by the conditions under which saleswomen worked. To head off controversy, the large department stores began in the early twentieth century to provide more for the welfare of the workers, including restrooms, lounges, lunchrooms, recreation facilities, and clinics.

Overall, the owners and managers sought to create "palaces of consumption" that would both cater to bourgeois taste and define it in the process. Although the department stores were open to everyone, they did not just display goods; they did so in ways that defined an opulent style of living. They created new "needs" and suggested how these needs could be satisfied, for example describing how to dress when cycling, or selling new kitchen appliances while offering classes on how to use them. Some store owners promoted cultural events in the stores, such as concerts after closing time. Store exteriors made use of architectural innovations in steel and glass to create display windows and let in light. Interiors of stores were adorned with fine woods and marble. Paris's Bon Marché store, engineered by the designer of the Eiffel Tower, Gustave Eiffel, and completed in 1887, became a tourist attraction itself (M.B. Miller 1981, p. 42). With goods, services, and cultural opportunities located in settings of luxurious splendor, the department stores portrayed shopping as a pleasure in itself.

Overall, the stores, aided by the development of mail-order departments, helped to break down regionalism and create national cultures of the good life – initially in Europe and the U.S., and later in cosmopolitan centers and outlying towns and mail routes around the world. Yet this process was not without its critics. Some observers worried about the increased uniformity and lower quality of mass-produced goods. There was also concern about the threat to morality represented by women frequenting public places. In both Europe and the United States in the early twentieth century, sensationalist accusations circulated about the vulnerability of department store saleswomen to sexual predators of various sorts. The open nature of the buildings and the vulnerabilities of the women who worked there, it was argued, attracted pimps and madams: in those accounts, saleswomen entered lives of debauchery when they became "ruined women" after subjection to sexual harassment by managers; or they craved the luxuries surrounding them, which they could not afford on their low wages, and prostituted their bodies for money to satisfy their cravings (M.B. Miller 1981, p. 195; Benson 1986, pp. 135–6). A parallel concern emerged about kleptomania among bourgeois women, based on the view that the department store provided an occasion of temptation that could not be resisted (M.B. Miller 1981, pp. 196–206). Both concerns reflected a view that department stores were sites of corruption:

> Bourgeois institutions were expected to uphold the moral order, not threaten it and yet this did not seem to be the rule in the department store.... [T]he pathological frenzy to which some women were driven had become simply the seamier side of the new consumer society, where the old virtues of thrift and self-control were giving way to a culture of gratification.
>
> (M.B. Miller 1981, pp. 206–7)

Department stores were aided in their efforts to create this culture of gratification by the development of advertising.

Advertising

Industrialization vastly increased the number and variety of goods available in the market, and the department store and other innovations offered new opportunities for consumption. However, for these innovations to work people had to want goods. Businesses thus became concerned about creating national markets for their goods and encouraging buying among classes of people who had previously been less engaged in the consumer economy. Accomplishing these goals entailed changing the ways that people thought about buying. Advertising was instrumental in promoting this cultural shift.

Advertising was designed to replace the values of Poor Richard and the Protestant ethic – saving and a certain asceticism – with the idea that consumption is an aspect of being a good person. In the United States advertising promoted this shift by helping to create a national culture in which the use of particular products carried moral weight. For example, a good American father is told that he must buy life insurance from Prudential if he cares about protecting his family. The insurance business, rather than the family or the state, is depicted as the source of true security.

Advertising is a pervasive part of modern culture, and a great deal has been written about it. Some authors celebrate advertising for promoting an ever wider availability of goods and product choices. Others excoriate it as the means by which capitalist producers manipulate and control the masses. Some defenders claim that advertising actually is not all that powerful: it can only provide information to aid consumers in making their choices. Here, we will take a brief look at these discussions concerning whether advertising influences people to buy things. However, our primary interest concerns questions about whether and how advertising contributed to a shift in values.

Ironically, the least controversial form of advertising is also the most effective: price advertising – that is, an ad that says a product is on sale or has a low price (Schudson 1984, p. 64). Instead of criticizing this form, the arguments against advertising mainly target national consumer goods advertising. But the effects of this kind of advertising are hard to assess because producers use it along with other marketing strategies and within a larger social context where many other factors can influence the sale of a given product. In addition to advertising, producers develop a marketing mix that includes both direct sales and promotions – in which customers receive material benefits for buying products, such as premiums or sweepstakes chances. The amount of money spent on advertising is tied to consumption, but not in the way that one might expect: there is a higher correlation between sales in the *previous* quarter and money spent on advertising in a *given* quarter than between advertising in a *given* quarter and sales in the *following* quarter (Schudson 1984, p. 17). In other words, success in sales seems to lead to greater expenditures on advertising, not the reverse.

What forces affect sales, then? The quality and the price of the product do seem important. Advertisers like to say that "good advertising drives out bad products," because even if advertising persuades people to buy a product once, they are not likely to buy a second time if they do not like it. Sales also depend on social forces such as demographic trends and the state of the economy, and on government policies. If new-car sales or housing starts go down in a recession, no one suggests that advertising campaigns are at fault. If fewer babies are born, the market for baby food goes down. In turn, mothers who are in the labor force have different buying patterns than mothers who are not in the labor force. Government tax credits for energy-saving home improvements influence people's decisions about whether to make those improvements. Although advertising may be the most visible persuader, it does not have consequences independent of other circumstances.

Furthermore, most customers are not defenseless when confronted by advertising. Benson has shown that department store customers in the first half of the twentieth century read advertisements with considerable caution (1986, p. 106). Other research indicates that in the 1980s only 9 percent of television viewers could identify the brand or product category they saw advertised just before answering a phone call from a market researcher. Not only are ads less than overwhelming in their direct impact, most people also "operate in an information environment" where they have considerable resources to bring to the interpretation of ads (Schudson 1984, pp. 3, 90–114). Consumers often have knowledge about a given product and other products like it that comes from their own personal experiences and those of people they know. They may have other information from sources such as internet consumer-opinion sites or consumer-education groups. They are also likely to see advertisements from rival products. They may hold skeptical views about the media in general and advertising in particular. And, as Schudson has pointed out, "price is a check on advertising claims" (1984, p. 114). Thus, the marked price may be interpreted by the customer as "too much to spend" for a given object or as so low as to cast doubt on the quality of the product.

Some people, however, have less information, and they are therefore more vulnerable to the claims that advertisements make. As Schudson noted, both highly mobile people and highly immobile people (including the housebound among the elderly), children, the poor, and "many of the relatively poor and poorly educated people in the third world" can have "situational or structural ignorance" (1984, pp. 117–25). Yet even for such groups advertising does not appear to have the direct effect of inducing customers to go out and buy a particular product.

Nevertheless, critics charge that advertising has power on another level. Advertising, they argue, tells people that consumption is a good thing in itself. It thus exploits established "needs" and creates new ones. Stuart Ewen has theorized that capitalism required the creation of a consumer culture for two reasons: first, to "feed and adhere to the demands of the production schedule" and, second, to "absorb, neutralize, and contain the transitional impulses of a working class" (1976, p. 52). Advertising, for Ewen, is the primary agent in a process through which individuals have lost their consciousness of "class" as an identity defined in relation to their work, and instead sought identity and self-expression in consumption. In Ewen's terms, "By transferring the notion of 'class' into 'mass,' business would create an 'individual' who could locate his needs and frustrations in terms of the consumption of goods rather than the quality of life (work)" (1976, p. 43).

Ewen's argument is too simplistic in several ways. First, at least early on, working-class wages were too low for them to have been as involved in the consumer culture as Ewen's argument implies. Second, as Schudson argued, large cultural shifts such as the growth of consumer culture have many determinants – changes in modes of transportation, communication, patterns of urban growth, and social and geographical mobility, for example (Schudson 1984, pp. 176–7).

However, for many people, advertising is the most visible spur to consumption. What, then, can be concluded about the overall effects of people being bombarded with the message that through consumption we can meet all our needs and desires? Schudson has provocatively suggested a parallel between the official art of the former Soviet Union – "socialist realism" – and advertising, which he characterized as a sort of "capitalist realism." Both forms of public culture simplify and typify life as it "should" be. The individuality of any person featured in an ad is muted; rather, people in ads embody some larger symbolic significance. As Schudson noted, the values that advertisements express are not usually capitalist in themselves. Instead advertisers usurp values in the culture – love, friendship, youth – and use them in a capitalist way to sell goods (Schudson 1984, pp. 210–21).

This analysis leads to two broader concerns about advertising. The first is about the effects of a cognitive distancing that people exposed to either the claims of socialist realism or advertising learn to carry out. For both socialist and capitalist realism, a common response is disbelief. Viewers "knew" those healthy, happy Soviet workers were not real people, just as viewers "know" that a new shampoo will not solve the problems of one's love life. Yet, if it is adopted, such a thorough-going suspension of belief leads to a certain detachment from reality, and advertising thus encourages an ironic stance (Schudson 1984, pp. 224–9).

The second concern is this: to the extent that advertising constitutes a pervasive public art form (though not an official one), it becomes the dominant mode in which thoughts and experiences get expressed. Schudson argued that advertising as pervasive art "brings some images and expressions quickly to mind and makes others relatively unavailable" (1984, p. 230). Alternative values and worldviews will certainly exist in a culture dominated by advertising, but it is harder to find expressions of them. Therefore advertising has a certain power to distort and flatten people's ability to interpret complex experiences that lie beyond its vocabulary. We can observe this flattening when advertising photographs are placed in magazines that also include documentary photographs. In the jumble of advertising and news stories, people may respond to both kinds of images with the same distancing mechanism. Both the documentary image and the advertisement become objectified and treated as commodities (see Figure 6.1). More than causing major changes in culture, advertising reflects culture. But it does so only partially, and in ways skewed toward a capitalist idealization of culture.

Mass consumption

Defining the beginning, the stages, and the end of the "consumption revolution" in the West depends on the stage of the revolution of interest. McCracken (1988) points to a beginning in Elizabethan England, with changes in the meaning of material things for

Figure 6.1 In modern mass media the boundaries between art, documentary, and advertising
   are increasingly blurred. In 2001 Benetton collaborated with the United Nations
   Volunteers program to create a series of images featuring the volunteer efforts of
   individuals from around the world, producing images with both the United Nations
   and Benetton logos. The images, what Benetton calls "communications," were
   disseminated globally in newspapers, magazines, and on billboards.

Source: James Mollison, © Benetton Group Spa.

the nobility, and he pinpoints a second major development in the eighteenth century,
when consumption spread to people in other classes (see Chapter 5). The third
moment in the history of consumption in McCracken's account came in the nineteenth century, in the period of rapid industrialization. Whereas in the eighteenth
century the middle class had for the most part imitated the wealthy, by the following
century different styles were emerging. Bourgeois styles dominated, but young dandies
developed their own taste culture in opposition, while the decorative-arts movement
associated with William Morris and his craft workshop sought to reform bourgeois
aesthetics. Consumption became a way of expressing more than status – or desired
status. It could also express one's attitude toward the dominant bourgeois culture
(McCracken 1988, pp. 22–8; Rosalind Williams 1982).

   As for later developments, in the U.S. some scholars point to a decisive change
during the 1950s, after government loans to G.I. families encouraged the growth of
suburban communities, thereby democratizing consumption on a scale hitherto
unknown (Ewen 1976). Whichever way one chooses to periodize the development of
consumption, it seems relentless. In recent years, markets have emerged for human
embryos and reproductive services, public education and prisons. It has become
increasingly difficult to point to any part of contemporary life that remains wholly

outside the processes of commodification and practices of consumption. Yet the emergence of consumer culture has been highly skewed in its consequences.

Class, gender, and consumption

Because social position has made a tremendous difference in how individuals are incorporated into consumer culture, to make sense of the consumer revolution it is especially important that we understand the significance of class and of gender. Overall, producers depend for their livelihood on the ability of people to buy the goods they produce. In the 1920s industrialists recognized that they had an interest in supporting the movement for higher wages and shorter hours, which would increase levels of consumption. Then U.S. President Herbert Hoover is cited as describing high wages as the "very essence of great production" (Ewen 1976, p. 28). But high wages for whom? Shorter hours and higher wages in the 1920s affected mostly salaried workers, including the expanding middle class; the wages of working-class people were still too low to allow for significant participation in consumption. According to data about the period, working-class wages were close to subsistence levels (Ewen 1976, pp. 56–7). Workers' consumption thus involved either buying on the installment plan or substituting one kind of purchase for another. In the typical American community of "Middletown" in the 1920s, for example, it was not uncommon for a family to mortgage their house to buy an automobile (Lynd and Lynd 1929, p. 254).

Daniel Bell has argued that mass consumption began to take off in the 1920s. He attributes this development to revolutions in technology and to three social inventions – assembly-line production, the development of marketing (including but not limited to advertising), and the spread of installment buying. Bell also linked the rise of mass consumption during this period with changes in values: "The concomitant revolutions in transportation and communications laid the basis for a national society and the beginnings of a common culture. Taken all together mass consumption meant the acceptance...of social change and personal transformation" (D. Bell 1976, p. 66).

An early form of installment buying predated World War I, but it was used only by poor people, and it carried the stigma of debt. In this form, people bought things from peddlers who came by every week to collect payment. Middle-class morality demanded a different approach: when people wanted something, they should save for it. Going into debt was viewed as "wrong and dangerous." A new culture of consumption thus could only take off with a shift in moral values. In the view of Lears (1983), such a new morality emerged on many fronts in early twentieth-century culture, including academic psychology and religion. Lears argues that in the U.S. the new service elites – psychologists, therapists, and liberal Protestant religious leaders – were offering a new therapeutic ethic in response to the anxiety produced by modern existence. This ethic promised personal fulfillment and it provided authoritative answers to questions about the meaning of life, by undermining the culture of guilt and legitimating consumption.

The shift in values could take hold, in part, because new forms of installment buying routinized the process of consumption and changed its moral valence: businesses billed monthly charges through the mail. This approach was efficient and impersonal. Businesses avoided using the word "debt," and both middle-class and working-class people took advantage of the opportunity to buy "on credit" (D. Bell

1976, p. 68). Given the low wages of the working class, however, they benefited less from this innovation than did the middle class.

Boorstin (1973) and others have suggested that mass consumption created a "democratization of goods." Schudson's account is somewhat different. Yes, goods became more uniformly available, more standardized, more convenient, and more likely to be consumed in public ways. Yet, although the goods displayed in a department store are in theory available to everyone, in practice they are available only to those with the resources to make the purchase. Schudson's analysis reminds us that the displays of mass consumption create a democratization of desire and envy (1984, pp. 181, 151). During the first half of the twentieth century, Western "national cultures" increasingly came to be organized around consumption. However, working-class and poor people remained mostly at the margins or outside the new cultures.

In everyday life, as Victoria de Grazia observes in *The Sex of Things* (1996), consumption practices are filtered through the household. Thus, looking at those practices through the experiences of households brings to light the complex ways in which social class and gender constrain people's ability to consume, and shows how the status positions associated with class and gender sometimes become reconfigured under a new regime of consumption culture.

De Grazia depicts a trajectory of changed meanings of the household stretching from the 1880s to the 1960s. The British rural cottage of the 1880s was a site of self-sufficient production. By contrast, in the 1960s American suburban household

> the father worked away from home, commuting by automobile to an office job, [while] the mother, isolated from relatives, friends, and even neighbors, operated a self-contained, all-equipped establishment-cum-decorative garden. Household co-manager with Mr. Breadwinner, Mrs. Consumer was an astute and mobile shopper, bringing her expertise to all aspects of consumer choice – from the schools for her children and her pet's veterinarian to the family's health insurance plan.
>
> (V. de Grazia 1996, p. 152)

The image of families before the industrial revolution as self-reliant three-generational units is largely a myth that emerged from functionalist social theory during the mid-twentieth century. Nevertheless, traditional preindustrial households in Western societies can generally be characterized as: (1) relatively more unified between home and work, public and private, sacred and secular, instrumental and expressive, and work and play than typical modern households; (2) patriarchal in their ordering logic, with legal and customary authority residing in males and kinship organized through strong, often economically based, paternal ties; and (3) gynocentric in the sense that activities were organized around the reproduction of the family, with women as significant partners in the work of the household. It was not until the nineteenth century that husbands and wives were likely to view each other as companions, or that males were defined as "providers," or that motherhood was seen as woman's sacred vocation.

As the industrial revolution took hold and work became an activity of men in extra-familial settings, women who were not employed outside the home increasingly found that consumption became defined as their work. This was true in two quite different ways. First, as production moved out of the household, women's work of reproducing their families came more and more to involve consumption activities. Clothing, for example, gradually shifted from being produced in the household to being purchased in stores. Second, among the affluent, women became the primary vehicles for "conspicuous consumption" – the exhibition of signals of status.

De Grazia argues that consumption, as it has developed in the West, is fundamentally gendered as female. She points to moralists in the early eighteenth century who described credit schemes and the volatility of the capitalist system in terms of the "feminine disposition," nineteenth-century novelists and modernist intellectuals who heaped disdain on commercial mass culture and its ability to "bewitch" consumers, and the ways that "commercial artists sprawl idealized female figures across twentieth-century advertising copy, designing their forms and faces to elicit desirous gazes. And marketing agents probe the calculations and caprices imputed to Mrs. Consumer to survey the entity of household spending" (V. de Grazia 1996, p. 1).

If viewed through sociological lenses sensitive to class, gender, and nation-state, the historical shift from the ideal-typical traditional household to the ideal-typical consumer one was anything but uniform. Housework itself changed very slowly: in the nineteenth century, the egg beater and the cast-iron stove were the only widely diffused labor-saving devices (Strasser 1982, pp. 33–49). Although gas lighting was available in most major American cities by the 1820s and 1830s, until the turn of the twentieth century only relatively wealthy people could afford to install it in their homes. Electricity was not commercially available until the 1880s. Sixteen percent of households had electricity in 1912, 35 percent in 1920, and 68 percent in 1930. But even by 1930 only 10 percent of farm homes were electrified. The majority of the latter did not have electricity until the then U.S. President Franklin D. Roosevelt's rural electrification program in the mid-1930s (Strasser 1982, pp. 68–83).

Changes in the nature of housework quickened in the twentieth century with the invention and diffusion of vacuum cleaners, electric irons, washing machines, and so on. Attempts to rationalize housework did not, however, depend solely on technological changes. By the end of the nineteenth century, women such as Catherine Beecher and Ellen Swallow had developed systems of "domestic science" for running households more efficiently (Sklar 1973). With the rise of scientific household management and labor-saving devices, fewer women did housework for wages. The number of women employed as domestic servants decreased dramatically between 1910 and 1920 – the period that includes the socially reorganizing watershed of World War I. Paralleling this development, fewer unpaid women – mothers and daughters of the housewife – helped out with domestic work. In theory, more effective household management and labor-saving devices reduced the need for labor from these sources. However, Ruth Cowan (1976) has argued, there is a catch: labor-saving devices increased expectations of how much housekeeping was "necessary." Clothing and linens, for example, could be washed much more frequently, and ordinary people came to expect freshly prepared hot meals three times a day. So women did not in fact end up spending less time doing housework.

Rising-consumption-based economies thus have been something of a double-edged sword. Moreover, the realities for women in different classes and in different societies have varied greatly. Belinda Davis (1996) argues that during World War I the gendering of consumption as female afforded women in Berlin the power to press the state for relief in the face of food shortages. When women demonstrated in the streets or even engaged in violent confrontation with merchants accused of food speculation, they were portrayed in police and press reports as acting within their rights. To be a consumer was to be a German, and as archetypical consumers women found themselves with a public voice and legitimacy that they had not previously experienced. This legitimacy, moreover, did not necessarily extend to working-class men, who were more easily dismissed as public drunkards or simple rabble-rousers. Central to the shift toward the modern welfare state of Germany's postwar Weimar republic, according to Davis, was the increasingly prominent idea that citizens contributed to the war effort by making sacrifices as consumers. In return the state had an obligation to acknowledge and meet the needs of its citizens.

The role of consumer thus may be empowering in some contexts. However, it can just as easily signal a decline in status, increased dependence on a male breadwinner, or some other reorganization of gender relations. In the years between World Wars I and II, in order to meet the economic burdens of the marketplace U.S. working-class families often used strategies that ended up subverting any clearly gendered division of labor in which the man produces and the woman consumes (B. Davis 1996). And, as Bull and Corner (1993) show, the transition to a consumer economy in Italy during the 1960s was just as likely to move women into roles in the labor economy as to push them toward adopting the "Mrs. Consumer" role in the home.

It is worth asking whether the situation in advanced capitalist societies is so distant from the range of dynamics found earlier in the twentieth century. Weinbaum and Bridges (1978) have described women as "consumption workers." Although a common stereotype has women consumers as neurotic products of modern society addicted to shopping, these scholars disputed that stereotype, arguing that women do not consume out of "psychological need" but rather because it is their job. As consumers, women must make decisions about when it is efficient to buy things at the market and when it is efficient to produce at home. Rejecting the common portrayal of housewives as their own bosses, Weinbaum and Bridges pointed out that housewives must observe schedules set by the state and economic institutions. Imagine the constraints of a woman with children to take to school, dry cleaning to pick up, groceries to buy, perhaps a special coffee or bread to purchase at another shop. In addition, she needs to get the car's oil changed and her driver's license has to be renewed. Assuming that she has the money to pay for these goods and services, and that she is not also working full-time in the labor force (as many women indeed are), she is still dependent on the scheduling processes of the enterprises providing goods and services. Even the increase in "self-service" has its drawbacks, for it pushes household managers into doing work previously performed by paid employees. Clearly, consumer society has altered the character of household life, often improving the quality of life – especially for the working poor. However, its effects are diverse, and not all of them can be deemed "progress."

Consumption and globalization

The consumption revolution begun in the West has also taken hold in non-Western societies. Because mass consumption mostly came later to societies outside the West and often under conditions of economic subordination, considering developments of consumer practices elsewhere reveals some interesting comparisons with – and relationships to – Europe, Britain, and the United States.

Studies of emerging non-Western practices have two basic orientations, both concerned with understanding the development of societies in relation to increasingly dominant mass consumer cultures. On the one hand, some scholars explained the late emergence of consumer economies outside the West as efforts to "catch up" – attempts by developing states to assert their independence by modernizing their economic and civil spheres and creating national identities in the service of *economic* autonomy (see Kang 1995 for a review of such arguments about the newly industrializing East Asian countries). This perspective assumes a particular world-historical narrative – a trajectory of modernization moving toward capitalism – and the absence or slow pace of development is often explained in terms of a "lack" (see, e.g., Rostow 1960; McClelland 1961). Late states, be they African, Latin American, or Asian, fall short in modernization, such arguments hold, because they lack the necessary resources – including material resources, natural resources, and capital, as well as cultural resources such as paradigms, ideologies, and practices – held to have been important for the West's transition to mass consumer capitalism.

By contrast, more recent and more culturally nuanced studies do not posit a unified global history of development with different societies at different stages along the same track. They seek instead to explore non-Western cultures on their own terms and to consider their relations with the West by focusing on how mass consumption practices have been used to assert *cultural* autonomy.

Let us consider East and Southeast Asia countries, which experienced rapid economic growth beginning in the 1960s. One aspect of the rise of consumption in the West – the contradiction between a moral discourse of thrift versus gratification – has its parallel in tensions between different generations of people in South Korea. According to Seung-Kuk Kim (2000), the rise of consumerism in South Korea is the result of factors that include: (1) rapid economic growth and democratization through the 1980s; (2) a demographic explosion of college students who were children of affluent parents from the rising middle classes (who sometimes increased their own purchasing power by providing tutoring for younger students); and (3) an age structure in which those between ages 15 and 35 make up close to half the population. Not surprisingly, according to Kim, the younger segment of the population quickly became the focus of both electoral propaganda and commercial advertising. As a result, the old (older than 35) and the young (35 or less) became not only politically divided as conservatives and progressives, but also culturally divided, with the older generation holding a predominantly productionist orientation while the young embraced a consumerist orientation (Kim 2000, p. 64).

The generational differences can be captured in cultural terms by the Korean sentiment called *Han*. Depicting *Han* as an aggregate sentiment, Kim reports a widespread view that most South Koreans, particularly those more than 50 years old, are emotionally or psychologically full of "tears and regrets, unsatisfied desires and discontents, and grudges and enmities." Such attitudes result, his argument suggests, from the hardships of twentieth-century history – Japanese colonialism, World War II, the Korean War. This complex of experiences and attitudes is invoked to explain the eventual rapid and successful industrialization and expansion of consumption in South Korea, which are described as resulting from a general achievement orientation and strong desire to emerge from a difficult past. Unlike Western capitalism, with its close religious connection to the ascetic Protestant ethic, South Korean capitalism had been socio-psychologically constructed on the basis of hungry spirits of Korean people full of *Han* (Kim 2000, pp. 64–5).

Parents in South Korea spend willingly for their children, especially on education. On the other hand, general surveys indicate a great ambivalence about perceived excesses of consumption and materialism. This moral ambivalence is similar to earlier (and ongoing) concerns in the West. But there is a key difference: the older generation's unease with the younger's consumption of popular culture is often expressed as concern about Westernization or Americanization. It seems unlikely that *Han* can explain all the complexities of South Korean development, but according to Kim it does explain quite well the country's particular age-differentiated pattern of consumption that is coupled with the older generation's ambivalence toward increasing consumption and leisure.

Chua Beng-Huat (2000a) reports on countries throughout Asia – Singapore, Malaysia, Japan, Indonesia, the People's Republic of China – that share the Korean moral ambivalence toward consumption and its potential to infect youth with the degeneracy of Westernization. Yet these countries also share consumption styles associated with status display much like those found in the West: "anyone who calls the latest Mercedes, purchased at inflated prices and maintained at high cost, merely a car clearly misses the symbolic point of such a possession" (Beng-Huat 2000a, p. 21).

Indonesia, because of its low level of development, throws the symbolic side of consumption into sharp relief. There, according to Solvay Gerke, the severely limited ability of the new middle class to consume results in visible forms of status display:

> For example, one could readily see young people and families spending hours sitting in strategic places, where they could be seen by all and sundry, at McDonald's or Pizza Hut drinking Coke or milk-shakes with a burger. They would take the empty hamburger bags with them, as they left the fast-food restaurant, so that everybody in the street could see where they had lunch or dinner.
>
> (Gerke 2000, pp. 146–7)

Gerke adds that young people will share fashionable sweaters, t-shirts, and jewelry. She uses the term "lifestyling" as a verb to highlight how their practices invoke symbols. Through active lifestyling people keep demonstrating group membership, often while trying to deny their social and economic circumstances.

As in the West, the shift away from producing goods to satisfy one's own needs to consuming goods produced by others has given social critics cause for concern. Beng-Huat's example of the sewing machine in Singapore echoes the Frankfurt School critique of the loss of authenticity and spontaneity in Western culture:

> Up to the late 1970s, one of the skills that many female Singaporeans acquired was dressmaking. In addition to commercial dressmaking schools, community centres all over the country had dressmaking classes to cater to this demand. Every household either owned or strove to own a sewing machine; it formed part of the bride's dowry in marriage. Dresses were largely homemade. By the late 1980s, it was rare to find any female Singaporean under 30 years of age who could sew. Clothing, reconfigured as fashion, is now purchased off-the-peg, according to one's consumption capacity, in stores of all sizes.
>
> (Beng-Huat 2000a, pp. 23–4)

Concern for a loss of authentic or indigenous culture in favor of a mass-produced one takes on increased significance when critics sound the alarm of Americanization or Westernization. With McDonald's and Disney theme-park culture spreading aggressively beyond the borders of the United States, for example, critics often warn of cultural imperialism, raising the fear that local cultures will be completely overwhelmed. However, as Shunya Yoshimi (2000) illustrates with the case of Disneyland in Japan and as Beng-Huat (2000c) shows by looking at McDonald's in Singapore, the picture is complex. When American firms confront anti-Americanism, or at least ambivalence about Americanization, they modify their images and align their practices with local custom. The result is less an imperialist imposition of one culture upon another and more a strategic modification of both imported and indigenous culture enacted in pursuit of profit.

The studies of Asian consumption considered here – whether they address identity dynamics of status-seeking or resistance to forces of Westernization – share a fundamental assumption, that industrialization and the rise of mass culture and consumption elsewhere need to be understood as reactions to what took place first in Europe and the United States. However, historians and literary critics associated with subaltern studies that originated in critiques of the colonial experience in India draw the unidirectionality of this assumption into question. In *Provincializing Europe*, Dipesh Chakrabarty argues for an approach to history that can transcend both the too simple dichotomy of developed West versus underdeveloped East, as well as the problematic argument that posits a sequence – first in the West and then elsewhere (2000, p. 6). For Chakrabarty, treating Europe as the fulfillment of a modernist ideal relegates non-Western cultures to the status of provinces – primitive or backward cultures in need of modernization. However, when the lived experiences of actual people in Europe are explored in relation to the ideal, Chakrabarty asserts, European culture looks as provincial as any other culture. In his view, a thorough understanding of the colonial and postcolonial experience outside the West requires an intellectual shift. Whereas processes like rationalization, progress, and the organization of modern societies around individual rights are typically presented as threads of a universal narrative of historical development initiated in the Western experience, in fact this narrative is not experienced as universal – either elsewhere or even in Europe. The everyday resistance and political struggles of subalterns – subordinated people – in colonial India, Chakrabarty argues, show us that universalist narratives of modernism simultaneously allow the powerful to rule and create opportunities for the oppressed to make claims for their own liberation. Subaltern-studies scholars thus urge a revision of history that allows historical narratives to be told from the perspectives of the colonized (see Prakash 1994 for an overview of the subaltern-studies project).

Cooper (1994) demonstrates how the subaltern critique of colonialism that was developed in relation to India may also be fruitfully applied to Africa (for Latin America, see Mallon 1994). In Africa, Cooper argues, women experienced colonialist modernization in contradictory ways:

> Before the conquest, women had once exercised considerable control over farming and the crops they produced, but the expanding slave trade made women vulnerable to kidnapping or to the control of their would-be protectors. Colonial rule – the decline of warfare and increased possibilities for cash cropping – for a time gave women space to reassert power within domestic economies, but the subsequent decline of village agriculture and the increasing importance of labor migration made women increasingly dependent on men's fortunes.
>
> (Cooper 1994, p. 1,534)

Cooper uses the African case to illustrate a broader dynamic in the subaltern experience of modernity and industrialization. Colonial powers initiated economic policies to attract laborers into an urban industrialized workforce, and they sought to socialize new generations of urban workers in ways that would distance them from the backwardness of rural village life. One unintended consequence was the development of trade unions. These unions, in turn, could draw from the same discourse of modernity as the colonialists – a discourse of rationalized productivity, predictability, stability, and order – to make claims to entitlements that officials found difficult to reject. From the subaltern perspective, the experience of modernization outside of the West is not a simple matter of resistance or acquiescence, and the critique of colonial rule thus provides an opportunity to deploy the very categories of knowledge typically associated with modernization to examine the contested nature of power and ideology.

Conclusion

The industrial revolution created a world of consumer goods beyond what would ever have been imagined by the early industrialists. Some writers argue that, in turn, mass culture has had broader ramifications for society and for how individuals constitute a sense of self. Fox and Lears point to the importance of three developments in the U.S. in the late nineteenth and early twentieth centuries: (1) the emergence of a national market; (2) the development of a new layer of professionals and managers enmeshed in a complex web of business and professional organization; and (3) the rise of the therapeutic ethic (Fox and Lears 1983, p. xi). Technological and economic changes resulted in a new form of material culture; they also set in motion changes in the cultural constitution of self and society.

As we have argued, the consumption culture that developed in the West during the era of industrialization was encouraged by the growth in a positive valuation of consumption. Advertising played on both the ethic of fulfillment through consumption and the anxieties of modern individuals. Observers in the 1920s noted a change from advertisements that essentially described the qualities of products to advertisements that appealed to people's insecurities. In *Middletown*, for example, the Lynds characterized modern advertising as:

> concentrating increasingly upon a type of copy aiming to make the reader emotionally uneasy, to bludgeon him with the fact that decent people don't live the way he does…. This copy points an accusing finger at the stenographer as she reads her motion picture magazine and makes her acutely conscious of her unpolished finger nails…and sends the housewife peering anxiously into the mirror to see if her wrinkles look like those that made Mrs. X in the advertisement "old at thirty-five" because she did not have a leisure hour electric washer.
>
> (Lynd and Lynd 1929, p. 82)

Entrepreneurs brought a host of personal grooming products on to the market, using advertising to inform people of new needs and then offering them chances to buy products that satisfied those needs. Ewen argues that advertisers saw their task as creating consumers' "critical self-consciousness in tune with the solutions of the marketplace" (1976, p. 38). As Lears's analysis suggests, such ads probably did not create anxiety as much as they exploited anxieties that were already there. Yet, even if ads are not generally taken at face value, the act of detaching or distancing oneself from them creates a cognitive perception of unreality that can be experienced as personally unsettling. Not only is the vision in the ad perceived as unreal, but the feeling that the self is real becomes more and more difficult to maintain (Lears 1983, pp. 8–9). In the context of a therapeutic culture, people came to experience the crisis of authenticity identified by the critical theorists as a personal crisis.

In thinking through arguments such as these, it is easy to conjure up "capitalists" or "advertisers" who manipulate everyone else, without people being able to do anything about it or even knowing that it is happening. We embrace a more nuanced view. From the beginning, the consumption revolution has been both fueled by many different sources and diverse in its consequences. Even if the consumption culture has been hegemonic in its dominating, absorbing reconstruction of culture, the capitalists, advertisers, and therapists whose actions helped promote it themselves were "driven by unfocused anxieties as well as deliberate strategies" (Lears 1983, p. 37).

In the end the important issues are what choices this culture of consumption allows people and under what circumstances. Certainly the consumer culture discriminates against poorer classes unable to participate fully in the market for mass-produced goods. Just as certainly, women are marginalized to the extent that consumption has been identified both as female and as an essential yet unpaid form of labor in the modern household. It might also be argued that less developed countries become ever more shaped by the diffusion of culture from the developed West, where mass production and the ethics of consumption first took hold. And yet, as we have seen, the picture is not so simple. As modern processes of economic rationalization and ethics of consumption spread to non-Western countries, the potential for new cultural forms and new kinds of critique emerged. Developing countries have not simply mimicked the West. True, their cultures have been profoundly influenced, but the assumed economic, political, and cultural dominance of the West has met with challenges – resistance to cultural imperialism, the development of trade unions, subaltern efforts to "provincialize" Europe. And for women in the West, especially working-class women, the identity of consumer in some contexts created opportunities – renegotiated roles in the division of labor in U.S. households, public political legitimacy in Germany.

To pursue further the question of how consumer culture shapes social life, we need to ask how pervasive forms of mass-produced and mass-mediated culture have become, and with what consequences. As the critical theorists and Lears evidence, these issues already matter for industrial society. Yet the developments that concern them can properly be understood as harbingers of a world often now called postmodern. It is to understanding this world that we now turn.

Suggested readings

In *The Sex of Things* (1996), Victoria de Grazia has compiled a wide-ranging collection of sociological, historical, and psychological essays examining the gendered nature of mass culture and consumption in the United States, Great Britain, and Europe.

Shopping for Identity: The Marketing of Ethnicity (2000), by Marilyn Halter, examines the history of consumption, marketing, and ethnic identity in the United States by investigating the variety of ways that American-ness can be produced and consumed while at the same time ethnic specificity can be maintained in the marketplace.

In *Cultural Consumption and Everyday Life* (1999), John Storey briefly examines the rise of consumer culture in the West and then organizes a lengthy discussion of consumption around two general theoretical perspectives: consumption as manipulation versus consumption as communication.

Histories of Leisure (2002), edited by Rudy Koshar, is a useful collection of essays offering an historical overview of leisure (cuisine, tourism, and sport, among other topics) in modern Europe.

Note

1   A movement in the arts (1916–22) characterized by fantastic and often playful expression of supposed unconscious content.

7 Deconstructing the postmodern

As our explorations of the historical formations of culture in the past three chapters have emphasized, no purely sociological analysis can be complete: understanding culture is a multi- and interdisciplinary undertaking. The explosion of interest in culture in the past half-century thus creates new opportunities for drawing the humanities into closer relation to history and the social sciences, and the social-science disciplines themselves into closer relation with one another. In the social sciences, issues of culture are now central to a variety of theories – focused on political, economic, and social structural analysis, on organizations, issues of social solidarity, social movements, and action. Across the humanities and social sciences, the growing commitment to examine culture – notably "popular" culture – in relation to society has roots in the emergence of cultural studies – investigations of culture that transgress supposed turf boundaries of academic disciplines.

Consolidation of cultural studies can be traced in significant respects to the work of researchers at Great Britain's University of Birmingham Centre for Contemporary Cultural Studies – the "Birmingham School," founded in 1964 (Centre for Contemporary Cultural Studies 1980; Johnson 1986–7; Kendall and Wickham 2001). This generative intellectual movement – which initiated important interdisciplinary research on culture, social stratification, and everyday life – was itself part of a much wider shift toward "camp" stances about culture. Beginning in the 1950s and 1960s, cultural producers along with everyday people began to strike increasingly self-conscious and ironic stances toward both "legitimate" and "pop" culture, treating advertising slogans as poetry, for example. The unlicensed appropriation of cultural forms – exemplified in Andy Warhol's art in the 1960s depicting well-known advertising logos such as soft-drink bottles – gave audiences a more "hip" and critically engaged relationship to culture (Stimson 2001). Yet there is an irony in how cultural studies itself has developed in the wake of the broader cultural shift: much of the intellectual momentum has come from the humanities, yet the sources of interdisciplinary enrichment in the humanities often have their origins in social philosophy, linguistics, history, structuralist anthropology, symbolic interactionism, social phenomenology, and ethnomethodology, and their topics are eminently social. "Cultural studies" displaces the conventional disciplines of social inquiry. But it does so in part by poaching from them.

Following the path-breaking work of Michel Foucault, one central movement of cultural studies depends on taking a "textual turn," by exploring the ways in which the social world is textually represented, categorized, and imbued with meaning through "discourses" – that is, publicly available and socially organized ways of textually representing, theorizing, and organizing social activity and its objects (see Chapter 8).

Texts, once understood as written materials, are now to be found in the "cultural scripts" by which people operate in the social world. Even social space – an urban area, or a suburb, a mall, a highway, an entire region – can be treated as a "text." To do so, it is only necessary to recognize that people orient actions on the basis of the "signs" we see as intelligible patterns in those worlds. *How* such "texts" are read, whether they have any stable meanings – these are questions of "reception." Some theorists embrace a poststructuralist and semiotic approach, arguing that texts and symbols themselves order and constrain the social worlds that people inhabit; other theorists take hermeneutic or interpretive positions, exploring how people make novel meanings in relation to the texts and symbols around them (see Chapter 10).

Despite the nuanced differences, poststructuralist and interpretive theories share the potential to link the *contents* of culture – its symbolic and meaningful dimensions – with the more material aspects of social life – concerned with stratification, power, economic patterns, and organizational features of cultural production. Thus, Foucault argued that culture is all about power, but the power in question is not centralized in some government or corporate office; rather, power is diffusely distributed in the myriad discourses through which people act in their social worlds in relation even to something as "private" as sexuality.

Influenced by Marxist theorist Antonio Gramsci (and later by Foucault), the Birmingham School researchers began in the 1960s to explore the power of everyday popular culture, arguing that the content of culture distributed through mass media often is infused with subtle ideological meanings that reinforce the status quo (Barrett *et al.* 1980; Bennett *et al.* 1981). Political resistance, then, is importantly concerned with the micropolitics of cultural resistance and countercultural movements – as we saw in the work of Paul Gilroy (1991) discussed in Chapter 3. Yet a number of critics have raised concerns that cultural studies too readily romanticizes populist resistance where a less entranced analysis might find people acting more like conformist consumers (Mulhern 2000). Indeed, one cultural analyst, John Docker (1994), self-consciously developed his own approach in opposition to the work of John Fiske (e.g. 1987), who had become most closely associated with the populist reading of popular culture. The critical points about populist romanticization are well taken, but they do not stand in opposition to cultural studies *per se*, for a number of cultural-studies researchers share the critical concerns (F. Webster 2001, p. 90). Rather, the tendencies toward romantic and populist optimism about resistance through and against popular culture alert us to the need for clear-headed and thoughtful empirical analysis about what people are up to when they engage with culture.

The textual turn is important to both cultural studies and the social sciences because it encourages a wide range of scholars to focus attention on relationships between culture and meaning, in the context of people's specific social locations and the webs of social organization that frame their life experiences. With the textual turn, we now are in a much better position to document the powerful ways in which culture mediates social life. Yet studying relationships between the symbolic and the social is hardly a new enterprise. Rather, the so-called cultural turn revisits a longstanding debate about the relative sociological importance of "material" (economic) versus "ideal" (symbolic and discourse-centered cultural) forces.

At the beginning of the twentieth century, Max Weber (1958a) argued that the Protestant ethic of self-sacrificing Christian asceticism reinforced the emergence of modern rationally organized industrial capitalism. He emphasized that he did not want to substitute a "one-sided" cultural analysis for a one-sided economic one. "Not ideas, but material and ideal interests, directly govern men's conduct," he wrote. Still, Weber reflected, "very frequently the 'world images' that have been created by 'ideas' have, like switchmen, determined the tracks along which action has been pushed by the dynamic of interest" (1946, p. 280).

At the high tide of structural comparative sociology, Theda Skocpol (1979) took the opposite view, asserting that culture – in the form of political ideology – was not relevant to the outcome of major social revolutions. Soon after, however, the textual turn provoked a renewed interest in the relation of culture to change. Lynn Hunt (1984), for example, argued that the French Revolution of 1789 depended on "the invention of a new political culture" that facilitated the formation of a new French political class, and consequently established a particularly modern kind of politics based on new forms of citizen participation in public affairs. Later, Hunt used a Freudian metaphor to explore the French political unconscious at work in what she called *The Family Romance of the French Revolution* (1992). To invoke the terminology of Ann Swidler (1986), in a wide range of studies culture has increasingly been construed as a "toolkit" that has particular flexibility and salience in times of rapid change. In this view, cultural reorderings can radically alter the "textual" meanings so central to social life. Such fundamental transformations of culture – what might be called "cultural revolutions" – may occur quickly and in conjunction with political upheaval, as Hunt suggests for the French Revolution, or, like the consolidation of the Protestant ethic in the modern personality, they may transpire as broad, glacier-like changes that take place over decades or even generations. Why do fundamental cultural transformations occur, and what is their significance for social life?

These questions could be addressed by reference to historical examples like the French Revolution or the Protestant Reformation. However, an especially relevant time to examine for thinking about how culture is connected to social change is our own historical era. The "textual turn" itself is often considered part of a proclaimed emergence of contemporary "postmodern" culture. In this book, we already have considered postmodern writers, but we kept the focus on their sociological contributions to cultural analysis. Here, we focus on debates concerning a broader postmodern cultural and social transformation. In following these debates, we distinguish between *cultural* postmodern*ism* and *societal* postmodern*ity*. The first term, postmodern*ism* can be used to describe a cultural movement – just as modern*ism* was an art movement that began in the late nineteenth century. On the other hand, postmodern*ity* links to a different binary opposition – modern*ity* as a broad societal transformation, with roots that go back at least to the sixteenth century. An important question, then, is whether the postmodern is only a passing style or mood, or whether postmodernity as a societal era involves more durable changes. To explore this issue, we will ask, first, about postmodernism as a cultural movement and, then, about the relation of postmodern culture to industrial and postindustrial society and to globalization, so as to consider whether the era of modernity has been superseded by postmodernity. First, then, the vexing question: what is postmodern?

The postmodern turn: no definition

Despite a lot of talk about postmodernism, people often have quite different conceptions of it. There are good reasons for this. The term "postmodern" has been used at different times and in different contexts – in architecture, in film, in art, politics, philosophy, and business. And it has attracted both passionate interest and pitched opposition. The significance of the postmodern thus depends very much on who is using the term, when, and how. Moreover, in each context separately, and in all of them together, the syllable "post-" causes problems. Post-anything implies a coming after, defined, not so much in its own terms, but by what has come before. Thus, on purely logical grounds, we would not necessarily expect a "post-" situation to have coherent, definable characteristics; it could easily amount to a jumble. And, indeed, such a jumble often is celebrated by postmodern thinkers as *itself* a defining character-istic of the postmodern.

Thus, in a path-breaking essay intended to confront the challenges of the new era for feminism, Donna Haraway (1985) argued that conventional boundaries – between humans and animals, between animal-humans and machines, and between the phys-ical and non-physical – break down. The emerging world is one of the "cyborg" – "a cybernetic organism, a creature of social reality as well as a creature of fiction" (1985, p. 65). Although Western civilization glorifies individual uniqueness, Haraway argued that we are all enmeshed in hybrid relationships, especially defined through connec-tions with microcomputers and biotechnology. Because we cannot wish away the new circumstances, Haraway suggested, we are better off politically and individually coming to terms with them.

Several years later, Todd Gitlin detailed what he regarded as key attributes of post-modernism. In his view,

> [it] is indifferent to consistency and continuity altogether. It self-consciously splices genres, attitudes, styles. It relishes the blurring or juxtaposition of forms (fiction–nonfiction), stances (straight–ironic), moods (violent–comic), cultural levels (high–low). It disdains originality and fancies copies, repetition, the recom-bination of hand-me-down scraps. It neither embraces nor criticizes, but beholds the world blankly, with a knowingness that dissolves feeling and commitment into irony.
>
> (Gitlin 1988, p. 35)

When did this postmodern sensibility surface, and what is its relation to the modern era? The emergence of a distinctly modern world can be traced to the global expan-sion of Europe and the Protestant Reformation beginning in the sixteenth century, to the Enlightenment as a philosophical movement of reason beginning in the seven-teenth century, and to the industrial revolution and resulting urbanization and proletarianization beginning in the late eighteenth and early nineteenth centuries. Whatever visibly might be called "postmodern," however, has been with us in any significant way only since the political and countercultural challenges to established social orders beginning in the 1960s and the explosion of popular culture that occurred during the same period.

But the timing is tricky. Postmodernism has antecedents in certain late-nineteenth-and early-to-mid-twentieth-century modernist and avant-garde philosophies and cultural movements focused on relativism, perspectivism, subjectivity, and language. True, modern thought has a side that emphasizes rationality, coherence, analytic science, and holistic theory, but in the latter part of the nineteenth century the human-ities and the arts began to revel in discordant and disjointed experience, contradictions, celebrations of the irrational, and attempts to reintegrate the human animal within the total human experience. These movements of their day were "modernist" in their breaks with a monolithic Victorian bourgeois worldview (Singal 1987). But they remained largely elitist, rejecting mass culture and advocating pursuit of "art for art's sake." Not surprisingly, such forms of cultural modernism remained largely separated from the general public and from history. Under these circumstances, avant-garde movements emerged in the efforts of surrealists, Dadaists, and others to offer a critique of elitist modernism by forcing art and culture into a confrontation with politics and history (Huyssen 1986; N.F. Cantor 1988, pp. 35–41).

Yet the potency of both the modernists and the avant-garde was undermined by their own successes. Impressionist, surrealist, and abstract-expressionist painters, for example, found their work displayed in major galleries and museums and collected by wealthy bourgeois patrons of the arts. Artists' support depended on an established gallery system, and the content of their avant-garde work seemingly could be absorbed within established modern culture so long as their careers did not threaten the institutional frameworks that orchestrated the aesthetic definition and reception of artistic work (cf. Bürger 1984). Elements of these "rebellious" cultural movements were incorporated first into elite and then into popular culture. Mondrian's abstract blocks of color, for example, were appropriated in high-fashion designer dresses in the 1960s, then in inexpensive "knock-off" imitations.

Because seemingly anti-modern movements are deeply implicated in modernism itself, some theorists, for example Lyotard (1984), have suggested that the postmodern – however construed – should be regarded as a "moment" of modernism rather than the time following the *end* of modernism. This approach makes sense because the culture of modernity itself facilitates cultural movements rejecting modernity, whether they be nostalgic, even reactionary, or, alternatively, avant-garde (cf. Lechner 1990). Flare-ups of the specifically postmodern challenge to modernity have had a checkered presence during the modern era: they are marked, in Lyotard's view, by rejections of modernity's two prevailing "master narratives" of historical progress – (1) the triumph of Liberty and (2) the march of Reason. These challenges have intensified in the two decades since Lyotard wrote, especially through the work of postcolonial, subaltern, and feminist theorists who argue that "grand narratives" construct women, the poor, and people of color as "the Other" on the basis of their alleged non-modern tenden-cies (see Chapter 4). Precisely to challenge such representations, people like the filmmaker Trinh T. Minh-Ha (1989, 1991) have worked to create new forms of narra-tive, no longer totalizing or grand.

As Lyotard understood, the modern ideals have not been abandoned in the face of postmodern challenges by figures like Trinh, Michel Foucault, and the deconstruc-tionist Jacques Derrida. To the contrary, one of the most eminent of contemporary social philosophers, Jürgen Habermas (1987), has made great efforts to salvage the modern values of reason and progress. Yet he has done so by criticizing modern scien-tific reason as inadequate to solving the problems of social life in an emancipatory way, and he has proposed communication among people as a basis for a higher form of reason better suited to human needs. Lyotard emphatically rejected Habermas's proposal. However, the two scholars share some ground: both regard scientific ratio-nality as suspect, both think that the institutional arrangements under which technical knowledge is produced serve the interests of the powerful over other people, and both see nonauthoritarian, uncoerced communication as a potential antidote to the tendency of technology and technical knowledge to overwhelm other social values (J.R. Hall 1999, pp. 56–62).

If the postmodern challenge is ultimately to prevail as a break with the modern, it will only occur on the basis of a fundamental shift in the cultural structuring of social institutions centered on the legitimation of aesthetics and of knowledge. Earlier avant-garde movements did not effectively resist the institutional frameworks of the modern era by which legitimacy is ascribed to art and social critique. Those who seek to promote the advance of postmodern culture have learned that to succeed they need to challenge the very sources of cultural equations and institutional arrangements of the established social order. Thus, we should chart the present and future significance of postmodern change by looking for something other than simply shifts in the *content* of art and culture and intellectual debate. If postmod-ern*ism* as culture is really taking hold, we would expect to find: (1) changes in the *forms* of "art" and "culture" that obtain currency and legitimacy among various social strata; and (2) alterations of the institutions by which culture is produced, distributed, and incorporated into daily life. If these cultural changes are associated with broader social transformations, such that we could speak of a new era of post-modern*ity*, we would also expect: (3) changes in the cultural structures of wider social institutional arrangements – of family life, politics, business, and even war. How do contemporary changes measure up to such benchmarks?

Artists' reactions to the exhaustion of the modernist avant-garde make up only one strand among a diverse array of often contradictory "postmodern" developments in film, photography, music, fashion, and other cultural media. Much of what has been called postmodern since the 1960s doubtless will turn out to have been ephemeral, passing fads. What of it might be significant or enduring? From early on, architecture has been an important avenue of postmodernist culture, and it offers a useful example by which to explore this question.

Self-consciously postmodern architecture, beginning in the 1960s and the 1970s, reintroduced certain classical forms (Roman or Egyptian columns, for example), juxtaposing them with modernistic elements in a way that seemed to break with the sleek aesthetic coherence of modern architecture. By now, these postmodern design motifs have been copied so widely (in neoclassical shopping malls, for example) as to become clichés, and some of the most appealing examples of new public architecture – Frank Gehrey's stunning Guggenheim Museum in Bilbao, Spain, or Norman Foster's neoclassical Queen Elizabeth II Great Court at the British Museum in London – lack the supposed postmodern penchant for pastiche. Yet, for all the passing fads of post-modern architecture, there may also be some more fundamental change at work.

For modern architecture, Charles Jencks has suggested, the factory and the machine offered the dominant metaphors; thus there was Le Corbusier's famous "home as a machine for living in" (Jencks 1981, p. 31). By contrast, Jencks described postmodern architecture as the product of treating design as a matter of "language." But the language is not the result of experts defining a single, elitist vocabulary to be imposed upon the public. In place of monumental, abstract, and formal rationalism associated with modern architecture, postmodern architecture is, as it were, a *conversation* between materials, motifs, people, and places. This conversation is situated among many dialects, "quoting" many sources: the vernacular vocabulary of popular culture, diverse revivals of earlier design motifs, the contexts of buildings, and their uses. Modern architecture was to be judged on the basis of its ability to rationalize a single, coherent aesthetic. Postmodern architecture – with its divergent sources and imple-mentations – could hardly be evaluated by such a standard. In its place, Jencks proposed "plausibility" (1981, p. 8). Postmodern architecture could be deemed successful if its aesthetic elements – however diverse – make sense in space (and of space) for the people who inhabit it.

In Jencks's account, postmodernism does not depend on any specific *content*, at least in architecture. Instead, it establishes a new *relationship* between the designer, the designed world, and inhabitants of that world. As a consequence, postmodern architecture does not aim toward construction of a single, coherent, rationally ordered environment. It celebrates playfulness and even contradiction. These charac-teristics are not tied in any necessary way to how buildings look (even if the juxtaposition of elements in certain postmodern buildings is immediately recogniz-able). Instead, they derive from a more fundamental – if complex – shift in the relation of architecture to society.

Whether the overall movement of postmodernism will become an enduring world-historical development on a par with the birth of the modern era remains to be seen by future generations. But clearly it would amount to a coming-after modernism that places root cultural orderings into question: at stake is nothing less than a transforma-tion away from formal reason as universal, from positivist science as objective knowledge unsullied by values or material interest, from the rational and formal imperatives of hierarchical bureaucratic organization – in short, the whole cultural fabric of modern society. For all the difficulties of definition, the postmodern turn would involve a fundamental reordering of how we experience and act in the world. The very power and authority of formal, objective knowledge would be challenged by situated knowledge.

By Jencks's standard, much architecture that was labeled "postmodern" simply placed a new "look" on to ongoing social practices of building design. By Jencks's standard, much that superficially looks and feels postmodern may not be so. If we hold to the idea of the rise of the postmodern as a fundamental shift, then any claims for its triumph would be premature. Moreover, the short history of the still-young twenty-first century – centered on terrorism and economic malaise – might seem to take the cultural wind out of postmodern sails. Yet to declare the "death of the post-modern" seems like an act of hubris that ignores pervasive changes that cluster under the flag of postmodernity. As the historical sociologist Peter Wagner argues, "orga-nized modernity" has undergone a substantial crisis that draws into question "the intelligibility and the shapeability (or manageability) of the social world" (1994, p. 175). Call the changes postmodern or not, but economic activity has shifted away from mass to flexible production, and the activities of organizations are increasingly carried out by teams rather than by hierarchies. The supposedly coherent values of modernity have been challenged by pluralistic and multicultural developments. And the modern idea that the world as a whole was on a trajectory toward increased liberty and political freedom now is subject to considerable doubt. Indeed, the modern nation-state has been undermined – from within by the fraying of political communi-ties; from below by nationalist movements; and from above by the emergence of supernational governing organizations such as the European Union. In other words, not just the popular culture of modernity but its institutions have undergone basic transformations. With no foreseeable conclusion to the present conflicts between the West and Islamicist challengers, any strong return to the values that ordered modernity can no longer simply be assumed. And with the changes in cultural structures documented by Wagner (1994, ch. 9), any institutional reconstruction of modernity as it came to be defined during the twentieth century seems highly unlikely.

By the sobering early light of the twenty-first century, some observers regard affir-mations of the postmodern condition as often unwieldy and overstated, or even naive about the strong political and economic forces that shape our history. The fierceness of the debate can be gauged by the assertion of Edward Rothstein (*New York Times*, 9/22/2001) that the 9/11 attacks require a disavowal of postmodernist relativism and a reaffirmation of objective truth – a claim that in turn prompted the prominent intel-lectual Stanley Fish (2002) to argue that the opponents of postmodernism willfully misunderstand postmodern claims because they want a world where their own values and political agenda can be advanced uncontested. Ironically, the sobering develop-ment to which Rothstein referred – the globalized war on terrorism – itself may be understood in terms that have a strongly postmodern cast, as Der Derian (2001) demonstrates by arguing that military war, global surveillance, and mediated war have become infused in a historically new conglomeration, no longer "war" in any conven-tional modern sense.

Postmodern ideas often fly in the face of conventional modern understandings. However, we live now in a world framed by, not just intellectual talk about the post-modern, but also broadly postmodern shifts in the social itself. The sheer bulk of discourse on "the postmodern" ambiguously signifies (or signifies by its ambiguity) the postmodern turn, which cannot be defined in any objective, totalizing way. Because the postmodern turn involves a collapse of totalizing objectivity, proponents of the postmodern often make a badge of honor out of their refusal to define post-modernism: it cannot be defined, for to define it is to subordinate it to the logic of modernism, exactly what postmodernist thinkers want to avoid. Thus, to understand the postmodern requires adopting one or another postmodernist perspective, in which the search for a definition no longer seems necessary.

The postmodern turn as a textual turn?

Even if definitions might seem worthless to postmodernists, the absence of definition creates its own difficulties. Since no one need agree about the features of postmod-ernism, doubts arise about boundaries. Almost anything trendy could get the label, it would seem. Thus, no specific viewpoint can be taken as "representative" of postmod-ernism and it is difficult to discuss postmodernism in general. However, one dimension of postmodern thinking – the "textual" turn – offers a vivid contrast to modernist assumptions about social processes. Considering it thus helps to show the sociological issues at stake.

The textual turn, in its strongest version, asserts that the social *is* textual. Thus, as Richard Harvey Brown put it, "selves and societies are constructed and deconstructed through rhetorical practices" (1990, p. 191). This view has deep roots in social theory – in linguistic and cultural anthropology, in the studies by symbolic interactionists, in Erving Goffman's work, in the social constructionism of Peter Berger, in the ethnomethodology of Harold Garfinkle, and, more recently, in the work of Michel Foucault and Jacques Derrida. In these views, the world is not accessible to us in its "natural" state. Rather, we mediate our connections to the world symbolically. To take a classic example in anthropological linguistics, "snow" is not apprehended by anyone as an intrinsically natural phenomenon devoid of its cultural packaging; instead, we experience it in different ways according to the symbols we use to represent snow and the meanings we attach to them (white Christmas? Skiing weekend? Caring for sheep in a blizzard?). If this argument has at least some plausibility even for the "natural" world, it seems even more compelling for the social world, where we live our lives in terms of categories (such as marital status: single, married, lesbian partner, divorced, and more detailed nuances) that structure our own and other people's reciprocal social actions. Diverse strands of sociological thought – from Durkheim's symbolic structuralism to symbolic interactionism and Weberian interpretive sociology – acknowledge the centrality of symbols and meaning to social life. What, we must ask, is so distinctive about the textual turn of postmodernism?

The answer is that the textual turn is not new to sociology. Instead, two things happened. First, among social researchers in the 1970s and 1980s it became increasingly evident that cultural and macrostructural perspectives have much to offer each other, and that research excluding either dimension is incomplete. The currents within and interchanges among such perspectives are diverse, but it is not necessary to catalog them in order to recognize the rich understandings that can result. The classic study of the Balinese cockfight by Clifford Geertz is an icon of the possibility: Geertz did not simply assert that the lived activity of carrying out cockfights is a ritualized representation of Balinese social structure. Instead, he maintained that the cockfight

> provides a metasocial commentary upon the whole matter of assorting human beings into fixed hierarchical ranks and then organizing the major part of collective existence around that assortment.... It is a Balinese reading of Balinese experience, a story they tell themselves about themselves.
>
> (Geertz 1973, p. 448)

For Geertz, the Balinese cockfight story is acted out by members of society in formulaic ways that comment on the world even while the tellers are enmeshed within it. After Geertz, for social researchers story and society have increasingly become a hall with facing mirrors where it is difficult to tell which is which.

There is a second important change in the relation of textual analysis to sociological thought. Outside of the once neatly bounded social sciences, literary critics and other humanists for some time now have drawn on linguistics, psychoanalysis, and the more interpretive, hermeneutic, phenomenological, and interactionist strands of social theory to create something of a revolution in the humanities, by awakening critics to the recognition that there are other texts than those like Goethe's and Jane Austen's, studied in courses on the canons of classic literature. On this basis, literary critics sometimes have turned their gaze to popular novels – mysteries, spy novels, romances, science fiction – both for their merits as literature and to get closer to the "social texts" of popular life. Thus, the line between "high" culture and "popular" culture tends to be erased by postmodernists (Jameson 1991, ch. 1).

With these broadening definitions of texts, it is only a small step toward what Richard Harvey Brown (1990) advocated – treating the social world itself as a text to be "read" rather than an objective reality to be apprehended. Such a move blurs (even erases) the difference between fiction and reality (between entertainment and news, for example), and symbolic interactionists within sociology typically avoided taking this move, for they had long struggled to establish their legitimacy in a field in which "idealism" was scorned. Literary critics, by contrast, suffered from no such censure: treating the world as a text actually *enhanced* their authority (R. Collins 1989, p. 131).

Ironically, then, the textual turn has significant precursors in various strands of social theory, yet the particular kinds of social theory that served as inspiration – interpretive sociology, phenomenology, symbolic interactionism, ethnomethodology – typically were treated as marginal to the social sciences in their modern phase, creating an odd contemporary spectacle: literary theorists have adopted (sometimes ersatz) sociological perspectives and techniques of analysis, and they have met with great success by doing so, while those same perspectives and techniques sometimes have been (and continue to be) resisted by "mainstream" sociologists!

In short, when the textual turn is brought full circle, *back* into sociohistorical inquiry, the implications are substantial and controversial. In one aspect, the literary shift is concerned with rhetorical critique and Jacques Derrida's technique of "deconstruction" – which inspects texts to show how they create a particular sense of reality, even in the absence of the capacity of any text to represent or correspond to reality. In the modernist scheme of things, literary critical tools were applied almost exclusively to fiction, but now they have been brought to bear on broader discourses that reveal the imaginative efforts required to construct nonfiction narratives and stories – about news, politics, gender, race, and within academic disciplines such as history, anthropology, sociology, economics, and even the physical and biological sciences. Taken to its logical conclusion, the textual turn suggests that all knowledge is metaphoric, offering images by which we understand the world. Those images no longer are deemed to be securely grounded in reality. Rather, they "float," without any direct and unambiguous relation to the world they are intended to describe.

A view that regards all discourse as inflected with imagination and metaphor is particularly devastating for objectivist sociological theories such as structuralist Marxism, structural functionalism, rational-choice theory, and structuralist theories of social organization, for they are supposed to use analytic concepts to get at "real" social processes that are invisible to everyday appearance (cf. Bogard 1990, and the symposium in *Sociological Theory* 9 [2], 1991). As Dick Hebdige framed the problem:

> It is no longer possible for us to see through the appearance of, for instance, a "free market" to the structuring "real relations" beneath (e.g., class conflict and the expropriation by capital of surplus value). Instead, signs begin increasingly to take on a life of their own referring not to a real world outside themselves but to their own "reality" – the system that produces the signs.
>
> (Hebdige, quoted in C. Norris 1990, p. 141)

If even formal knowledge is based on metaphor, other less formal public discourse and everyday knowledge would bear similar fates. The world as directly accessible becomes obscured behind imagery.

The textual turn, as we have described it so far, really is a philosophical argument. It is not so much an argument about reality; it is an argument that critiques the modernist assumptions about how (or indeed whether) we know about reality. If the philosophical argument is given credence, then what symbolic interactionists and other sociologists have been saying for decades has merit: well before postmodernism, modern societies and indeed societies in general were centrally structured by symbolic constructions of reality, even though objectivist sociologists resisted this analysis.

However, there is an even stronger claim based in the textual turn. The rise of post-modern society, it is argued, amounts to nothing less than a shift in the nature of social reality. At first glance, this argument seems self-contradictory on two counts. First, if the basic thesis about discourse is correct, societies always have been discursively constructed. Second, it seems odd to insist that texts are nonrepresentational and then use texts to talk about "real" changes (even real changes in the arrangements of texts). Despite these seeming contradictions, some postmodernists want to say that the world/texts now are organized in new ways.

In part, discursive arguments about an emergent postmodern form of society mirror sociological analyses developed independently of the textual turn. Thus, Herb Gans (1974) disputed the special character of "high" culture on the basis of both content and form: he could not help but note a long history of borrowing by high culture from popular culture, for example with the use of popular tunes in "serious" music. Moreover, Gans noted, much elite culture now depends upon popular-culture mechanisms of mass production and distribution – the recording industry, television, film, the internet.

Other sociologists also pointed to what we now call postmodernization, but without taking a textual turn. Daniel Bell, for example, argued in *The Cultural Contradictions of Capitalism* (1976) that the spheres of work and leisure were becoming disconnected from one another, such that people have become something like Jekyll-and-Hyde figures playing contradictory roles while they are at work versus when they play. Sociologists have also shown that with the rise of a service economy, culture has been recreated as work. Thus, Arlie Russell Hochschild (1983) described how service workers – airline flight attendants – have been subjected to "the commercialization of human feeling" in their jobs. In the opposite venue, Ann Swidler (1980, p. 135) observed that personal emotional relationships now require "work," and Barry Glassner (1990) has pointed to how people use leisure-time in a highly disciplined pursuit of "fitness" through exercise and diet. In an ironic and quintessentially postmodern way, the pursuit of selfhood becomes work – the therapeutic meeting by people sharing a common personal problem, the organized yoga classes of individuals seeking personal fulfillment, the visit to the health club for regimented exercise and socializing – all carefully distanced from any hint of productive labor such as mowing the lawn. In short, sociological studies of work and leisure suggest a notable shift in cultural practices since the high-water mark of modernism in the 1950s. But what makes the cultural changes specifically postmodern?

Architecture again provides a clue. In 1968 a group from the Yale Architecture School conducted a studio exercise called "learning from Las Vegas." They wondered whether studying the American commercial strip could teach architects something about new architectural forms that were emerging next to the strip highways, expressways, and interstate highway system. Their field trip to Las Vegas revealed that commercial architecture of the strip was redefining the relationship of building forms to space and to signs. In the nineteenth century, the sign had simply *identified* the building – a hotel, a store, or an office. To be sure, building style communicated something about its use and status. But in the early twentieth century, small-scale entrepreneurs began to experiment in radical ways with vernacular commercial buildings. Sometimes they made the shape itself represent a building's function. Thus, in the 1930s some coffee shops were built to look like coffee pots (see Figure 7.1), and there were hotdog stands in the shape of hotdogs, gasoline stations that loomed up as giant gasoline pumps, and so on. In Las Vegas, the Yale architects noted a related development: the signs in front of buildings were overwhelming the buildings, to the point where the buildings themselves were becoming caricatures of their signs. Ultimately, buildings became enclosed signs, decorated on the interior as continuations of the signs. The visitor to a Las Vegas gambling casino enters a fantasy experience theme park like "Caesar's Palace," goes on a "safari" into Saharan Africa, or enters a scaled-down Venice or Paris. Overall, an inversion had occurred – "the victory of symbols-in-space over forms-in-space" (Venturi *et al.* 1977, p. 119; for a sociological discussion, see Larson 1993, pp. 53–61). The architectural critics thus trace a fundamental shift: as new suburbs, malls, and vacation meccas continue to rise up around us, we live no longer in space. We wend our way through symbols.

Figure 7.1 The building-as-icon of the 1930s established an important precedent for subsequent strip- and consumer-oriented building development; New Bedford, Pennsylvania, photograph by Esther Bubley.

Source: Library of Congress, Prints & Photographs Division, FSA–OWI Collection.

The French social critic Jean Baudrillard has championed this view more generally, by consolidating an argument made by Daniel Boorstin, that the relation of images to reality has undergone a series of transformations. Images once might have more or less accurately reflected reality. Even if they did not, people drew a strong distinction between reality and fantasy, for example when going to a play or movie. However, as Daniel Boorstin argued in his book *The Image, or What Happened to the American Dream?*, the rise of public relations early in the twentieth century amounted to a self-conscious exercise in the manipulation of images that foreshadowed a more pervasive change. "A new kind of synthetic novelty," he announced, "has flooded our experience" (Boorstin 1962, p. 9). For example, Boorstin suggested, authentic heroes are more and more difficult to find in the midst of celebrities "well known for their well-known-ness." Today, we have the likes of Anna Kournikova – the Russian tennis player, who, despite never winning a major tournament and posting an unimpressive overall record, still earns between $10 and $15 million a year through endorsements and modeling. Already by the 1960s such developments had proceeded to the point where, as Boorstin put it,

> everybody's reliance on dealers in pseudo-events and images cannot – contrary to highbrow clichés – accurately be described as a growing superficiality. Rather these things express a world where the image, more interesting than its original, has itself become the original.
>
> (Boorstin 1962, p. 204)

Today, Boorstin would have to recognize that during the 9/11 attacks a number of people on one of the airplanes acted heroically, causing the plane to crash rather than letting it reach its target. But he might point out that because these real heroes tragically died in the attacks they have been spared the relentless media attention that tends to turn even heroes into celebrities.

For Jean Baudrillard, there are two ways to think about what Boorstin calls pseudo-events: it may be that an image "masks and perverts a basic reality," or, more radically, that it "masks the *absence* of a basic reality." Even in the latter case, the assumption of an existing reality can be maintained by efforts to simulate a reality that doesn't exist, as in the case of advertising that depicts a utopian world: we would be hard put to find such a world in reality, but nevertheless can imagine it as real. But for Baudrillard there is a stronger version of the second possibility, in which the image "bears no relation to any reality whatever: it is its own pure simulacrum" (1988b, p. 170). "Simulation," Baudrillard tells us, "is no longer that of a territory, a referential being or a substance. It is the generation of models of a real without origin or reality: a hyperreal" (1988b, p. 166). For both Boorstin and Baudrillard, the everyday world of our lives has become overshadowed by images that give the appearance of reality, but without having to have any necessary correspondence to the world beyond their realms.

These ideas can be given concrete form through the example of tourism (Boorstin 1962). Perhaps it is still possible to travel without being a tourist. But tourism has grown to the point where it often overshadows travel. It is now an enormous industry. Certain places – the Caribbean, Hawaii, and so on – are essentially "tourist destinations." Organizers of tourism thus work to create images depicting the tourist destinations on websites and posters in order to pique tourists' interest in an experience of novelty that does not require great personal risk. Yet the world is a risky place, and the effective marketing of such images requires a reorganization of the tourist destination experience itself as a pseudo-event. The tourist has to be able to return from a trip and proclaim satisfaction that everything was as the website portrayed it. In the ongoing real world, however, this is not always easy to achieve. Kenya, for instance, is a great tourist destination, but if tourists look behind the facade of the tour they may see social and political conditions at least unsettling to the idea of "vacation." Vacationing can be something like visiting a Potemkin village, a socially constructed corridor to be experienced as the real world which nevertheless masks the real world.

In the tourist industry, the danger of offensive reality intruding can be controlled by an altogether different solution: rather than establishing a tourist destination within a real place like Kenya or New York City, it is possible to create tourist destinations that are, to use Baudrillard's term, simulacra. Thus, Disney World and Las Vegas are not real worlds prior to tourism; they are places where the controlling reality is the reality of tourism (cf. Zukin 1991, ch. 8). But for Baudrillard Disneyworld – tremendous achievement of controlled imagery that it is – only begins to unveil the possibilities. Disneyworld has boundaries: we know when we are going to visit it. But what if the world at large has become a Disneyworld, a simulacrum? For Baudrillard, this is the current condition: "It is not the least of America's charms that even outside the movie theaters the whole country is cinematic. The desert you pass through is like the set of a Western, the city a screen of signs and formulas." To unravel the mysteries of the city, he adds, "you should not, then, begin with the city and move inwards to the screen; you should begin with the screen and move outwards to the city" (Baudrillard 1988a, p. 56).

The possibilities of a postmodernized world are difficult for us to absorb as individuals, for we are quite capable of entering into new realms of symbolically constructed realities, at one and the same time recognizing their "constructed" character yet nevertheless "naturalizing" our relationship to them as ordinary. Thus, the worldwide web establishes new conventional ways by which people interact with one another, yet people quickly become adept at negotiating its reality. Images become the world, yet their connections to one another operate according to different logics than those of social interaction in the face-to-face world. Few people, if anyone, mistakenly think that the web "represents" the "real" world. Something much more radical has occurred: it no longer matters whether the medium and content of the internet can be claimed to represent the real world. The simulacrum is a real world.

Yet it would be a mistake to think that only a separate reality such as the internet can be a simulacrum. Consider the fusion of "entertainment" and "shopping" in relation to "tourism." Increasingly, tourist destinations are providing elaborate shopping environments, and shopping is becoming much more than simply the act of acquiring the necessities of life and objects of desire. Instead, in tourist destinations the act of shopping is itself a form of leisure entertainment. Similarly, many "ordinary" shopping malls have restyled themselves as what might be considered local tourist destinations, complete with restaurants, coffee shops, multiplex movie theaters, and of course stores owned by companies like Disney that sell children (or their parents) items derived from movies, cartoons, and theme parks (Hannigan 1998, ch. 5; Gottdiener 2001).

And what of the purchases themselves? In one approach to shopping, the objects become overwhelmed by their significations. Take the images of the past that Ralph

Lauren offers through its home-furnishings line – "from Scottish manor houses to African safaris, from Caribbean beach houses to clapboard cottages" (*New York Times*, 2/2/1992). These images are simulacra in which we can immerse ourselves, detached from the present moment of history by their nostalgia, even as they detach themselves from the unevenness of the real world of the past by their utopian perfection. At a personal level, the implication thus is as disconcerting as the cultural claim: surrounded by consumer choices that create personal simulacra, in Baudrillard's vision individual people too must be simulacra – simulations of images of personhood that construct identities possessing an illusory sense of reality.

Carried to its logical conclusion, the simulacranetic analysis would hold even for the events of public life. Of course there are still real events, as was demonstrated on a world-historical scale by the 9/11 destruction of the World Trade Center's twin towers. An enormous number of people were directly and tragically affected by the attack. Yet, even for such a dramatic and all-too-real event, the old relationship between reality and image threatens to become inverted: events of historical significance can be swallowed up by the simulacra that present them to us. Indeed, in the initial weeks after the attack television clips of the collapse of the towers were shown repeatedly. However, soon thereafter airing of such images was reduced dramatically (in contrast to other video clips shown repeatedly, for example of then President Bill Clinton shown meeting Monica Lewinski on the rope line). For once, reality was already too daunting without media hype. Yet media executives' decisions to stop airing video clips of the World Trade Center buildings collapsing affirm the importance of the simulacrum, for they demonstrate an emergent collective understanding about the power of mediated reality to envelop the public.

In the strong Baudrillardian account of postmodernization, behind the surface image lies, not some reality that it represents, but only the backstage. Most everyone knows that images are produced by backstage work, but this knowledge no longer discounts the image, and so the image is what counts. Yet, because the image is not discredited by exposure of its construction, it no longer represents or obscures reality; the image *is* "reality." Whether or not any of us is willing to follow Baudrillard through this looking-glass, one thing has become increasingly evident: many people have by now become quite sophisticated about the constructed nature of frontstage realities. However, even this sophistication, when it occurs, does not allow people to reach past the simulacrum to some ultimate unmediated reality. We have undergone a dramatic shift to the point where reality and media images (some representational, others not) are tied together in a tangled web of often blurred relationships that create a new "reality," what Bruno Latour (1993) called, in a different context, a "hybrid," neither one thing nor the other.

The upshot of Baudrillard's analysis is to suggest that a dramatic cultural shift has taken place. On his view, we can no longer understand the world by using the modern tools of analytic knowledge. And the world we would understand no longer works as it once did. Such claims are striking. Paradoxically, however, they evoke the idea of a totalistic change, and the plausibility of this idea depends upon an essentialist view of the world – the very viewpoint that postmodernists criticize when they find it in modernist theories. Only if the social world has a prime cause, one or another basic animating force, can a change in one realm totally reshape the world in general. Some versions of postmodernism do indeed shift the prime mover, from economics to media and symbols. Yet a more relativistic postmodern view would dismiss any such essentialist and holistic theory. Whatever the outcome of these theoretical debates, it is important to consider the empirical issue of whether – and how – postmodernism as a cultural movement might be tied to a broader social transformation toward postmodernity.

Postmodernity: is everything different now?

A theory of contemporary society proposed in the 1970s suggested that changes in the economies of so-called "developed" or "advanced" nation-states represented the emergence of a "postindustrial" order based on production of services and knowledge at the expense of manufacturing – changes strongly driven by dramatic and self-reinforcing innovations in technology, especially computers (D. Bell 1973; Touraine 1981). The working class was declining in the industrialized countries, the argument went, and a "new middle class," living in the suburbs, was taking form on the basis of expanded service occupations in social welfare, financial services, travel and tourism, computer software, restaurants, and a host of other nonindustrial (at least not heavy-industry) sectors of the economy. Although the details and significance of these changes have been hotly debated, by now there can be little doubt that a fundamental and long-term shift occurred. As Nigel Thrift (1999) points out, capitalism itself has taken the "cultural turn," not only in the turn to marketing entertainment and lifestyles, but also in the emphasis within the workplace on New-Age ideas about personal growth and fulfillment. Because of the radical nature of the postindustrial transformation, understanding its contours requires careful consideration.

One way that the transformation can be charted is by examining change in occupational structures of advanced societies: in the U.S., for example, already by 1970 compared to 1940 agricultural employment declined from 17.4 percent of the labor force to a mere 3.1 percent of the labor force, while employment of manual workers slightly decreased – from 39.8 to 36.6 percent. By contrast, in the same time period there were solid increases in middle-class jobs, many of them in relatively new occupations. For example, professionals went from 7.5 percent to 14.5 percent of the labor force, and clerical workers rose from 9.6 percent to 17.8 percent. These basic trends have continued more recently. Thus, the U.S. Census Bureau reports that for the period 1983–94 the greatest occupational declines in numbers of workers occurred in mining (−4.1 percent), tobacco manufactures (−4.2 percent), and leather and leather products (−5.2 percent), while greatest growth took place in health services (10.6 percent) and personal supply services (12.5 percent). Projecting to the year 2005, the Bureau predicted the greatest job growth in health services (5.7 percent), computer and data-processing services (4.9 percent), and business services (4.4 percent) (U.S. Census Bureau 1975, series D182–232; 1983, Table 89; 1996, Table 642). Along with Japan and countries in Europe, the United States is no longer simply an industrial nation-state; its economy increasingly is based on middle-class, non-manual, and service work.

As striking as the statistics are, they are only indicators of a much more pervasive shift. The old styles of hierarchical corporate organization and mass production are giving way to organizational forms where authority is de-emphasized in favor of teamwork and production is organized in "post-Fordist" ways that de-emphasize factory production lines and mass production and consumption in favor of "flexible specialization" and "just-in-time" production. In turn, these changes are tied to increasing product differentiation oriented to ever narrower consumer niches (think of the diversity of car, sport-utility-vehicle, and hybrid automotive choices). These developments are made possible by ever closer business monitoring of consumer choices, for example by tracking inventories and sales through product barcodes and credit-card purchase data. Overall, the changes are substantial enough that not just cultural analysts are charting the emergence of postmodern society. Though the terminology used to describe the changes is diverse, a wide variety of observers would agree with historical sociologist Peter Wagner that there has been a "breakup of the order of organized modernity" (1994, p. 123).

Yet there are complications to any theory about postindustrial society relevant to postmodernization as a social transformation. These can be considered by exploring the relation of postmodernity to modernity and to processes of globalization.

Persistences of the old regimens: modernity and industrialism

For all the undoubted significance of the changes since the 1960s, a sociological perspective necessarily suggests that no social change is total. The effects of even quite dramatic changes tend to be uneven and incomplete. How fundamental a change, then, is the rise of postindustrial society? The work of two sociologists shows that we should at least recognize important continuities between the industrial and the postindustrial. Krishnan Kumar (1978) made an early and direct assault on postindustrial theory. He argued that a close examination of claims about postindustrial society showed changes, yes, but changes that were of the same character as the changes in industrial society. For Kumar,

> Beneath the postindustrial gloss, old, scarred problems rear their heads: alienation and control in the workplaces of the service economy; scrutiny and supervision of the operations of private and public bureaucracies, especially as they come to be meshed in with technical and scientific expertise. Framing all these is the problem of the dominant constraining and shaping force of contemporary industrial societies: competitive struggles for profit and power between private corporations and between nation states, in an environment in which such rivalries have a tendency to become expansionist and global.
>
> (K. Kumar 1978, pp. 230–1)

Kumar's probing commentary builds upon a wide sociological literature tracing back to the works of Weber and Durkheim, which describe the processes of functional differentiation and specialization (see also Luhmann 1982; J. Alexander and Colomy 1990). And developments since Kumar put forward his analysis, if anything, confirm it. Indeed, when Kumar (1995) revisited these issues at the end of the twentieth century, he depicted the collapse of communism in 1989 as a harkening back to a specifically modern agenda of building democracy in the world. Although Kumar did not dismiss theories about the information society, post-Fordist organization of society, and the advent of postmodernity, he again affirmed continuities amidst change.

An analysis by Peter Berger, Brigette Berger, and Hansfried Kellner – *The Homeless Mind* (1973), written even before Kumar's earlier book – mounts a challenge similar to Kumar's, but one more directly concerned with culture, specifically the culture of modernization. Of course the term "modernization" has long been controversial because it is often treated as carrying the ideological freight of "progress" as a social value and narrative of modern history. To avoid this meaning, Berger *et al.* made no judgment about progress; they defined modernization simply as "the *institutional* concomitants of technologically induced economic growth" (1973, p. 9). Most telling, Berger and his colleagues noted the cultural consequences of two long-term secular trends of modernization – the rise of technologically based production and the ever advancing bureaucratization of organized activity. These trends have had specific implications for the character of people's consciousness: our very ways of experiencing the world, they argued, are mediated by technology and bureaucracy.

Two points are important here. First, the trends that Peter Berger *et al.* describe under the rubric of modernization continue to operate today, in the supposedly postindustrial and postmodern situation. If anything, the implications of technology for consciousness have spilled over outside of production. Now many people interact with technology in everyday life in quite intimate ways – by use of ever more complex and specialized devices such as computers, cell phones, and personal data assistants. Similarly, bureaucracy not only mediates our consciousness in the workplace; increasingly, it orders our experiences of leisure, through the bureaucratized service economy's penetration of everyday life in tourism, entertainment, market research, recreation, and the like. Indeed, the revolution in computer data processing, coupled with the emergence of business and government sites on the worldwide web, has produced a situation in which people deal with bureaucracies seamlessly, on a daily basis, often without giving it a second thought. If anything, bureaucracy has become pervasive because it has become articulated through computer technology. Thus, the social forces of modernization continue to structure social life under postmodernization through the deployment of newly available technologies.

Second, long before the debate about postmodernism heated up, Berger and his colleagues identified certain cultural consequences of modernity that more recently have been proclaimed as signifiers of postmodernity. Modern identity, they argued, does not depend on a coherent self, but on the playing of roles in situations segmented from one another. Under these circumstances, an attempt to define the ultimate meaning of one's life would require the establishment of a "home world." But this enterprise is both "hazardous and precarious." Already in modern times, identity depends on an open-ended project of self-definition in a pluralistic set of overlapping and interpenetrating worlds. People respond to these unsettling circumstances, the Bergers and Kellner suspected, by personally taking on technological and bureaucratic sensibilities and becoming career counselors for their own lives, in both occupational and leisure aspects. "The family unit thus operates as a life planning workshop" (P.L. Berger *et al.* 1973, p. 72).

The Homeless Mind may overstate the roles of technology and bureaucracy in accounting for innovation and eclecticism in popular culture. Moreover, the book's argument did not anticipate how the boundaries between once segmented arenas (such as the public and private) would blur when "meanings" or symbols became increasingly freefloating in relation to "things." But their analysis establishes a framework in which such "postmodern" changes may be understood. The very features often associated with postmodernism – the quality of pastiche, the juxtaposition of cultural elements that lack coherence, the disjuncture between culture and any moorings in concrete situations – these are all features that *The Homeless Mind* identifies as characteristic consequences of modernization, not postmodernization.

The view of Krishnan Kumar and the Bergers and Kellner – that postmodernity cannot be viewed simply as a total and qualitative shift in the cultural patternings of contemporary societies – is neatly captured in an observation by Steven Best and Douglas Kellner: "Frequently, what is identified as a postmodern development can be seen to be a prototypical modern trait" (1991, p. 278). Our discussions in the previous three chapters reinforce this point about continuities: changes in how culture is produced do not necessarily change the content of culture or the processes of its reception and use by people. Conversely, changes in content of culture do not necessarily reorder the world so drastically that the old processes are no longer significant. As we argued in Chapter 5, the emergence of new technologies of distribution – television and film – did not destroy the basic dramatic devices by which audiences have become cathartically engaged in drama since well before industrialization. By the opposite token, the spread of postmodern sensibilities and culture does not happen by magic: as we will detail in Chapters 8 and 9, culture is produced under particular political and economic conditions, through collective activities that are socially organized.

Globalization and the postmodern condition

For the most part, theorists of postindustrial society focused their attention on the developments they saw emerging in the most technologically developed societies at the core of the capitalist world economy. However, as researchers who study the world economy point out, the changes in capitalist core societies cannot be separated from changes elsewhere in the world. Thus, postindustrialization involves a global redistribution of economic activity in which many industrial and manufacturing activities are being relocated to poorer countries, where wages and other costs are lower and environmental regulations may be less strict. Moreover, the changes associated with the postindustrial information society are hardly confined to capitalist core countries. Postindustrialization, then, is part of a wider development that has been described by the term "globalization."

If globalization is defined broadly as the development of ever more closely knit connections between peoples and regions around the world, it must be recognized as a process that has been going on for millennia, and intensively since the so-called voyages of discovery beginning in the fifteenth century. Yet the contemporary interest focuses on the period since the global economic crisis of the late 1970s, after which economic elites of the economically most powerful nation-states adopted a "neo-liberal" economic policy, increasingly pushing for an internationalization of economic production based on the reduction of trade barriers between countries (cf. Wagner 1994, p. 126). The economic, social, and cultural changes associated with globalization are complex, and they are the subject of widespread discussion (Sassen 1998; Hardt and Negri 2000; Cooper 2001; P.L. Berger and Huntington 2002; Kellner 2002). But the broad outlines are evident.

Clearly, a global network of capitalist production has emerged, with significant consequences for the nature of work – and who does the work – both in advanced and less developed countries. In addition, the nation-state – the basic building block of the modern international order – has been challenged: (1) from above, by the emergence of supranational regulatory organizations such as the European Union and the World Bank (van Ham 2001), and (2), from below by the challenges of nationalist social movements, such as that in Quebec, and the devolution of political authority, for example in Scotland (Elazar 1998). Workers – ranging from the highly skilled to completely unskilled – have increasingly engaged in transnational migration to pursue employment or business enterprise, resulting in a globalization of the population within nation-states around the world (Kyle 2000). And the global movements of capital, production, and people have been coupled with increasing global flows of culture, both through the globalization of media and globalized marketing of products (see Figure 7.2) (Mahoney 1989; A. Smith 1991).

Thus, the postmodern cultural tableau is a globalized one. Nigerian pop music groups are achieving distribution and popularity in the U.S., and Arabs are watching television "Westerns" produced in Italy. American jazz musicians performing in Switzerland are inviting African drummers to sit in on their sessions. Japanese teenagers adopt American Hip-Hop fashion styles. In the news business, according to some observers, the information network is becoming consolidated into a world information order dominated by multinational corporations and the most powerful nation-states (R.L. Stevenson and Shaw 1984).

Figure 7.2 Globalization has blurred the cultural horizons of even indigenous peoples. In this highland Peru market, a *mestiza* (mixed heritage) woman sells synthetically dyed wool yarn amidst tennis shoes and other goods shipped from around the world, while an indigenous woman carries her child in a traditional sling.

Source: J.R. Hall photograph, 1982.

Yet discussions of globalization, like any social trend, tend to get carried away with pointing to all the changes rather than noting all the things that have not changed very much. Nation-states remain fundamental units of governance, hardly swept away by the emergence of global and subglobal governing entities. Many people manage to live their lives without cell phones or personal data assistants, and a breakfast in rural Ireland remains quite Irish. Globalization is not a relentless and uniform process with cultural consequences all of one piece. Instead, there are a variety of developments, driven by quite different interests, shaped by diverse processes, and with different consequences in various societies and regions of the world.

Peter Berger (2002) has usefully begun to disentangle the "many" globalizations. When he started to study the phenomenon, he thought that globalization would amount to something initiated in the West, especially the U.S. This globalization could be described in positive terms as the spread of "an international civil society, conducive to a new era of peace and democratization," or it could be regarded more perniciously as "the threat of an American economic and political hegemony, with its cultural consequences being a homogenized world resembling a sort of metastasized Disneyland" (2002, p. 2). In either event, the question of interest would be how societies in various parts of the world respond to a global diffusion of culture, either accepting it, trying to wall it off, or creatively adopting and adapting it.

However, Berger ended up finding a much more complicated situation. Without doubt, an international business and governmental elite promotes global coordination of economic and political development. And another elite sector based in the West – the intelligentsia – has created a web of scholarly and critical exchanges that shapes academic and political agendas around the world. Business globalization promotes the diffusion of corporate-produced popular culture that establishes McDonald's restaurants in India and a Disney park outside Paris (partly financed by Arab investors!). Unevenly associated with the governmental elite and intelligentsia, global social movements also have emerged, to address human rights, AIDS, and a variety of other issues (see Chapter 11). Less widely noted, but equally important, Berger insists, evangelical Protestant Christian missionaries have made converts in a number of regions around the world – from Latin America to Africa to East Asia, and in the bargain they have spread a culture of individualism among hundreds of millions of people.

All of these are vectors of globalization that have their origins in the West, especially the U.S. However, they do not simply envelop the world, and they are not the only globalizing tendencies. In the first place, contributors to Berger and Huntington's edited book (2002) and other observers (see Skelton and Allen 1999) have shown that globalizing culture is received in various societies around the world in radically different ways. Some states, like North Korea and that of the Taliban when it ruled Afghanistan, make every effort to shut out alien cultural influences. And, even where Western cultural objects and practices are adopted, they can blend with local culture in what Berger calls "localization." Thus, McDonald's has had to adapt its menu to India, and, even at that, Indians seem to prefer Indian food over the McDonald's menu, vegetarian options notwithstanding. This is not a matter of localization but of "hybridization." The fast-food format has taken hold in India, but Western corporations are not its most successful purveyors. In four years, McDonald's had sold a paltry 7 million hamburgers, whereas Indians consume 7 million *dosas* on a daily basis (Srinivas 2002, pp. 94–7). Similarly, despite concerns about the global reach of

Hollywood, India has its own thriving popular commercial film industry, dubbed "Bollywood," and Indian-produced films do not simply imitate Western genres. Rather, they are strongly centered in the diverse cultures and issues of Indian society (Tyrell 1999). Indeed, hybridization is not only driven by Western diffusion; it also moves in the opposite direction. For example, the rise of New-Age culture in the West can be traced to creative reinterpretations of Hindu, Buddhist, indigenous American, and other non-Western traditions that have been going on for more than a century (P.L. Berger 2002, p. 14). Similarly, in recent decades in the West, music from non-Western cultures has become subsumed under the general label of "world music." Such music ranges from ethnomusicologists' recordings of relatively authentic indigenous music to music that has taken on the Western format of popular culture, to groups that draw on diverse influences to create synthetic world music (in a way that parallels "California" fusion cuisine).

When hybridization emanating from outside the West is sufficiently coherent and vigorous as a cultural movement, Berger points to "alternative globalizations," sometimes based on alternative conceptions of modernity (2002, pp. 12–13). For example, Islam encompasses diverse cultural movements. The Taliban and warlords in Afghanistan and al-Qaeda's wider Islamicist movement, along with the Islamic regime in Iran, are all anti-modern in their own ways. Yet some states – for example in Indonesia, Egypt, and Morocco – have sought to develop modern political and economic institutions while maintaining Islam at the center of cultural life. How can the latter approach be understood in relation to modernity? In Peter Wagner's (1994) view, a narrow definition of modernity would center its ideals in democracy, equality, and individual liberty, coupled with the creation of structures of state, educational, and other regulatory institutions appropriate to society based on such principles. However, Wagner argues that no society has ever fully realized the ideals of modernity; any actual society was always incompletely modern. In this light, perhaps all modernities should be regarded as "alternatives," each with its particular mix of contradictions between modern ideals and actual social organization. In this light, we can imagine competing civilizational efforts to dominate globalization, notably from the West, Islam, and China.

Writing before 9/11, Peter Berger doubted any imperialistic account of globalization mimicking ancient Rome. He argued that the U.S. did not really have the power to impose culture globally. Against the imperialistic model, he proposed an alternative model of ancient Greece, a civilization that was widely influential because of the predominance of its language. Further, Berger distinguished between "sacramental" and "non-sacramental" cultural consumption. Sometimes, the adoption of a Western practice (eating that McDonald's burger, for example) amounts to an embrace of Western culture in a deeply meaningful – thus sacred – way. But much consumption of Western culture, Berger argues, is routine. Sometimes a burger is just a burger. By these arguments, Berger tends to treat the global spread of Western culture as less pernicious than it seems to those who lament the "Disney-fication" of the world.

Berger is certainly right to point to the complex and contradictory forces of globalization. If anything, in the wake of 9/11 the contradictions intensified: first, because the U.S. became much more engaged in international affairs militarily; second, because outside the U.S. the inevitability of its domination of international politics in the long run was opened to question; and, third, because heightened international tensions make global cultural interchange more problematic. After September 11,

2001, the scope and character of globalization – and whose globalization – are even more open questions than they were before.

Conclusion

In this chapter we have made a distinction between postmodern*ism* as a cultural movement and postmodern*ity* as a broader social transformation. For a time, the cultural movement outran itself, such that postmodern*ism* became passé. More recently, T.J. Clark (2002), the art historian of modernism, has wanted to ask new questions about postmodernism. Clark asserts that the critical role of modern*ism* as a cultural movement in relation to modernity is finished, because modernity is finished, swallowed up by the emergent information culture symbolized – and made visual – by the worldwide web. Whether or not, in Clark's sense, the word postmodern*ism* is retained to describe critical cultural engagement with the conditions and ideologies of the contemporary era, in our view postmodern*ity* encompasses a set of transformations – both cultural and social – that are profound and irreversible. Just as Clark proclaimed the end of aesthetic modernism, the era of what Wagner (1994) calls "organized modernity" is also over, in the specific sense that computers and communication technologies, along with social organization of their use, have transformed the world in an irreversible way. Just as people of the twentieth century could not roll back history to the era of the horse and buggy, people of the twenty-first century cannot easily contemplate a world where large organizations do not carry on their activities and relations to the world by way of computers.

However, we should be suspicious of any "essentialist" argument that the advent of the postmodern transforms everything. Such an argument, decidedly idealist, can only be advanced by averting one's gaze from the concrete, sensuous activities of people at work, attempting to control the production and "spin" of culture. Postmodernist and globalizing developments themselves extend certain features of modernization – bureaucratic and technological rationalization, pluralism, and so forth – into new domains and configurations. Therefore, it is best not to see either postmodernity or globalization as a fundamental shift and passage beyond modernity. Rather, the insight of Jean-François Lyotard (1984) cited above is reaffirmed: the postmodern should be understood as a "moment" of modernity. Similarly, Peter Berger's account "suggests that globalization is, *au fond*, a continuation, albeit in an intensified and accelerated form, of the perduring challenge of modernization" (2002, p. 16).

In short, theories of totalistic social change are almost always wrong. Thus, this chapter has sketched the continuities as well as the changes involved in the advent of postindustrial postmodernity and the globalization that has accompanied it. To be sure, the power of culture may be altered by postmodernism, and the production and distribution of culture may take new forms. But these points simply reinforce the argument: the "textual turn" does not happen in a semiotic vacuum somehow detached from the material and social circumstances of its production. The significance of the postmodern turn relative to modernity thus can only be assessed by looking closely at the social organization of culture in the contemporary era – the power relations involved in culture, the social activities by which it is produced, how audiences make meaning in relation to culture, and what the significance of culture is in everyday life and developments of social change. It is to these questions that we turn in the following four chapters.

Suggested readings

What might postmodernity mean (and not mean) on the ground? In *Inside Subculture: The Postmodern Meaning of Style*, David Muggleton (2000) interviews youths using a neo-Weberian methodology to explore whether once-identifiable subcultures such as punk have imploded with the emergence of postmodern irony. His study is a paragon of the potential for sociologically informed cultural studies.

To explore the meanings of postmodernity outside Europe and North America, one can read Beatriz Sarlo's *Scenes from Postmodern Life* (2001), in which she uses close social observation and critical observations of culture to reflect on television, video games, the arts, film, and other topics in Latin America.

Cultural studies, as a transdisciplinary enterprise, has been the subject of considerable development and debate. One book, *Understanding Culture*, by Gavin Kendall and Gary Wickham (2001), sketches the development of the field, proposes that cultural studies should be regarded as the study of social activities of "ordering", and draws on Foucault to define the domain in these terms and on a variety of topics. Toby Miller's edited book *A Companion to Cultural Studies* (2001) provides an initial gateway to the diverse topics, the substantive debates, and the relationships between cultural studies and a variety of fields, as well as regions of the world.

There has been a flood of books and articles about globalization, but not many scholars link the different aspects – cultural, economic, and social – to show how the lives of people are (and are not) changed by broader developments. A concise theoretical overview is that of Kellner, in "Theorizing globalization" (2002); an empirical study that links various aspects is Carla Freeman's *High Tech and High Heels in the Global Economy* (2000), which shows how women in the Caribbean who take globalized high-tech jobs are also transformed in their consumption patterns, lifestyles, and gender identities.

Part 3

Cultural forms, processes, and change

8 Power and culture

What is the relation of culture to the exercise of power – the subordination of individuals and groups to the will of others or to the constraints of an established social order? Karl Marx once held religion to be the opiate of the people. Granted, Marx's view was more complex than this remark would suggest. But this strong version of class domination through cultural domination remains a useful benchmark by which to examine relationships between culture and power. This chapter explores the social and technological forces that shape the conditions under which culture might prove powerful, and then examines various theories of power and culture. These theories are diverse: one view holds that the power of culture is beyond the control of any group or social stratum. Alternatively, the patterns of culture by which people live are seen as shaped in one or another way by the influence of powerful interests.

Any theory that explains culture in relation to power faces widespread opposition. Humanists, especially those concerned with high culture, have long resisted accounting for the content and form of cultural objects by "reducing" them to the social conditions of their production. This sort of impulse also suggests that the best of culture ought to transcend the political conditions of its making. In this line of thought, art, literature, poetry are timeless: once produced, they exist outside of history, hence at a distance from the social conflicts of an era. A great painting by Picasso, for example, cannot be reduced to economic, political, or other circumstances of its having been painted; nor ought it be judged aesthetically on the basis of political criteria (cf. Wolff 1987; Zolberg 1990).

The scholarly balance shifted during the 1980s. For postmodern critics interested in the politics of culture, even seemingly apolitical culture, precisely in its claim to be apolitical, fills the media with apolitical material, thereby crowds out political discourse, and thus operates in a deeply political way. Now, postmodernists assert, all texts, all cultural objects have to be understood in terms of how they are socially produced, by whom, at what historical moment, and with what political implications.

This controversy in turn suggests a problem that derives from the social implications of power. Cultural analysts sometimes want to identify an unambiguous relationship between a posited coherent shared societal culture (e.g. "British culture") and particular cultural objects. If we simply assumed that objects of "high" culture – for example the novels of Jane Austen – were produced by the force of individual genius, and if we assumed that critical acclaim accurately distinguished great work from the trivial and ephemeral ("trashy" novels), then culture – produced by individual genius – would at the same time represent a society's essential enduring accomplishments and transcendent values. A parallel argument could be made about popular culture. Pop music would be the music *of* youth; Hollywood movies, a *reflection* of their predominantly middle-class audience; and fast food, the *response* to increasingly mobile lifestyles. Culture – high or popular – could be interpreted in terms of its meaningful relation to its audience as society.

However, this approach to the content of cultural objects can only proceed in the absence of questions of power and its relation to cultural diversity: who produces and distributes culture, which of diverse cultural possibilities gets established as a society's culture, whose interests are served by its content, what social strata are empowered by its ideas, and how (and how much) does culture shape action? Apolitical theories of culture typically make one or the other (or both) of two assumptions: either there is a relatively free market in cultural objects such that people get what they want in culture (within their financial and cognitive abilities to acquire culture), or the culture of a society (or a social group within a society) has a consensual basis and the culture exists for all members equally, as the set of ideas and values and aesthetics that bind them together. Under these assumptions, cultural objects reflect the values and meaningful concerns of their audience.

However, the question of power gets in the way of this straightforward equation. As we saw in Chapter 2, with the issue of community, and Chapter 3, with patterns of social stratification, culture can be a basis for participating in social strata and social groups, and it yields labels, as well as boundaries that include and exclude. The capacity for labeling and exclusion/inclusion infuses culture with a kind of power, by groups and society as a whole over individuals, and of some groups and strata over other groups and strata. Thus, as contributors to Lamont and Fournier's edited volume *Cultivating Differences* (1992) show, symbolic boundaries between high and low culture, ethnicities, gendered identities, and political affiliations help create and maintain relations of power.

Power, however, is not an abstract and automatic social phenomenon. It is manifested in concrete activities. To understand power in relation to culture, it is necessary ask whether and how specific individuals and groups derive benefit from their disproportionate abilities to produce and distribute culture. Once we acknowledge, first, that it takes resources to disseminate music, to paint, to publish, to produce and distribute television programming, and to make and show films, and, second, that these resources are not equally distributed in any society, then it becomes possible to investigate the political economy of culture: how the production and distribution of culture are economically supported, and how these activities are connected to the structure of political interests and power in a society.

These questions are entangled with other pieces of the sociological puzzle. As Wendy Griswold (1987a) has observed, the audiences and patrons of culture may influence how cultural producers and distributors act and what they produce; in different ways, producers and distributors of culture shape and affect their audiences. Thus, in Part 3 of this book we analyze the entire ensemble of relations between the exercise of power, how cultural objects get produced, and how people act as "audiences" in the meaningful reception of culture. Cultural *production* and *audiences* are addressed in Chapters 9 and 10; in the present chapter we will touch on those topics only insofar as they affect our understanding of the relation between culture and *power*.

Questions of power may be addressed in two broad ways: (1) by looking at *power aspects of the established order of culture* and (2) by investigating the *political economy of cultural production*. The latter approach explores how the form and content of cultural objects may be shaped by the economic and political control of cultural production. The former issue, to which we now turn, is about the power implications of a society's cultural patterns.

Power and the established order of culture

Sociologists widely recognize the importance of the ability to produce and distribute culture, but there is considerable disagreement about how much, how, and which powerful interests control the content and form of culture for their own benefit. One theoretical possibility is that an overall *established order* – the ongoing institutional arrangements – of cultural production has *functional* consequences for the power of different social groups, independently of any individual's, organization's, or stratum's capacity to control the shape of the established order. For example, although the field of media industries is dominated by a mere handful of organizations, we must also recognize that the overall structure of media production is the product of multiple forces, and that it is thus "relatively autonomous" of any given company's or corporate sector's ability to organize or transform the established cultural order. For example, although certain organizations seek to manipulate the structure of the music recording industry and thus benefit disproportionately from the established order, crucial factors contributing to the shape of that order – the shifting relative importance of verbal, written, printed, and visual communication and the development of digital technologies – are in important ways beyond the control of particular organizations and groups.

The established order of culture thus may be understood in two ways. First, technology and the interplay of a variety of social forces may produce cultural patterns that allocate power. Second, independently of these processes, it is possible to understand the cultural order as a realm of ideas and symbols that powerfully shape society.

Technology, social forces, and the cultural order

Is there a difference between a culture based largely on print and speech communication and one where people routinely watch television and use DVDs, VCRs, computers, and wireless communication? Do authoritarian societies have different cultural patterns from democratic ones? Posing questions about technology and social forces in such stark terms yields a ready affirmative answer. The more subtle question has to do with whether and how these differences condition the power arrangements of societies.

Technology

Marshall McLuhan's (1964) famous formulation that "the medium is the message" suggests a sort of technological determinism. For McLuhan, the content of what we hear on the radio is not so important as the way that the radio organizes our worlds, both in the capacity to transmit information and entertainment and in the ways we incorporate sounds from beyond our immediate life-worlds into our everyday activities. With radio, patterns of human interaction are changed to the extent that music (and a wide variety of it) becomes accessible to us without much effort – certainly without the need to assemble musicians, attend a concert, or make music ourselves. Other technologies – the automobile, television, the VCR, the computer – also reconfigure the ways we interact with one another.

Joshua Meyrowitz (1985) extended McLuhan's analysis by looking at the information we get through various media. Instead of assuming that information comes into a social world that itself is unchanged by the process, Meyrowitz asks how one or another particular medium shapes social relationships. In his view, print media – books, magazines, newspapers – offer a depth and detail of information that makes each person something of a specialist on the basis of what he or she reads, whether astrophysical theory, home hobby books, or gossip columns. With print, we each get to know a great deal about selected topics, but what we know and what others know can be quite different, because people burrow into many different topics. Television, on the other hand, is oriented to more general audiences, and it lacks the capacity to convey detailed information yet offers its audiences a wide awareness of things previously known only by specialists (rituals of warfare among Pacific island natives, for example). General audiences also become familiar with knowledge previously held largely by people with distinctive status positions; for instance, children can become conversant with the "backstage" worldview of parents.

Technological and economic changes shaping media industries during the 1990s amplified the importance of Meyrowitz's argument. The veritable explosion of cable channels and the internet (and the emerging convergence of the two) rapidly have increased the availability of often highly specialized content. Citizens not only get to read newspaper accounts of politicians' speeches; they get to inspect very intimate details in the life of the president of the United States, as when Bill Clinton's affair with a White House intern became the focus of media attention in the late 1990s, or when George W. Bush lost consciousness, and nearly his life, after choking on a pretzel while alone watching a football game on television in the White House.

For Meyrowitz, such developments blur the distinctions between backstage and frontstage, and between expert and lay person. Thus, frontstage presentations by public figures – how they want to be seen – compete with images about backstage activities. As a variety of commentators have noted, public life obtains the dramatic quality of a soap opera that feeds on previously secret "scandal" or other plots that are easily serialized. In a similar way, the expertise of professionals becomes subject to second-guessing because television offers everyone a patchwork of expert knowledge in diverse fields. Overall, television and streams of information available online have made many people much more sophisticated about "performances," and, possibly for that reason, people sometimes do not easily impress. Ironically, though, awareness of the constructed character of public images brings people to recognize that images do make a difference. For example, in the weeks following the 9/11 attacks in the United States in 2001 considerable television airtime, column inches, and server space were given over to a debate about the appropriate name for the war on terrorism. The original name coined by the Bush administration, "Infinite Justice," was criticized as vengeful, and the administration then chose a new name, "Enduring Freedom," both to reflect better on the motives for war and – importantly – to avoid alienating potential members of the international coalition the administration was forging to prosecute the war (cf. Arundhati 2001; Rosenberg 2001).

Meyrowitz's focus on television can obviously be broadened to include other technologies that followed – the video cassette recording, the compact disc, the digital video disc, electronic computer mail, and so on. Each technology gives rise to a distinctive set of possible relations between individuals and culture, and each shapes social relationships among the people who participate in it. McLuhan grandly imagined a sort of "global village" in which people would be united into one large community by the enveloping web of communication. The worldwide web and the huge audience for events like the World Cup seem like unifying developments, yet the opposite image – of alienation – also seems relevant: people become separated from one another by their ability to select and experience culture individually through technology like MP3, which allows individuals to download and store music from the web on portable hard drive/players, or the "TIVO" and devices like it, which can instantly record and time-shift television programming and even make programming choices in response to the history of a given user's viewing habits. Rapidly changing technologies that alter the web of communication thus may either increase or decrease the degree to which people are connected.

How are these changes related to power? The answer depends on both the nature of culture under various technologies and the relation of technologies to the established order of culture. Participants in what began as the Frankfurt School of critical theory (discussed in Chapter 6) have argued since the 1930s that there can be no single theory of how power operates in societies because every change – even toward freedom – establishes a set of conditions in which new arrangements of domination can take hold. There are dialectical shifts in the exercise of power. For example, a well-established democracy can be subverted by the rise of propaganda. Similarly, free choices in the marketplace can be constrained by the social conditions under which they are made, such that the range of choices cannot be assumed to match buyers' wants and needs.

In the dialectic of power identified by the critical theorists, people interested in minimizing the non-legitimate exercise of power need to identify specific sources of power that operate in their immediate circumstances. Early on, the critical theorists wondered why the working class lacked the revolutionary fervor that Karl Marx had expected. One answer pointed to the new technological possibilities of cultural domination. Already in the 1930s, Walter Benjamin (1969) identified a key divide in culture, noting the increasing prevalence of mechanically reproduced recordings, art prints, films, and so on, distributed on a mass basis. In our era, the mass production and distribution of culture is the central arrangement by which people have access to culture, and this is as true for much of high culture as it is for popular culture (Gans 1974; Halle 1993). Both classical composers and the latest offerings of the pop music industry are available on compact discs and as MP3 files. What, then, was Benjamin's concern? As we saw in Chapter 6, for Benjamin a real cultural object has "authenticity," a special "aura," and a kind of "authority" that are diminished by mass copying. In his view, the shift to mass production – from live to recorded music, from theater to film and TV, from painting to art prints and reproductions – has dire consequences. Art loses its significance as a critical activity when mass reproduction makes it more of a commodity subject to the same forces of manufacturing and marketing as other commodities – cars or laundry detergents, for example. "To an ever greater degree," Benjamin wrote, "the work of art reproduced becomes the work of art designed for reproducibility" (1969, p. 224).

Of course, Benjamin had not seen the half of it. Television and streaming video delivered via the worldwide web may appear to represent the world, but acting, the technologies of animation and editing, and the possibilities of embedding images in a variety of textual and graphic contexts mean that the world as it is depicted on television and via the web need not have any existence beyond the screen, even though, as a Baudrillardian simulacrum, the screen reality paradoxically threatens to overshadow the significance of everyday life. The images brought into our homes by television and the web create a new claim of authenticity. We are dazzled by the experiences made possible by the new technologies: they allow us to see and hear things in ways unavailable in our everyday worlds. Yet for Benjamin our individual responses to the fascinations of mass-produced culture are prefigured in their design. Indeed, the successful producers of popular entertainment and advertising have developed substantial lore about how to use media techniques to create particular effects in mass audiences. Benjamin was not completely opposed to the new developments. He recognized that mechanical reproduction could free art from its "parasitical dependence on ritual," thus contributing to the possibility for autonomous artistic practice (1969, p. 224). But mainly he worried that the mass production of culture heightened the potential for promoting entertainment over critical thought and offered a distraction from the circumstances of actual social life by spreading new kinds of (debased) ritual values – those of mass spectacle – with affinities both to fascist politics and to consumer capitalism.

Overall, technology shapes culture in important ways: it establishes the media of cultural interchange; it may make culture more accessible to some groups and less accessible to others; it can shift our connections to culture and change how we view the world. However, technology itself is an insufficient basis on which to explain the power effects of an established order of culture. In response to the technology argument, critical theorists Max Horkheimer and Theodor Adorno observed in the 1940s: "No mention is made of the fact that the basis on which technology acquires power over society is the power of those whose economic hold over society is greatest" (1982, p. 121).

Social forces

Despite the significance of technology, empirical sociological research suggests that the established order of culture cannot be reduced to its technological basis. To the contrary, as Benjamin (1969) indicates clearly in the epilogue of his famous essay, technology, artistic schools, and political movements are interrelated. Whatever the consequences of a cultural order for the distribution of power, diverse social forces help shape its emergence.

We might assume, to take one example, that technological innovations in printing brought the modern newspaper into being. But Michael Schudson has argued that it is just the reverse: in the U.S., various social forces of change came to a head in the 1830s, creating demand for a new kind of newspaper, and this demand in turn motivated technological innovations that made printing easier (1978, pp. 31–5). What were these social forces in the nineteenth-century U.S.? Schudson points to three: the emergence of a broadly based market economy, the diffusion of political participation among wider and wider sectors of the population, and the eclipse of small-scale community by a more complex society. When increasing numbers of people become drawn into the market economy, they begin to have an interest in news of commerce that previously was important solely to business people. Similarly, the growing interest in politics could not be adequately served by the party-organ newspapers of the day, which primarily published the views of the political parties without offering what we today think of as "news." Finally, even if in small communities face-to-face conversations could serve as a medium of communication that helped bind people together, a complex society created wider social ties beyond the world of people's immediate neighbors: what happened in another state or country became of interest to people whose horizons were expanding. In the nineteenth century, forces were at work changing the social world and people's ties to it; these changing conditions, Schudson argues, created circumstances in which "news" gained a sufficient audience to fuel the birth of the first modern newspapers.

What about other kinds of societal arrangements, for example of material culture? Let us take the case of the American motel. It would be easy to argue that technology gave rise to the motel. At the end of the nineteenth century, hotels were a form of travel accommodation appropriate to cities and to forms of travel such as trains that served urban places. With the early-twentieth-century advent of the automobile – a technological innovation – motels might be explained as hotels moved out to the highway. But this commonsense explanation is drawn into question by Warren Belasco (1979), who shows that motels indeed originated by catering to the motoring public, but not simply as hotels at the edge of town. Instead, the motel form of overnight travel accommodation emerged as a byproduct of status competition between elite vacationers and other people with whom they shared the road. When the grand American spas and resorts began to attract a less elite clientele in the latter part of the nineteenth century, some patrons began to seek out other forms of leisure. Motivated by the desire for a nostalgic return to nature and embracing "the strenuous life" recommended by President Theodore Roosevelt at the turn of the twentieth century, some people used the first automobiles for "auto-camping," going, as they said, "a-gypsying" to escape the constraints of the increasingly industrial, bureaucratized, and urban social landscape. To cater to this trend, city campgrounds gradually became established, and then private ones, which charged a fee, thus excluding vagrants and the migrating poor. By the 1920s entrepreneurs were offering tourist cabins and cottages on campgrounds as more comfortable accommodations for their paying clients. It was at these autocamping/cabin facilities that the first motels were established. Thus, the motel as a business format for lodging was born of changing tastes among automobile tourists engaged in status competition with one another.

The importance of diverse social forces can also be seen in long-term and global developments toward contemporary culture. At the beginning of the twenty-first century, complex interactions between global media technologies, consumer capitalism, international tourism, and migration are reshaping social relationships within and across nation-states, including the very notion of citizenship. People's identifications with communities have become defined less in political terms and more in terms of what cultures they consume and how they become tied to new hybrid cultures that have developed out of increasing social interchange across national boundaries. As Nick Stevenson argues,

> citizenship becomes less about formalized rights and duties and more about the consumption of exotic foods, Hollywood cinema, Brit. pop CDs and Australian wine. To be excluded from these commercial goods is to be excluded from citizenship (that is full membership) in modern western societies.
>
> (N. Stevenson 1997, p. 2)

On the flip side of this international consumption dynamic are the emerging imperatives of relations between culture and the market. To be a full member of the global
community is to offer up one's images, practices, language, and other cultural artifacts
to those with the power and resources to consume them (buy them, watch them, eat
them, study them). Thus, to understand globalization it is essential to recognize that
mass-mediated communications technologies which make culture available to a wide
audience are operating in a globalized social climate of consumer capitalism and
tourism. In this globalized circumstance, social relationships to culture increasingly
become defined as relationships between performances and audiences. The relationships of individuals and groups to cultures beyond the boundaries of their own
societies may have political effects as well. Just as Meyrowitz argues that relations
between individuals are reshaped when television makes formerly "expert" knowledge
available to lay persons, globalizing media may be transforming the nature of citizenship by making social and cultural resources available that allow individuals to
distance themselves from their own official state-centered discourses and connect
transnationally with other bases of identity (J.B. Thompson 1994; 1995).

Emergent patterns of culture as diverse as the newspaper, the motel, and globalized
identity discourses cannot be explained by technology alone. Cultural developments are
shaped by social forces at work in the societies where they appear. We may suspect that
further research would show the significance of social forces for diverse kinds of culture
– popular music, film, craft fairs, literature, motorcycle gangs, and so on. Yet to explain
the origins of an established cultural order by either the influence of technology or
social forces does not necessarily explain that order as a basis of social power. This is
true for two reasons. First, whatever the origins of a cultural order, once it is established
it may have consequences as a set of meanings and objects that inscribe power within
society. Second, individuals and groups that own or control key organizations in the
established social order may be able to exercise power through cultural production.

The established cultural order as a medium of power

Do the institutionalized patterns of culture that inform our actions themselves
amount to orders of power? If so, why and how? Sociologists like Durkheim (1995)
focus on culture as a force of social integration. Yet this does not deny the power of
culture. To the contrary, culture can thereby define the boundary between social integration versus alienation or deviance. At least implicitly, this means that culture is a
medium of power: people who operate within the boundaries of a culture are dominated by its categories and meanings; those who deviate from cultural expectations
may be subject to sanctions both at the hands of authority and of other people who
conform to the established cultural order.

Sigmund Freud confronted the coercive power of culture much more directly than
Durkheim. As we saw in Chapter 2, Freud argued the existence of a fundamental
conflict between the individual's subconscious desires for sexual pleasure and the
demands in a civilized world for the individual to knuckle down to the responsibilities
of family and work. The superego, representing normative social demands on the individual, had to be accommodated by the individual ego, or society could not exist. As
with Durkheim, the victory of culture over the individual is a functional necessity in
any society. For Freud, the persistence of culture requires the repression of individual
freedom.

In the view of critical theorists, the "necessity" of cultural domination is organized within contemporary societies by the necessity of channeling social life along lines that gear into capitalist-organized satisfaction of wants that substitute for the freedom to satisfy individual desires. As Chapter 6 showed, for theorists like Benjamin mass production of culture played into this possibility: production, distribution, and consumption crystallized as an organized complex that gave rise to specifically capitalist styles of life. Some twenty-five years later, Herbert Marcuse argued for the connection between capitalist cultural domination and the lifestyles of specific social strata – working-class youth, suburban professionals, and so on – by suggesting that consumption may be an act of free choice, but the choice is "spurious": it conceals the "universal coordination" of consumers, and it has consequences for all kinds of people, even the affluent.

> The high standard of living in the domain of the great corporations is *restrictive* in a concrete sociological sense: the goods and services that the individuals buy control their needs and petrify their faculties. In exchange for the commodities that enrich their life, the individuals sell not only their labor but also their free time.
>
> (Marcuse 1962, pp. 90–1)

Like Horkheimer and Adorno, Marcuse emphasizes the role of corporate business interests in the structuring of a world organized to surround and envelop consumers. In this view, power is based on the ability to shape the world so that people will freely choose to define their needs, wants, their entire existence, through consumption. Yet this power is hardly total: as can be seen from global ramifications of the Asian market collapse in 1997 and the U.S. economic slowdown in 2001 and 2002 – exacerbated by the terrorist attacks of 9/11 and business scandals – the spending practices of consumers may shift radically from time to time, with dramatic consequences for a capitalist-organized consumer order.

Though critical theory offers mostly interpretation rather than concrete research, its interpretations are not without empirical support. Sociologists who have studied commercial architecture, for example, have found that restaurants and stores often are designed to maximize sales, maintain customer turnover after purchase, and meet other corporate goals, such as appealing to multiple customer values with a strong yet inoffensive "business format" (see Figure 8.1). At franchise restaurants, we enter worlds designed as extensions of their advertised images, on the basis of market research (Wright 1985). Similar considerations go into the design of shopping malls, which recreate the civic space of downtown shopping streets, but under totally private auspices, which can maximize control of a thematically integrated environment, excluding nonconforming business activities, the homeless, or political controversy, and thereby sustaining a sense of "mall gentility" in which "nothing unusual is happening" (Jerry Jacobs 1984, pp. 13–14).

The success of shopping malls across the U.S. came largely at the expense of downtown shopping areas. Efforts in response to revitalize downtown shopping areas – and later to create entire "gate-guarded" communities – have in some sense transferred the ideology of mall gentility into actual civic spaces. The planned community of Celebration, Florida, for example, began selling houses in 1995 amid accusations that its funder – the Walt Disney Corporation – was plotting "to lure unwitting citizens

Figure 8.1 While walking through a mall, consumers may find themselves immersed in an
environment that mimics public space and civic interaction but that is, in fact, private
and designed to structure experience around shopping and entertainment. This
photograph, taken at the Mall of America in Minnesota, shows off the centerpiece
of the mall – an indoor amusement park called "Camp Snoopy," replete with giant
hovering Pepsi logo. The mall also includes an aquarium, marriage chapel, post
office, and high school.

Source: Chris Gregerson, http://www.phototour.minneapolis.mn.us/1911.

into living in theme parks" (Jerry Adler 1995, p. 44). In 2001, the grand opening of
"The Village," a housing development in Northern California, offered prospective
homebuyers the opportunity to live in a community entirely modeled after the paintings of Robert Kincade – a highly successful artist roundly criticized for creating
mass-produced art sold to the middle classes through a chain of retail galleries in
suburban malls.

In the early 1840s, before Karl Marx developed his theory of capitalism, he
engaged in a philosophical critique of bourgeois society that warned against a situation in which private interests would come to structure the organization of civic space
(1978, p. 33). But Marx could not anticipate the world of the mall and the planned
community that so many shoppers – and citizen-consumers – would find so attractive.

The designs of restaurants, stores, malls, and towns are physical manifestations of a
culture created by business corporations. Yet this is not the end of the matter. As
Robin Leidner (1993) shows through participant-observation research on service
workers, human interaction itself, not just physical structure, is constructed and

scripted to serve business interests. By studying insurance sales and McDonald's restaurants, Leidner demonstrated the subtle and not so subtle ways that scripted interactions – which are an attempt to control both workers and clients – have consequences for identity and self-image. Corporate scriptings transform the affective display of emotions into work (cf. Hochschild 1983). Routinizing those displays may violate everyday norms of authenticity, autonomy, sincerity, and individuality, but if the practices become commonplace, they routinize a public culture of inauthentic authenticity (see Figure 8.2).

Of course, not everyone responds to any given script enacted by service workers, and therefore even for a given material need different products and marketing strategies are required to satisfy a diverse population. Market research is able to identify "clusters" of consumers to "target" with goods, services, and business formats designed specifically for them. Malcolm Gladwell (1997) has described a very sophisticated version of this targeting with respect to the highly lucrative U.S. teen market. He calls it "cool-hunting." Coolhunters fancy themselves as anthropologists who observe teen subcultures in order to define newly emerging trends. Coolhunters sell the information they gather to culture-producing firms (a one-year subscription to one of the most

Figure 8.2 Just as physical space can be scripted to serve business interests, so too can human interaction. As the affective display of emotion is incorporated into service work and increasingly routinized, as with the smile and posture of the woman working at this cosmetics counter, there is a risk of violating norms of authenticity, sincerity, and individuality.

Source: J.R. Hall photograph.

well-known sources of cool, *Look-Look*, runs at $20,000). Perhaps, one could argue, such research procedures are democratically oriented toward insuring that producers respond to the needs and desires of consumers. But, as media critic Mark Crispin Miller (in Goodman and Dretzin 2001) points out, producers are not always interested in giving consumers what they want or need. They are often concerned with devising ways to sell some image that they already control to a very lucrative market whose members like to imagine themselves to be independent of the corporate marketing of culture. After all, what is "cool" often is by definition outside of convention.

In the final analysis, a critical theory of power does not assume the existence of a single, cohesive, powerful group; nor does it depend upon centralized control of communication. Advertising, market research, and capitalist consumer production are significant elements of a wider set of social institutions that includes politics, government bureaucracies, information-processing organizations, planning agencies, and scientific laboratories. The power of these institutions may lie in their diffuse yet pervasive character – in their ability to structure everyday experience. Thus, in the view of the contemporary critical theorist Jürgen Habermas (1987), the social world of everyday life – the "life-world" – has become overshadowed by the "system." In part this change occurs because systematic rationalization of social life has invaded the life-world to the point that much of life is overwhelmingly organized via corporate and governmental bureaucratic systems. These systems produce goods, services, and information in ways that affect the environment, the character of cities and towns, what we eat, how we maintain health, how we care for the sick, and so on. Habermas's argument is largely theoretical, but it makes sense when one recognizes, for example, the use of "under-the-radar" techniques of youth marketing like hiring teens to log on to internet chat rooms and surreptitiously promote products or hiring college freshmen to throw parties and pass out promotional materials. The life-world has shifted from once having been the location from which action proceeded to the reverse: the realm of everyday life is now organized increasingly from the outside, by the "system."

The model of power illuminated by critical theory argues that organization of the social world yields a de facto domination of society's members through its cultural arrangements, shaped especially in the arena of large-scale economic and political organizations. Such a theory can be put into sharper focus by asking how cultural arrangements yield such a form of power. The most insightful answer to this question has been provided by Michel Foucault, who moves in a quite different direction from critical theory.

In a fascinating array of studies on prisons, mental illness, and other aspects of social life, Foucault (1965, 1975, 1979, 1978–86) consolidated an important account of the diffuse institutionalized power of culture. Other strands of research already had begun to explore this terrain. Labeling theorists had shown, for example, that "madness" is not simply a psychological fact; it is a shifting social construction of meanings that coordinates institutionalized arrangements designed to identify and deal with people at the fringes of society. The matter of who is at the fringes of society depends on time and place (Goffman 1961; Scheff 1966; Laing 1967; Szasz 1987). Foucault deepened this fundamental insight, as we saw in Chapter 5, by positing a time before the emergence of the modern world in which neither "reason" nor "madness" described the average person. In this view, the emergence of modern reason as a category of popular personality at the end of the sixteenth and into the seventeenth and eighteenth centuries had two implications for the social order. In the first place, it allowed reasoning *about* madness. However, for Foucault, the power of reason does not guarantee truth and it has not yet tamed madness. Perhaps this failure stems from the second implication of reason's emergence: that madness was uncommon in an earlier era because reason was uncommon. The birth of reason made possible the delineation of madness, in that reason established a standard of comparison by which madness could be identified.

Because madness and reason are intimately connected with each other, changes in what counts as reason will change what counts as madness too. Foucault's account suggests that we are trapped in the very boxes established by social efforts to create valid categories. The social arrangements for processing people through treatment or incarceration or monitoring have the effect of constructing the specific conditions of madness, from the warehousing of schizophrenics in the back wards of mental hospitals to the "mentally ill" homelessness of today. In other words, institutionalized practices based on reasoned knowledge in the disciplines of psychiatry and psychology, social welfare, and police procedure construct both the life circumstances and the meaningful categories of "madness" (Foucault 1965, 1979). It is this critique of reason itself, and our entrapment in and through its unfolding, that separates Foucault from the social constructionists.

For Foucault, even one of the most intimate aspects of personal life – sexuality – is "deployed" from outside the sites of its practice. But Foucault did not follow Freud in regarding civilized power as an exercise in repressing sexuality. To the contrary, there is a flood of discourses on sexuality – in movies, advertising, in the newspapers and magazines, in therapy groups, and with doctors. These discourses are powerful, not because they offer rules of conduct, but because they establish the web of meanings that embed sexuality within society. Sexual activity, at its core an animalistic behavior, has become imbued with specifically moral attributes. Thus, we do not simply act sexually as animals. Sexual practices carry specific culture freight. Forms of heterosexual, monogamous, marital, homosexual, and other sexual conduct transpire within fields of meaning organized by professional and mass-mediated discourse (Foucault 1978–86). To take but one example, Mark Monteiro (1997) examined discourses of masculinity in the popular Brazilian magazine *Ela Ela: uma revista para ler a dois* ("Him Her: a magazine to be read by the couple"). This magazine was published between 1969 and 1972 – a period when Brazil was facing sociohistorical changes associated with the rise of countercultural social movements advocating feminism, gay power, and the entry of women into the once male-dominated workforce. Monteiro finds that the visual and written discourse on men undergoes a shift over the period: there are more pictures of male models, more articles dealing with male vanity, new cosmetics marketed to men, and treatments of male homosexuality. However, a durable undercurrent of male social dominance remains, for social changes are represented as running counter to norms of heterosexual patriarchal power. The image of the "real man" persists as a yardstick against which to measure social change.

For madness, sexuality, and other aspects of social life as well, Foucault connects "reason" to disciplines of knowledge, and disciplines of knowledge become the basis of another "discipline," the bodily exercise of power over the subjects of disciplinary knowledge.

Foucault's emphasis on knowledge has informed the work of a wide variety of scholars. Notably, the Subaltern Studies Group that emerged in the 1980s made an effort to rewrite the history of India from the perspective of groups oppressed by colonial rule.

As Chapter 4 showed, this effort required that the group critique the discipline of history itself, in particular for its complicity in extending the discourses of colonialism, nationalism, and modernity. "The inescapable conclusion from [the group's] analyses is that 'history,' authorized by European imperialism and the Indian nation-state, functions as a discipline, empowering certain forms of knowledge while disempowering others" (Prakash 1994, p. 1,485).

Gayatri Chakravorty Spivak (1988) raised the relevant question: "Can the subaltern speak?" Spivak, who both champions and critiques postcolonial studies, draws from Jacques Derrida to deconstruct the rhetorics and images of colonialism and postcolonialism, and argues that without an explicit critique of the disciplinary bases of knowledge subalterns simply become, once again, subordinated to the discourses of modernism and modernization, and to those who might speak for those discourses – Western intellectuals. Such an argument is particularly disarming because it depicts a cultural domination that operates without conspirators yet reduces the agency of acting subjects to mere reflections of the cultural categories that frame social life. The consequence of such domination, in the case of the subaltern, is that efforts to liberate the dominated subject simply reinscribe the hierarchy of dominant/dominated positions.

Both in subaltern studies and elsewhere, Foucauldian analysis can seem to create an intellectual impasse for the less powerful. We all seem trapped within culturally constructed standpoints that imprison both our reasoning and our selves. For this reason, the efforts of the Subaltern Studies Group have gained importance outside India (see Chapter 6). Florence E. Mallon (1994), in surveying their influence in Latin American studies, has urged scholars to remain focused on the tension between postmodern discourse analyses and emancipatory politics. Otherwise, there is no privileged standpoint like that asserted for the working class by Marxists, and power and domination eclipse both objective analysis and subjective agency.

Any given societal arrangements rarely benefit everyone equally. Instead, they work to the advantage of particular social classes, ethnic groups, professions, and one gender (almost universally men) over another. How are these inequalities to be explained, and what is the significance of culture? Some theorists emphasize the cultural patterns as products of a capitalist consumer society. Others, like Habermas and Foucault, see the cultural power basis of contemporary society as grounded in a wider set of institutions than purely economic ones. Yet one feature of theories about how culture helps sustain an established order is especially worth noting. Privileged groups that benefit from the cultural matrix do not necessarily achieve this benefit by the direct exercise of power, and people from disprivileged strata are not necessarily excluded from participation in the apparatus. What matters is that a diffuse but pervasive set of meanings, objects, and arrangements establishes a de facto power by the incorporation of culture into our everyday lives.

Insofar as the power of culture is diffuse, as Foucault suspected, political change and even a shift in economic organization would not change the powerful operation of culture in daily life. Indeed, for Foucault, even broad cultural change – a change in sexual mores, the end of colonial rule – seems only to herald a new set of categories that entangle us. Thus, Foucault has been read both as a conservative theorist, pessimistic about the possibilities and benefits of cultural change, and as a new radical who produced a fundamental critique that must be reckoned with if meaningful social change is to occur. If Foucault is right, efforts at social change must be directed toward the categories of culture, their consequences, and the implications of changing their operation in social relations. Only if he is wrong, and the content of culture is connected to specific economic and political interests, does the question of who controls cultural production make very much difference.

The ownership of cultural production

A venerable tradition in sociology confronts power much more directly than Foucault does. If power is defined as the ability to make people do things whether they want to or not, then power to shape culture can be traced to those people and organizations that produce culture. Obviously culture is directly produced by cultural workers – artists, journalists, film producers, novelists, fashion designers, teachers, and sociologists. The questions then become, whom do cultural workers work for, and how does the ownership of cultural production affect culture?

The close of the twentieth century saw unprecedented growth in media industries brought on by waves of mergers made possible by wide-ranging deregulation. A brief look at the economic value of the biggest media-company mergers that took place between 1980 and 2000 reveals the dimensions of this startling consolidation. In 1983 the largest merger, achieved when Gannet Newspapers bought Combined Communications (billboards, newspapers, and broadcasting) was worth $581 million (in constant 2000 dollars). Six years later the largest merger created a $19.4 billion company, bringing together Time Incorporated and Warner Communications. Two years after that, AT&T combined with TCI for $56 billion, and when AOL got together with Time Warner in 2000 the deal was worth $166 billion (Croteau and Hoynes 2001). The fourth largest international media conglomerate, with 1998 sales of $12.8 billion, was Rupert Murdoch's News Corporation, which brings together the Fox channels (news, sports, Fx), a string of television stations and newspapers, including the *New York Post*, book publisher HarperCollins, several sports teams, including the Los Angeles Dodgers, and British Sky Broadcasting (Demers 1999).

As Croteau and Hoynes point out, media empires are nothing historically new. What make today's empires different is their enhanced opportunities for media integration. Today they seek to integrate both horizontally, by owning many different types of media products, and vertically, by owning or controlling all phases of the creation, distribution, and marketing of a particular media product. Although "product placement" (placing a product within the story of a film or TV in exchange for an advertiser's money) has been an accepted business practice for some time, the new profit-making strategies almost completely blur the boundary between advertisement and product. Now, for example, internet players of "The Sims Online" video game find a handy McDonald's kiosk where busy cyber-social individuals can stay happy eating fast food. "Synergy" or "cross-promotion" – the new industry buzzwords – is made possible by ownership and business alliance patterns that create what some media critics refer to as the "integrated communications mix."

When the Disney Corporation makes a feature film about a youth hockey team called the "Mighty Ducks," when they actually own part of a National Hockey League team called the Mighty Ducks, and when they own the ESPN cable network that televises hockey games, when they use their ESPN network and Disney stores to sell jerseys (licensed by the League and worn by both fictional players on the film screen and professional players on the TV screen), and when this all somehow gears together nicely with the Disney character Donald Duck, it becomes difficult to tell what is a promotion, what is a product, and what is culture. There might not be any difference. As Douglas Rushkoff puts it:

> Look how Viacom leverages [Howard Stern] across their properties. He is syndi-cated on 50 of Viacom's Infinity radio stations. His weekly TV show is broadcast on Viacom's CBS. His number one best-selling autobiography was published by Viacom's Simon and Schuster, then released as a major motion picture by Viacom's Paramount Pictures, grossing $40 million domestically and millions more on videos sold at Viacom's Blockbuster Video.
>
> (Rushkoff, in Goodman and Dretzin 2001)

Growth and conglomeration of mass-media outlets have contributed to the direct political power of owners and to the consolidation of media under the dominance of large-scale, consumer-oriented corporate capitalism. In turn, the latter development has shaped the content and formats of mass media. This consolidation, of course, has taken place as part of a wider consolidation of corporate capitalism – in food brands, shopping-mall chains, department stores, and so forth. The power entailed is not simply that of direct authority and influence. Instead, it is a power to design, produce, and distribute culture on a mass basis.

The political economy of cultural production

Culture is not produced solely by capitalists, of course, even if global capitalist enter-prises have been increasingly organizing the process for a long time. The culture that gets made is the product of complex social relations among diverse people who do not necessarily share the interests of the owners or managers of the means of cultural production. A question arises, then, about the nature and degree of power over the *work* of cultural production, for it is possible that producers of culture might act in ways beyond the *control* of owners and managers. This question can be addressed in two different ways: first, by asking who produces culture and, second, by investigating the degree to which political and ideological considerations affect production.

Cultural workers

Two classical early-twentieth-century sociologists – both Italians – theorized in path-breaking ways about cultural workers. One, Vilfredo Pareto, was a political radical for a time, who eventually came to support Mussolini's fascist regime. The other, Antonio Gramsci, remained a committed communist, even to his death in one of Mussolini's prisons. Despite their political differences, both thought that political power is closely linked to domination through culture, and each addressed the role of cultural workers in the process.

Pareto's theory of power distinguished between elites and masses, with the elite controlling mass cultural interpretations of events. He argued that elites maintain their legitimacy and the legitimacy of controversial policies and actions (tax policies, mili-tary actions, etc.) by appealing to popular sentiments that connect with "residues" – deep psychological orientations of the masses toward such symbols as family, commu-nity, self-sacrifice, respect for hierarchy, and fears concerning bad events, the unknown, and the nonconforming (Pareto 1966, p. 222ff.). In Pareto's view, in-group and out-group elites "circulate" – that is, replace one another – on the basis of their relative abilities to appeal to cyclical waves of changing popular sentiments that are tied to the deeply held residues. An elite that bases its appeal primarily on sentiments of justice or equality, for example, can only maintain power in the shifting currents of popular sentiments if it recruits new members from its elite opponents, who may try to gain power on their own by appealing to the rising tide of newly emergent sentiments such as patriotism or security. Pareto maintained a clear distinction between what the powerful actually *do* and how they *justify* what they do; he saw justifications as proceeding by appeal to sentiments rather than by appeal to reason, and he held that elites survive by successfully recruiting (elite) cultural workers who can appeal to popular sentiments.

Antonio Gramsci, like Pareto, was concerned with the role of culture in a ruling group's domination of a social order, which he termed "cultural hegemony" (cultural domination). Though Gramsci was a Marxist, he did not regard the ruling ideas of an era as the ideas of a ruling class. Instead, he suggested that cultural hegemony is maintained by the promotion of *any* culture that accommodates people to their social fate, so long as it does not threaten ruling-class interests. Country-and-western music probably appeals to relatively few members of the corporate capitalist class, for example, yet its content thematizes personal troubles among the people to whom it appeals, without amplifying dissatisfactions in ways that challenge the established social order.

For Gramsci, cultural hegemony is closely linked to the recruitment of workers for the staffing of positions of cultural production. He identified two polar opposite types of people doing significant cultural work: *organic intellectuals*, who are actively linked to the problems and aspirations of concrete social groups (for example Martin Luther King, Jr., with black Americans or, perhaps, the Subaltern Studies Group in postcolonial India), and *traditional intellectuals*, who fill routine cultural roles in relatively conventional and predictable ways. If we broaden the use of the term "intellectuals" to include cultural workers in general, Gramsci's theory suggests a basic goal for any ruling class: it must insure that *traditional* cultural workers staff the production of culture for a wide range of taste publics, so that produced culture, whatever its specific content, will pacify the public. In this view, the elite has no interest in imposing elite culture on other people; its interests are satisfied so long as other people's culture does not threaten their power. Thus, since *organic* intellectuals representing dissatisfied social strata pose a threat to the established order, a ruling class has an interest in undermining their effectiveness. Such an interest might be fulfilled in a number of ways. "Traditional" culture itself may be promoted in order to moderate external cultural challenges. Or organic cultural workers may be recruited into traditional cultural production roles, where they tend to become cut off from the aspirations of concrete social groups, and instead represent a "diversity of opinion" within the mix of traditionally produced culture (Gramsci 1971).

Neither Pareto's nor Gramsci's theory is easy to test empirically, for the cultural material that might be hegemonic changes over time, as do sentiments and the significance of traditional and organic intellectuals. Yet it is instructive to explore briefly a kind of cultural production where the political stakes are particularly high – the news. When we ask who becomes a reporter in the U.S., and how, the answers suggest that news personnel are drawn disproportionately from the upper-middle class, and that their secondary socialization – in college and sometimes graduate school – shapes professional orientations that may produce the "traditional" cultural worker described by Gramsci. As Michael Parenti notes, "Only one in five [journalists] comes from blue-collar or low-status white-collar families," and "most newspeople lack contact with working-class people, have a low opinion of labor unions, and know very little about people outside their own social class" (1986, pp. 40–1). These social horizons shape reporters' outlooks, according to Herbert Gans's study of major news outlets such as the "NBC Nightly News" and *Time*. One thing Gans found was that news people, like the rest of us, have outer limits to their social circles. The consequences are important:

> Journalists obtain their information about America from their customary sources; from what they themselves read in the paper; and, because they have trouble crossing the social barriers that separate them from strangers, from what they learn from peers and personal contacts, notably relatives and friends.
>
> (Gans 1979, p. 126)

To be sure, many journalists are liberals, but, interestingly, their liberal views typically do not get reflected in their news accounts (Parenti 1986, pp. 40–1).

Based on research like that of Gans and Parenti, and the theories of Gramsci and Pareto, we have good reason to suspect that the social locations and alignments of cultural workers with the interests of particular social groups have important consequences for the culture that gets produced. What is true for journalists may hold for other cultural workers – artists, religious personnel, novelists, and others. Comparative research on the social locations of cultural workers thus represents an important subject for further inquiry.

Social control and cultural production

Another important issue can be explored through research about journalists: if the social origins, politics, and personal networks of cultural workers matter, they must have their effect on actual culture that is produced. Indeed, any political economic effect is significant only if it finds its way into the form and content of culture. As we already have seen, the line between advertising and content has been blurred by corporate interests. However, more subtle processes also seem to be at work. They have to do with how worldviews get publicly established as legitimate in the first place.

Public opinion, for example, cannot be assumed to exist independently of the mass media, its practices, and its distribution of information. Benjamin Ginsberg has argued that the establishment of democratic nation-states over the past two centuries has been accompanied by a reconstruction of popular opinion, its sources, and its expression. He describes an "idea market" dominated by "the most powerful producers of ideas" – "upper- and upper-middle-class groups and the organizations and institutions they control" (Ginsberg 1986, p. 89). In Ginsberg's view, processes of public-opinion formation are connected to this idea market: opinion once was closely linked to social groups, but techniques of mass polling have individualized it, undermining oppositional groups within society. The ways in which people form opinions have also shifted due to the emergence of mass-media polling techniques, which affect opinion both by the ways questions are framed and by the consequences for the general public of receiving reports about the opinions of a statistical sample of individuals remote from their own lives. Ginsberg reports revealing research from 1980: of the people in lower-income groups in the U.S. who watched television news "every day," 66 percent "believed that inflation was an 'extremely' serious problem," compared to only 56 percent of lower-income people who "almost never" watched television news (1986, p. 101). Interestingly, the opinions of people in higher-income brackets seem to have been much less affected by watching television news.

Overall, Ginsberg's argument suggests that the production of culture is shaped by the long-term emergence of a particular institutional pattern of relationships between government, the media, and the most powerful social classes. This broad institutional pattern has its parallels in the organization of more concrete practices. As Michael Schudson has shown, professional standards of factuality that emerged in the 1890s tended to exclude journalists as persons on the scene of events from offering their personal insights. In a parallel way, more recently the emphasis on "objectivity" in news reporting has lent official news sources an aura of legitimacy that unofficial sources lack (Schudson 1978, pp. 71–87, 160ff.). In the view of Daniel Boorstin (1962), the news production process increasingly has come to depend on press releases that subordinate journalism to powerful public-relations techniques of press management conducted by corporations, governments, politicians, and celebrities. It is no longer possible to draw a sharp distinction between the news that is reported and the "pseudo-events," as Boorstin called them, that are staged by organizations and individuals in the news. Local news features on the health and technology beats now sometimes use entirely packaged news stories, including video and scripts for anchors and reporters to use in voiceover. These packages are produced by corporate public-relations firms that often coordinate dissemination of them to coincide with the introduction of new products (electronics, pharmaceuticals) into the market.

Journalists, of course, are careful to document their "facts," often by two-source corroboration. But the choice of which facts to include affects the story, and even prior to the choice of facts comes a decision of what Herbert Gans calls "story selection" – whether to cover a given set of events at all. Gans's (1979) study of newsrooms at *Time*, *Newsweek*, CBS and NBC shows little in the way of direct political control of news, but it does reveal a less obvious effect of "enduring values" that strongly shape news content. Gans identified a number of central values that inform how news is reported: ethnocentrism, altruistic democracy, individualism, and moderatism, among others. However, these value structurations of the news "are rarely explicit and must be found between the lines – in what actors and activities are reported or ignored, and in how they are described" (Gans 1979, pp. 39–40). Overall, Gans concluded that these values amount to an ideology that, though not inflexible, promotes "responsible capitalism" (as opposed to greedy, polluting, and other irresponsible kinds) while maintaining "respect for tradition" and "nostalgia for pastoralism and rugged individualism" that are "unabashedly conservative" (1979, p. 68).

How can the effects of subtle value structurations be measured? Political scientists Pippa Norris and David Sanders (1998) describe standards of practice used by newsmakers, political party strategists, media critics, and regulators in Britain to gauge balance in political news reporting. They found that three common approaches are employed. The first, and most common, is "stopwatch balance" – a simple evaluation of proportionate time given to particular political candidates, parties, or groups. Next is "directional balance" – an evaluation of the content of news reporting in terms of its positive, negative, or neutral perspective. Finally, there is "agenda balance," which builds upon the observation that political parties tend to have "ownership" of particular issues. If, for example, there is disproportionate news coverage of an issue "owned" by a particular party (say, crime, which tends to be a hot-button issue for conservative parties), then a bias toward that political agenda, and party, is created even though the reporting is not explicitly political.

Norris and Sanders's research finds that neither agenda bias nor the relative amount of news coverage for a particular political party has much effect on support for that party. What does seem to matter is directional bias – *how* the parties are covered. Given these findings, Norris and Sanders argue that the most commonly used evaluative tool, stopwatch balance, may, "at best, be irrelevant, and, at worst, may obscure any real biases in British television journalism." Still, the researchers antici-pate the continued use of stopwatch balance measurement because it is the easiest tool to use and, "if nothing else, it provides a modest fig leaf of impartiality to clothe naked and unprotected journalists hit by the chill winds of charges of party bias" (P. Norris and Sanders 1998, p. 17).

Norris and Sanders's research would seem to confirm for Britain what Gans asserted concerning the U.S. In Gans's view, values and ideology establish an implicit contextual climate that influences news reporting on events such as oil spills, military actions, changes in hostile countries, foreign-trade problems, and the like. Is cultural hegemony mainly a matter of subtle value influences, then? A study of how the *New York Times* and CBS News reported the Vietnam War suggests a more direct process also at work. In a detailed analysis of news accounts about the war, Todd Gitlin (1980) showed how media use "news frames" to place events within the narrative structures of stories about the news that are greater than the sum of their factual parts. Gitlin found that early protests against U.S. involvement in the Vietnam War were reported, to be sure, but the importance of the events was discounted by the use of "framing devices" such as trivi-alization and disparagement of protesters' effectiveness. News coverage portrayed the antiwar movement as marginal, radical, poorly organized, and polarized by internal dissension. In the long run, the grassroots character of the movement was undermined by the "spotlight" effect of news coverage and the identification of radical "celebrities."

Gitlin's research describes a striking example of *reflexivity*, in which a given course of events is affected by the ways in which events are reported. But Gitlin offers strong evidence that, in coverage of the anti-Vietnam War movement, the reflexive effect of reporting supported interests of hegemonic control. All the same, the eventual partial success of the antiwar movement shows that cultural hegemony does not always completely shape popular opinion on controversial issues. The case of news reporting on the Vietnam War shows the hegemonic process to be real, nevertheless limited, yet still ultimately powerful in shaping public ideology, values, and attitudes.

The research agenda on hegemony has been pursued more broadly in a study that compares U.S. news coverage of different world regions. Writing toward the end of the Cold War, Herman and Chomsky (1988) described a pattern of U.S. media "self-censorship" that resulted in a double standard. They found one kind of coverage for issues that advanced U.S. propaganda interests, for example anti-government protests in Eastern Europe and the then Soviet Union. There was a much different treatment of news about delicate foreign-affairs matters that might reflect negatively on the American public's image of their own country and its government – Vietnam, El Salvador, and the Iran/Contra affair.

The subtle structuring of U.S. propaganda that Herman and Chomsky documented may be attributable to military media-management strategies enacted in the wake of the Vietnam War. According to Croteau and Hoynes (2003), after Vietnam the U.S. military

[handwritten margin note: more dumbing down than omitting, distracting]

put in place a twofold approach to their interactions with journalists. First, they developed an extensive public-relations machine by hiring press personnel at officer status to advise the Pentagon on how best to disseminate a positive image of military action and foreign policy. In addition, the military devised a strategy for direct control of access to information during military action. The press pool, tested during the U.S. invasions of Panama and Grenada, and then put to effective use during the Gulf War and the 2001 offensive against al-Qaeda and the Taliban in Afghanistan, allows the military to restrict the number and kind of journalists working in a war zone and limit their access to the battlefield (Jeffords and Rabinovitz 1994; Mowlana *et al.* 1992).

News is a cultural product of central importance for the public sphere, but it is not just the news that is subjected to processes of social control. Analysts from the British Birmingham School and other practitioners of cultural studies have drawn on the theoretical perspectives of Gramsci and Foucault to analyze television, movies, advertising, magazines, and other mass or popular culture forms. A variety of studies show "ideological work" in popular-culture media that promote public stereotypes about gender, race, class, and other problematic issues in the U.S., the developed nation-states more generally, and the entire postcolonial world (Artz and Murphy 2000; Goldman 1984; Angus and Jhally 1989; M.C. Miller 1990; Grossberg *et al.* 1992). This research shows pervasive ideological subtexts in everyday culture. The content of popular culture is complexly coded, and it thus can create an invisible ideological climate that seems natural when we are immersed within it, but which contains powerful – because implicit and therefore unchallenged – assumptions about how the world is and ought to be.

Even highbrow art is created, distributed, and appreciated within established arrangements that affect its content. Thus, Judith Adler (1979) has offered a cautionary tale about the utopian and radical origins of an art school – California Institute of the Arts – and the ways in which the patronage of the Disney Foundation colored the scene there. During a period when Disney was offering seed money, Adler observed,

> In the absence of a substantial endowment, any activities or "manners" which could be construed as making fund raising difficult were likely to become the subject of major controversy, until eventually the imperatives of institutional survival defined "reality" for the artists who came to the school.
>
> (Judith Adler 1979, p. 61)

Within an organization, such exercise of control can be quite direct. In theory, the *least* external influence or control would operate in free markets, where the only influence on artists depends upon their willingness to respond to the tastes of buyers. However, research demonstrates that even art markets are subject to social controls. In a study of art photographers, for example, Barbara Rosenblum showed that access to the market itself was highly controlled by gatekeepers, who staffed the fine-arts photography schools and operated the galleries where photography was shown (1978a, 1978b). And the buyers' side of the market is not a random "public": today, a significant proportion of art purchases are made by museums and corporations interested in defining public art. Indeed, the quantity of acquisitions by corporations has now attained a level that establishes a separate "corporate art" market. In this market, the subjects of art tend toward noncontroversial topics such as pastoral scenes of beauty and abstract experiments with form (cf. Martorella 1990).

Even aside from the social control of who gets to produce for a given art market, "money talks" in the market and art thus tends to be shaped by those individuals and groups wealthy enough to buy it. At the extreme, art is subsidized by wealthy organizations such as churches or the state (Raymond Williams 1982, pp. 36–56). Museums play an important intermediary role between those who fund art and those who create it, and being included in a museum collection or exhibition has a direct and sometimes dramatic effect on an artist's reputation and career (as well as on the value of patrons' collections). Thus, Victoria Alexander (1996a, 1996b) has studied U.S. art museums and the ways that funding has affected the content and style of exhibitions. The process she describes is complex. The mix of funding sources includes wealthy individuals, corporations, government, and foundations, all of which have interests in particular kinds of exhibitions. Curators especially encourage scholarly exhibitions founded upon traditional art-historical merit and research. Although some funders do support such exhibitions, there is significant pressure for popular shows that will attract large audiences by providing content easily accessible without specialized training in art history. One outcome of this pressure is that museums increasingly mounted large-scale "blockbuster" exhibitions throughout the 1980s and 1990s. But the dynamics behind the change are more complex than a simple model of coercion brought on by economic dependency would suggest:

> It is important to recognize that museums must continue to win legitimacy both from funders and from other actors internal and external to the organization, especially curators, critics, and scholars who are oriented to the art historical merit of museum operation.... [M]useum curators operating within an institutional context actively manage external pressures so as to keep museums functioning *as closely as possible* to curators' normative requirements.
> (V. Alexander 1996b, pp. 830–1; emphasis added)

Social control can be of a very direct sort, but the examples of journalism, popular culture, and art show that it can also involve subtle processes ranging from the ideology of "objectivity" and implicit ideological subtexts of popular song lyrics to the varied effects of cultural workers responding to implicit controls of organizations and the marketplace. These issues are rightly the subject of continuing research, for they are central to the question of whether and how freedom of speech and artistic expression are meaningfully exercised within societies in which flows of information and ideas are increasingly channeled through large organizations and mass media.

Conclusion

Research and theories that show culture to be shaped by political and economic forces can be countered in most developed societies by arguments that point to freedoms of the press and expression. It is also easy to show that diverse opinions are represented in journalism, and that consumers face a dazzling array of choices in music, art, entertainment, clothing, home furnishings, and the like. Yet three points must be recognized. First, the diversity is greater in theory than it is in actuality. Second, the existence of a diverse culture does not disprove analyses either about the diffuse power of established culture to inscribe the meaning of the world or about the political economic structuration of culture. The character of cultural diversity, its accessibility, its boundaries, as well as the choices of consumers may all be shaped by social control and by the ownership and staffing of dominant media outlets. Third, even if "proof" about these theories remains elusive – in part because of the complexity of the issues – the questions they raise are so important that we ignore them at the peril of misunderstanding the social conditions of our existence.

Today, there are few scholars of culture and the mass media who would deny the general arguments that culture is intimately connected with power and that it is conditioned by the political and economic conditions under which it is created, distributed, and consumed. As we have seen, the debate is not about *whether* these effects occur: it is about *how* they occur. Yet the focus on the power of culture raises other questions. Given that production of culture is socially organized, how do social activities give shape to it? And since we cannot assume that people readily absorb and act on the basis of all the ideas that surround them, what is the relation between culture and its audiences? It is to these questions that we turn in the following two chapters.

Suggested readings

David Croteau and William Hoynes, in *Media Society* (2003) develop a sociological perspective on mass media in an encyclopedic overview that nicely summarizes the latest findings and debates. They frame the book around a model of media/society interactions not unlike Wendy Griswold's heuristic device (the cultural diamond) for examining culture more generally.

In *Selections from the Prison Notebooks* (1971) Antonio Gramsci develops the notion of power and domination through consent with his concept of cultural hegemony. The ideas presented in this book are essential reading for understanding the dynamic of ideological power in mass-mediated societies.

Lee Artz and Bren Ortega Murphy present an interdisciplinary analysis of Gramsci's contributions to studies of ideological power in *Cultural Hegemony in the U.S.* (2000). The authors delineate the intellectual history of the concept of hegemony, examine the complex and varied relationships between Gramsci's ideas and other theoretical schools (especially the Frankfurt School of Critical Theory), and review applications of Gramsci's ideas in contemporary empirical studies of mass culture.

Questions of culture and power are now entangled with issues of globalization; for an excellent review of the central debates on globalization in the sociological, anthropological, economic, and political literatures, see Mauro F. Guillén's "Is Globalization Civilizing, Destructive or Feeble?" (2001).

For a theoretical examination of cross-national cultural differences, see *Rethinking Comparative Sociology: Repertoires of Evaluation in France and the United States* (2000), edited by Michèle Lamont and Laurent Thévenot. The empirical studies presented in this book analyze how people in France and the United States use cultural schema to make judgments about politics, economics, morals, and aesthetics.

The *Columbia Journalism Review* is useful reading for students of the media. The stories in this bimonthly publication illuminate how professional journalists confront issues of power as they respond to the political, economic, technological, and social forces explored in this chapter. Articles from the *Review* are available online at http://www.cjr.org/.

9 The production of culture

The commonsense idea of how culture is produced emphasizes the individual. One story has the artist, like a shaman in a premodern society, partaking of the sacred: the artist and the art are divinely inspired. Another narrative, which gained credence with the growth of individualism in the nineteenth century, imagines the artist as romantic hero – a person of genius, alienated from society, toiling alone in a garret to create a great work. Both these images emphasize the artist's unique vision, talent, and work. Both neglect the activities of multitudes of less distinguished individuals who make their living doing art work. Neither view is sociologically informed.

The sociology of culture in recent decades offers an alternative account of how culture gets produced. This account can be credited in large part to the application in recent decades of two quite different analytic frameworks – organizational theory and symbolic interactionism. Each of these approaches downplays the content of a cultural work – and its meaning to the artist or the public – in favor of looking at art as a "product" that requires the cooperation of multiple actors in a collective process for its completion. Both approaches thus inform a research agenda concerned with what sociologist Richard Peterson (1976) called the "production of culture." Peterson coined this term as part of his effort to use a rethinking of culture to reinvigorate sociology (Battani and Hall 2000). He wanted to sidestep a theoretical impasse between highly abstract functionalist and Marxist theories of culture by concentrating on empirical middle-range studies of how expressive symbols are created. His strategy was to employ a set of sensitizing concepts to examine the complex relationships between cultural objects and social organization.

The two analytic frameworks that inform the analysis of cultural production – organizational and interactionist – are somewhat different in their orientations. This difference can be pinpointed by considering an issue they both address – how to think about social groups and their boundaries. Within the sociology of organizations, cultural analysis about the production of such things as music, books, and scientific reports especially spoke to the question of how the "boundaries" of organizations become established. In many industries, technological issues about production are most problematic. By contrast, in culture industries – made up of profit-oriented firms that produce cultural products for distribution – the most problematic issues have to do with deciding what to produce and how to market and distribute it. For organizations to solve these problems often requires that they coordinate with other organizations. Studying cultural production thus presented an opportunity for development of organizational theory about the tasks bundled within various organizations and the boundaries between them. But organizational theory was not the sole beneficiary of this research. When organizational sociologists took up cultural production as their subject, they changed how other sociologists think about culture.

Whereas organizational theory is largely concerned with business organizations (Padgett 1992), symbolic interactionists have conceived of social organization more broadly. Addressing boundary questions, they developed the concept of the "social world" to refer to a diffuse network of people who have a variety of patterned and emergent relations with each other (Shibutani 1955). Sometimes a social world comes to share more of the properties of formal organizations, as when it is focused on production, and a particular kind of production requires a tightly coordinated division of labor (Strauss 1978). But typically, on a continuum, social worlds are more organized than social movements and less organized than formal organizations. There is an ongoing collective activity (for example a recreational activity such as hiking) to which all participants are committed, but the participants carry out diverse actions, both within, and often outside, multiple organizations, some of them only loosely connected, if at all. Social worlds thus lack sharp boundaries of either location or membership.

Generally speaking, studies of cultural production concentrate on identifying the social arrangements and activities necessary to create cultural objects, and analyzing how these shape the content of objects. In this chapter we apply the production perspective primarily to the arts and to popular-culture industries, where it counters popular myths about the lone creative individual. We will also explore relationships between cultural production and broader aspects of social organization – culture industries, reward structures, the state, and audiences. Looking at the creation of art – even when credited to a single individual – is a good starting point for thinking about the production of culture because works of art are almost never created without the coordinated activities of more than one person, typically many people, in "art worlds."

Art worlds

Working out of the symbolic-interactionist tradition, Howard Becker uses the term "art world" "to denote the network of people whose cooperative activity, organized via their joint knowledge of conventional means of doing things, produces the kind of artwork that the art world is noted for" (1982, p. x). Recall the stereotype of the lone struggling artist. Let's assume that a particular singer-songwriter is both inspired and talented. To be as successful as her talent warrants, she needs a way of making enough money to live on, instruments to play, a way of communicating to backing musicians about what they have to do, a place to rehearse, places to perform, perhaps a manager or an agent, a recording company, a distributor who will get CDs into the right stores, favorable reviews in the right places, and an appreciative audience. Of course there is variation in how deeply artists are integrated into art worlds. Our singer-songwriter could sing her songs to herself as she drives to work in the morning, accompanied only by her own drumming on the steering wheel. She might produce her own downloadable digital music files on a website and stage performances in a local music scene where her audience is made up of friends, other musicians, and local aficionados. And she might see taking part in this scene as an end in itself. She might, however, see it the way participants in a corporate music world see it – as a proving ground out of which musicians emerge into careers connected with a national or global market. In other words, the horizon of her participation in an art world is open to a range of possibilities. All of them, however, even the seemingly most solitary, depend on immersion in social networks.

Focusing on social networks in art worlds raises questions about how activities are coordinated through a division of labor. In some cases the division of labor is visually displayed. People who go to see a movie may be enticed by an ad that announces stars, producers, and directors; if they stay to the end they will view the "credits" – an often lengthy list of people involved in the making of the film, down to the hairdressers and baggage handlers. Yet collective activity is part of cultural production even when it is not so directly acknowledged. A painter may work alone but he usually has a supplier from whom he can buy paints and other materials. If he wants others to acknowledge his work, he will probably choose to work in an established tradition, and this tradition will be socially defined in part by commonly understood aesthetic "rules" that help critics and buyers decide how to judge whether or not work is "good." Our artist also needs people who will show his work to others, and an audience who will buy it for themselves or to display in public places.

In any art world, Becker pointed out, some activities are usually regarded as at the "core" of the overall enterprise while others are treated as peripheral (1982, pp. 16–18). People tend to assume that the person who does the core activity is the artist. However, there can be ambiguity about who that person is. For the conductor of a symphony orchestra, the performers are her "instrument." Yet members of the audience may single out performers as artists. In a different venue, the success of visual artists like Andy Warhol, Jeff Koons, and Mark Kostabi depends on their promotional skills and ability to manage "factories" full of assistants producing the objects that they claim as their own art. Similar practices of shop production have occurred at other times and places, for example in eighteenth-century Europe. In these examples and more generally, art is collectively produced, and who gets designated as an artist is a question open to different answers.

Moreover, what gets defined as the "core" artistic activity can change as technology changes. In many performance contexts it is now standard for performers to use recorded music and lip-synching. The voice that one hears on a favorite CD results from an interaction between (at least) a vocalist, various engineers, and a variety of technologies deployed in a recording studio. The sound that the audience is used to hearing would be impossible to replicate in a live performance. And, with these changes, recording engineers who mix sound have increasingly gained status as artists (Kealy 1979).

Given the collective activity required to produce art, who counts as the artist is fundamentally a social question. And this question is tied to another one – who is part of an art world? The singer? The recording engineer? The remastering engineer? The CD production-line worker? The audience? The boundaries of art worlds are not as easy to pin down as membership in a formal organization. The core activity encompasses those people who are socially defined as the artists. Their "suppliers" are broadly understood to include the people who provide resources that help artists accomplish the core activity. Then there are people involved in distribution – the agents, impresarios, concert-hall managers, museum curators, website moderators, disc jockeys, and reviewers. Finally, there are consumers. However, even here we do not find an undifferentiated mass. The most knowledgeable consumers – those having some training or experience in the art form – often make up an important segment of the audience. For the fine arts, one study cited by Becker (1982, p. 53) found that between 40 and 60 percent of those who visit galleries are either artists or art students. In turn, patrons and "serious" members of the audience can be distinguished from the occasional attendee.

Conventions

As the gradations of people's involvement suggests, art worlds are like other culturally defined social worlds such as science or religion: they are organized around specialized knowledge. Participants are distinguished from other people in the society by their familiarity with this knowledge. Such specialized knowledge of an art world encompasses various aspects, but it is centrally concerned with "conventions," where a convention is defined as "a common practice constructed through a tacit agreement process" (D. Lewis 1969, cited in Gilmore 1990). Conventions are especially important for coordinating activities because art worlds lack clear membership and authority relations. Knowledge about them is also important for audiences: just as it is more fun to watch a soccer match if one knows the rules, knowing the conventions of other cultural forms enhances a person's enjoyment of them.

People learn conventions in part through engagement with cultural products. For example, cultures differentiate music from noise on the basis of music's adherence to recognizable conventions. People in Western cultures learn the widely used eight-note scale very early. Simple songs such as "Twinkle, Twinkle, Little Star" train children to "hear" – that is, to recognize and expect common musical progressions. Another set of conventions involves musical notation. Writing music that performers who play instruments can read is one way to coordinate the activity of making music. Serious members of the audience, of course, can also read music. However, some knowledge is so specialized and technical that few members of the audience are likely to possess it. Musicians, for example, need to know how to tune instruments, whereas this knowledge would add very little to the appreciation of the music by a member of the audience. So conventions within an art world range from general ones shared by an audience to highly technical ones used to coordinate the activities of artistic production.

Artists also group themselves into different "schools" on the basis of adherence to certain conventions (and rejection of others). In fact, people at the core of an art world often experiment with conventions quite different from generally familiar ones, and rebellion against standardized conventions can become the basis for innovation (see, for example, Hagaman 1996). Appreciation of many art forms thus requires knowledge about whether and how conventions are being challenged or violated. When the composer John Cage played a recording of street noise on a concert stage, appreciation of his experiment depended both on being able to tell how the staged performance departed from daily life and on how it departed from classical Western music conventions.

Even closely related scenes within a broader art world become differentiated from one another on the basis of how relations between conventions, coordination, and innovation are structured. Gilmore (1987) has explored these relations in the concert-music world of composers, performers, and support personnel in New York City. He found three different scenes there. In the largest and most heavily financed ones – *Midtown* – classical music is played in the Lincoln Center and Carnegie Hall by major symphony orchestras and touring groups.

As a consequence, Midtown participants have a strong organizational interest in musical conventions with which to coordinate concert activities. Concert collaborators have rationalized the production process through the use of a performance "repertory" that standardizes musical notation, instrumentation, and performance techniques. These strong conventions create efficiency, but limit musical innovation. Midtown concerts thus emphasize virtuosity as an aesthetic focus.

(Gilmore 1990, p. 157)

By contrast, *Downtown* – where avant-garde music and performance art is found – includes nonspecialists and composer-performers who use lofts and alternative performance spaces in Greenwich Village, SoHo, and Tribeca. Here, the division of labor is collapsed: composers often perform their own works, and support personnel and collaboration are arranged through exchanges within informal networks. In this scene, Gilmore observed, "New instruments and radically new performance techniques are constantly being introduced." Finally, *Uptown*, serious academic contemporary music is composed and played by musicians affiliated with universities. There, "new performance practices are introduced but on traditional instruments. Notation remains predominantly conventionalized, but new symbols are introduced to represent new sounds" (Gilmore 1990, p. 157). As we would expect, Gilmore found that conventions enhance cooperation between artists and supporters of the core activity. But their importance varies depending on how a scene is organized. The Midtown scene, which requires the cooperation of large numbers of people, is strongly dependent on conventions, whereas innovation thrives in the scenes that are less dependent on them.

Conventions are equally important for audiences. As British critic John Berger has shown for the visual arts, they package cultural content in recognizable forms, and these forms in turn condition how members of the audience perceive and respond to the worlds in which they live. Berger's argument is that there are established conventions for portraying various subjects – the wealthy, the poor, men, women – and that seeing *representations* of these subjects establishes a context for how people see the *subjects* themselves. Conventions concerning depiction of the nude in Western art, for example, treat women as objects to be observed by men. Portrayal of women and non-Europeans as "other" helps men, who are dominant, feel more powerful (J. Berger 1977, pp. 45–64). On a different front Berger argued that in the early modern era specific techniques of oil painting emphasized the materiality of objects in the paintings, in effect rendering those objects as things to be possessed by early capitalists. By staying within these conventional techniques, artists produced works that were recognized as "good" and worth buying and selling through the art market (1977, pp. 83–112). Thus, in Berger's analysis, art-world conventions can simultaneously shape audiences – with regard to how they perceive content – and artists – with regard to how they depict forms.

In deciding how closely to adhere to conventions, cultural workers make choices between maximizing possibilities for distribution and doing something more innovative but "risky." Innovative projects are risky in part because they fall at the boundaries of or outside standard conventions, and thereby tend to appeal to a much smaller audience. Mass culture production is risky in a different way, one that reduces innovation:

The audience is unpredictable, and the people who produce and distribute the work have no real contact with it. They market the work in large quantities, as with books and records, or through a mechanical system, as with radio and television, so that they could not, if they tried, know audience members personally.

(Becker 1982, p. 125)

When there is so much distance between artists, producers, and audience, it is difficult to determine what tastes and conventions might be shared. Therefore, the least risky path is to use well-established conventions known to be effective – such as standard sight gags or dramatic music at a suspenseful moment.

Artists and art worlds

Understanding the relations between conventions, innovation, and coordination makes it possible to identify different kinds of people who engage in creative activity. Whereas psychologists and aestheticians tend to look at talented individuals – although in different ways (Zolberg 1990, pp. 115–24) – it is also possible to classify artists in relation to art worlds and their conventions. Becker has suggested four basic types – integrated professionals, mavericks, folk artists, and naive artists.

The *integrated professional* knows and uses the conventions of the art world and engages in cooperative activities in a routine way. As Becker observed, integrated professionals

> define the problems of their art similarly and agree on criteria for an acceptable solution. They know the history of what previous attempts to solve those problems generated.... They, their support personnel, and their audiences can understand what they have attempted to do and to what degree it works.... Integrated professionals can produce work that is recognizable and understandable to others without being so recognizable and understandable as to be uninteresting.
>
> (Becker 1982, p. 230)

Because integrated professionals are tied into strong cooperative arrangements that have the goal of producing art, not surprisingly, they produce most of what is recognized as art within art worlds.

Maverick artists also have had experience in the art world, but unlike integrated professionals they find conventions too constraining. Mavericks sacrifice cooperation in favor of innovation, and other members of the art world often do not recognize their innovations as art. Because mavericks ignore conventions that make cooperation easy, they can have difficulty getting their work produced. Even if they produce their work themselves, they can encounter difficulty with distribution – getting it seen by critics and accepted by the public. If the work is something to be performed, they may find themselves recruiting and training support personnel – including the audience – from outside the conventionally bounded art world (Becker 1982, pp. 234–5).

The deliberate choice of mavericks to operate outside of an art world again highlights the tension between convention and innovation. As Becker noted, the work of mavericks suggests either ignorance or "blatant disregard for conventional practice" of other artists (1982, p. 233). Their stance can be disturbing to others in an art world because it calls attention to the constraining nature of the art world's conventions. Yet sometimes the maverick's innovation is successful and it is taken into the art world. The compositions of composer Charles Ives are a case in point. Ives wrote music that performers would not play. But instead of forcing Ives to conform to the conventions, their refusal had the opposite effect: he felt free to write music without paying attention to the practical issue of whether or not it was possible to play the music as he imagined it. Despite the difficulties, some of Ives's work eventually became part of concert repertoires. However, Ives is the exception: the work of most mavericks is probably lost (Becker 1982, pp. 233–42).

The third of Becker's types, *folk art*, consists of "work done by ordinary people in the course of their lives, work seldom thought of by those who make or use it as art at all" (1982, p. 245). Singing in a group, dancing at a social event, cooking, and sewing are all activities that socially competent people may learn to do as part of participating in particular communities. These activities could be judged in aesthetic terms, but aesthetic criteria are not usually the primary basis on which they are evaluated in those settings. The point of singing "Happy Birthday" to someone is seldom to achieve a virtuoso performance. Yet the possibility of aesthetic evaluation means that folk objects can become "art" if they are lifted into another context where aesthetic judgments are central, as happens, for example, when quilts are no longer used on the beds of friends and family members to keep people warm but purchased for display by museums or art collectors.

Becker's analysis of folk art points to the role that aesthetic theory plays in creating and defining art worlds. For Becker "art-ness" does not inhere in the object, but rather in the relation of the object to an art world. Ordinary people make aesthetic judgments in their daily lives. They may occasionally comment when someone at church sings off key, and they note that someone is an especially good cook or that a cake is beautifully decorated. But fulfilling social roles competently does not require artistic abilities or performances. In fact, in some circumstances it is considered impolite either to judge things by aesthetic standards or to "show off" one's own abilities. Furthermore, even when aesthetic judgments are made, they are usually not articulated in terms of a well-developed aesthetic theory that specifies in detail how to evaluate an object. This all changes when everyday cultural objects become defined as "art."

Finally, Becker identified *naive art*. In this form of production, producers of work view their creations as art, but they lack knowledge about the conventions of an art world and usually do not receive recognition within it. Naive art work is thus idiosyncratic (see Figure 9.1). In Becker's account, "The reasons for doing [the art] are personal and not always intelligible…. These works, not belonging to any tradition of artistically defined problems or solutions, seem to spring out of nowhere. No one knows how to respond to them" (1982, p. 264). Naive artists operate outside of any art world, and their works often use nonstandard materials and nonstandard methods of construction. Consider the house in Houston made out of 39,000 beer cans (P.L. Brown 1991), or the 25-acre mosaic sculpture garden in Chandigarh, India, that was created over a period of forty years by Nek Chand, a transport worker (Rawvision.com 2002). Such objects, if they receive any recognition, are likely to end up in *Ripley's Believe It or Not* or a website devoted to oddities, rather than an art museum. They demonstrate a creative impulse, but they do not fit conventional ideas about art.

Becker's categories emphasize differences, not in the quality of the product, but in the relation of artists and their work to one or another art world. The work of inte-

Figure 9.1 During the 1960s, in Sleepy Hollow, Kentucky, Henry Dorsey welcomed visitors who
wanted to see his electric-powered yard-sculpture garden composed of found objects.
His enterprise could usefully be viewed through the lenses of the surrealist, neo-
Dada, and kinetic-art movements, and it paralleled much in the movements of Pop
Art and found-object composition among professional artists integrated into high-
culture art worlds. However, he expressed his vision well outside any established art
world.

Source: J.R. Hall photograph, 1968.

grated professionals receives the most support and rewards, and it is the most likely to
be recognized and preserved as art. However, since the boundaries of art worlds are
not fixed, works by mavericks, folk artists, and naive artists occasionally are incorporated into art worlds, as, for example, when an art world's boundaries change.

Boundaries

The conventions that define art also provide a basis for defining who is inside an art
world and who is not, who is eligible for rewards and who is not. These boundaries are
important because, although there is much cooperation in art worlds, there are typically
more artists than resources – including financial support for developing projects,
performance space, gallery space, promotion, and recognition. Under these conditions,
artists will compete for resources. In doing so, they will be well served by making efforts
to determine whether potential collaborators operate strongly within the conventional
boundaries of the art world. Observance of conventions alerts an art-world participant
to how much effort will be required to work with a potential collaborator.

As important as the boundaries of art worlds are for collaboration, however, they are not static, in part because art worlds themselves are in competition with one another. Especially when innovation is valued, there is some pressure for conventions to change. The work of mavericks and even naive artists is occasionally incorporated into an art world. Activities previously considered crafts or folk arts may become defined as serious art. Take, for example, the incorporation of clay as a medium into art. Becker (1982) describes how artists who had little concern for traditional craft virtuoso standards began to experiment with using clay. To distinguish their own work from craft production, they made deliberately nonfunctional art objects. In a related development, very skilled craftspeople working in clay began to compete with artists for gallery and museum space. Such transitions have an impact on the conventions of both the craft and the art world.

Boundaries, however, are not solely marked by conventions about how things are done. They are also sometimes based on other considerations, notably the characteristics of participants. Women and minorities have been excluded from many art worlds, in some cases by being prevented from learning the conventions. Women in Western societies, for example, were not allowed in life-drawing classes in the nineteenth century. According to Linda Nochlin (1971), one result of this exclusion was the nineteenth-century institutionalization of an image of women artists as "lady painters." Living outside the boundaries of established art worlds, these women would "dabble" in media like watercolor, thus displaying the Victorian feminine ideals of being well rounded, refined, and not too intellectually engaged in an activity that, though worthwhile, could certainly be put down at a moment's notice in favor of wifely and motherly duties.

The model of the lady painter contrasts strongly with the mythic image of the "artist as male hero." How, then, do women artists position themselves in relation to these opposing cultural constructs? Bette J. Kauffman (1995) has interviewed members of women's cooperative art galleries in Philadelphia and New York City to address this question. She finds that the way women talk about their artistic careers sometimes reifies the stereotypical distinction between male and female spheres of activity, and at other times explicitly politicizes the differences. In either case, the gendered boundaries of institutionalized art worlds have important effects for participants.

Native-American artists also have had to confront dominant cultural constructs of the artist, as Leuthold (1995) has shown. By examining video documentaries about native-American artists made by both natives and non-natives, Leuthold identifies two different sets of assumptions about native-American artists, their art, and their relations to ethnicity and tradition. In videos highlighting "traditionalist" approaches, art work is not separated from other spheres of life, and it is often indistinguishable from religion. As Leuthold observes, "The traditional society allows for individual styles and artistic developments but legitimates art through the recognition of a communicative code that has endured across time. Perseverance takes precedence over progress and innovation" (1995, p. 279). On the other hand, documentaries about "contemporary" approaches focus on the innovative, personal, and autonomous aspects of art making. Native-American artists thus confront a choice between two different approaches to art-world success. Their choices have consequences not only for their own careers but also for tribal traditions and relations between cultures.

Leuthold's analysis illustrates a principle asserted earlier by Paul DiMaggio (1987, pp. 449–51) – that groups located at different places in culture industries make classifications about art on the basis of different principles, even in relation to more or less the same work. Victorian novelists, for instance, wanted to mark off the high-culture novel as an art form distinguished from popular novels written by women. By such strategies of "professional classification," artists often try to control the development of their own and others' reputations. But cultural distributors who sell art for profit may develop quite different "commercial classifications" of the same materials. And those who deal with government regulation develop "administrative classifications."

Struggles over classification schemes are revealing episodes in contestations over culture more generally. For example, consider photography soon after it was introduced to the United States in the nineteenth century. As people began experimenting with the new technology, and especially as the business of making photographic portraits began to take off, practitioners sought to define their own and others' activities in relation to boundaries of practice that they sought to conventionalize. The earliest period of photography in the United States was dominated by one process and one type of practice – the daguerreotype and commercial portrait photography. But when amateurs began experimenting with photography in the 1860s, and subsequently, as manufacturers developed simplified technologies and turned their efforts to creating a mass market of casual amateur photographers in the 1880s, pitched battles ensued over who deserved the title of photographer and, ultimately, who among them could claim the status of artist. Early and successful daguerreotypists sought distinction by promoting an image of their studios as places of refined culture. The success of this strategy is evident in the lasting reputations of "high-class" daguerreotypists who already in their own time were rewarded with professional recognition, profitable business, and the ability to dictate to the photographic supply houses. Later, these same practitioners gained prominence in histories of photography as art (Battani 1999; cf. Christopherson 1974; Bourdieu *et al.* 1990). By a range of such strategies, nineteenth-century U.S. photographers sought to endow their practices with cultural capital, and thus gain status and economic advantage.

The drawing of art-world boundaries may also have powerful ordering qualities that differentiate insiders from outsiders within a broader society (Zolberg and Cherbo 1997). Anne Bowler (1997), for example, has drawn on Foucault to show how in the early twentieth century experts in European, British, and eventually U.S. art worlds began to find aesthetic value in the works of asylum patients. For the gate-keepers, this outsider art was emblematic of the modernist avant-garde, which found inspiration in the powerfully critical idea that madness and genius were linked in their resistance against a dominant culture increasingly ordered by instrumental reason. The irony, according to Bowler, is that the critical character of asylum art depends on its marginalization, thereby affirming the deviant character of the asylum patient and strengthening what Foucault described as the disciplinary power of rational medical and scientific discourses. In this case, and no doubt more broadly, art-world boundaries are dialectically connected with broader formations of cultural boundaries.

Culture industries

The art-worlds approach to cultural production, by thematizing conventions, activities, and boundaries, brings to light the social construction of cultural practices and their symbolic creations. An alternative approach comes out of the sociology of organizations. Sociologists who studied formal organizations in the mid-twentieth century sometimes misused Max Weber's ideal type of bureaucracy to conceptualize modern organizations as "rational." James Thompson (1967), however, argued that an organization's ability to act rationally was "bounded" by "uncertainties" stemming either from the environment or from technology. Culture-producing organizations – for example book publishers or music-recording producers – came to the attention of organizational theorists in part because uncertainties in these industries come from the environment rather than technology (on books, for example, see Coser *et al.* 1982). Thus, although technologies for recording music and producing books change, Paul Hirsch (1972) has argued that culture producers face greater uncertainty over which performing artists to record or which books to publish. This is the "input boundary." Even more problematic is the "output boundary" – where judgments must be made about how to distribute a product and whether to promote one product over another, including how to decide which products have the greatest chances of becoming "hits." Activities at the input boundary organize resources for the *production* of cultural objects, and activities at the output boundary organize the *distribution* of cultural products.

Organizing resources and distributing product

Hirsch's model assumes that artists are in excess supply (there are more individuals whose work producers can choose from than could ever be produced) and that choosing among them is a difficult process. Hirsch argued that organizations deal with this uncertainty in part by distributing risks. Thus, organizations may use agents or talent scouts based outside of the organization to pre-screen talent for them. They may also pay artists through royalties instead of either buying the products outright or putting artists on salary. Organizations also minimize risks by producing far more objects (e.g. films) than they intend to distribute and promote, and deciding at a later juncture which ones will be most profitable and therefore which ones should receive the greatest effort in distribution and promotion.

The issue of distribution is complex because cultural products often are "marginally differentiated" from one another rather than radically dissimilar, and, as the popular saying has it, "There's no accounting for taste." This situation creates uncertainty at the "output boundary," an uncertainty further compounded by relations with "cultural gatekeepers." Gatekeepers typically operate within mass-media outlets that present cultural products to a wider audience, and they promote only a small portion of the items that are produced. Traditionally, such gatekeepers – reviewers, talk-show hosts, disc jockeys, and the like – do not work directly for a culture-producing organization. Yet such organizations could not survive without them.

Although gatekeepers have some goals that overlap with those of producers, in general the gatekeepers seek to make independent judgments about the worth of a product (Ahlkvist and Faulkner 2002). On the one hand, as Hirsch (1972, pp. 654–5) pointed out, mass-media gatekeepers are unlikely to be coopted by culture producers because their interests differ in two respects. First, there is a "norm of independent judgment" among gatekeepers, which discourages them from simply endorsing a product. Second, this norm is reinforced because mass media have a greater interest in delivering an audience to advertisers than in promoting specific cultural items.

Hirsch, however, also described a symbiosis between mass media and culture industries, and this symbiosis undoubtedly has increased in the years since Hirsch's analysis was published. Recent changes in culture industries – namely, intense vertical integration and technological convergence (discussed in Chapter 8) – tend to undermine the role of gatekeepers as autonomous actors in distribution networks. Although the norm of objectivity among critics and journalists is still strong enough that a critic charged with reviewing a film produced by his or her parent company is likely to seek to assert an independent judgment, culture-industries companies have found ways to coopt the gatekeeping process that do not involve directly influencing critics. Entertainment news, for example, offers a format for regular reporting on film open-ings, box-office figures, and music popularity – without the need to offer any form of review or endorsement. The effect can be considerable, especially for big-budget films that often succeed or fail based on opening-week revenues.

Other strategies for reducing risk – integration and cross-promotion – further blur the distinction between product and promotion. Take, for example, the popular U.S. television show from the late 1990s, *Making the Band*. The production company for this show, working in collaboration with ABC and MTV, used a nationwide talent search to find a few dozen aspiring young male singers and dancers. These young men then went through try-outs held to select members of a pop band with a recording and touring contract under the tutelage of Lou Pearlman, a famous producer of already highly successful groups. *Making the Band* followed the trials and tribulations of the contestants. In sociological terms, searching for and developing talent – activities that are conventionally located at the input boundary of the producing organization – were brought inside and treated as a product (the television show). Similarly, promotion was effectively collapsed into a product: the show advertised the band. In turn, the networks' entertainment-news divisions interviewed the contestants, reported on the innovative new show, and announced the release of the compact discs produced and distributed by another division of the media conglomerate. How routine such integra-tive cross-promotion configurations might become remains unclear, but a parallel approach has been employed in the so-called reality shows produced in both the U.S. and Europe – *Survivor, Big Brother,* and *The Greatest Race*. These shows center on non-unionized contestants who are much less expensive than actors. A season-long contest among them is charted in dramatic weekly one-hour installments and shad-owed by a steady stream of former contestants, who, upon having been eliminated from the competition, appear on various of the network's talk shows.

Quite apart from new forms being introduced based on risk reduction, established patterns of distribution sometimes change in other ways, and such changes can affect the cultural content of a particular form. Richard Peterson (1978) explains changes in country music in these terms. In 1959 a group of industry executives formed the Country Music Association to promote their music, and they convinced a number of radio-station managers to adopt a full-time country-music format. The number of country-music stations tripled by 1965 (Peterson 1978, p. 299). This success, however, created a problem. Before 1960, not only did country music have a distinctive sound (with regional variations), but country-music programmers – disc jockeys, music direc-tors, and station managers – also had a distinctive style. They knew about the music, presented material in a conversational "folksy" manner, and played a variety of performers and kinds of music. With the expanding number of stations, however, the demand for country programmers outran supply. At the same time, as stations adopted the country format they had an interest in shifting the style of the music, based on a difference between the traditional country audience – working-class males – and the radio advertisers' ideal market – female consumers.

In something of a hybrid solution, many stations found themselves shifting to a country format while staffing the new programs with personnel who had formerly played rock or easy-listening music. Because the DJs knew little about country music, "modern" country radio stations adopted a "top-40" format with much more emphasis on new releases, to the neglect of older music. Under the new system, a few country performers became "stars" to a degree previously not possible, but many older performers got less airplay, and the lines between country and other musical genres blurred because the new DJs favored crossover artists. In one direction, Waylon Jennings and Dolly Parton crossed over *from* country to pop. Conversely, John Denver and Olivia Newton-John crossed from the pop charts *to* country. Top-40 country-music stations began to sound much more like other top-40 stations. The record industry changed as well. Country music – once the most stable market sector, with known recording artists who had predictable if not spectacular sales – became very unstable. Before the big changes, with a smaller but known audience, promotion was not so important, and a record with modest sales could still make money. In 1965 records rarely sold a million copies. However, by 1977 a record had to sell a million to be "successful" because promotion had become more expensive (Peterson 1978, pp. 307–8).

As Peterson's analysis demonstrates, we cannot assume that changes in cultural styles are driven only by changes in the tastes of consumers or innovations by artists. For country music, changes in styles were caused by industry changes that resulted in the creation of new audiences for new kinds of music. Similar forces have come into play in Hollywood movie production and promotion (Baker and Faulkner 1991). These and other studies along these lines show that transformations in the organization of production can shape the kinds of culture audiences receive.

Innovation in culture industries

As country music and the composition of its audience changed, participants in the country-music world faced a dilemma. How is it possible to create innovative and original music – a requirement of the commercial-music industry – while maintaining the sense of tradition and heritage that has been central to the authenticity of country as a genre? In *Creating Country Music: Fabricating Authenticity* (1997b), Peterson shows that country musicians negotiating this dilemma repeatedly have had to face the charge that authentic country music was dead. As early as 1910 the displacement of balladeers with string bands was declaimed as signaling the end of the music. Nearly a century later, a critic in the mid-1990s, Tony Scherman, asserted that country music was no longer authentic because the social conditions that spawned the genre had been eclipsed: "Country music was born of the trauma of rural people's adjustment to industrial society, but that fight has been fought" (quoted in Peterson 1997b, p. 222).

Peterson argues that authenticity is not a static quality. It is, rather, a renewable resource that is historically reworked and changed through ongoing interactions between audiences, creators, and industry operatives. Creating a sense of authenticity, according to Peterson, takes effort. Early country musicians conveyed their authenticity by playing traditional forms of music. From the 1950s onward, they were encouraged to demonstrate that the music they were performing was part of their authentic rural experience. By the 1990s, a self-reflexive collective memory of what constitutes country music had become available in books, photographs, recorded music, documentaries, and places like the Country Music Hall of Fame. With the codification of a country-music heritage, artists today can affirm authenticity by showing that they know and respect the tradition, and want to carry it forward (Peterson 1997b, p. 225).

Thus, even while the country-music industry establishes innovations in musical distribution (e.g. the shift to a top-40 format), performers can affirm their authenticity as country artists by affecting a certain accent, vocabulary, grammar, and general working-class identification, and by adhering to certain performance conventions like reprising early hits and introducing the hometowns of band members. Industry publicists contribute to the process by producing press packs for local newspapers that include praise from established country artists, descriptions of great fan acceptance in the southern U.S., and folksy histories of artists' early family musical experiences. Overall, country musicians seek to perform original new work while simultaneously demonstrating their authenticity relative to a fairly explicit model – the established country conventions that have become increasingly codified since the 1950s.

By looking at the social construction of a genre in a particular industry, Peterson deepens our understanding of the processes of cultural power discussed in Chapter 8. The project of consolidating claims of authenticity for country music, according to Peterson, requires building an institutional system, and one of the best ways to obscure this act of arbitrary power is to propagate the idea that the institutional system builds upon a "natural" category – country music (1997b, p. 212). It would be worth asking whether this fabrication of authenticity in country music works in a way analogous to the creation of other apparently "natural" distinctions – of race, gender, class, and region – that are constructed on a wider and more diffuse basis. But this is not a question to pursue here. In terms of specific cultural production, Peterson's analysis explains innovation in country music as deriving from changes in the structure of the industry, while conventions are deployed to maintain distinctions that keep the identity of country music separate from other genres (especially pop music) in the commercial field. Innovations in culture-industry production are mediated by the construction and maintenance of cultural genres that are aligned with audiences and their conventionalized constructions of cultural categories.

Rewards

Given the power of industries to shape cultural genres, what motivates artists to participate? One answer is that art worlds, like other social worlds, offer their participants both material and symbolic rewards. Diana Crane (1976) has suggested that an important dimension of reward systems in cultural worlds – including art, science, and religion – concerns who controls the evaluation process for allocating rewards. In her analysis, the more that insiders control rewards, the more innovation will occur. Crane distinguishes four kinds of reward systems: (1) *independent* reward systems, where producers themselves define appropriate problems and solutions and allocate symbolic and material rewards; (2) *semi-independent* reward systems, where producers define problems and allocate symbolic rewards, but consumers allocate material rewards; (3) *subcultural* reward systems, in which work is produced for a small, relatively homogeneous audience that allocates rewards; and (4) *hetero-cultural* reward systems, where cultural production depends on new ideas originating in one of the other three systems that are then are reproduced for a heterogeneous mass audience.

In Crane's view, innovation within an art world is less likely when rewards are scarce. Mavericks, folk artists, and naive artists may be wildly innovative, but their relation to the art world is such that they tend to remain outside of its reward system. In order for a system to produce both variety and continuity, she argues: (1) there has to be a balance between the availability of resources and the number of innovators; and (2) symbolic rewards must be as important as material rewards. The hetero-cultural system is the least likely to produce innovations, according to Crane, because although consumers allocate symbolic rewards, entrepreneurs allocate material rewards, and the material rewards are more important than symbolic rewards (see Figure 9.2).

Empirical studies of material rewards for creative artists are few. Work on the topic is complicated both by the difficulty of determining a representational sample of artists (do we count all the people who have ever sold things they made for crafts fairs?) and because it is difficult to assess their earnings. One study of artists' earnings used labor-income data collected by the U.S. Census in 1979 to compare a sample of artists with non-artists. In marked contrast with the stereotype of the struggling artist, the study found that artists on average earned only 6 percent less than non-artists, although there were differences among types of artists, with actors being the best paid, and musicians and dancers the worst paid (Filer 1986, p. 61).

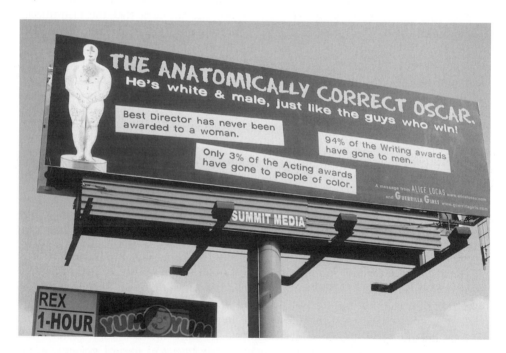

Figure 9.2 This billboard, erected in Los Angeles for the 2002 Oscar ceremonies, was created by the "Guerilla Girls" to focus attention on the gender and ethnic bias of the American Motion Picture Academy's reward system. Calling themselves "the conscience of the art world," the Guerilla Girls use a variety of activist strategies to critique the way that economic and symbolic rewards are apportioned in art worlds, in this case by making the coveted trophy look more like "the white males who take him home each year."

Source: Courtesy of the Guerilla Girls.

Compared to material rewards, symbolic rewards might seem more likely to offer evidence of the "extraordinary" nature of artistic work. But, here, the production-of-culture perspective shows how reputation is "socially constructed." In one view, people who interpret a work of art become participants in creating the meaning of the work; those who take this view are sometimes called "death of the author" theorists (e.g. Bakhtin 1968; see also Becker 1982; Zolberg 1990). This thesis is controversial for its dismissal of artistic creativity, but it rightly emphasizes that the reputations of works of art, artists, and even art forms are not established facts based on universally affirmed standards of excellence, but, rather, judgments open to contestation and reassessment. Thus, for instance, a study of the rise of the modern auction for art works found that "only in the past hundred years has the market ennobled paintings to a rank above objects whose major virtue was the lavish materials, skill, and ingenuity that went into them" (Faith 1987, p. 95). Before 1890 works of Renaissance silversmiths could be worth more than paintings by old masters such as Raphael.

A study of etching between the 1880s and 1940 by Lang and Lang (1988) pursues the issue of specific artists' reputations. They ask what factors increase the likelihood that an individual with a reputation in etching when the art form was at its height would be remembered today. They find qualities inherent in the art to be less important than other factors. Artists with a reputation as etchers who also achieved fame in other mediums – for example James Whistler or Mary Cassatt – were more likely to be remembered. Among artists who worked primarily in etching, the likelihood that they are still remembered increases when: (1) artists, during their lifetimes, made efforts to preserve their work, for example by producing in quantity and keeping good records of their working process and sales transactions; (2) other individuals, during the artists' lifetimes and after, undertook a conservator's role, preserving the work and reputations of the artists; (3) an artist is linked to circles of people of historical interest, such that the reputation of others may enhance interest in the artist; and (4) "retroactive interest" in the artist's work arises because it can be viewed as an indicator of "emerging cultural or political identities." These factors, Lang and Lang find, worked against women etchers: women in their study often produced fewer objects and were less likely to have a spouse outlive them and take on the conservator role. The Langs conclude:

> What obviously matters most in the long run is the proximity of the deceased to institutions with organized arrangements for the archiving and restoration of the historical evidence. Particularly those who have enjoyed power and influence in their lifetimes are also more likely to have friends with influence and connections to archives.
>
> (Lang and Lang 1988, pp. 101–2)

In sum, the Langs' and other studies emphasize that institutional and structural factors, including the labor market, affect how artists are rewarded, not only financially, but symbolically as well.

The state and culture production

In our considerations of cultural production to this point, we have focused mainly on cultural workers and the organization of their direct activities. But national and local governments have an impact on the arts as well. State funding provides significant financial support for art and art institutions. Governments also have directly influenced the content of art through censorship of individual artists and works of art, as well as by promoting certain styles (such as socialist realism in the People's Republic of China) and by condemning other styles (such as modern expressionism under the Nazi regime, or the wide range of art and expression deemed un-Islamic under the Taliban in Afghanistan). Legal restrictions of various kinds can also shape the environment in which cultural production takes place.

Legal restrictions

Mass-culture industries with public avenues of distribution operate in an environment shaped in part by government regulations. Broadcasting in the U.S., for example, must be licensed by the Federal Communications Commission, and many restrictions apply, including how powerful a signal a station can use in broadcasting. Before U.S. deregulation in the 1980s, there were other restrictions concerning content. Broadcasters were required to subscribe to norms about "fairness" and "equal time" when presenting controversial issues, and to air a certain number of "public service announcements."

Restraint-of-trade rules in the U.S. until recently also restricted vertical integration in the movie industry and limited the number of television stations that network broadcasting companies could own and operate. Presumably such separations between production and distribution promote competition and enhance both opportunities for cultural production and choices for consumers. However, culture-industry representatives successfully argued the opposite view during the 1980s and 1990s. In their account, technological changes – especially digital technologies – opened up new opportunities for production and distribution on such a scale that monopoly and restraint of trade are no longer likely scenarios (see Croteau and Hoynes 2001 on the disingenuous nature of this argument).

Another domain of state regulation is copyright law, which regulates legal ownership of art works, thus affecting who can use an art work, how it can be sold, and who profits. A study of the American novel by Wendy Griswold (1981) provides a striking example of how copyright law can influence cultural content. Literary critics have long explained the uniqueness of the American novel as a reflection of uniquely American character traits. One version of this argument suggests that, whereas European novelists write about love and marriage, "classic American fiction is about men removing themselves from society, especially from women who seem to represent the constraints of social and domestic life" (Griswold 1981, p. 743). To evaluate such claims, Griswold studied a random sample of 130 novels written by American and European authors and published in America during four time periods, beginning in 1876 and ending in 1910. She found that most authors, American and European, did write about love and marriage. Significant differences could be found in the content of American and European novels in the earlier periods, but styles converged after 1890. Griswold argues that the early differences in novels are not explained by differences in national character, but rather by differences in the market positions of European and American writers. Before a change in copyright laws in 1891, U.S. companies could republish works previously published elsewhere without paying royalties. With competition from abroad, U.S. writers were pushed "to deviate from the norm, to write on nontraditional themes that the European authors had not effectively monopolized." After the change in copyright laws, competition leveled out, "the novelistic imperatives took over, and the American authors swung into line with everyone else" (Griswold 1981, p. 760).

State cultural production, censorship, and funding

Artistic freedom of expression is highly valued within most art worlds today, and censorship of any kind is anathema to artists. Although we can cite a few explicit cases of censorship – such as the Afghan Taliban's strict prohibitions on television, video games, and popular music – censorship is rarely so direct or blatant. Nonetheless, public media such as television, radio, and film do confront regulations designed to restrict the availability of certain content – notably sex, violence, and profanity. Although the application of such restrictions causes controversy, the failure to control content also causes controversy. As mechanisms of censorship, restrictions are probably most important in the ways that artists (and their suppliers and distributors) include them in their calculations, thus engaging in self-censorship in order to avoid possible problems.

The dominance of the action-adventure genre in Pakistani film can be at least partially explained as the result of such "problem avoidance." Pakistan's Lahore region, "Lollywood," is one of the most prolific commercial film centers in the world, although clearly subordinate to India's "Bollywood." According to Elphicke (2001), filmmakers in Lollywood suffer from extreme censorship by the government, yet they are also protected by the government's tight restrictions on imported films. Because of the censorship, Lollywood filmmakers essentially make one conventional action film over and over again, while more innovative Pakistani filmmakers have moved their operations to India to take advantage of the television market there (one effect in India of the success of the Bollywood feature-film industry has been a depletion of television programming). Here, the content of the artistic product is strongly shaped by the conditions under which it is produced, in this case state regulation.

According to Becker, "The state is primarily interested in the way art affects mass mobilization – it supports art so that the population can be mobilized for the right things and suppresses art because it fears people will be mobilized for the wrong things" (1982, p. 187). As Victoria Bonnell frames the problem in her study of Soviet political posters between 1917 and 1953, "The critical issue facing the Bolsheviks in 1917 was not merely the seizure of power but the seizure of meaning" (1997, p. 1). When the Bolsheviks took power they faced the problem of communicating with a largely illiterate population under conditions unfavorable to cultural production. The revolution had resulted in paper shortages, closings of printing plants, and transportation disruptions. It was difficult to publish newspapers, and their effectiveness was limited by the size of their audiences. So the new Soviet rulers turned to visual media. Mass-produced posters that united political ideology and traditional religious iconography were used to promote social cohesion, legitimate authority, and socialize the population into new values and behavior. In the initial years of the revolution, artists who had training in either religious or political painting produced the propaganda posters. By the 1930s, however, state schools were graduating political artists under direct supervision of the Soviets, and image production became increasingly centralized (Bonnell 1997, p. 12).

Despite its attraction as a source of power, centralizing the production of art or its funding can have unintended consequences for states attempting to remake themselves.

Following independence in 1947, India confronted issues similar to those faced by the Soviets. As Vera Zolberg (1993) has shown, the Indian government worked to help create a new public culture by funding state museums mandated to provide equal access to the arts and folkways of India's diverse tribal and religious subcultures. Over 400 such state museums were established by imitating similar museums in the West. Through imitation, Zolberg argues, the Indian museums tended to recreate the intellectual logics of colonialism, in part by reifying ethnic differences through a "fuzzy essentialism" (1993, p. 245). Rather than blurring parochial differences and bringing formerly excluded groups into a common national culture, making cultures the objects of museum study exacerbated differences and thereby exposed the state to criticism. Similarly, in the Soviet-satellite (East) German Democratic Republic (GDR) vigorous state funding of the arts helped create a situation in which artists and audiences could begin to identify with modern art, and, on this basis, critique the state's hegemonic official culture and advocate cultural reform. "Ironically," comments Rueschemeyer, "over the years, nonconformist artists acquired a strong voice precisely because art had been established as an important component of official culture" (1993, p. 230–1).

The cases of India and the former GDR show that controlling society by controlling aesthetic production does not always work. However, there are other possible relationships. In totalitarian states, art and politics have often been close allies. Simonetta Falasca-Zamponi shows, for example, how Mussolini's fascist government in Italy applied an aesthetic theory (*l'art pour l'art*) and practice (Italian futurism) to create a powerful logic that constructed politics *as* art. Mussolini presented himself unapologetically as the state leader/great artist who shaped his raw material – the crowd – by saturating their senses with a state aesthetic and directing them toward the ultimate choreography of the state – warfare (Falasca-Zamponi 1997; see also Berezin 1997; Bowler 1991). A somewhat different alliance of art and politics toward totalitarian ends can be found in Saddam Hussein's Iraq. In *The Monument: Art, Vulgarity, and Responsibility in Iraq*, Samir Khalil (1991) describes the ubiquitous portraits and monumental images of Saddam as a variation on Pop Art – a celebration of an advertising aesthetic. In a way analogous to modern corporate advertising, Hussein's use of official art saturates the environment with a populist egalitarian image. The image of Saddam is seen speaking for the people and their desires (rather than openly dominating them), while the proliferation of images simultaneously exerts control by crowding out possible alternatives to the official line.

Of course, it is not just totalitarian regimes that shape, use, support, and control the arts. In the U.S., government funding of the arts began in the nineteenth century with sculpture and architecture projects celebrating the ideals of democracy (city halls, capitol buildings). Later, during the 1930s, the government-funded artists who were enlisted to help legitimate reformist social programs (Stange 1989). Then, after World War II, arts funding dramatically increased when celebration of the modern arts emerged as an important foreign-policy instrument used to demonstrate the advancement and triumph of American culture on the global stage (N. Harris 2001).

When it comes to limiting the influence of the arts, democratic governments are most likely to regulate distribution networks. In the U.S., for example, literary works have been in effect "censored" through application of the Comstock law – an 1873 statute that prohibits sending lewd or obscene works through the postal system. This law shapes censorship in the U.S. down to the present day. In 1957, Samuel Roth, the publisher of the literary magazine *American Aphrodite*, was convicted of violating the

Comstock law by printing and sending through the mail an issue with an excerpt from an unpublished manuscript, "Venus and Tannhauser," written in the 1890s by Aubrey Beardsley. Although Roth's case was appealed all the way to the Supreme Court, he lost and served five years in prison. Justice William Brennan, writing for the majority in the case, established criteria that still stand. Obscene materials do not enjoy first-amendment protection of free speech, he wrote, but for materials to be judged obscene they have to "violate community standards" and be "utterly without social importance." Although the community-standards provision is ambiguous, free-speech advocates in the 1950s and 1960s effectively used a number of test cases to fight against censorship by arguing that particular works had redeeming social value (E. de Grazia 1991).

Supreme Court rulings left an opening in the U.S. for states or communities to engage in censorship. Thus, at the local level works are sometimes prohibited: certain books may not be allowed in a local library, or a local board may set standards for screening motion pictures in public theaters. Although judgments about sex and violence have been the most frequent targets, censorship has also been used against works believed to incite hatred toward minority groups. For example, D.W. Griffith's film *The Birth of a Nation* (made in 1915), which portrayed the Ku Klux Klan in a positive light, was banned by the governor of Ohio, partly in response to campaigns by the National Association for the Advancement of Colored People (NAACP). More recently, in 1990 a painting ridiculing the now deceased Chicago Mayor Harold Washington was removed from a student show at Chicago's Art Institute by members of the city council (Dubin 1992). Such local censorship tends to arouse less concern among advocates of free speech because copies of the work typically are available elsewhere.

Overall, the popular arts are more likely than fine arts to be controlled by censorship, because censorship typically operates by regulating distribution. This, however, is only one aspect of potential state interference with culture. Another possibility derives from state support of the creative activities of artists. It is here that elite arts are more likely to be controlled – by withdrawal of Federal funds. In some arguments currently put forward within art worlds, for the state to withdraw financial support because of objections to the content of art work is, in effect, censorship.

In 1999 Rudolf Giuliani, then mayor of New York City, sought to cut off all city funds to the Brooklyn Museum in response to an exhibition called "Sensations" that featured work by an often controversial group known as the Young British Artists. At the center of the controversy was a painting by Chris Ofili that incorporated elephant dung and pornographic images in a canvas depicting the Virgin Mary. Supporters of the piece argued for a complex interpretation affirming the Catholic faith of the artist, but Mayor Giuliani and some religious activists saw it as an attack on Catholics. In the end, their attempt to cut off funding to the museum was unsuccessful. Analyzing the controversy, David Halle (2001) concludes that efforts to reduce government funding for the arts are most successful in the *absence* of any popular perception of censorship. He cites surveys showing that the public is ambivalent about Federal funding for the arts, but very strongly supportive of first-amendment rights to free speech. Still, controversy over U.S. government funding of the arts increased so much during the 1980s and early 1990s that people routinely spoke of the "culture wars" (Hunter 1991).

An implicit assumption undergirds arguments that the arts should be supported with public funds – namely, that arts constitute a public good. Supporting this view is a study by Judith Blau (1989), which argues that, while the arts were once concentrated in cities with the greatest amount of inequality, that is no longer the case. On the other hand, employing a cultural-capital argument, DiMaggio and Useem (1978) argue that historically the arts have primarily benefited elites – by providing them enjoyment and enhancing their status. Because of the tension between the arts as a public good and elite domination of the arts, DiMaggio and Useem suggest that the public and policymakers in the United States need to think about barriers and incentives to democratization of the arts.

Producing people's culture

What if there were a popular cultural form that was democratic, at least in the sense that it provided a forum for everyday folk – people typically excluded both from representation in mass media and from participation in the elite arts? What might such a forum look like, how might it function, and what effects could it have? In *The Money Shot: Trash, Class, and the Making of TV Talk Shows* (2002), sociologist Laura Grindstaff uses a production perspective to examine what is arguably just such a form – the daytime television talk show. Grindstaff's study is important to consider here because it is emblematic of the potential that Richard Peterson saw in the production perspective when he coined the term in the 1970s.

Daytime talk shows feature real people, their life experiences, and the true stories they have to tell. Shows within the genre range from "trashy" to "classy," depending on how sensational their subject matter and featured guests might be. The move in the 1990s toward a more trashy approach (and higher audience ratings that went along with it) led to considerable criticism of talk shows in the popular press. These criticisms have some persistent themes – that the genre and the people participating in it exhibit very poor taste, coarsen the culture, and offer little more than a contemporary version of the nineteenth-century circus freak show.

The criticisms target basic aspects of the shows' formats and content that derive from how they are produced. Creating talk on TV, as Grindstaff shows, depends on routinized production techniques that constrain what people can and will say and how they can say it when they appear as guests or experts on one of the shows. All the shows, regardless of their status as classy or trashy, share a concern for producing what Grindstaff calls the "money shot," the moment when guests on the show deliver raw emotion – joy, sorrow, remorse, or sometimes rage and physical violence. The money shot affirms the authenticity of what the viewer is seeing. In a way, Grindstaff argues, television more generally shares this interest: "Most media texts, in fact, are organized around moments of dramatic revelation and emotional intensity – organized, that is, around some version of the money shot" (2002, p. 20).

The need to gather guests together on a routine basis and get them to tell real stories in a compelling way makes the work of producing a talk show similar to news production – supposedly a very different activity. Talk show producers, like news reporters, have beat territories that they search for potential stories, and they have routinized sources through which they track down potential guests. The supply of newsworthy events is unpredictable (despite the growth in the staging of media events), so editors want to have ready supplies of " 'timeless features,' which are not 'pegged' or connected to a specific event and thus can be run at any time; these are called pegless wonders, or evergreens" (Gans 1979, p. 109). TV talk shows are even more reliant on previously told stories for their material. As Grindstaff observes,

Producers will unabashedly take a news item or an idea from elsewhere and personalize it, making it "friendly" to a talk-show audience, or they will take a topic from another talk show and put a different twist or spin on it.

(Grindstaff 2002, p. 83)

Although there are structural similarities between the production of news programs and TV talk shows, there are also significant differences. First, granted, news talk shows such as those on Fox News employ some techniques that parallel those of daytime talk, going for their own "money shots." Still, talk shows feature ordinary people and occasional experts, not celebrities or people involved in notable public events – or claiming to offer informed public comment on them. Second, in the search for the all-important money shot, talk-show producers strongly encourage the display of unrefined emotion and physicality over and above civil and thoughtful discussion. Indeed, what makes ordinary folks authentically ordinary in the context of these shows is the money shot, and this is the principle on which all production is organized. Ordinary people are explicitly coached ("fluffed" in industry terminology), as Grindstaff observes, to "discuss mostly personal matters pertaining to sexuality, identity, interpersonal relationships, and victimization or abuse, and their expertise stems from firsthand experience rather than formal educational or professional credentials" (2002, p. 19). This "everyday" expertise potentially has subversive implications, as Joshua Gamson (1998) has shown in relation to sexual identities. However, according to Grindstaff, even though the genre inverts the usual hierarchies of mass media by giving ordinary folk a chance to speak as experts, it also provides those very people with a narrowly defined voice through which to speak – a voice that tends to reproduce societal stereotypes of class and status.

The centrality of production goals and their consequences for the shows' cultural significance hardly imply that guests are dupes of the production process. Although their deep emotions are treated as raw material by producers in search of the money shot, the guests – both ordinary people and the experts who do appear – are often aware of the manipulations taking place. As one guest says, "You may not be completely cognizant, but, subliminally, viscerally, you know. You sense that you've gotta be a good talker, that you've gotta have a dramatic story, that you've gotta point fingers, express outrage, things of that sort" (Grindstaff 2002, p. 166). Guests experience ambivalence about the trade-offs that they often see themselves facing. They are willing to endure the manipulation of a process that dominates them in order to get their stories heard. But as Grindstaff comments, "This is precisely how hegemony works. If it were otherwise, then popular culture would not be so popular. And, if popular culture were not so popular, it would be easier to dismiss or ignore" (2002, p. 33).

The result of the trade-off is a reinforcement of a stereotype – "white trash" – that connotes an interlocking set of devalued behavioral, cultural, and aesthetic qualities. In turn the white-trash stereotype maintains symbolic distinctions of status (Grindstaff 2002, p. 264; see Goad 1997 for a discussion of the term). Thus, when mainstream critics disparage the daytime talk-show genre, according to Grindstaff they are not decrying the exploitation of underclasses but are, rather, reinforcing symbolic distinctions between trash and class by treating televised representations as evidence of people's natural inclinations – inclinations held unworthy of public display.

Grindstaff's study demonstrates the potential of the production perspective that Richard Peterson saw early on – to use middle-range studies about the production of expressive symbols to reveal cultural dimensions of broader social processes. Grindstaff's examination of talk shows reveals a complex relationship between the situated actions of individuals in media production and the reproduction of broader societal culture. The interactions of producers, guests, and audiences are constrained by the organization of production. These constraints, in turn, are forged in the exercise of power. In negotiation around such constraints there is potential for democratic communication in the public sphere raised by Habermas, the exercise of hegemony as defined by Gramsci, and the role that Bourdieu showed cultural capital to play in the cultural reproduction of status differences in society.

Conclusion

The production-of-culture perspective changed the focus of the sociological study of culture from emphasizing the uniqueness of artists and art works to analyzing the social processes through which art and popular culture are created, and how these processes are like (and unlike) those found in other forms of social organization. This shift away from concern with the content of cultural forms in turn helped undermine the distinction between high arts and popular culture. Indeed, within the production-of-culture perspective the high-versus-popular distinction itself has to be understood as a social construction based on art-world conventions rather than on inherent differences in culture.

Together, the interactionist and organizational approaches to the production of culture have altered the ways that we think about the relations between society and culture. Studies coming out of the sociological study of organizations have yielded new understandings of formally organized parts of art worlds and their structural features. Those coming out of a symbolic-interactionist perspective bring to light emergent processes and the forms of coordination among activities. Yet explanations of culture in relation to production do not tell the whole story. Wolff (1981, 1983) argues that the sociology of culture cannot entirely put aside "the specificity of art" – that is, its meaningful aesthetics and significance. In the fullest applications of the production-of-culture perspective, there is little if any difference between the arts and other socially organized activities. This is an important insight, yet sociologists also need to consider the meaning of cultural objects' content, style, and aesthetics, both for their creators and their audiences. Examining cultural objects in this way raises issues that lie largely outside of the production-of-culture perspective.

Suggested readings

To understand the nature of religious controversies about art in the United States – often referred to as culture wars – it is worthwhile to read three works together. Max Weber's "Religious rejections of the world and their directions" (in *From Max Weber*, 1946) illuminates historical tensions between autonomous art worlds and salvation religion; Emile Durkheim's *Elementary Forms of the Religious Life* (1995) offers an accounting of classification schemes that would suggest inevitable, in fact necessary, conflict between sacred and profane spheres of life; while the contributors to *Crossroads: Art and Religion in American Life* (2001), edited by Alberta Arthurs and Glenn Wallach, examine points of contention as well as (potential and actual) alliance between art and religion.

The Guerrilla Girls are a group of masked (literally) women artists, writers, and filmmakers engaged in art-world activism. They wear gorilla masks when appearing in public and produce posters, printed projects, and actions to expose sexism and racism in politics, the art world, and culture at large. Their website (http://www.guerrillagirls.com/) and their book *The Guerrilla Girls' Bedside Companion to the History of Western Art* (1998) provide excellent documentation of the contentious gender and ethnic boundaries in art worlds and pop-culture industries.

The chapters in *Outsider Art: Contesting Boundaries in Contemporary Culture* (1997), edited by Vera Zolberg and Joni Maya Cherbo, and *On the Margins of Art Worlds* (1995), edited by Larry Gross, examine in detail the roles played by status, ethnicity, gender, and nationality in the processes of attaining artistic recognition.

Steven C. Dubin's *Bureaucratizing the Muse: Public Funds and the Cultural Worker* (1987) should be read as a classic exemplar of the production-of-culture perspective. The Chicago-area Artists-in-Residence program – active from 1977 to 1981 – represented the largest use of U.S. government funds to create employment since the 1930s. In his study, Dubin brings together the sociology of complex organizations with symbolic interactionist theories of labeling, deviance, and social control to illustrate how the bureaucratic processing of art transformed the identities of artists participating in the program.

Richard Peterson's *Creating Country Music: Fabricating Authenticity* (1997b) and Laura Grindstaff's *The Money Shot* (2002) are illustrative of a broader potential of the production perspective. Both of these books offer detailed and nuanced insight on the workings of particular spheres of cultural production, but go beyond those particulars to examine larger social structures and cultural processes that both constrain and are potentially transformed by cultural production.

"Richard Peterson and cultural theory: from genetic, to integrated, and synthetic approaches," by Marshall Battani and John R. Hall (2000), traces the importance of Peterson's ideas about cultural production for sociological theory more generally. (The issue of *Poetics* in which this article appears is devoted entirely to the work of Peterson.)

Diana Crane's *The Transformation of the Avant-Garde: The New York Art World, 1940–1985* (1987) considers, among other issues, how artists manage to obtain funding. *Paying the Piper: Causes and Consequences of Art Patronage* (1993) is a collection of essays by Judith Huggins Balfe that explore the sociological implications of arts funding. Empirical studies from the U.S., Europe, and Asia cover a variety of funding models, including direct patronage by private individuals and institutions, direct city and state funding, and indirect support from the state.

10 Cultural objects, audiences, and meaning

How does culture that is distributed from outside our immediate social worlds figure in our lives? The differences between urbane cosmopolitan individuals and people of "country-and-western" sensibilities show that personality and lifestyle have cultural aspects. If this is so, it follows that somehow individuals "take on" some elements of the culture that they experience. That people are influenced by culture is an obvious truth. People often live the culture. We need think only of the rock-music fan whose life revolves around concerts and new releases of music. And what about all those romance novels available at the drugstores? Someone is buying them.

At the extreme, the boundary between one's own personal world and the world of distributed culture is blurred. As one researcher reported, she bought a copy of *Soap Opera Digest* at the supermarket checkout stand with the magazine's cover featuring two stars from the television soap "General Hospital." Seeing the magazine cover, the cashier commented, "I think Grant and Cecilia will work it out, don't you?" and then proceeded to offer her views on how the soap couple might deal with their problems (Rosen 1986, p. 43). When this soap-opera fan enters into a fictional world and treats the characters as acquaintances, it may seem to destroy the line between reality and fantasy. Yet such a practice is hardly unusual. To the contrary, what critics sometimes call "the suspension of disbelief" is a minimal requirement for entering into the "reality" established by a cultural object such as a soap opera. We refuse to be distracted from the show's reality when we have to do something as mundane as waiting for the end of a commercial break. Perhaps not as fully as the cashier caught up in the soap-opera world, we all suspend our everyday assumptions about reality (e.g. that the characters are just acting) whenever we go to a play, watch a television commercial, or read a novel.

We do the same thing even when we shift from our everyday world to cultural objects that are supposed to represent events in the real world (as opposed to fictional creations). Thus, watching television news or news talk shows requires us to "enter into" a world that is organized in different ways from the world of our direct, everyday experience. Some sort of shift also occurs when we take in cultural objects that are not directly representational. Thus, listening to music or looking at an abstract painting or sculpture does not depend on a belief that the object represents anything, even a fictional world. Nevertheless, to appreciate the music or the painting or the sculpture requires paying attention in a way that differs from other everyday activities such as talking or shopping. The very activity of viewing or listening itself changes our way of being in the world at the moment when it is occurring, and perhaps later on. The salience of culture is even more pronounced when we actively engage in cultural practices such as dancing, playing music, bowling, or riding horseback.

Culture is central to our daily life. What, then, are the processes by which specific culture becomes part of our personal repertoires of appreciation, knowledge, motives, and actions? Somehow, the classical music aficionado finds one composer much more compelling than another. Similarly, a person with particular tastes in clothes will take on one new fashion trend much more readily than another.

For the sociological understanding of culture, explaining such processes of interaction between people and culture are important because the significance of other theories about culture depends upon whether and how culture becomes incorporated into our personal repertoires. One way or another, normative theories of culture, cultural theories about social stratification, and theories of the political economy of culture all assume the existence of cultural influences. Thus, research on class, ethnicity, and gender (Chapter 3) yields explanations about how culture operates for various social strata and their interrelations. But left largely unanswered is the question of how people become "enculturated" in the first place. In a parallel way, if culture is a basis of normative integration, as some theories discussed in Chapter 2 suggest, society obtains cohesion to the extent that its members share central values. There may even be mechanisms, such as ritual, held to transmit values. Yet, despite the research inspired by normative theories of culture, the actual relationship between ritual and people's solidarity is not well understood. Finally, the theories of political economy considered in Chapter 8 suggest that powerful interest groups may try to affect the production of culture for their own purposes. But cultural domination in turn depends on the processes by which culture figures in social life, and accounting for such processes remains outside the domain of political economy. In short, these key approaches to the sociology of culture require that we pose – but themselves do not answer – a central question: how are individuals' thoughts and conduct influenced by their participation in culture?

Nor is the question simply academic. In public debates, people often want to argue that culture has (or does not have) direct, strong, and clear "effects." The widespread assumption seems to be that in the absence of such effects culture would not be worth so much public concern. In the polarized public debate about the mass media, either video games "rot the brain" or they are "harmless."

For their parts, the producers of cultural objects often assume that culture does have some sort of influence. Thus, novelists and artists sometimes have wanted to change their audiences' understandings of the world. And corporations must think that they are getting something for their money, or else they would not be spending so much on advertising. Critics of the mass media often share their assumption. It is implicit in concerns expressed by the U.S. Surgeon General and civic groups in 1990 about cigarette-company advertising campaigns for new brands meant to target young, "virile" women with low levels of educational attainment ("Dakota") and blacks ("Uptown"). On a different front, some parents and religious groups have worked to control violence on television; others have sought to regulate "explicit" popular-music lyrics or the formats and contents of television programs for young children. And, for decades, a debate has raged about the effects of pornography.

For certain groups, there are very high stakes in how the question of cultural consequences is answered. Advertisers of alcoholic beverages and cigarettes sometimes find themselves in government hearings where they carefully argue that advertising does not create new consumers of a product; instead, among existing consumers it influences a particular product's market share over its competitors. This claim notwithstanding, however, advertisers often target the young and presumably new consumers of their product category. Advertising agencies and mass-media organizations that depend on advertising revenues are caught in something of a double bind: they must convince product sellers that advertising works, and yet they must not let the popular view of advertising accord it so much power that they can be accused of manipulating people against their own best interests (Schudson 1984, pp. 9, 15).

Controversies over the potential negative consequences of culture – from advertising to pornography – create a highly charged civic context for the sociological debate over the relationships people have with distributed culture. It is therefore important to consider the question carefully, and independently of the public pressures. But research efforts are often garbled, for one thing, because the effects/no-effects formulation does not offer an adequate conceptual framework. It is one thing if someone enjoys a song by a wholesome "boy band," something else again if song lyrics drive us to criminal acts that we would not otherwise carry out. There is a broad range of possible effects.

The so-called effects controversy, then, should be abandoned in favor of an alternative approach that poses three related questions. First, there is the question of whether cultural objects have unambiguous meanings and messages, and how these meanings and messages might be related to the intentions of those who produce the cultural objects. Whatever the answer to this question, a good deal of research has been devoted to a second question – how culture affects its audiences; here, the research findings often are in conflict with one another, partly because the methodologies for studying effects are poorly conceived. Nevertheless, it is instructive to see the variety and types of effects that researchers have identified. Finally, the first two issues need to be understood in relation to a third one: within any given audience, it seems that not all individuals pay attention to cultural meanings in the same way. Theories and research on audiences thus alter our understanding of the meanings of cultural objects and the processes by which culture influences individuals. Considering these issues offers a basis for starting to figure out how cultural meanings become part of our lives.

The question of meaningful content

To look at a painting or watch a film or listen to music is to experience a cultural object that has been produced through an interaction of ideas with organized social activity under concrete social and historical conditions (see Chapter 9). These cultural objects often are distinctive and easy to identify. Some people can name a popular song just from hearing the first few notes, and people who have studied paintings sometimes can identify a Cézanne or a Rubens at a glance, even when they have never seen the specific painting before. Yet assessing the meaning of a cultural object is a much more difficult matter. In the first place, it is always possible that a particular painting or sculpture is a forgery or a copy, and the significance of a counterfeit cultural object is very different from that of an original work (Jones *et al.* 1990). But this issue, intriguing as it may be, is not nearly so important to cultural studies as the question of whether a cultural object in itself possesses any clear and unambiguous meaning.

The cultural object – a photograph, a film, a dance, a fashion style – often stands on its own, sometimes rich in content yet difficult to "read." As Chapter 9 implies, the distinctiveness of any cultural object is somewhat arbitrary, in the sense that it could have been produced in a different way. The painting of the *Mona Lisa* could have a different expression on her face. A television situation comedy could have a different cast of characters – say, workers and customers at a fast-food restaurant, rather than neighbors on a suburban street. The fact that choices are made in the production of cultural objects raises the question of what meaning those choices might have. Even if the choices are made "unconsciously" – that is, without deliberation – they still may tell us something. And if the choices are conscious ones, then it is possible to inquire about the intention that gave rise to a particular choice, and to the meaning of the object that is the result of many such intentional choices. Just focusing on the cultural object, two broad approaches to analysis of meaning have gained importance. One approach, *hermeneutics*, points to the problem of uncovering the ideas and intentions by which the object was produced. The other broad approach, *semiotics*, examines the relation among various symbols within the cultural object itself, considering the intentions of its creators only to the extent that they are structured by existing codes of meaning.

Hermeneutics and the problem of intended meaning

"Hermeneutics" – the Greek word for interpretation – has its origins in the idea of translating, and traditionally the term was used to describe Biblical exegesis. This original focus of hermeneutics easily conjures up images of scribes guarding the faith by protecting sacred texts and excavating their "real" meanings through scrutiny of intra-textual evidence and comparison with other ancient scrolls. Yet the idea of "translating" – whether from one language to another or simply from a preexisting version to a new rendition in the same language – raises a thorny problem. How can any particular translation be validated as "correct" or "true"? If there can be no single valid translation, then special claims by "experts" lose their force. Everyone who reads translates. That is, we each interpret cultural texts. And in turn, our texts – things we say and do, our cultural creations – are interpreted by others.

The hermeneutic attempt to understand the intended meanings of cultural objects is plagued with obstacles. One problem is that the cultural creators are not always clear about their intentions. Moreover, these ambiguous intentions can change over time. An author may think she has one purpose while she is writing, yet after having completed a novel may come to see its meaning quite differently. This problem can only be compounded by a second one: when more than one cultural worker is involved in production, their intentions may come into conflict with one another. There are, for example, the legendary battles between film directors and the stars doing the acting. A third problem is especially daunting: whatever the intentions of culture creators, how can other people learn what those intentions were? Sometimes all we have to go on is the cultural object itself, and even when it is possible to interview cultural producers we cannot be sure how well they remember their intentions, or whether they are willing to reveal them. Many artists will want to let the art just "speak for itself."

These difficulties suggest that it is impossible to arrive at the definitive intended meaning of a cultural object. Does this mean that we should not ask? Engaging a longstanding debate in sociology, Robert Wuthnow (1987, ch. 2) has argued that the subjective meanings of action are very difficult to learn, that purely subjective meaning is not necessarily important to sociological analysis, and that alternative approaches might be more fruitful. Wuthnow's critique notwithstanding, only empirically, and for particular cases, can we answer the question of whether the study of situated meaningful social action and interaction is important. In some cases, people rework cultural meanings in their personal lives in ways that yield culturally based but unanticipated outcomes. Wuthnow takes the position that sociologists ought to be primarily concerned with shared meanings – meanings as they are communicated through "discourse and behavior." Despite Wuthnow's efforts to differentiate subjective meaning and shared meaning, however, the analysis of shared meanings, of course, is as much a matter of interpretation as is the study of subjective meaning, for there is no unambiguous way to determine what of culture is really shared among an analytic category of people or a real social group, and what the meanings of any such culture are. Thus, neither subjective nor public meaning can be privileged as the site of sociological interpretation.

All the same, the choice of looking for meaning in intentions versus object is not without consequences for how people make sense of culture. As John Berger (1977) has pointed out, some art critics point to the difficulties of interpreting artistic intentions in order to emphasize formal properties of art, thereby trying to maintain the purity of art as art, divorced from its historical and social circumstances of creation. Such art critics may seem to raise procedural difficulties about historical and social contextualization, but their real bone of contention concerns what will count as legitimate standards and criteria of cultural criticism.

No doubt hermeneutics is something less than an exact science (though no less exact than cultural criticism in general), yet the difficulty of interpreting intended meanings does not diminish the importance of trying to do so. Moreover, matters are not hopeless. The cultural object itself may yield a good deal of information, and there may be other clues that help to clarify the intentions behind a painting, musical composition, or play.

One method is to use Michael Baxandall's (1985) approach of constructing a "Brief" for a cultural object. The Brief identifies various problems and issues toward which the cultural object is directed as a solution. In Baxandall's model, a cultural producer follows through on such a Brief under practical constraints and opportunities related to a medium and its techniques, relevant economic conditions, personal circumstances, and other conditions affecting the production of a cultural object. Thus, a film is done either in black and white or in color; it is based either on a previous story or on an original screenplay; it is shot in some combination of studio sets and locations outside the studio; particular actors are used; and so forth. As Chapter 9 shows, a good deal of cultural production is coordinated by reference to conventions – previously established routine ways of doing things. Moreover, conventions mediate between the cultural object and the people who experience it (Becker 1982). Thus, if the film producer uses a particular kind of musical score, say "triumphant music," at a dramatic juncture in the film, the effectiveness of that choice of music depends on the audience's shared knowledge of the music's conventional meaning. Beyond using of conventions, any given cultural worker operates in the context of other cultural workers, distributors, and the audience – all of whose interests and demands may shape the production of culture (Griswold 1987a). By constructing a Brief for a cultural object, an analyst can identify features of the object that give clues about the intentions behind the creation of the object and the relation of these intentions to various factors and circumstances.

As an example, Baxandall reconstructs a Brief for a 1910 painting by Picasso, *Portrait of Daniel-Henry Kahnweiler* (see Figure 10.1). Part of the Brief offers a description of issues that painters faced at the beginning of the twentieth century. One question concerned how to represent the depth of three dimensions while honestly acknowledging the two-dimensionality of the canvas surface. Another issue was what importance to give to form versus color. Third, there was the problem of time: how could an artist avoid the fiction that a painting can be like a photograph – capturing an instant just as it is – when the painting itself is created over a much longer period of time? The intentional project behind Picasso's painting can be grasped by identifying his innovative solutions to these problems of importance to early-twentieth-century painters. Other considerations came into play in how this Brief was realized: the particular social circumstances and personal idiosyncrasies of Picasso as a painter, the market for paintings that Picasso had to confront if he was to be economically successful, and so forth. In making his own choices, Picasso implicitly constructed his own unfolding Brief, and he acted in terms of it, but he did so in a concrete cultural, social, and economic situation that affected the character of the cultural object produced on the basis of the Brief. In turn, Baxandall argues, Picasso's painting itself

Figure 10. 1 Pablo Picasso, *Daniel-Henry Kahnweiler, autumn 1910*, oil on canvas. Baxandall's idea of the "Brief" helps explain the style of this painting by examining the way it solves particular problems. Among these problems for Picasso were the economic demands of the art market as well as aesthetic issues particular to the early twentieth century – especially how to represent three dimensions on a flat surface and how to capture a moment of time in painted form.

Source: Gift of Mrs. Gilbert W. Chapman in memory of Charles B. Goodspeed/image © The Art Institute of Chicago; painting © Estate of Pablo Picasso/Artists Rights Society (ARS), New York.

became one basis upon which his own and other artists' subsequent Briefs came to be defined (1985, pp. 41–73).

Despite the obstacles to hermeneutic analysis, Baxandall shows that it is possible to formulate an account of the intentions of cultural workers and their effects on cultural objects. To come to such an account requires a good deal of research and speculation. At the conclusion of considering evidence and argument, some critical interpretations of intended meaning may seem more plausible than others. However, interpretive questions are difficult to resolve in any definitive way, and the intentions of the person making the interpretation can themselves be subjected to interpretation. So it is with what Hans-Georg Gadamer (1975) called "the hermeneutic circle."

Indeed, Malcolm Barnard (2001) suggests we consider the circle – interpretations of interpretations – in light of Gadamer's thinking on the subject. For Gadamer, hermeneutics is only problematic to the extent that we embrace too positivistic an idea of the social sciences. If we are searching for an objective understanding – one proceeding from the assumption that a historically located interpreter with her own worldview (sometimes called prejudices or horizons) can somehow gain access to the creator's different set of prejudices or worldview – then we are doomed to failure. Objective understanding would require that the interpreter reconstruct him- or herself, in effect, to duplicate the world of the creator. Instead, it is more appropriate to think of meaning as produced by a "fusing" of the horizons of the interpreter and the creator – neither of which is necessarily fully understood (Barnard 2001, esp. ch. 2). Meaning is inherently open to variation because it emerges from a specific interaction between an interpreter and the creator through the cultural object.

Even assuming one could tease out the intentions of a cultural producer, such an effort hardly exhausts the problem of meaning. Indeed, although puzzling over intended meanings may help us reach a better understanding of a cultural object, analyzing its meaning does not necessarily depend on knowing the most private intentions of its producers (Wuthnow 1987, p. 65). Especially when there is widespread appreciation of a painting, a piece of music, or a play, we must suspect that it has some public meanings. That is, it must deal with issues of some cultural significance by use of symbols, conventions, and aesthetics that are socially understood and appreciated. Only in this way does a cultural object seem likely to capture the interest of some general public. According to Wendy Griswold (1987a), however, it would be a mistake for sociologists to turn away from "the problem of meaning" to focus solely on the social arrangements through which cultural objects are produced and appreciated – what she calls the "institutional approach." As we suggested at the conclusion of Chapter 9, just such a strategy, the production perspective, runs the risk of treating cultural objects as if they are just like any other sort of object. Griswold warns, "An approach to culture that is uninterested in meaning, or in how cultural objects differ from porkbellies, seems destined to continue to play a marginal role in cultural, though perhaps not social, analysis" (1987a, p. 3).

Griswold argues for bridging the gaps between sociology, cultural anthropology, art history, and literary criticism by focusing analysis on the point at which individuals interact with a cultural object. This analysis is properly organized around intention, reception, comprehension, and explanation. *Intention* (here she draws from Baxandall) is "the social agent's purpose in light of constraints imposed on him or her," whereas *reception* addresses how individuals "consume, incorporate, or reject" a given cultural object. *Comprehension* requires the analysis of symbolic patterns of culture (e.g. in relation to conventions), and *explanation* involves "drawing connections between comprehended cultural objects and the external social world, connections that are mediated by reception and intention." Griswold's hope is that organizing cultural analysis in this way allows sociology to "both subject its cultural interpretations to the definitional precision and validation criteria typical of the social sciences and be as sensitive to the multi-vocal complexity of cultural data as art history or theology" (1987a, pp. 4–5). In the face of Wuthnow's appeal to move beyond subjective meaning toward mapping the significant relations between symbols at the level of the cultural system, Griswold argues for recognizing that meaning need not be reduced to either a purely individual phenomenon or the public meanings of entire social orders.

Semiotics and the structure of public meaning

The fact that producers of culture routinely draw on conventions about the meanings of various motifs in an object offers a bridge from considering the meaningful intentions of producers to "decoding" the conventional meanings of a cultural object. Words, for example, have some general range of meanings, or else it would not be possible for you to make any sense whatsoever out of this sentence. In much the same way, the ability of viewers to "read" a painting or photograph depends on conventions concerning color, texture of paint, the character of brush stokes, the representation of dimensionality, and, sometimes, the symbolic content of the elements of the painting as a composition. The same is true for music, where pitch, timber, harmony, rhythm, melody, and other devices can be employed in conventional ways to convey certain moods and sensibilities. In the theater, certain gestures may be used by actors to convey surprise, anger, joy, or sinister motives in ways that will be readily understood by an audience, even though the same gestures in everyday life probably would seem contrived or overdone.

Because cultural objects are "read" on the basis of conventions, it is possible to describe them in terms of their use of (and play upon) conventions. In semiotics, then, the meaning of a cultural object is embodied in the structured relations of its conventional elements – the characters, costumes, setting, genre, plot, acting, camera angles in a film. That is, the meaning of a cultural object as a whole can be analyzed independently of questions about how and why it was produced. Yet there is a problem here that parallels the problem of knowing the cultural producer's intentions: to understand a cultural object's structured meaning assumes a good knowledge of the conventions, symbols, signs, motifs, aesthetics, and other elements that make the object hold together (e.g. as a painting or a piece of music). As Terry Eagleton has pointed out,

> For the structuralists, the "ideal reader" of a work was someone who would have at his or her disposal all the codes which would render it exhaustively intelligible. The reader was thus just a kind of mirror-reflection of the work itself – someone who would understand it "as it was."
>
> (Eagleton 1983, p. 121)

Such an "ideal reader" cannot exist, of course. Nevertheless, as with the problem of hermeneutics and the intentions of the cultural producer, the semiotic analyst of structure may make the attempt at a reading, and, whatever the flaws of such a reading, it may reveal a good deal about the meaningful character of a cultural object in its own terms.

Whether valid or not, assumptions about coherent meaning and the possibility of more or less objective reading have offered a foundation for a substantial amount of research on the effects of culture. Such research opens up the possibility of decoding meanings of cultural material to which even large numbers of people are exposed. Advertising offers a ready subject for such studies because, after all, advertisers have a high degree of self-interest in affecting people's actions. Their communication therefore presumably is designed to have accessible significance for the public, whether that accessibility depends upon conscious or less than conscious understandings by the public. What, then, are the codes and conventions of advertising? The sociologist Erving Goffman (1979) asked this question specifically for the issue of gender by examining still photographs in advertisements. Exploring the photographs in Goffman's study shows how advertisers communicated gendered relations at the time Goffman analyzed them. He was able to demonstrate that gender ranking between men and women can be accomplished through framing, perspective, and the size and positioning of models. Details are important. With the device of "head cant," "the level of the head is lowered relative to that of others, including, indirectly, the viewer of the picture. The resulting configurations can be read as an acceptance of subordination, an expression of ingratiation, submissiveness, and appeasement" (Goffman 1979, p. 46).

Using Goffman's analytic approach requires simultaneous interpretation on two different levels, what Roland Barthes (1977) calls "denotation" and "connotation." In the act of denotation the interpreter must be able to make sense of an image simply and directly: what is this thing an image of? On the other hand, in connotation the cultural significance of the image is considered. In *Mythologies* (1972), Barthes identified basic meaningful patterns ("mythologies") of mass culture in a wide range of cultural phenomena – things like advertising, food, automobiles, and professional wrestling.

The structuralist analysis of cultural meaning also has focused on broader societal "structures" – enduring meaningful patterns – of culture to see if they share a common code. Following the structuralist tradition of Emile Durkheim, the anthropologist Claude Lévi-Strauss (1966), for example, suggested, first, that cultural systems of classification exist prior to the individual and, second, that activities of social life are mapped on to already existing classifications. In a similar vein, Dayan and Katz (1988) have explored the commonalities of media events such as the wedding of Prince Charles and Lady Diana, the first landing on the moon, state funerals, and political hearings such as Watergate and Iran-Contra. The range of such events is diverse, yet according to Dayan and Katz they all share the character of "televised ceremonies" that ritually reaffirm the social order by staging a collective witnessing of the social order's moments of transformation. With live television coverage, ceremonies serve a "religious" function for a society as a whole. Such events, usually carefully staged, nevertheless come to represent history-in-the-making. Each one offers an idealized dramatization that reworks the meaning of the social order in a particular time of social change. Dayan and Katz state, "Without using this phrase in a pejorative sense, media events are 'symbolic manipulations.' They describe a striking affinity to the techniques used in therapeutic contexts by traditional 'shamans' [healers]. Through ceremony, a problematic situation is redefined, transcribed to another language" (1988, p. 167).

Jeffrey Alexander and Philip Smith have analyzed public political debate in the U.S. to understand that "other language" – what they consider the underlying cultural system of meaning: "We argue that culture should be conceived as a system of symbolic codes which specify the good and the evil" (1993, p. 155). In their analysis, debates within American civil society are historically contingent reflections that play off a more fundamental and enduring cultural code, which, in turn, is structured as a set of binary oppositions between sacred and profane – as Emile Durkheim (1995) argued. Perhaps most striking in Durkheim's approach to sociology is his idea that cultural objects (his focus was religious ceremonies) offer an idealized version of the social world. According to this view, we should not expect culture to represent or mirror the world as it "really" is. To the contrary, culture may be expected to present the world in some normative version of how it "ought to" (and, sometimes, ought not to) be. In this perspective, critics of the mass media are often correct when they point to television and the movies as offering fantastic distortions of the subjects they treat. Yet from the Durkheimian point of view this is hardly surprising. The important question concerns the specific meaning that any such idealized version of reality has.

Cultural critics have decoded everything from advertisements (Barthes 1972; Goffman 1979; Leiss *et al.* 1988), news (Manoff and Schudson 1986), television (Gitlin 1986), Hollywood movies (M.C. Miller 1990), and clothes (Lurie 1981) to popular song lyrics and high-culture paintings and plays. Sometimes studies address particular themes across cultural objects – gender in music lyrics, ethnicity in movies, and so forth; other studies offer interpretations of a single cultural object as a whole.

What is at stake in the latter efforts – to get at the meaning of a whole cultural object – can be seen by examining different critical interpretations of the same film, *Boys Don't Cry*, starring Hilary Swank, released in 1999. The film, based on actual events, tells the story of Brandon Teena, born Teena Brandon, who was raised as a woman but spends everyday life passing as a man. The story follows Brandon in Lincoln and Falls City, Nebraska, as he/she befriends a rough group of pool-shooting beer drinkers and becomes sexually involved with a beautiful and highly sought-after local woman. Eventually Brandon's sexual identity is discovered and he/she is raped and then murdered.

One critic, Michele Aaron (2001), portrays the film as a radical exercise that reveals the performativity of gender. For Aaron, the film can be understood as a reworking of the conventions that mark the Hollywood genre of the cross-dressing or transvestite film (she alludes to *Some Like it Hot* from 1959, *Victor/Victoria* from 1982, and *Mrs. Doubtfire* from 1993). These films, almost always comedies, "derive their effect from the slapstick, sexually suggestive or supposedly absurd scenarios resulting from the central character's passing within the diegesis and the audience's privileged position of knowledge (being in on the disguise)." Usually the genre is conservative, according to Aaron, in that all transgressions of gender boundaries are used to eventually affirm rigid categories and a return to order (when the central character's "true" identity is revealed). But *Boys Don't Cry* is different: "Brandon is not so much trying to pass as someone else as trying to be 'him' self. Passing is not, therefore, a means to an end, as in the comedies, but an end in itself" (Aaron 2001, pp. 93, 94). Importantly for Aaron's interpretation, there are critical moments in the film where other characters become complicit in Brandon's passing. The film is a radical reworking of the cross-dressing genre because it operates with a "transgendered gaze" such that "[i]n being made aware of the characters' suppressed knowledge about Brandon, the spectator joins them as a community of witnesses to Brandon's passing/failing." The film thus avoids the reification of gender categories. "Where in cross-dressing comedies the relationship between passing and failing reeked of reassurances for the no-less titillated spectator, in *Boys* their interaction constructs and confirms knowingness, the implication, of all those witnessing Brandon's activities" (Aaron 2001, pp. 95, 96).

Another critic, Judith Halberstam (2001), mostly agrees with Aaron's interpretation, but focuses on a particular scene not highlighted by Aaron to argue that the radical nature of the transgendered gaze in *Boys* is ultimately undermined, with the result that conservative understandings of gender distinctions are affirmed. The key to the film for Halberstam is a scene in which Brandon's girl friend Lana finds him hiding out after being raped. The dialog and interaction in this scene are all directed toward portraying the encounter as one of lesbian love:

> They both agree that [Brandon's] whole journey to manhood has been pretty weird and then they move to make love. While earlier [the filmmaker] created quite graphic depictions of sex between Brandon and Lana, now the action is hidden by a Hollywood-style dissolve as if to suggest that the couple are now making love as opposed to having sex.
>
> (Halberstam 2001, p. 297)

This scene is crucial to understanding the film, according to Halberstam, because it is here that the filmmaker "suddenly and catastrophically divests her character of the transgendered gaze and converts it to a lesbian and therefore female gaze" (2001, p. 297). Because of this conversion, Halberstam argues, the murder that marks the end of the story appears as the result of homophobic rage. Ultimately, conventional distinctions between male/female and heterosexual/homosexual are affirmed.

If Aaron or Halberstam really were "ideal readers" as described by Terry Eagleton their decodings of *Boys Don't Cry* would accomplish two things. First, they would provide a reliable account of the film's symbolic structure and, second, the reliable account would affirm the potential of structuralist readings of cultural objects. But, in fact, neither Aaron nor Halberstam can be assumed to be an ideal reader, because *Boys Don't Cry* remains the subject of critical controversy. Julianne Pidduck (2001) shows us a considerably different film by reading it in relation to the "road-movie" genre. Brandon Teena becomes "a quintessential outsider whose transgressive choices are understood against the backdrop of the flat Midwestern landscape" (2001, p. 98). In Pidduck's view, a poignant love story is structured around the iconography of the road movie's ideal of romance and escape. But, of course, there is no escape in this story, and Pidduck understands this as an effect of class. "Tragically, class curtails the character's horizons, defeating the transcendence of fantasy and the transformative powers of love" (Pidduck 2001, p. 99).

The divergent interpretations of Aaron, Halberstam, and Pidduck stem from a shared commitment to looking ever more closely at the film. Each interpretation is an effort to incorporate more – to understand more relations between characters, more relations between scenes. Jennifer Devere Brody (2002) takes a different approach. She analyzes what the film does *not* offer. "I am interested in thinking about the 'negative' space of the film; indeed, about material so absent it never even appeared on the cutting-room floor" (2002, p. 91). What is absent? Race. For Brody the film is most closely associated with the conventions of documentary, yet with respect to race it has changed the historical events dramatically. In real life, when Brandon Teena was murdered so too was a young physically disabled black man named Phillip DeVine. For Brody, the filmmaker's decision to leave DeVine and the history of race in rural America out of the story (despite the film's documentary look) and critics' failure to highlight the importance of raced interpretations are strange, questionable, and even unethical lapses:

> In her reading of the film, Pidduck includes a snippet of dialogue between Brandon and Lana. The two discuss Brandon's decision to participate in the violent "redneck"' ritual that results in his being "tied to the back of a truck and [being] dragged like a dog." This conversation screens a reference to an event, utterly current at the time of the film, in which a black man, James Byrd, was dragged to his death in Jasper, Texas, in what many consider to be a lynching. In this sense, [the filmmaker] participates, however unwittingly, in a larger pattern of leaving race out of the picture so that other identity categories appear stable and queerness is represented in a way that makes it synonymous with whiteness.
>
> (Brody 2002, pp. 93–4)

Brody argues that making race absent is a larger problem with the emerging genre of "queer cinema," and that any reading of the film without a consideration of race is necessarily partial.

The existence of multiple readings of *Boys Don't Cry* suggests that any particular structuralist reading of a text is generated by specific thematic concerns and methods of criticism. Any reading thus necessarily excludes meanings that are available in alternative approaches to reading the text. Yet the same thing can be said about the text itself: any narrative or account depends on a wide range of choices concerning plot, characterization, exposition, and so forth. The meanings available in the narrative depend on the particular choices made; other meanings are excluded by those choices. To oversimplify, the recent critical method of reading a text known as deconstruction involves, in part, searching for the exclusion of meanings from the text. Asking what is not in the text yields a revealing mirror-image of what is in the text; they are, in effect, a paired opposition. Thus, in discussing *Boys Don't Cry* Brody considers the significance of race: even though race is not a theme of the film, the hidden relationships between race, gender, class, and sexual identity structure her encounter with the film. Terry Eagleton has pointed to the rationale for this interpretive approach in deconstruction: "Since the meaning of a sign is a matter of what the sign is not, its meaning is always in some sense absent from it too" (1983, p. 128).

The acknowledgement of multiple readings based on complex meanings that exist both in the text and in its suppression of other meanings has moved critical textual analysis past structuralism to "poststructuralism." Critics no longer can aspire to the definitive decoding of a text, for other critics are waiting in the wings to decode the critical interpretations themselves! Poststructuralist interpretation continues the structuralist focus on public issues of meaning in the structure of the text, rather than the hermeneutic search for the producer's intentions. But the controversies show that poststructuralist interpretation faces the same problems as hermeneutic interpretation, namely the difficulty of getting at the "real" meaning. Nevertheless, controversies of interpretation sometimes reflect overall agreement about a text. None of the critics doubts that *Boys Don't Cry* is about sexual identity and gender relations. They dispute particular points about the meaning of the relations depicted in the film that may go well beyond the critical analysis of the general audience. But these differences depend on "highbrow" analyses of popular culture that don't necessarily have anything to do with how an audience experiences either a film or any other cultural object. All critical readings – hermeneutic, structuralist, or poststructuralist – leave fundamental questions unanswered: whatever the sources and supposed real meaning of the cultural object, what relation does the object have to its readers, and how does that relation to readers get formed? It is to these questions that we now turn.

Uses, effects, and agendas

Trying to understand the relations between cultural texts and their audiences is not easy. After all, using a cultural object such as a cell phone or a television has obvious effects, in the sense that using the object alters behavior from what it would be otherwise. But the relations that people have with symbolic culture are necessarily more elusive. People experience culture through the senses – by reading a book, watching a video, going to a concert. No doubt people go through cognitive changes from such experiences. But under what circumstances might these changes alter a person's more settled ways of thinking or acting? Three broad approaches to the relationship between cultural objects and audiences have informed the debate: (1) a "uses and gratifications" approach that emphasizes the audience's role in choosing culture; (2) an approach that explores the more-or-less direct effects of exposure to particular cultural objects; and (3) an approach that points to the audience's formation of general worldviews and frameworks of interpretation on the basis of "agenda-setting" in the mass media.

The obvious problem encountered by any strong theory of cultural effects is that people may – to a greater or lesser degree – select from among alternative experiences of culture those that somehow "speak to" them. In this sense, people choose what may, in turn, affect them. Also, since culture depends on an audience, producers of culture often try to shape the cultural object to gain that audience. To take an extreme but not uncommon example, Hollywood producers sometimes test-screen films, and it is not unusual for them to make significant changes to accommodate a trial audience's reactions. In a less obvious way, writers take into account their readers; painters, their gallery dealers and patrons. In turn, when culture is marketed in an economy, patrons contribute to the success and failure of cultural producers by deciding to buy or not to buy, watch or not watch. In short, audiences may have an influence on culture, as well as the other way around. What diversity there is in television genres is to be explained in part by the absence of a monolithic mass audience and the existence of a wide range of "taste segments" (Cantor and Cantor 1986). In the context of technological changes – especially the increasing availability of dozens of cable television channels – the term "narrowcasting" describes programmers' strategy of targeting small specific audiences as opposed to large mass audiences (Turow 1997).

What do audience choices reveal about culture? The assumption that cultural objects reflect an audience's values and interests faces a critical challenge, for, as Wendy Griswold (1981) has shown, the production of culture is influenced by other factors besides the composition of the audience. However, if this difficulty can be resolved, content analysis can be used as a methodology to identify the thematic dimensions of specific cultural objects such as novels, comic strips, and films. In turn, the themes identified through content analysis can serve as an approximate gauge of the concerns and interests of the audience that chooses to consume them – as a taste public, social group, community, or society. Thus, Elizabeth Long (1985) has studied what best-selling novels during the period 1945–75 reveal about the American dream by premising her research on the assertion that these particular novels "are primarily a social rather than a literary phenomenon." This implies, for Long, that what counts is the popularity of novels, which "suggests that they are finding resonance with broad segments of the reading public, rather than appealing only to certain subsections of the audience." For the task of exploring general features of cultural continuity and change, "best sellers are a particularly useful source of information because they represent a sort of common denominator of our literary culture" (Long 1985, pp. 5–6). Such an approach, focused on overall popularity, tends to explore culture as a reflection or barometer of society. However, it does not address the question of whether culture influences people, and, if so, in what ways.

If the focus on the popularity of cultural objects is shifted from social interpretation to the issue of individual choices, a slightly different theory of culture and audience emerges. Specifically, the idea that cultural artifacts tell us something about the people who use them can be turned into a strong theoretical claim. In the "uses and gratification" model, people are theorized to choose culture that confirms, extends, and enriches their own perspectives. Thus it would seem that, if culture has an effect, the effect is merely one of reinforcing previous sentiments. Such an approach can find favor both with media executives, advertisers, and the general public, and with sociologists like Gans (1974, p. 32) who defend popular culture. The model would seem to sidestep the menace of media manipulation, reassuring us that we exercise choice rather than make Pavlovian responses to media stimuli. However, the simple reinforcement of previous views would hardly be politically insignificant. To the contrary, the consequence of such an effect, in relation to a freely choosing public, would be to enhance the stability of the status quo.

Because culture seems to some extent to be both a reflection of its audience and shaped by it, an even stronger causal hypothesis about effects of culture also has received a great deal of attention, especially from those whom sociologist Howard Becker (1963) has termed "moral entrepreneurs" – people on the lookout for the pernicious effects of decadent culture on innocent people. Just as rock and Hip-Hop lyrics are singled out today, at the turn of the twentieth century dire warnings surfaced about the role of player-piano roll music in corrupting youth (Berlin 1980). Similar concerns have been raised about violence on television and in video games, pornography, children's television, comic books, "obscene" art, indeed whatever cultural material denigrates or challenges the values and worldview of the moral entrepreneurs. But moral entrepreneurs do not come from any single social sector. Religious fundamentalists, political liberals and conservatives, intellectuals, radicals, and feminists have all at one time or another bemoaned the effects of popular culture.

Yet the project of developing an empirically robust theoretical demonstration of the effects that moral entrepreneurs warn against has proven challenging. "Copycat" crimes, in which an individual imitates an act seen in the media, are sometimes taken as proof of media effects, but they show quite the reverse: a combination of factors, rather than violence depicted in media alone, must be at work, or else a much larger number of people exposed to particular media content would imitate it. Advocates of the effects thesis are thus careful to acknowledge that violence and crime "result from several forces at once" (Liebert and Sprafkin 1988, p. 161). Given the huge sizes of mass media audiences, if there are (contingent) media effects even a very low percentage of imitative behaviors could result in a significant increase in violent crimes such as murder. Although their findings are controversial, some researchers have found evidence supporting this thesis (Phillips and Bollen 1985; Stack 1987).

Still, skepticism persists. Based on a review of effects research on children, news, violence, and a variety of other subjects, Herbert Gans concluded:

> So far, it is difficult to attribute any large-scale permanent effects of specific items or types of media content, although it seems likely that the media may have negative effects on "media addicts," people whose entire emotional and cognitive life is centered almost entirely on the media, and others predisposed to pathology who find their behavior publicized by media content.
>
> (Gans 1974, p. 39)

For Gans, the critics' stereotype of a society of zombies plugged into mass media did not hold up under the scrutiny of research: the gap between critical claims and findings was "sizable."

A decade later, Joshua Meyrowitz (1985) also reviewed effects research. He found that quantitative researchers over the years added more and more variables controlling for personality, social class, peer influence, and other factors. On this basis they hoped to increase their ability to show a relationship between the media stimulus as cause and a research subject's action as effect. But, like Gans, Meyrowitz asserted a "general failure of researchers to demonstrate clear and direct effects of media content on social behavior" (1985, p. 13). Gans readily admitted that mass media have more fundamental effects, changing the mix of culture available, reorganizing the information access of individuals, and so on. As we saw in Chapter 8, Meyrowitz extended this analysis by arguing that mass media reorganize the social life of people who participate in them. Important as such consequences may be, however, they do not resolve the issue that is of such concern to media critics – whether there are direct effects of media content.

As Gans recognized, further research might refine knowledge about media effects. One study of long-term effects found a negative statistical correlation between children's amount of television viewing and their scores on reading-comprehension and language-usage achievement tests: the more television, the lower the achievement scores. But, as Hodge and Tripp (1986) commented, it is not clear whether television actually dampens achievement or, instead, whether children of low achievement watch more television. To Hodge and Tripp, it seems plausible that some children in intellectually impoverished environments are affected positively by television. As they note, although television overall has a statistically negative effect, other factors must be much more important, since television accounted for less than 5 percent of the total variation in the children's scores (Hodge and Tripp 1986, pp. 163–5).

Other research further underscores the complexity of media effects. One study argues that some people become socialized toward media "dependency" for useful information about the world. Such viewers of television watch carefully, and on this basis they are more likely to respond to media content than are viewers who get distracted by one thing or another (Ball-Rokeach *et al.* 1984, p. 136). Similarly, Gerbner and his colleagues (1980) advanced a "cultivation theory," which suggests that the "mainstream" worldview offered on television tends to provide specific embellishment of ideas to people already holding mainstream values, while when less socialized individuals engage in heavy viewing it results in their cultivation of mainstream viewpoints. In this analysis, people look for role models and ways of being, and they select from the images that appear and imitate those which appeal to them.

By these accounts of viewing behavior, television can be a powerful tool of socialization, or possibly manipulation. If this is so, then we need to consider a crucial issue – the particular political or other value significance of the medium's content. To do so, let us return to the question of violence on television. It might be assumed that programming depicting violence would offer role models for viewers, who would, in turn, live more violently. But the reverse seems to be true. One study concerned about children suggests that they do not necessarily understand media violence in the same way as real violence; media violence may be a cultural metaphor that signifies conflict, with the result that children will recognize conflict as an important part of social life (Hodge and Tripp 1986, p. 217). Similarly, a study of television crime programs has found that heavy viewers indeed cultivate the worldview of the programs, but they do so in specific ways. Given that they learn about the legal system predominantly from television and that television provides an unrealistic portrayal of the criminal justice system, heavy adolescent viewers have less knowledge of criminal justice processes than light viewers. Moreover, the heavy viewers reflect the television-police viewpoint that places more emphasis on "crime control" than on considerations of "due process" based on the U.S. constitution's bill of rights: "In fact, crime shows appear to promote antiheterodoxy – the desire to punish those who deviate from accepted norms." Quite the opposite from promoting violence, the depiction of violence in crime television shows that "crime doesn't pay": heavy viewers are more likely to view the world as a "threatening" place, and they come down in favor of "law and order" (Carlson 1985, pp. 189–90). This sort of "television imaginary" constructed on the basis of fictional programs can also take hold on the basis of how news is framed. Thus, surveying crime coverage in over 2,000 Irish newspapers, Michael O'Connell (1999) found that a bias toward stories focused on extreme offenses, helpless victims, and pessimistic accounts of the criminal justice system leads to distorted public opinion. Despite relatively low crime rates, the Irish public believes itself to be experiencing a crisis of law and order.

The effects of violence on television crime shows and news programs do not seem to be what a "copycat" theory would predict. The reason probably is that people pay attention to culture in ways that are more complex than copycat theories suggest. Audiences do not just absorb cultural material "whole hog." Instead, they actively participate in selecting and making sense of cultural objects. For example, a study of news audiences suggests that people are quite selective in what they will bother to watch in the first place. When they do watch they sort through information received, discarding much of it. The flood of journalistic information available thus is filtered by people who do not go past the headlines of many stories, read only the lead paragraphs of others, choose only a few stories to peruse, and absorb even fewer: "On an average, out of 15 to 18 stories in a television newscast, no more than one is retained sufficiently well so that it can be recalled in any fashion shortly afterwards" (Graber 1984, pp. 201–2). Even for a news story that can be recalled, people don't absorb the entire story; instead, they compare what they see with one or more framing "schemas" that organize existing knowledge, and they even add information under certain conditions.

Selective recall of media content does not suggest the absence of media influence, of course. To the contrary, if only certain cultural material receives "play," then the media can be powerful in focusing the collective attention of the audience by giving emphasis to certain topics. In this vein, an "agenda-setting" hypothesis argues that the media do not affect the opinions of individuals so much as they help to establish the circumstances in which the public and politicians pay attention to certain issues in the first place. Consider crime reporting: according to the Center for Media and Public Affairs (http//www.cmpa.com), network news coverage tripled in the U.S. at the same time that the country was experiencing an overall decline in violent crime.

The research on agenda-setting implies that the amount of media news coverage does not necessarily derive from some intrinsic importance of a topic. That is, changes in the coverage of civil-rights issues do not necessarily reflect a sudden shift in abuses of civil rights. Yet there is a methodological problem: how can researchers know about the real incidence of events if the news cannot be assumed to be a reliable reflection of actual events? It would be useful to have some standard by which to measure the "objective" importance of topics – that is, their significance independent of the amount of media coverage they receive. One such standard might concern the deaths per thousand people from various causes. If media coverage reflected objective risk, alcohol-related deaths would receive a certain amount of coverage, drug-related deaths a certain amount of coverage, job-hazard deaths their "fair share," and so forth. The difference between the "fair share" and actual coverage would reflect the media's disproportionate attention (and, equally important, inattention) to various issues, and this information would clarify its role in agenda-setting. Studies of local communities, for example, have shown how media coverage sets the public agenda concerning rape, and influences the way justice-system officials deal with particular criminal cases – by plea bargaining or going to trial (Pritchard 1986; Protess *et al.* 1985). Such influence can take place in subtle ways. When Nicola Gavey and Virginia Gow (2001) analyzed national media coverage and public opinion regarding false rape allegations in New Zealand, they found that even the most liberally biased coverage of the issue – they focus especially on an article with clear feminist sympathies – has a tendency to reproduce conservative myths about rape, rapists, and victims.

Studies of agenda-setting in turn raise the question of who sets the agenda of the agenda-setters. It is at least theoretically possible that journalists reflect and respond to the concerns of the public or some segment of the public (to say nothing of interest groups' public-relations initiatives). The public and interest-group concerns, however, do not always calibrate with the relative scale of various problems (cf. Gans 1979, ch. 3). In fact, research shows that particular mobilized groups with sophisticated knowledge about media story-coverage decisions can influence the agenda of the media by their own activities. Thus, the "missing children" issue that received extensive coverage beginning in the 1970s was something of a media-created "urban legend" (Brunvand 1981). The legend was propagated through the interplay of certain journalistic and mass-entertainment predispositions toward sensationalism (e.g. daytime TV talk shows) and the activities of moral entrepreneurs who had a vested interest in exaggerating the issue in order to legitimize their own organizations as dealing with a social problem of epic proportions. The success of this agenda-setting depended, in turn, on playing to deep-seated public anxieties about children (Fritz and Altheide 1987). More recent public concerns about satanism in the U.S. and Great Britain (Bromley 1991;

deYoung 1998; P. Jenkins 1992) and artists' treatments of Christianity (DiMaggio *et al.* 2001; Halle 2001) reflect much the same process.

In sum, the clearest evidence about the "effects" of culture shows that agenda-setting can influence media content. But, in turn, the effects of content depend to some extent on "uses and gratification" – the ways that people choose to experience culture, and how they interpret what they experience based in part on their interests, previous knowledge, and experiences. Although it is clear that certain kinds of culture do affect audiences in measurable ways, the uses-and-gratification focus on the predispositions of people to take in culture begins to turn the question around. Rather than simply assuming that a cultural object possesses objective cultural content and asking how this content affects people, analysts now also ask about how audiences shape their own reception of culture.

Theories of audiences

Interest in audiences has its origins in theories that have converged on the problem from different directions. Because these theories have their own distinctive explanatory concerns and approaches, the audience question often replicates larger theoretical debates. Nevertheless, the debates crystallize the theoretical issues on a topic that all sides have recognized as important, and sociologists have conducted sophisticated research that informs the debates. Certain theories – hermeneutics and phenomenology – by their very nature assume a significant role for audiences in relation to cultural objects. Other perspectives – Marxism, poststructuralist semiotics, and various postmodern theories of literary criticism – have become elaborated and transformed in significant ways through their considerations of audiences.

In contrast to a structuralist theory that assumes the possibility of reading a text objectively, a hermeneutics of the audience follows the same approach employed in interpreting artistic intention – namely, theorizing the audience as actively making new meanings in relation to whatever cultural objects they witness. Of course, hermeneutics cannot escape its own assertion that all interpretations are partial, and it thus does not offer a methodology of definitive interpretation.

Phenomenology – a theoretical stream with affinities to hermeneutics – is specifically concerned with the nature of ideas as thoughts or mental events – that is, with how the world "appears" to us as phenomena in our minds. The early-twentieth-century phenomenologist Edmund Husserl sought to establish a basis for achieving true knowledge without resorting to presuppositions or assumptions. Phenomenology has never succeeded in this quest. Nevertheless, Alfred Schutz's (1970) social phenomenology of thought processes is a useful tool that suggests some important things about culture and the audience.

First, the cultural object "out there" – the film or musical performance – cannot be meaningful in its own right, for different people may pay attention to different aspects of it. In this view, people make meaning out of culture, rather than apprehending the meaning in culture. Taken to the extreme, this perspective leads to the viewpoint of literary critics, such as Stanley Fish, who regard every critical reaction to a text as founded in misinterpretation. Reading is an activity of creative misunderstanding, and criticism is no more an objective activity than is writing novels or poetry. In this approach, it would seem that everyone who reads also "writes," through the activity of reading.

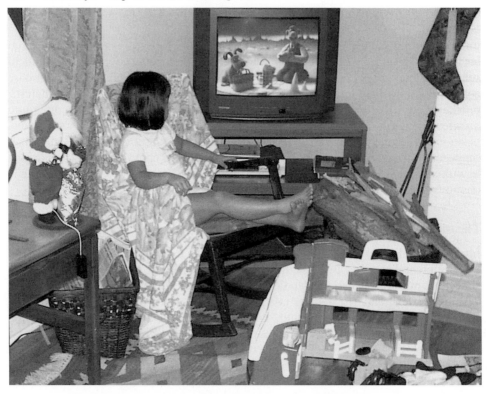

Figure 10.2 Sociologically informed research recognizes that the significance of images transmitted via television screens cannot be understood without also understanding how particular audiences engage those images in specific contexts. This photograph reminds us that, while the television is a technological device for transmitting images, it is also an object of the life-world, and that its images are always seen in relation to that world.

Source: Marshall Battani photo.

Second, how people make meaning out of culture very much depends upon their own reservoirs of knowledge and on their own immediate situations (see Figure 10.2). For example, a worshiper in a church will attach a different significance to the art displayed there than will a tourist or a visiting art historian, just as a politician likely will attach significance to television news programs that differ from the "reading" of the news by someone else. Reading a cultural object, then, is not just a passive process of "taking it in." Instead, the reader is actively engaged in making new meanings based on the conjuncture of various relevant considerations.

Third, and perhaps most important, phenomenology helps to overcome the analytic distinctions that separate the cultural producer, the cultural object, and the audience. Rather than treating each as a separate entity that somehow "affects" the other, phenomenology offers a way of recognizing the cultural object as a medium that connects the producer and audience in a special kind of intersubjective relationship. The activity of "reading a book" offers a generic example. When we read, we pay attention (more or less) to a stream of words on paper. The stream of consciousness (as opposed to the stream of words on paper) is constituted through the activity of the reader, who is paying attention to thematic topics, raising interpretive points of relevance, partly directed by the writer's goals and motivational relevancies. To the extent that readers "give themselves over" to the writer's stream of words, they can follow and explore the writer's own train of thought (filtered, of course, by readers' diverse ways of making meaning). But "giving oneself over" to reading amounts to "taking on" the writer's stream of words as though they were one's own (cf. Holub 1984; Maclean 1988). The activity of reading, then, makes the cultural object a part of one's own stream of consciousness. To take extreme examples, when we watch a television commercial enough times or listen to a popular song over and over again we absorb the cultural material: it becomes part of our own memories, ready to come to conscious awareness again if, somehow, it becomes "relevant" to some topic that comes up. For health-food activists "you are what you eat." For cultural phenomenologists "you are what you read," but "what" you read depends on how you read.

Theories about audiences range widely in their emphases and nuances. One approach includes the audience within the text. In others, the text disappears through the work of audiences. Such "armchair" theorizing stands in sore need of empirical research. Until recently, however, empirical studies about audiences were poorly conceived: rather than studying the actual audiences in the process of engaging with texts in the wider world, researchers often tried to create "laboratory" experiments. For example, an audience of college freshman – available for research because they happened to enroll in some introductory social science course – would be exposed to texts, and attempts then were made to measure their changes in attitudes and values. Fortunately, recent research has used more sophisticated methods to get at the ways actual historically constituted audiences make sense of cultural objects. For example, as we saw in Chapter 3, Radway (1984) has studied the ways in which romance novels played into the worldviews and lifestyles of women who became readers of their own volition.

In a parallel vein, Wendy Griswold (1987b) examined how different book reviewers based in the West Indies, Great Britain, and the U.S. reacted to the work of a Barbadian novelist. West Indian reviewers tended to focus on issues of individual and national identity in the novels. In contrast, "Americans revealed their obsession with race by talking about it so much, while the British indicated their preoccupation with colonialism by avoiding the subject so persistently and by concentrating on style rather than content" (1987b, p. 1,102). For Griswold, it would be a mistake either to assume a fixed content to a cultural object or to suggest that every reading is idiosyncratic and unrelated to the object's content.

How do divergent interpretations arise? Marjorie DeVault (1990) has addressed this question by studying how various readers follow divergent textual cues in interpreting a single novel – *The Late Bourgeois World*, by South African writer Nadine Gordimer, published in 1966. Liberal readers who wrote reviews immediately after the novel was first published were concerned about the "human tragedy" of South African society, and they found that the novel's fictional narrator, Liz, got in the way of their capacity to appreciate the book. Later, literary scholars in the 1970s and 1980s expressed interest in the contradictory feelings of white Europeans about black activism; these critics could more easily accept Liz's narration. Finally, a feminist reader not only accepted Liz's narration, but considered Liz's life as an important aspect of the story in and of itself. For DeVault, various readers make different arguments about a novel and its meaning, based partly on information available in the text. The diversity of arguments is possible because "the conventions of literary realism mean that the fictional situation is portrayed in a way that includes much more than is necessary for any single argument" (DeVault 1990, p. 915).

There is now a growing trove of sociological studies that address relationships between social position and audience interpretation. In *Women Watching Television*, Andrea Press (1991) has studied interactions of gender and class in the U.S. Looking at race, Darnell Hunt (1997) has shown how dramatically different were the interpretations by black versus white audiences who watched news coverage of the 1992 Los Angeles riots following the acquittal of white police officers accused of beating an African-American motorist. Diana Crane (2000) has employed cross-national comparisons of the production and consumption of fashion to highlight the very different ways that diverse audiences make use of clothing in the crafting of identities. And Tamar Liebes and Elihu Katz (1993) have explored how audiences make meaning in relation to the fictional realism of television drama.

Liebes and Katz compared how six different ethnic groups from three different countries interpreted *Dallas* – a television drama produced in the U.S. that attracted audiences around the world in the 1980s. The show's popularity concerned many critics, who saw it as an instance of cultural imperialism in which the values of U.S. culture were being spread about the globe. Liebes and Katz tested this cultural-imperialism hypothesis by studying the show's reception among groups of Russian immigrants, Moroccan Jews, Arab citizens, and kibbutz members – all in Israel, as well as audiences in the U.S. and Japan. Was there a U.S. cultural message being transmitted to audiences? The short answer is no. Liebes and Katz found a variety of interpretations. In retellings, some participants in the study focused on the linear progression of the story-line to the exclusion of everything else, while others were wholly engaged with characters rather then story or plot. The same media text was seen by some as an affirmation of tradition and the authority of family structure, by others as a display of hegemonic Western ideologies, and by still others as a depiction of a complex psychological game. Each of these different approaches to reading and retelling, the researchers found, was correlated with the specific stocks of knowledge that members of a particular ethnic or national group brought to their interaction with the program. Like Griswold and DeVault, Liebes and Katz reached conclusions that broadly square with phenomenological theories: readers play active roles in making meaning out of texts, partly on the basis of their own social circumstances of reading.

Conclusion

Semiotic and phenomenological approaches, as well as the new work on audiences, converge from different directions on social mediations between producers, objects, and audiences toward cultural constructions of reality that are marked by a lived and incessantly reworked tension between public symbols and meaningful individual conduct. It remains for future theorizing and research to clarify these complex relationships further. Whatever directions such research may take, one point already is firmly established: audiences no longer can be considered simply as the passive recipients of culture. Instead, they are themselves engaged in cultural work. Yet that work is not restricted to the social role of "audience."

The whole range of culture–audience approaches focus on cultural users in relation to particular cultural objects produced for distribution. But people do not just "consume" culture as "audiences." In fact, people partake of a broad range of cultural objects from many different sources, and any single cultural object is just one of many that a person engages. People need to be considered holistically, not just as recipients of culture. It is thus important to invert the culture–audience question, as it were, and explore the ways in which people engage in the active cultural work of social life on a daily basis.

Suggested readings

The emerging field of visual studies can provide useful sociological insight on the construction of meaning. Malcolm Barnard's *Approaches to Understanding Visual Culture* (2001) offers an in-depth comparison of theoretical positions on meaning and visual culture (especially tensions between structural and hermeneutic approaches), as well as numerous empirical studies relevant to the various theories.

In *Picture Theory: Essays on Verbal and Visual Representation*, W.J.T. Mitchell (1994) explores the fundamental problem of trying to theorize about pictures by using verbal discourse. By examining the ways that pictures function in theories of culture and consciousness, Mitchell proposes a novel way to think about theory – as a kind of "picturing." His ideas are worked out in relation to a wealth of theory as well as empirical cases from film and television.

For a comprehensive historical examination of the role that vision plays in Western theory and philosophy, see Martin Jay's *Downcast Eyes: The Denigration of Vision in Twentieth-Century French Thought* (1993). Jay moves from Plato, to the French Enlightenment, and finally to modernism as he interrogates the often contradictory discourses of vision – how it is cast as a provider of universal access to the world and as a tool of domination – in Western (especially French) social thought.

Two examples of empirically grounded sociological work that effectively bridge perspectives on cultural production and cultural consumption or reception are Diana Crane's *Fashion and Its Social Agendas: Class, Gender, and Identity in Clothing* (2000) and *Bearing Witness: Readers, Writers, and the Novel in Nigeria*, by Wendy Griswold (2000). Crane looks at nineteenth- and twentieth-century fashion in the U.S., U.K., and France, and addresses the complex interplay of class and gender in a way that poses challenges to postmodern theories of identity and culture. Griswold's analysis of Nigerian novels, writers, readers, publishers, and booksellers reveals the complex interplay of global and local culture in the creation and recreation of Nigerian fiction.

11 Culture, action, and change

Uses of culture are both personally meaningful and socially symbolic. When a daughter argues with her mother about appropriate dress, this argument about tastes also implies assertions about the daughter's independence from her mother and her identification with the culture of her peers. This book has explored the processes by which culture gets produced and deployed, as well as the ways that it constrains or shapes action, and how it affects people when they take it in. In these discussions, as object or meaning, cause or effect, culture has been at the center. We have often touched upon the uses to which culture is put. For example, we considered how people use culture more or less unconsciously in the enactment of traditions and taken-for-granted everyday practices, and we examined how cultural distinctions about class, ethnicity, and gender structure people's status assertions in everyday life.

In this concluding chapter we give fuller consideration to how people directly engage culture, and with what consequences. Looking more directly at how people use culture requires shifting the focus of analysis from culture to action. Here, we raise issues about the relations of individuals and groups to subcultures, countercultures, social movements, and cultural change. We thereby explore more directly how people deploy culture in active, self-conscious, and even contentious ways. This shift both depends upon and extends the reconceptualization of culture as symbolic expression that has taken place since the 1960s.

The broad definitions of culture circulating in the social sciences in the first half of the twentieth century – notably, defining culture was the whole way of life of a people – served the task of distinguishing what is biologically based from what is "superorganic." By the middle of the century, Talcott Parsons and Alfred Kroeber argued that this task had been accomplished, and that it was time to refine the definitions to better differentiate the "social" from the "cultural." To this end, they wrote:

> We suggest that it is useful to define the concept *culture* for most usages more narrowly than has been generally the case in the American Anthropological tradition, restricting its reference to transmitted and created content and patterns of values, ideas, and other symbolic-meaningful systems as factors in the shaping of human behavior. On the other hand, we suggest that the term *society* – or more generally, *social system* – be used to designate the specifically relational system of interaction among individuals and collectivities.
>
> (Kroeber and Parsons 1958, pp. 582–3; emphasis in original)

Kroeber and Parsons thus distinguished the concept of culture from the concept of society, and they did so in a way that centered on culture as an overarching system of values. In his own scholarship Parsons devoted his efforts to developing the concept of the social system, and in relation to the social system he thought of cultures as values – essential and abstract but socially pervasive meanings that motivate human action. As Ann Swidler interprets Parsons's theory: "Social systems exist to realize their core values, and values explain why different actors make different choices even in similar situations," yet values themselves are "the unmoved mover in the theory of action" (Swidler 1986, p. 274).

In recent years sociologists have moved away from the focus on values, toward theorizing culture as expressive symbols. This change in orientation is central to the shift beginning in the 1970s, from discourse on moral culture as rules to conceptualizing moral culture as practices and constitutive narratives. This shift can be identified in approaches ranging from the neo-Durkheimian inquiries by scholars such as Jeffrey Alexander (see Chapter 2) to production-of-culture research (see Chapter 8).

In the work of Parsons's student Clifford Geertz culture is treated as the publicly available symbolic forms through which people experience and express meaning. Geertz's wonderfully evocative analyses helped advance the new definition of culture. His portrayal of the Balinese cockfight (discussed in Chapter 7), with its layers upon layers of meaning, did much to legitimate the study of popular culture. Geertz (1973) showed how the cockfight both revealed solidarities and divisions in Balinese society and offered men the opportunity to work through those relationships in a sporting situation. Geertz's portrayal of the cockfight exemplifies his notion that expressive symbols do not simply reflect relations in a society; they are both "models of" and models for" behavior. The richness of Geertz's analysis of this popular cultural form opened the way for anthropologists and sociologists to turn their attention to popular culture in their own societies.

The emergent focus on culture as expressive symbols has consequences for thinking about how people use culture. Here, we examine both how individuals use culture to express their individuality (taste) and how groups struggle over and express their collective identities through objects and sites of cultural memory. We then explore some alternative ways of thinking about (1) a dominant culture in relation to relatively autonomous subcultures and (2) a dominant culture in relation to oppositional cultures – that is, countercultures. These considerations raise questions about the relation of culture to social movements, and of social movements to cultural change.

Material culture, consumption patterns, and communities

Material goods become important as aspects of culture according to the meanings they are assigned. In Chapters 5 and 6 we discussed the development of consumption both in terms of a change in attitude by which consuming became defined as socially valued, and in relation to changes in people's buying habits. As we saw, in the course of this "consumption revolution" people began to use consumption to express themselves to a far greater degree than had been possible before, both as individuals and in relation to social strata and groups. As we saw, producers, advertisers, and merchants promoted these changes. Yet it is important to turn the analysis around and ask about the meanings of consumption to consumers. To do so, we first consider research on individuals' attributions of meanings to things and then examine how groups – sometimes unself-consciously but sometimes with explicit intention – express themselves through consumption patterns and styles, thereby turning cultural "things" into meaningful "culture."

As Chapter 3 suggests, in modern societies distinctive patterns of consumption, especially when they are recognized by participating individuals as symbolically constitutive of social groups and boundaries, are important bases by which social structuration occurs through the struggle over status. It is also worth considering whether culture is stratified by geographic location and how proximity in physical space enhances the possibility of social community. Despite the emergence of national and international consumer cultures, there is a difference that persists between the cultures of small towns, exurbs, and the countryside, compared to the cosmopolitan culture of urban life, where sheer density of social interaction encourages certain cultural solutions – aloofness, reserve, and a blasé attitude (classically described by Simmel 1950). Moreover, within a given society there is substantial cultural variation from region to region. In the United States there are still regional differences between New England, the urban Northeast, the South, the Midwest, the West, and the West Coast. In France there are differences between the cultures of Brittany, Alsace, and Provence. Whether in London or Cyprus, local denizens will be able to acquaint the outsider with the subtle but locally important cultural differences in "who we are" and "who they are."

A number of community studies have documented the distinctive cultures of urban neighborhoods, of small towns, and of suburbs. For example, Herbert Gans (1962) showed how second-generation Italian-Americans in the West End of Boston carried forward certain traditional ways of doing things. The relatively poor Italian-Americans in the neighborhood that Gans studied formed a "peer-group society" where the privacy and consumption so valued in the suburban middle classes were not so important. Instead, people placed great emphasis on visiting among family and friends, on maintaining relationships of reciprocity in gifts and favors, and on rejecting the upward social mobility – and move to the suburbs – that would undermine the solidarity of the community. These enduring qualities of ethnic-community life have been immortalized in films such as *My Big Fat Greek Wedding*. Yet, for all the specifically ethnic symbols and customs, Gans asked whether the community was an ethnic or a class phenomenon, and he concluded that class was the fundamental determinant of the culture: even though the culture was elaborated in specific ethnic terms, it was structurally equivalent in its worldview and practices to those of other working-class ethnic communities. Nor, as Bennett Berger already showed in 1960, are suburbs monolithically middle class or above in their class composition. More recently, people from the suburbs move even further, to exurbs, or back to the city. Thus, suburbanization is hardly a monolithic trend, even if it remains unrelenting, and where it occurs, many kinds of people make the move, bringing diverse lifestyles from cities, small towns, and other countries.

At least since suburbs began to be built en masse by developers at the end of World War II, they have been the source of great controversy. Both members of the urban working class and cosmopolitan sophisticates often have disdained the suburbs of the middle classes for their supposed homogeneity, alienation, and boredom. Yet Gans argued that this is something of an outsider's stereotype. True, most suburbs tend to be more homogeneous than cities or towns, where a greater variety of people can be found within an equivalent amount of geographic space. It is true also that suburbs lack the vitality of culture and the density of social interaction found in the cities. But

Gans pointed out that many people choose to live in the suburbs precisely to escape these features of the city. Further, his research on Levittown, where construction began in 1947, suggests that even in a nearly "instant" suburb public space is more friendly than that of the city, and a new pattern of sociability quickly becomes centered in people's homes – outside of public space. Perhaps because of the relative homogeneity of Levittown, combined with the fact that inhabitants chose to move there, interpersonal relations could obtain a depth and vitality that is not always easy to sustain in the more tradition-bound world of the working-class city neighborhood or the often fleeting contacts of professional upper-middle-class urban life. Moreover, Levittowners quickly became immersed in a complex web of formal and informal organizations, from the Cub Scouts to babysitting exchange associations (Gans 1967; see also Seeley *et al.* 1956; B.M. Berger 1960).

The critique of supposed homogeneity in suburbs in turn raises the issue of individual freedom and autonomy. What kinds of choices are available in the suburbs? How is living in a suburban environment a "commitment" to a constraining set of practices? On the other hand, how do people make varied use of the material objects they acquire? Early critics of the sameness of Levittown were surprised to find that within a decade owners had altered the appearance of their houses – changing the siding, constructing additions, doing landscaping, and so on – to create more personal and distinctive houses. Later suburban tract-housing contractors sought to take this interest in the expression of taste into effect, and offered minor variations in the housing they built.

The gentle suburban resistance to homogeneity in the context of a choice that limits difference can be treated as one end of a continuum. At the other end of this continuum are to be found some countercultural groups that position themselves explicitly at odds with a dominant culture and adopt self-conscious "in-your-face" confrontational styles. When Willis (1977, 1990) examined youth subcultures in Britain, he documented the push for autonomy through the creation of various subcultural expressions – most importantly, music, dress, and styles of banter. These sorts of expressions – clothing, for example – are often taken as trivial, but Willis maintains that they are vital for the sustenance of individual and group identities. Thus, despite the differences between the two ends of the continuum, there is also a similarity. Levittowners who altered the appearance of their houses were expressing their individuality in asserting their own taste preferences within the confines of the suburb, just as the youth with blue hair is expressing hers.

Collective memory

Not only do individuals express their identities and preferences by using material culture in demonstrations of "taste," but social groups attach cultural meanings to places and objects in efforts to convey intended messages to a receptive public. For example, buildings and streets are often named to invoke memories of persons. Alderman's (1996) discussion of the renaming of streets in southern states in the U.S. after Dr. Martin Luther King provides an interesting example. By such processes, material objects – statues, buildings, places – become part of the discourse about what it is to be a member of a nation or a community (see Figure 11.1). It is thus important to consider how cultural meanings get attached to places and events in the service of collective identities.

Figure 11.1 At the state capitol building in Jefferson City, this bronze monument titled *Missouri* is intended to call up in the mind of the viewer both general and particular references to water symbolism and associations between the river's bounty, the state, and all that is good and beautiful in the Western tradition. The young woman's pose calls to mind classical statues, yet there are several twists that give *Missouri* a distinct local flavor: the wreath around her head is made of cattails found along the banks of Missouri's rivers; the corn is native to the new world, and the fish behind the cornucopia is a Missouri catfish.

Source: photo by Charlene Adkins, 2002.

Scholars across various disciplines have begun writing about how art, popular culture, activism, and consumer culture intersect in the narratives and cultural objects centered on public spaces. "Collective memory" is the term they use to refer to such stories about the collective identities of groups, communities, and societies. Controversies such as the one about how to rebuild on the site of the World Trade Center's twin towers in New York City reflect tensions about how to construct collective memory.

The sociologist Jeffery Olick has traced two sociological traditions dealing with cultural representations of the past which have come down to us. One, from Emile Durkheim, emphasizes "collective commemorative representations and mnemonic traces." In the other, from Halbwach, "collective memory" refers to "collectively framed individual memories" constituting an "active past that informs our identities." Olick suggests that Durkheim's and Halbwach's ideas are connected to two different definitions of culture – culture as "patterns of publicly available symbols objectified in society" versus culture as subjective meanings in peoples' minds (Olick 1999, pp. 335–6). In order to emphasize the connections between these two aspects of "social memory," he advocates using collective memory as "a sensitizing term for a wide variety of mnemonic processes, practices, and outcomes, neurological, cognitive, personal, aggregated, and collective" (1999, p. 346).

In Olick's formulation and more generally, collective memory is different from personal recollections, official historical discourse, or academic history. As Sturken has observed, the point of analyzing cultural memories is not to try to discern "what really happened" in a given set of events in the past, but to look at "what its telling reveals about how the past affects the present" (1997, p. 2). Sturken prefers the term "cultural memory" over "collective memory" because she is interested in the relatively self-conscious processes through which memories get produced and attached to "objects of memories." Her point is well taken no matter which term is used. Remembering – and forgetting – does not simply happen. Rather, these are outcomes tied to the intentions and actions of people, who often work within institutional frameworks of an established social order, and also sometimes within marginalized groups or even oppositional movements.

Space and time

Studies of collective memory often examine cases of commemoration. In these studies, place acquires a special importance because sites can be used to anchor, preserve, or define memories. Thus, Pierre Nora's (1989) notion of "sites of memory" reflects his view that memory attaches itself to sites rather than to events. Nora's work privileges place over time, and he posits an opposition between history and memory. History is "perpetually suspicious of memory." Other scholars regard history and memory as "entangled." As Zelizar points out,

> The study of collective memory has little to do with the passage of time in its expected form. Rather, collective memory is predicated upon a disassociation between the act of remembering and the linear sequencing of time.... Time's *recreation* is so central that studies of collective memory are often constituted by their very invocation of nonsequential temporal patterning.
>
> (Zelizar 1995, p. 222)

Thus, collective memory works to inform group identities by offering a shared past linked to particular events. Yet temporality is rearranged.

How memory disrupts the linearity of time can be seen in practices such as "retrospective nominalization," which involves the renaming of events that occurred at one point in time, following events that occur later. For example, World War I only became known by that name after World War II. Before then it was known as the Great War. Zelizar notes that the constant linear flow of calendar time has the potential for undoing community, whereas collective memory allows a community to use time in a way that works to its benefit.

Collective memory is itself a process, continually unfolding, as with tradition (see Chapter 4), always subject to further transformation. Some authors have focused on particular moments of commemoration, but later commemorations can cover or overturn earlier commemorative work. For example, Barry Schwartz (1987) has shown that George Washington's reputation continues to evolve rather than having been fixed by any particular commemoration. Ironically, new memories thus depend on forgetting old ones. Not that forgetting is necessarily bad. As Sturken (1997) reminds us, the desire for coherence and continuity produces forgetting. The narrative form itself entails forgetting because narrative closure requires that only some events – those that "fit" within the coherent story – get remembered.

Yet the question of what gets remembered and what gets forgotten is important. Although studies often emphasize how collective memory creates and maintains group identities, we cannot assume that everyone has the same interests in remembering particular events. Painful pasts create ambivalence, as became apparent in the debates in Germany following the destruction of the Berlin Wall in 1989. Did this event signal unification (of the two Germanies, East and West) or reunification (of one Germany, temporarily separated in the aftermath of World War II)? Interpretations differed. Germans also faced the question of whether Berlin or Bonn would be the capital of the new Germany, and, if Berlin, whether it would be the Berlin of Hitler or the Berlin of Kaiser Wilhelm.

In order to consider the political nature of memory, Sturken borrows Foucault's notion of subjugated knowledges. She cites Foucault's point: "Since memory is actually a very important factor in struggle (really in fact, struggles develop in a kind of conscious moving forward of history), if one controls people's memory, one controls their dynamism" (Sturken 1997, p. 6). But Sturken cautions against the assumption that collective memory is inherently a site for resistance. How the process of collective memory plays out is highly dependent on the particular place and context.

One study that displays the complexities is Lyn Spillman's (1997) comparison of centennial and bicentennial celebrations in the United States and Australia, which examines how the process of developing national identities occurred in these "settler countries" (as opposed to nation formation in the first European nation-states or in postcolonial countries). In Australia and the United States, national identity was not built through nationalist movements. Instead, Spillman argues, national identities came into being "as the result of a slow process of cultural innovation and diffusion" (1997, p. 19). At the time of the Australian centennial in 1888, for example, there was no formally unified state, only six British colonies.[1] Yet a shared identity had been emerging over the previous fifty years, beginning with the common usage of the term "Australia," first suggested in 1814. In the 1880s, federation was expected but not yet achieved.

The centennial celebrations in both the U.S. and Australia were only loosely related to governmental sponsorship. By and large, they amounted to "intense episodes in an uninstitutionalized and diffuse field of cultural production" (Spillman 1997, p. 33). Many groups participated in activities in the public sphere, but not everyone had the same goal. Although studies of collective memory often emphasize consensus, Spillman finds not consensus but rather shared cultural repertoires in the commemorative process.

Commemoration without consensus

The Vietnam Veterans Memorial in Washington, D.C., is a very different case, but it is one in which consensus was markedly lacking. As Wagner-Pacifici and Schwartz (1991) show, both the content and the symbols themselves were contested. Although the memorial was to be a public symbol that would confer recognition on those who had died in the Vietnam War, the sponsors of the monument faced the difficult task of commemorating a military defeat that ended a war for which there had been no public consensus. Rather than uplifting, tall, vertical, and white, the design they chose for the Vietnam Veterans Memorial was black, and it cut into the earth. As a result of their choice, the sponsors became caught up in a series of negotiations regarding the unconventional style of the planned memorial. Wagner-Pacifici and Schwartz argue that the planning and construction of the Vietnam memorial brought into play conflicting views both about the meaning of the war and about what is appropriate within the genre of the war memorial. In their analysis, the Vietnam Veterans Memorial's break with the conventional genre corresponds to a collective break with previous interpretations of memorialized wars.

In addition, however, Wagner-Pacifici and Schwartz point out that after the memorial was completed the conflicts over design became overlaid with new meanings that arose in the use of the memorial by the large numbers of people who visit it. To make sense of these new meanings, they draw on Durkheim's influential analysis of the social functions of ritual (see Chapter 2), which seeks to explain how various kinds of expressive rites and commemorations – religious and other – produce individuals' feelings of identification with a group and its members. For Durkheim (1995), the feelings are produced not by abstract values but by symbolic acts and expressions.

The collective use of the Vietnam memorial in symbolic acts makes it, in Durkheimian terms, a sacred space. Yet Wagner-Pacifici and Schwartz argue that the wall evokes a particular response, a kind of ambivalence, that is not typical of sacred spaces:

> In the Veterans Memorial, then, we see none of the hegemonic influence that forms the basis for…"manipulative theories" of secular symbolism…. If the Memorial were in fact a tool of state power, if it were adopted by the state in order to maintain allegiance to an elite and to promote authoritative ways of seeing society…then that tool has not been used very effectively.
> (Wagner-Pacifici and Schwartz 1991, pp. 406–7)

Instead of hegemonic glorification, Wagner-Pacifici and Schwartz describe a different social process: people may need ritual to deal with the Vietnam War as a painful and controversial part of the past, even though the rituals "are not rituals that Durkheim would have recognized," since they do not reinforce common sentiments (1991, p. 417).

As social analysts increasingly recognize the multicultural basis of modern societies, it becomes important to have theories that address both the claims made for any given dominant culture, as well as cultural challenges, and where and when they are likely to occur. Wagner-Pacifici and Schwartz significantly expand Durkheim's formulation in this regard by suggesting that rituals do not necessarily reinforce common sentiments. Still, their analysis presents the Vietnam memorial as a national symbol, and they depict the ritual as promoting a unifying healing. Yet critics such as Zolberg have questioned whether the groups in American society who found themselves on opposing sides about the Vietnam conflict have been reunited (1990, p. 103).

A situation of even greater unresolved conflict is embedded in multiple memorials constructed in Israel to honor its assassinated prime minister, Yitzhak Rabin.

Following his death in 1995, a majority of people wanted to honor Rabin as the hero of the 1948 Israel War of Independence and mourn the killing of their head of state. A smaller group also honored his work negotiating for peace with Palestinians. In this case, the disagreements about how to memorialize a "difficult past" led to a contestation among memorials. At the time of Rabin's assassination, Israelis already were divided into right and left, hawks and doves, divided by how to resolve the conflict with the Palestinians. Vinitzky-Seroussi argues that, although Rabin's death was mourned by many Israelis, fewer people mourned his political assassination, and this divergence had an impact on memorialization (2002, p. 36). A memorial that had a restricted meaning, only calling to mind the person and the date of his death, reached the widest audience. Memorials that evoked the wider context of his death, including his pursuit of peace in the Middle East, aroused a more conflicted response and a smaller number of supporters. In contrast with the Vietnam Veterans Memorial, which is located on a single site, there are several different sites for Rabin, each representing a different narrative.

Vinitzky-Seroussi argues that multivocal and fragmented commemorations express social conflicts rather than resolving them:

> A fragmented commemoration that consists of multiple and diverse times and spaces, and in which different discourses of the past are enacted and expressed in order to appeal to different groups, does not enhance social solidarity. And more than representing social conflicts, it may sharpen them by offering contentious collectives what they scarcely could have laid claim to before the monuments were erected and the memorial days were set: a place to meet, a time to share, a discourse to cherish…it is about reinforcing, even building dissensus.
>
> (Vinitzky-Seroussi 2002, p. 48)

Fragmented commemorations, in other words, cannot be analyzed successfully within a Durkheimian perspective.

A final example of collective memory concerns the public space of Tiananmen Square in Beijing, China. Wu Hung (1991) recounts how this site has been a place where, throughout the twentieth century, Chinese mass movements staged demonstrations, including the one most familiar to Westerners, the 1989 student uprising. Yet the authorities could demonstrate their power in Tiananmen Square, as the watching world saw. As with the Vietnam and Rabin memorials, there is a narrative of "dissensus," but, here, the power of the state was paramount in shaping the outcome.

Tiananmen, originally one of a series of gates in the walls of the capital city, served as the formal entrance to the interior of Beijing. First built during the Ming dynasty (1368–1644), it was part of a system of walls and gates that symbolized the emperor's distance from his people (Wu Hung 1991, p. 85). Mao dramatically altered the meaning of Tiananmen when he appeared above the gate in 1949. According to Wu,

> No other gesture could more effectively prove the newness of the Communist leadership, and no other act could more convincingly seal the title of the People's Republic. From that moment, Tiananmen was no longer one of many gates, but a monument where yearly parades would refresh the memory of the country's founding.
>
> (Wu Hung 1991, p. 88)

Between 1949 and 1989, Tiananmen served as an emblem of the state, and displays of state power occurred there. But so did grassroots demonstrations, including an unplanned assembly of 100,000 people mourning Zhou Enlai 100 days after his death in 1976. Wu points out that although the place remains the same the meanings change over time. When police and soldiers attacked Zhou Enlai's mourners gathered at the Monument to the People's Heroes in the square, the monument, which had been erected by and identified with the state, became identified as the place for protests. The events that occurred in 1989, including the students' demonstrations and the display of the Goddess of Democracy, followed by her destruction by the armies of the state, do not stand alone. Events at Tiananmen are a part of a larger Chinese struggle about national identity and the locus of power.

Studies of difficult commemorations suggest that theories restricted to considering what things mean to people are not fully adequate in their understandings of public expressive culture. Such understandings also need to be informed by analysis of the conditions under which people choose one expressive symbol over another. Important conditions for such choices are rooted in the relation of an individual or group to the dominant culture.

Culture and action

Rethinking culture in relation to expressive symbols has implications for two long-standing debates that have shaped the discipline of sociology. One debate is about whether material interests or ideal (normative and value) concerns motivate individual behavior. For this debate, it is important to consider the implications of shifting the focus in the analysis of culture from values and norms to practices and narratives. The other debate is about the relation between the individual and the society, variously conceived as an issue of "order" or a controversy about "agency," depending on whether the debate centers on the ways that choices are socially constrained or on choices that individuals make. Matters relevant to these two debates have surfaced throughout the present book, for example, in our discussions of the self, stratification, power, and audiences. Here, we explicitly address the consequences of conceptualizing culture in relation to expressive symbols and meanings for three approaches that address one or both of the two debates. We examine, first, a reconstruction of the Parsonian action framework by Ann Swidler and others, then a symbolic interactionist reformulation of the concept of subculture by Gary Alan Fine, and, finally, a semiotic analysis by Mark Gottdiener that reconfigures Marxist theories of cultural hegemony.

Culture as a toolkit

Ann Swidler directly challenged the view expressed in action theory "that culture shapes action by supplying ultimate ends or values toward which action is directed" (1986, p. 273). Like other theorists at the time when she wrote on the topic, she recognized the importance of examining expressive symbols rather than values in the sociology of culture. However, she worried that the interpretive approach "skirts the issue of explanation." In discarding earlier explanations of how cultural values motivate action, interpretive theorists had – unnecessarily in Swidler's view – abandoned any kind of causal analysis. Swidler's alternative formulation holds that culture should be seen as a "toolkit." Analysis then focuses on culture as a causal agent, not in defining ends (i.e. values), but "in providing cultural components that are used to construct strategies of action" (1986, p. 273).

When Weber spoke of meanings as undergirding action, he was concerned with specific historical instances in which ideas and actions were shaped by complex sets of material and ideal interests. Swidler argued that the foremost modern theorist of action, Talcott Parsons, transposed historical ideas into "global, ahistorical values" (Swidler 1986, p. 274). Swidler suggested that the theory of culture as values persisted because the claim that "culture shapes action by defining what people want" is intuitively plausible. But she countered that knowing "what people want" is "of little help in explaining their action." This conception of values equates them with preferences, hardly what Parsons had in mind. By the 1980s, the confusion between values and preferences – born out of economic and psychological models of human behavior – had become so pervasive in American ways of thinking that sociologist Robert Bellah (discussed in Chapter 2), although interested in how ideals shape behavior, did not use the term "values" anymore, not even when describing "justice" or "success" as aspects of the good society.

For Swidler, a Weberian formulation argues for ideas shaping action. By contrast, for Swidler "continuities of style" and "the way action is organized" are more enduring. For instance, she pointed to Weber's own example of the Protestant ethic and argued that "reliance on moral 'work' on the self has been a more enduring feature of Protestantism than the particular ends to which this work has been directed" (Swidler 1986, p. 276). From Calvin to Benjamin Franklin to modern sex manuals, there have been changes in the "ends" with which the Protestant work ethic has been aligned, yet something of the ethos continues to be culturally recognizable across these changes.

To think about "the way action is organized" means trying to understand how different actions of individuals are linked to one another. Many social theories (both idealist and materialist) present action as though people choose one action at a time. Swidler, on the other hand, argued that people choose one or another "strategy" (which means, not a plan, but rather a "way of organizing action"). This strategy model parallels the idea of commitment in symbolic interactionist theories: taking one action may "commit" an individual to other actions in the future, or make other actions easier or more likely as a consequence (Becker 1960). Swidler held that people "do not build lines of action from scratch." Rather, they use at least some "prefabricated links." Yet the links are not completely constraining. In Swidler's view, "All real cultures contain diverse, often conflicting symbols, rituals, stories, and guides to action" (1986, p. 277). People choose among the "tools" available within a culture – and there are always more such tools than can be used in any given situation.

However, patterns of use will vary according to social conditions. Swidler distinguished how culture works in situations of continuity (when people have settled lives) from how culture works in times of change (when people have unsettled lives). In stable times cultural experiences and socially structured situations reinforce each other, but when times are unsettled ideologies that emerge can establish new styles or strategies for action.

Conflicts such as the one over abortion illustrate Swidler's toolkit metaphor. Two ideologies – each coherent, each prescribing strong control over action – compete with one another. However, each ideology continues to depend on preexisting cultural "traditions" and "common sense" for resolution of various issues that it does not explicitly cover. This relation of ideologies to other cultural "tools" is apparent in Faye Ginsberg's (1990) study of pro-choice and pro-life movements in Fargo, North Dakota. In this small Midwestern city, the women who found themselves on one or the other side in one of the most bitter controversies of our times nevertheless seemed to have a difficult time casting those on the opposing side as "the enemy." Individuals who had lived their lives in Fargo continued to be enmeshed in relationships that were not determined by the ideologies of the abortion movements, and there was always the possibility of face-to-face contact with someone on the other side who might live on the same block or have kids in the same schools.

In order to understand why one ideology wins out, however, analysis must move beyond the cultural toolkit model. Ideologies have to be understood in context, in relation to particular structural constraints and historical circumstances in which they operate. Swidler's thesis about settled and unsettled times is partially an attempt to do just that. But it leaves many issues to be addressed. In Swidler's model there is little exploration of how individuals actually choose from among the tools in the toolkit. Strategies carry costs to individuals and to groups, but Swidler offered little discussion of this issue. Furthermore, as the abortion example shows, it is not necessarily the *times* that are settled or unsettled. It may be the *circumstances*. With many "single-issue" social movements, individuals can find themselves in highly ideological situations. Yet other people may avoid such situations and live more culturally settled existences.

In contrast to unsettled times (or circumstances), in settled times (or circumstances) cultures are "more encompassing," but, Swidler argued, they exercise less direct control over action. Under such conditions the tool metaphor is especially fitting: people select cultural elements and invest them with meaning. A family's holiday celebration may combine selected "traditions" from both the husband's and wife's pasts, as well as elements picked up from the newspaper. Thus, for Swidler, "the influence of culture in settled lives is especially strong in structuring those uninstitutionalized, but recurrent situations in which people act in concert" (1986, p. 281).

Swidler's discussion of the development of ideology suggests that in unsettled times societies contain competing cultures. Also, the notion of the toolkit implies that cultural expressions will not be the same for everybody. Still, Swidler's model seems to assume a "dominant culture" that is "taken for granted" to varying degrees, its very existence sometimes challenged by contesting ideologies and sometimes placidly accepted. Other sociologists of culture have questioned to what extent a shared taken-for-granted (and therefore dominant) culture exists anymore, even in settled times or circumstances. Many contemporary societies are characterized by high degrees of heterogeneity, in which different groups have different degrees of commitment to any supposedly dominant culture. Social theories therefore need to be capable of analyzing whether and how various groups actually come into conflict over cultural expression. Swidler's settled/unsettled-times formulation does not fully address this issue. At any given time, some subgroups are likely to gain advantage by having a relation to the dominant culture that they can take for granted: their positions of relative privilege protect them. Other groups, in different social locations, may challenge the dominant culture.

Subcultures and expressive symbols

Like Swidler, symbolic interactionists have participated in the critique of the emphasis on culture as values. They too have moved toward examining culture in its expressive aspects. Their work on subcultures focuses on symbols. This approach is consistent with a well-established line of symbolic interactionist research that treats action as contingent and emergent while exploring how certain choices increasingly commit a person to a line of action (Becker 1960; Becker *et al.* 1961).

The concept of subculture was first used in sociology to talk about ethnic groups; later it was applied to youth culture. In these investigations, deviant groups were often the focus. Early Chicago School sociologists Fredrick Thrasher and Edwin Sutherland argued against the idea that particular ethnic groups were inherently more likely to commit crimes. They observed that the ethnic composition of neighborhoods in Chicago changed, whereas crime rates in the neighborhoods continued at the same levels. They argued that deviant behaviors were learned through a process of cultural transmission through primary groups – friends in the neighborhood – by what they called differential association. In their analysis, members of delinquent gangs not only learned to engage in deviant behaviors; they also learned to value deviant activities over a conventional life. The theories of subculture developed by sociologists studying delinquents thus emphasized socialization into encapsulating groups that embraced value systems at odds with conventional values (e.g. Cohen 1955).

Gary Alan Fine and Sherryl Kleinman (1979) offered a reformulation of the concept of subculture that departs from the pejorative tendency to associate them with deviant or lower-class groups in society. They made four points in their critique. First, they argued that most analyses confuse "subcultures" and "subsocieties." Membership in a group often is lumped together with sharing values, knowing behaviors, and conscious identification with the group. Fine and Kleinman argued (as we have in Chapter 1) for an analytical distinction between group and culture. Second, they suggested that it is important to know who among a population participates in a subculture. They found the usual demographic markers misleading: for example, not all people of a certain age will share in youth culture. Third, Fine and Kleinman argued that a subculture tends to be perceived as "homogenous, static, and closed," whereas, in reality, information "flows across the boundaries" of subcultures. Their fourth point was that work on subculture had focused on values to the neglect of behaviors, norms, and material culture.

Fine wanted to explain both cultural diffusion and local variations in cultural content. Fine (1979) described the process of culture creation in small groups; Fine and Kleinman (1979) suggested how subcultural elements spread beyond groups. Although the mass media are instrumental in this latter process, like other researchers (discussed in Chapter 10) Fine and Kleinman resisted the notion that individuals or groups simply absorb whatever is transmitted by the mass media. Thus, they pointed to cultural materials available through the mass media that do not get picked up, and they noted how cultural materials such as jokes, stories, and urban legends can diffuse rapidly outside the mass media.

Earlier theories described subcultures as exclusive, but Fine and Kleinman made the essential point that participants in any given subculture are likely to belong to multiple groups. Even though cultural content is often defined through processes of negotiation in small groups, it is through social networks that cultural forms diffuse to other individuals and groups. Here, as in other aspects of social life, weak ties between people are important, in this case for how they promote the spread of subcultural forms (1979, pp. 10–12). Diffusion occurs through contact between people who participate in particular subcultures and others who do not.

The kinds of subcultural participation and group membership described by Fine and Kleinman raised questions about (1) the degree to which individuals identify with any given subculture and (2) how broader communities respond to subcultures. Fine and Kleinman distinguished between *knowledge* of a cultural form and *use* of a cultural form: "culture usage consists of chosen behaviors" (1979, p. 12). Enacting the behaviors, they suggested, depends upon identification with the subculture, and it is possible for a person's identification to remain latent much of the time. Identification also may vary both in centrality – the degree of "commitment to the population segment" – and in salience – the frequency of identification (1979, p. 13).

A distinctive appearance can mark subcultural participation to outsiders, making identification both more costly and more exclusive. On the other hand, negative responses by outsiders can have the effect of increasing the salience of identification with the subculture (Fine and Kleinman 1979, p. 15). In turn, to avoid consequences of negative labeling participants may develop subtle ways of signaling their involvement to one another. Thus, Judy Grahn has written about gay culture in high schools when she was growing up in the 1950s, where wearing purple on Thursdays or rings on particular fingers signified one's identity to other gay students (1984, pp. 1–20).

Analyses of subcultures open up ways of thinking about groups that possess their own cultural forms and symbolic expressions. According to Fine (1987), each little-league baseball team has its own particular culture. Little-league baseball teams across the country also share some symbolic forms in common. Although subcultures do not have the explicit character that Swidler attributes to ideologies, neither are they part of some taken-for-granted generalized culture: they offer alternative cultural "tools" to participants.

Cultural conflict and countercultures

Other researchers have considered heterogeneity of culture within a society by focusing on "oppositional cultures" or "countercultures" – subcultures that become defined in opposition to a dominant culture. Ironically, one criticism of Marxist formulations about cultural hegemony is that they fail to appreciate the possibilities for cultural conflict because the hegemony framework tends to assume that the dominant culture effectively precludes alternatives (Tuchman 1974; Gitlin 1980). However, as Mark Gottdiener has pointed out, even when elites control the production of culture they cannot control the interpretations that individuals give to cultural products: "ideological domination of mass culture industries is…not guaranteed to control or even affect an audience's behavior" (1985, p. 989). Not only is there variation among individual interpretations of mass culture, but – more important to Gottdiener – interpretations vary with the degree of involvement in one or another particular cultural milieu.

Understanding the relation between various cultures and the wider society is crucial to Gottdiener's analysis of any supposedly dominant mass culture. In his view, "before there is 'mass culture' there must be 'culture,' that is, the conceptual forms and accumulated knowledge by which social groups organize everyday experience within social and material contexts" (1985, p. 991). In modern societies, individuals are involved in social groups and networks with their own cultural forms. British working-class youth, for example, developed a distinctive culture in resistance to both their working-class parents' cultures and the dominant culture (Hebdige 1979; Willis 1977). American

Buddhism has taken a different form than either the dominant American culture or the Asian parent culture of Buddhism (Boucher 1988; Numrich 1996).

Gottdiener grounded interpretive processes of culture forming in the concrete group life of individuals. He was particularly interested in those cases where a group's cultural form is taken over by mass-culture industries. Although he rejected a thesis of cultural control or hegemony as too simple, he described a process where groups with their own distinctive cultures have to struggle if they are to maintain autonomy in the face of mass culture. The threats to autonomy can be seen not only when local cultural forms are taken up and reproduced in a sanitized version by the mass media, but in a more extreme way when previously autonomous cultural producers end up producing for the market – as we saw in Chapter 4 with indigenous artists who learn to produce "tourist art" to the exclusion of their own cultural production. Gottdiener's model has implications both for talking about autonomous subcultures – those whose participants see themselves as separate from the dominant culture – as well as cultures that become defined in outright opposition to a dominant culture.

The issue of autonomous culture production among oppositional cultures can be pursued further by considering a particular youth culture – New York City graffiti writers. Combining interactionist and Marxist approaches, Richard Lachman (1988) has explored both the "careers" and "ideology" of its participants. Largely through contact with "mentors," he found, would-be participants develop a sense that they could achieve fame through graffiti writing. Once they learn the basic skills, "taggers" work to write their names (tags) on as many subway cars as possible in order to become "king of the line." There is an element of danger involved since graffiti writing is illegal, and taggers must engage in their practice covertly to avoid getting caught and arrested or beaten up by the police. Taggers have relatively short careers of intense activity during which they establish their fame, and then, according to school counselors whom Lachman interviewed, they rest on their laurels and go back to school. Tagging is a cultural form appreciated by a local audience – other taggers and high-school students – and occasionally adopted by gang patrons: one gang will recruit and hire a tagger with "style" to establish the gang's "tag" in territories where it is involved in a dispute with another gang.

Yet during two brief periods, in 1973–4 and 1982–3, graffiti artists who went beyond writing their tags and painted entire murals on subway cars were embraced by art dealers in the New York art world. Lachman argued that the dealers were not really interested in coopting the particular alternative aesthetic and social form of these muralists. Rather, their interest was a product of the continual demand in the art market for stylistic innovation. However, the murals "violated so many of the post-modernist canons" that art-world interest in them did not last long. In the 1970s muralists formed their own art world, gathering in "writers' corners" in subway stations to view and judge the work of other graffiti artists. In this period, the "writers at all career levels agreed that a writer's standing was determined by his subway work…and that gallery shows and sales were the rewards, not the arbiters, of writers' graffiti reputation" (Lachman 1988, p. 427). Lachman argued that the destruction of meeting places by the police also destroyed the collective base of graffiti writers' art world and opened the way for the possibility of cooptation.

Lachman followed the work of the Birmingham School (S. Hall 1977; Hebdige 1979), and he suggested one set of circumstances in which commodification succeeds in cooptation: "Only by undermining the organizational bases for sustaining belief in the subculture's alternative view of reality could graffiti writers, or anyone else, be attracted to a conception of reality they had previously rejected" (Lachman 1988, p. 249). Yet this does not necessarily occur. Consider what happened when graffiti writers' style was adopted as a decorative motif within mass-culture industries. This was an act so distant from the realm of the graffiti writers themselves that they could not be coopted by it, in part perhaps because, as Lachman suggested, it did not undermine members' beliefs in the oppositional culture. Thus, although mass-culture industries often do coopt *products* from autonomous and oppositional cultures and produce sanitized versions for mass consumption, the *participants* who first produced the item may sometimes remain untouched by the cooptation.

Culture and change

Sometimes, dissent and opposition to a dominant culture become central organizing themes in social movements that seek to change some aspects of a society. Indeed, "culture" would seem to lie at the heart of social movements, regardless of their purpose. In all kinds of movements, people with shared ideas and feelings join together to pursue social change by expressing their hopes and grievances in one or another public way. Such expressions typically include strong symbolic components. Yet in research on social movements there was a long period when cultural aspects were treated narrowly or neglected entirely. In the 1990s this situation began to change. Culture reemerged as a significant dimension of research. Theories changed in part as a response to changes in the world, including globalization, the emergence of new issues and kinds of movements, and new information technologies used for mobilization (Johnston and Klandermans 1995; Johnston *et al.* 1994; Jasper 1997; Darnovsky *et al.* 1995)

Research on social movements incorporates analysis of culture in several ways. In early formulations culture surfaced as ideology. More recently, alternative approaches have emerged. Although various ways of considering culture overlap, it is useful to distinguish several approaches. Research connecting ideology and practice looks at the cultural life within movements. Framing and emergent-meaning approaches focus on how movement organizations use symbols to attract people or tap into their values and beliefs in order to motivate them to join movements or forge coalitions. Collective-identity approaches tend to start with individuals' experiences, expressions, and desires for recognition. Cultural-movement approaches look at movements oriented toward cultural change.

From ideology to ideological work as practice

Scholars during the 1960s into the 1970s who studied the labor movements of the nineteenth and early twentieth centuries tended to explain participation in terms of ideologies and interests. Ideologies were described in cognitive terms as belief systems, but also as originating in and reflecting interests, based in class or economic situation. Participation was theorized to result from strains and conflicts in social structure. However, movements that arose in the latter half of the twentieth century posed problems for this framework.

For example, a comparative study of communal-living groups in the counterculture during the 1960s and 1970s, *The Ways Out* (J.R. Hall 1978), argued that the many young people who formed or joined the groups sought to fulfill values such as community or spiritual growth that they did not believe could be easily attained in the wider society. But the study shows that the diverse cultures of countercultural communal groups cannot be reduced to values, norms, or ideologies in any narrow sense. Values often inspired communal endeavors, but as groups became established they enacted different types of collective life involving fundamentally alternative forms of time consciousness and orientations toward the construction of social reality. In some groups, the "here and now" was the locus of social life and a collective consciousness was enhanced by the process of "going through changes" together: people worked together and conflicts tended to be brought into the arena of public life. Other groups achieved great personal freedom, but at the expense of a shared collective life: work tended to be coordinated outside the "here and now" by use of bureaucratic planning methods, and conflict tended to remain outside the public realm or it became the focus of special meetings and occasions. Only some groups – usually larger and more visible ones – tried to enact highly elaborated ideological visions of utopia. Thus, it was not just values and norms that made for the diversity among groups. Communal groups went beyond ideology, living radically different realities by cultivating unconventional practices of being in the world.

Another study of communal life, by Bennett Berger, analyzes ideological conflict that surfaced in concrete practices. Berger's book about a Californian commune, *The Survival of a Counterculture* (1981), takes issue with the "debunking" argument found in many social scientists' analyses of ideology – that even when people claim to be motivated by values they are really acting out of self-interest. By now, debunking has become a central element of a certain cynical American mythology. Thus, the politician who claims only to want to serve the people (and knows what to do because of his enlightened perspective) is routinely exposed as driven by his own ambition and greed. But, debunking to the contrary, the interests of individuals often do become aligned with a more encompassing group or institution. How does this happen? For Berger the terrain of ideology is a contested terrain. Thus, groups have good reason to want to legitimate an alignment of ideology and individuals' interests. The group's survival depends on developing ways of doing things – dividing up the labor, making decisions – that work for the group by both making sense to members and getting the job done. Not withstanding sociologists' penchant for debunking, Berger suggested that interests and values need not be opposed: it is possible for people to act both in their own interests and according to their values. In fact, people do "ideological work" to reduce the conflict that they feel both between self-interest and transcendent values and between one value and another. Here Berger's approach draws close to conceptualizations of "practice" such as those developed by Bourdieu (1977) and Sahlins (1976). In these formulations, practices are defined as cultural resources that people draw on in constructing courses of action. Practices are not norms, values, or ideologies; nor are they simply materially determined. Among the multiple possible ways of accomplishing a task, practices are the conventional ones that are culturally available.

Framing and mobilization

A different question about social movements – whether they succeed or fail – yielded a different line of analysis among other researchers in the 1960s and 1970s. These scholars argued that standard approaches centered on collective behavior or ideology had made little progress in explaining movement outcomes. Using tools loosely tied to economic theory, these theorists argued for changing the focus from social movements – large, amorphous, hard-to-define entities – to social-movement *organizations*. Looking at relatively bounded entities on the basis of structural-resource and rational-choice models, they recast collective identity as "a valued commodity that is worth the commitment of time, resources, the 'capital' of individual autonomy, and the risk of presentation of self because the group from which it is derived is also valued," (Johnston *et al.* 1994, p. 18; see also Friedman and McAdam 1992). Resource-mobilization theorists produced important work on the impact of resources on social-movement success. Yet their analyses were criticized for overemphasizing rationality and neglecting culture.

However, some researchers working within the resource-mobilization approach incorporated a symbolic interactionist dimension and turned to the question of grievances. They asked how a social movement develops a message describing its cause in such a way that people see a fit between the cause and their own sense of what needs to be changed in the world, and join the movement. David Snow and his colleagues (1986) addressed this issue by developing the idea of "frame alignment." Their approach offers a way of linking social psychological analysis of individual actions with structural analysis of organizations. The concept of "framing" (borrowed from Goffman 1974) refers to the organization's packaging of an issue in a way that becomes aligned with the concerns of people who are potential recruits (cf. Pareto 1966).

Snow and his associates described several types of frame-alignment processes. "Frame bridging" is a recruitment strategy that involves using techniques such as mass mailings to carry a movement's message to groups of people who might be sympathetic to the movement. "Frame amplification" operates on already held beliefs and values, strengthening them in order to overcome "ambiguity and uncertainty or indifference and lethargy." "Frame extension" is the use of some kind of an initial "hook" – potentially quite distant from the core activities of the movement – to arouse the interest of potential recruits. Finally, "frame transformation" involves the planting and nurturing of new values that radically transform the individual.

Snow himself did not focus on culture as an independent dimension. However, insofar as the framing approach deals with meaning construction and interpretation on the parts of organizers and (often implicitly) potential recruits to the movement, the approach opened the door to explorations of relationships between mobilization and cultural elements such as beliefs and values, as well as emotions. As a result, the framing concept became adapted to a diversity of analytic uses (see Rhys Williams and Benford 2000 for a critical review).

Although Snow and his colleagues usually placed more emphasis on interpretations and activities within movement organizations, framing is not always exclusively controlled by a movement's organizers and activists. In democratic countries with an independent press, much "framing" occurs in the mass media. William Gamson's work on nuclear technology (1992) and Press and Cole's work on abortion (1999) retain aspects of a resource-mobilization approach but also examine how media and the broader culture shape what people think, apart from the movement framings.

Attention to similar cultural processes has surfaced in the work of scholars outside the resource-mobilization perspective as well. As Chapter 8 discussed, Todd Gitlin (1980) portrayed mass media as using "news frames" that shaped public understandings of the anti-Vietnam War movement. On a different front, Anne Kane (1997) demonstrates the importance of cultural processes of meaning formation in a social movement where diverse people come together and construct a shared ideology. She looks not at a new social movement, but at a nineteenth-century movement concerned with Irish land rights. In different ways, historical studies and framing studies make possible cultural analysis of social movements that connects meaning-making, movement process, and participant mobilization.

Collective identity and the new social movements

If the cultural meanings of social movements emerge through processes of framing and related activities of meaning construction, it is also the case that individuals who see themselves sharing a condition, value, or interest with other people can come to share an identity, and this identity can become the basis for mobilization into a social movement. Although movement identities no doubt have been important historically, scholarly attention to the linkage between individual identity and social-movement participation is a relatively recent development, one that has occurred alongside the rise of the new social movements, which call particular attention to issues of identity.

Analysis of the new social movements initially relied heavily on an opposition to the older, class-based movements. For example, Johnston, Larana, and Gusfield use language that presents the new movements in terms of eight characteristics, showing how they differ from older movements:

1   The membership of the new social movements "transcends class structure."
2   New movements "exhibit a pluralism of ideas and values, and they tend to have a pragmatic orientation" of working for reform in civil rather than political institutions of society.
3   They are "associated with a set of beliefs, symbols, values, and meanings related to sentiments of belonging to a differentiated social group."
4   "The relation between the individual and collective is blurred" so that social-movement action includes expressive activities that confer or confirm identity as a group member.
5   They "extend into areas of daily life," blurring the boundaries of the personal and political.
6   Compared to the older movements, they draw on different strategies, often "characterized by nonviolence and civil disobedience."
7   They tend not to be affiliated with party politics, and their rise is related to "the credibility crisis of the conventional channels for participation in western democracies."
8   Their organizations tend to be "segmented, diffuse, and decentralized."

(Johnston *et al.* 1994, pp. 6–9)

Studying the new movements posed problems, not only for theories developed to explain European class-based movements, but also for theories that focus on the strategic mobilization of resources – including participants – in social-movement organizations.

Recent research argues that biography, emotion, and moral understanding are important aspects of social movements. The "newness" of the new movement characteristics listed by Johnston, Larana, and Gusfield can be debated. Some of the characteristics may have been exaggerated by movement activists in order to make activism enticing to particular populations (Polletta 1998). In addition, the characteristics of the "new social movements" have become more visible in the "older" movements now that scholars have developed a theoretical sensitivity for them. Thus, some writers advocate avoiding the new/old terminology entirely. James Jasper (1997), for example, differentiates "citizenship movements" that engaged the state in ways characteristic of industrial society from postindustrial "post-citizenship movements" that have engaged civil society in an attempt to change cultural sensibilities. What interests Jasper is that the latter movements often involve relatively privileged people who are already integrated into the basic political, economic, and educational institutions of their societies. "Because they need not demand basic rights for themselves," he suggests, "they often pursue protections or benefits for others, including on occasion the entire human species" (1997, p. 7). Jasper turns the focus from how organizations use interpretive frames to draw people into a movement to looking at movements' logics of cultural expressions and practices. He argues that culture is an important dimension in its own right. In their studies of social movements, including those of animal-rights activists and environmental activists, Jasper and his colleagues describe the pleasure of protest and the passion of moral engagement as cultural features of social movements (Goodwin *et al.* 2001; Polletta and Jasper 2001).

Beyond new social movements

Although the debates about new social movements have centered on the United States and Europe, like the work of Jasper and his colleagues, contemporary studies of popular movements in other countries suggest that the distinction between new versus old social movements may be too limiting. One way to see this is by observing the ways that movements with expressed political goals use the media, where the cultural and the political interpenetrate. In Mexico, for example, the Zapatista National Liberation Army has acted very differently from Latin American political movements like the one that got the socialist Salvador Allende elected in Chile in 1970 (only to be overthrown in a U.S.-promoted coup in 1973) or guerrilla armies like the Sandinistas who led a popular uprising and seized power in Nicaragua in 1979. In contrast to earlier political and guerrilla movements, the Zapatistas have used the internet and global news media to influence civil society (Yudice 1998). People like Subcomandante Marcos, leader of the Zapatistas in the Mexican state of Chiapas, play to an international audience by using an "artful guerrilla media war" to challenge conventional interpretations. In one incident, when two photographers came to photograph peasant life Marcos took the camera and photographed the photographers. In a communiqué explaining his action, he talked about wanting to break down the distancing process whereby the images of Zapatistas become representations of "others" to be consumed by international news-media viewers. As Yudice explains, "Marcos propels the viewers and readers into the story as actors who must chose a side: to engage in the always institutionalized quagmire of representation or to act out the relations to civil society in a different way" (1998, p. 371).

Contemporary Latin American social movements thus present alternative conceptions of citizenship that bridge the distinction between citizenship movements and new ("post-citizenship") social movements. As Alvarez, Dagnino, and Escobar explain, "an alternative conception of citizenship…would view democratic struggles as encompassing a redefinition not only of the political system but also of economic, social, and cultural practices that might engender a democratic ordering for society as a whole" (1998, p. 2). This conception implies a broad understanding of democratizing politics that pursues issues of economic development and the eradication of inequality based in race and gender. As the actions of Subcomandante Marcos demonstrate, even when issues are local or national a movement may operate on a globalizing basis. Thus, political issues of the "public sphere" and issues of the "private sphere" concerning identity and group belonging are negotiated in processes of "transnational cultural brokering" (Yudice 1998, p. 270). Alvarez, Dagnino, and Escobar thus emphasize an interplay between the material world of "politics" and the cultural and the textual. For social movements of very poor and marginalized people, they note, the first goal of a struggle is often to "demonstrate that they are people with rights, so as to recover their dignity and status as citizens and even as human beings" (1998, p. 5). In these analyses, social movements are sites simultaneously of political mobilization, cultural production, and identity construction (see Figure 11.2).

Cultural movements

Is the study of social movements an adequate way to conceptualize the relation between culture and social change? Swidler's (1986) discussion of "unsettled times" suggests that changes in cultural practices occur during periods of social upheaval.

Figure 11.2 Highland Indians protesting neoliberal reform in Ecuador. Their protest was one of
many nation-wide marches to the capital in October 1997 to denounce
International Monetary Fund policies and fight for constitutional reform.

Source: photo by Suzana Sawyer, cultural anthropologist, 1997.

Although this is no doubt true, our discussion of ritual and tradition in Chapter 4 shows that changes in practices are ongoing cultural activities. Thus, Stanley Lieberson (2000) has shown that the names people choose for their children can be modeled as rather predictably changing processes of taste. More generally, cultural change does not always occur at the same time as social revolutions, or necessarily by the same processes.

Some European sociologists have suggested that the sociological analysis of postindustrial societies should shift from a narrow focus on political movements to encompass cultural movements (Touraine 1985; Offe 1985; Beckford 1989). Part of the reason is that "contemporary social conflicts are not just political, since they affect the system's cultural production" (Melucci 1985, p. 798). The forms of contemporary movements are often different from those of older political organizations, and, Melucci argues, the form is the message. Militant activity occasionally occurs, but in many cases ongoing personal involvement in an alternative culture is the central phenomenon.

"Structureless" cultural movements challenge a dominant culture but they do not depend on the organization and hierarchy of traditional social movements. Consider again the countercultural movements of the 1960s and 1970s. Certainly countercultural issues about the practice of everyday life surfaced in concentrated form in communal groups. Yet these groups were part of the wider counterculture, and the practices they promoted, such as vegetarianism, are now to be found in many different social locations. Analysis is likely to miss more diffuse and widespread processes of cultural change if it concentrates solely on organized groups. Cultural transmission and cultural change is facilitated by the movement of transformed individuals, not only through groups, but through social networks. Indeed, to the extent that groups are tightly bounded, any broader culture change – going beyond the borders of the group – may be less likely (Neitz 1994).

For example, consider the Voluntary Simplicity movement in the United States. This movement is based on a critique of American consumption patterns. It embraces the goals of reducing individual consumption, reducing paid employment, and increasing enjoyment of life with more time and less money. Although organizers seek to persuade people to become FI-ERs (financially independent, living without paid employment), the activity of movement participants consists largely of daily practices focused on living frugally with attention to reducing consumption (Grigsby 2003).

In addition to looking at organized groups, those seeking to understand cultural movements can approach them in two other ways. First, it is possible to study the individuals who are carriers of a culture. Second, the ideas and practices that make up the culture can be explored. One model useful for these analyses recognizes that each individual has a somewhat different package of diverse cultural objects and practices. People put different parts of the package into use in situations where they are salient. The emergence of new interests can lead an individual to challenge previously taken-for-granted cultural practices that had been widely shared with others. It is in this spirit that we can trace the history of cultural ideas and motifs as they become reworked by individuals facing new circumstances, when they sometimes coax new meanings out of longstanding cultural themes. Revising Swidler's (1986) thesis about the constraining nature of ideologies during times of transition, a more interactionist approach to cultural movements suggests that the choices about which tools from the toolkit to use – and how they work – will often be emergent.

Both ethnographers and students of popular culture and cultural studies have interests in the question of how people create and interpret cultural objects. At one time ethnographic accounts tended to focus on social networks and social relations, sometimes neglecting analysis of cultural content in favor of identifying generic social processes. People in cultural studies, on the other hand, focused on cultural content, sometimes without any reference to the interpretations of people who use culture. The perspectives explored in this chapter show the importance of analyzing cultural objects in relation to users. Conversely, an understanding of users must include knowledge of the cultural objects and expressive symbols themselves. This synthesis becomes possible because a focus on cultures as symbolic expressions shows the users of cultural objects taking on the characteristics of agents. Although constrained in a number of ways – by material resources, by their degree of integration into mass culture, by the limits on their knowledge – "users" of culture emerge as something more than "consumers."

Conclusion

If there is any broad conclusion to the present inquiry into culture it is this: societies are not organized simply in material terms, and their characteristics are not simply the products of material social forces. Rather, in diverse ways culture is a mediating and even ordering force. Yet, in comparison to material forces, cultural processes can be unstable, mercurial, and shifting in their significance. Meanings and symbols, often enduring, sometimes become quickly and dramatically reorganized. This means that the tasks of understanding society are more complex than the modernist social scientists ever admitted. It also means that the cultural practices of individuals and groups are potentially much more consequential than was once recognized. As Bennett Berger (1991) has observed in a wise essay worth reading, the freedom and constraint of culture exist in an uneasy tension forged by the choices that people make about what culture to embrace, and how. We cannot say whether this power of culture can, will, or should be taken up or left inert, or whether, when taken up, it will work for good or ill. The possibilities of some negative utopia are always with us, and they do not lie just at the margins of established society, like some apocalyptic nightmare – whether a mass suicide at Jonestown or the terror of 9/11. Rather, dystopias are latent possibilities always available (and too often enacted) in a broader society (J.R. Hall 1987). But we suspect that, whichever cultural currents predominate and whatever the channels and courses, they will change the world as we now know it. New people will enter the stage, acting in ways alien to the present, using new symbols and technologies, affecting new styles, enacting new ethics. Yet, even as all this transpires, it will not transform everything. The old regimens will persist amidst the new. Moreover, changes in culture will not take place independently of other aspects of society.

The explanations of social change by Karl Marx and Max Weber differed, but they both recognized that the Protestant culture of self-disciplined individualism and the economic and organizational features of capitalism developed in tandem. And they each saw that the persistence of any given institutionalized set of social arrangements partly depends on the ways people might culturally make sense of their situations. Questions about social order, culture, and change thus depend for their answers on a set of more specific and situational issues. How do people act – individually and collectively – on the basis of their consciousness of social circumstance? Are people satisfied with their lot? What is their way of life, and what is its significance to them? Do they adopt rhetoric and ideologies that justify acceptance of their social fate? Do they try to impress others with their status? Do people individually seek social mobility that will change their personal life chances? Or do they pursue collective action to change the life chances of their group? How change in the future will be channeled by the cultural meanings people attach to their social situations remains an open question. However, it is not a question that will be resolved in the abstract realm of culture as a sphere unto itself, but in the concrete socially organized world. Because of the intimate connection between culture and social life, understandings of sociology on culture offer important leverage for both personal and public action. In a world at the modern/postmodern pass, when the modern no longer is what it used to be, cultural studies are necessarily sociological studies.

Suggested readings

Colleen McDannell's book *Material Christianity: Religion and Popular Culture in America* (1995) offers a series of case studies of Protestant, Catholic, and Mormon religious objects that show how material culture and mass consumption are part of the history and meaning of American religious life over the last 150 years. McDannell thus provides an understanding of religious experience as created through devotional images, built environments such as churches and cemeteries, and objects.

In *Hidden Heritage: The Legacy of the Crypto-Jews*, Janet Jacobs (2002) studies collective memory among the descendants of Jews who fled the Spanish Inquisition. Jacobs interviews Crypto-Jews in the United States and in Latin America, and documents their constructions of their Jewish identities.

Poor People's Politics: Peronist Survival Networks and the Legacy of Evita is a study by Javier Auyero (2000) of the different meanings of Peronist politics among the urban poor living in a shanty town, and gives attention to historical, economic, and cultural contexts.

In this chapter we address cultural aspects of social movements, where people choose to work for social change. An ethnography by Nina Eliasoph, *Avoiding Politics: How Americans Produce Apathy In Everyday Life* (1998), studies the cultural and social factors that inhibit engagement in politics among middle- and working-class Americans.

Note

1   As Spillman remarks, from the point of view of nationalist politics "it is not clear…why the Australians celebrated a centennial event at all" (1997, p. 25). The centennial marked 100 years after the British government's founding of the first settlement, a penal colony, at Sidney Cove on January 26, 1788.

Bibliography

Aaron, Michele. 2001. "Pass/fail." *Screen* 42 (1): 92–6.

Abu-Lughod, Lila. 1998. *Remaking Women: Feminism and Modernity in the Middle East.* Princeton, N.J.: Princeton University Press.

Adler, Jerry. 1995. "Paved paradise." *Newsweek* (May 15): 42–5.

Adler, Judith E. 1979. *Artists in Offices: An Ethnography of an Academic Art Scene.* New Brunswick, N.J.: Transaction Books.

Adorno, Theodore. 1945. "A social critique of radio music." *Kenyon Review* 7: 208–17.

Agnew, Jean-Christophe. 1986. *Worlds Apart: The Market and the Theater in Anglo-American Thought, 1550–1750.* New York: Cambridge University Press.

Ahlkvist, Jarl A., and Robert Faulkner. 2002. "'Will this record work for us?': Managing music formats in commercial radio." *Qualitative Sociology* 25: 189–215.

Alderman, Derek. 1996. "Creating a new geography of memory in the South: (re)naming of streets in honor of Martin Luther King, Jr." *Southeastern Geographer* 36: 51–69.

Aldrich, Nelson W., Jr. 1988. *Old Money: The Mythology of America's Upper Class.* New York: Random House.

Alexander, Jeffrey, ed. 1988. *Durkheimian Sociology: Cultural Studies.* New York: Cambridge University Press.

—— 1995. "The reality of reduction: the failed synthesis of Pierre Bourdieu." Pp. 128–217 in Jeffrey C. Alexander, Fin de Siècle *Social Theory: Relativism, Reduction, and the Problem of Reason.* London: Verso.

Alexander, Jeffrey, and Paul Colomy, eds. 1990. *Differentiation Theory and Social Change: Comparative and Historical Perspectives.* New York: Columbia University Press.

Alexander, Jeffrey, and Philip Smith. 1993. "The discourse of civil society: a new proposal for cultural studies." *Theory and Society* 22: 152–207.

Alexander, Victoria D. 1996a. *Museums and Money: The Impact of Funding on Exhibitions, Scholarship, and Management.* Bloomington: Indiana University Press.

—— 1996b. "Pictures at an exhibition: conflicting pressures in museums and the display of art." *American Journal of Sociology* 101: 797–893.

Allahyari, Rebecca. 2000. *Visions of Charity: Volunteer Workers and Moral Community.* Berkeley, Ca.: University of California Press.

Allsen, Thomas T. 1997. *Commodity and Exchange in the Mongol Empire.* Cambridge: Cambridge University Press.

Alvarez, Sonia, Evelina Dagnino, and Arturo Escobar, eds. 1998. *Cultures of Politics, Politics of Cultures: Re-Visioning Latin American Social Movements.* Boulder, Co.: Westview Press.

Amis, Martin. 2002. "The queen's heart." *New Yorker* (May 20): 106–10.

Angus, Ian, and Sut Jhally, eds. 1989. *Cultural Politics in Contemporary America.* New York: Routledge.

Arthurs, Alberta, and Glenn Wallach, eds. 2001. *Crossroads: Art and Religion in American Life.* New York: New Press.

Artz, Lee, and Bren A.O. Murphy. 2000. *Cultural Hegemony in the U.S.* Thousand Oaks, Ca.: Sage.

Arundhati, Roy. 2001. "The algebra of infinite justice." *Guardian* [United Kingdom] (September 29). Guardian Unlimited: http://www.guardian.co.uk/Archive/Article/0,4273,4266289,00.html.

Auyero, Javier. 2000. *Poor People's Politics: Peronist Survival Networks and the Legacy of Evita.* Durham, N.C.: Duke University Press.

Baker, Wayne E., and Robert R. Faulkner. 1991. "Role as resource in the Hollywood film industry." *American Journal of Sociology* 97: 279–309.

Bakhtin, Mikhail. 1968. *Rabelais and His World.* Cambridge, Ma.: MIT Press.

Balfe, Judith Huggins, ed. 1993. *Paying the Piper: Causes and Consequences of Art Patronage.* Urbana, Il.: University of Illinois Press.

Ball-Rokeach, Sandra J., Milton Rokeach, and Joel W. Grube. 1984. *The Great American Values Test: Influencing Behavior and Belief Through Television.* New York: Free Press.

Banner, Lois W. 1983. *American Beauty.* Chicago: University of Chicago Press.

Barnard, Malcolm. 2001. *Approaches to Understanding Visual Culture.* New York: Palgrave.

Barrett, Michèle, Philip Corrigan, Annette Kuhn, and Janet Wolff, eds. 1979. *Ideology and Cultural Production.* New York: St. Martin's Press.

Barth, Fredrick. 1970. *Ethnic Groups and Boundaries: The Social Organization of Culture Differences.* Bergen, Norway: Universitets Forlaget.

Barthes, Roland. 1972. *Mythologies.* New York: Hill & Wang.

—— 1977. *Image, Music, Text.* New York: Hill & Wang.

Battani, Marshall. 1999. "Organizational fields, cultural fields, and art worlds: the early effort to make photographs and make photographers in the nineteenth-century United States." *Media, Culture, and Society* 20: 601–26.

Battani, Marshall, and John R. Hall. 2000. "Richard Peterson and cultural theory: from genetic, to integrated, and synthetic approaches." *Poetics* 28: 137–56.

Baudrillard, Jean. 1988a. *America.* New York: Verso.

—— 1988b. *Selected Writings.* Stanford, Ca.: Stanford University Press.

Bauman, Gerd. 1996. *Contesting Culture: Discourses of Identity in Multi-Ethnic London.* Cambridge: Cambridge University Press.

Baxandall, Michael. 1985. *Patterns of Intention: On the Historical Explanation of Pictures.* New Haven, Ct.: Yale University Press.

Becker, Howard S. 1960. "Notes on the concept of commitment." *American Journal of Sociology* 66: 32–40.

—— 1963. *Outsiders: Studies in the Sociology of Deviance.* New York: Free Press.

—— 1982. *Art Worlds.* Berkeley, Ca.: University of California Press.

Becker, Howard S., and Michal McCall, eds. 1990. *Symbolic Interaction and Cultural Studies.* Chicago: University of Chicago Press.

Becker, Howard S., Blanche Geer, Everett C. Hughes, and Anselm L. Strauss. 1961. *Boys in White: Student Culture in Medical School.* Chicago: University of Chicago Press.

Beckford, James. 1989. *Religion and Advanced Industrial Society.* London: Unwin Hyman.

Belasco, Warren J. 1979. *Americans on the Road: From Autocamp to Motel, 1910–1945.* Cambridge, Ma.: MIT Press.

Bell, Catherine. 1997. *Ritual: Perspectives and Dimensions.* New York: Oxford University Press.

Bell, Daniel. 1973. *The Coming of Post-Industrial Society.* New York: Basic.

—— 1976. *The Cultural Contradictions of Capitalism.* New York: Basic.

Bellah, Robert. 1970. *Beyond Belief: Essays on Religion in a Post-Traditional World.* New York: Harper & Row.

Bellah, Robert, Richard Madsen, William Sullivan, Ann Swidler, and Steven Tipton. 1985. *Habits of the Heart: Individualism and Commitment in American Life.* Berkeley, Ca.: University of California Press.

Beng-Huat, Chua. 2000a. "Consuming Asians: ideas and issues." Pp. 1–34 in Beng-Huat 2000b.
—— ed. 2000b. *Consumption in Asia: Lifestyles and Identities.* London: Routledge.
—— 2000c. "Singaporeans ingesting McDonald's." Pp. 183–201 in Beng-Huat 2000b.
Benjamin, Walter. 1969 (1955). *Illuminations.* New York: Schocken.
Bennett, Tony, Graham Martin, Colin Mercer, and Janet Woollacott. 1981. *Culture, Ideology, and Social Process.* London: Open University Press.
Benson, Susan Porter. 1986. *Counter Cultures: Saleswomen, Managers, and Customers in American Department Stores. 1890–1940.* Urbana, Il.: University of Illinois Press.
Bentley, G. Carter. 1987. "Ethnicity and practice." *Comparative Studies in Society and History* 29: 24–55.
Berezin, Mabel. 1997. *Making the Fascist Self : The Political Culture of Interwar Italy.* Ithaca, N.Y.: Cornell University Press.
Berger, Bennett M. 1960. *Working Class Suburb: A Study of Auto Workers in Suburbia.* Berkeley, Ca.: University of California Press.
—— 1981. *The Survival of a Counterculture.* Berkeley, Ca.: University of California Press.
—— 1991. "Structure and choice in the sociology of culture." *Theory and Society* 10: 1–19.
Berger, John. 1977 (1972). *Ways of Seeing.* Berkeley, Ca.: University of California Press.
Berger, Peter L. 2002. "Introduction." Pp. 1–16 in Berger and Huntington 2002.
Berger, Peter L., and Samuel Huntington, eds. 2002. *Many Globalizations: Cultural Diversity in the Contemporary World.* Oxford: Oxford University Press.
Berger, Peter L., and Thomas Luckmann. 1966. *The Social Construction of Reality.* Garden City, N.Y.: Doubleday.
Berger, Peter L., Brigitte Berger, and Hansfried Kellner. 1973. *The Homeless Mind: Modernization and Consciousness.* New York: Random House.
Berlin, Edward A. 1980. *Ragtime: A Musical and Cultural History.* Berkeley, Ca.: University of California Press.
Bernard, Malcolm. 2001. *Approaches to Understanding Visual Culture.* New York: Palgrave.
Best, Amy. 2000. *Prom Night: Youth Schools and Popular Culture.* New York. Routledge.
Best, Steven, and Douglas Kellner. 1991. *Postmodern Theory: Critical Interrogations.* New York: Guilford Press.
Biernacki, Richard. 1997. "Work and culture in the reception of class ideologies." Pp. 169–92 in J.R. Hall 1997.
—— 2000. "Language and the shift from signs to practices in cultural inquiry." *History and Theory* 39: 289–310.
Biggart, Nicole Woolsey. 1989. *Charismatic Capitalism: Direct Selling Organizations in America.* Chicago: University of Chicago Press.
Black, Jack. 1988 (1926). *You Can't Win,* foreword by William S. Burroughs. New York: Amok Press.
Blau, Judith. 1989. *The Shape of Culture.* New York: Cambridge University Press.
Blau, Peter. 1955. *The Dynamics of Bureacracy: A Study of Interpersonal Relations in Two Government Agencies.* Chicago: University of Chicago Press.
Bogard, William. 1990. "Closing down the social: Baudrillard's challenge to contemporary sociology." *Sociological Theory* 8: 1–15
Bonacich, Edna. 1972. "A theory of ethnic group antagonism: the split labor market." *American Sociological Review* 37: 547–59.
Bonnell, Victoria E. 1997 *Iconography of Power : Soviet Political Posters under Lenin and Stalin.* Berkeley, Ca.: University of California Press.
Bonnell, Victoria E., and Lynn Hunt, eds. 1999. *Beyond the Cultural Turn.* Berkeley, Ca.: University of California Press.
Boorstin, Daniel J. 1962. *The Image, or What Happened to the American Dream.* New York: Atheneum.
—— 1973. *The Americans: The Democratic Experience.* New York: Random House.

Boucher, Sandy. 1988. *Turning the Wheel*. San Francisco: Harper.

Bourdieu, Pierre. 1974. "Fractions of the dominant class and the modes of appropriation of works of art." *Social Science Information* 13: 7–31.

—— 1976. "Anatomie de gout." *Actes de la Recherche en Sciences Sociales* 2: 5–81.

—— 1977 (1972). *Outline of a Theory of Practice*. New York: Cambridge University Press.

—— 1984 (1979). *Distinction: A Social Critique of the Judgement of Taste*. Cambridge, Ma.: Harvard University Press.

—— 1991. "Four lectures." *Poetics Today* 12: 625–69.

Bourdieu, Pierre, with Luc Boltanski, Robert Castel, Jean-Claude Chamboredon, and Dominique Schnapper. 1990 (1964). *Photography: A Middle-Brow Art*. Cambridge: Polity Press.

Bourke, Joanna. 1994. *Working-Class Cultures in Britain 1890–1960*. London: Routledge.

—— 1997. "Asylum art: the social construction of an aesthetic category." Pp. 11–36 in Zolberg and Cherbo 1997.

Bowler, Anne. 1991. "Politics as art: Italian futurism and fascism." *Theory and Society* 20: 763–94.

—— 1997. "Asylum art: the social construction of an aesthetic category." Pp. 11–36 in Zolberg and Cherbo 1997.

Brasher, Brenda. 1998. *Godly Women: Fundamentalism and Female Power*. New Brunswick, N.J.: Rutgers University Press.

Braudel, Fernand. 1973 (1967). *Capitalism and Material Life, 1400–1800*. New York: Harper & Row.

Brody, Jennifer Devere. 2002. "Boyz do cry: screening history's white lies." *Screen* 43: 91–6.

Bromley, David G. 1991. "Satanism: the new cult scare." Pp. 49–72 in James Richardson, Joel Best, and David Bromley, eds., *The Satanism Scare*. Hawthorne, N.Y.: Aldine de Gruyter.

Brown, Patricia Leigh. 1991. "Living for folk art, and in it too." *New York Times* (January 3): B1, 4.

Brown, Richard Harvey. 1990. "Rhetoric, textuality, and the postmodern turn in sociological theory." *Sociological Theory* 8: 188–97.

Brunvand, Jan. 1981. *The Vanishing Hitchhiker: American Urban Legends and their Meanings*. New York: Norton.

Bryson, Bethany. 1996. "'Anything but heavy metal': symbolic exclusion and musical dislikes." *American Sociological Review* 61: 884–99.

—— 1997. "What about the univores?: Musical dislikes and group-based identity among Americans with lower levels of education." *Poetics* 25: 141–56.

Bull, Anna Cento, and Paul Corner. 1993. *From Peasant to Entrepreneur: The Survival of the Family Economy in Italy*. Oxford: Berg.

Bürger, Peter. 1984 (1974). *Theory of the Avant-Garde*. Minneapolis, Mn.: University of Minnesota Press.

Burke, Kenneth. 1950. *A Rhetoric of Motives*. Berkeley, Ca.: University of California Press.

Burke, Peter. 1978. *Popular Culture in Early Modern Europe*. New York: New York University Press.

Burns, Elizabeth. 1972. *Theatricality: A Study of Convention in the Theater and in Social Life*. New York: Harper & Row.

Butler, Judith. 1990. *Gender Trouble*. New York: Routledge.

Calhoun, Craig, ed. 1994a. *Social Theory and the Politics of Identity*. Cambridge, Ma.: Blackwell.

—— 1994b. "Social theory and the politics of identity." Pp. 9–36 in Calhoun 1994a.

Cannadine, David. 1983. "The context, performance, and meaning of ritual: the British monarchy and the 'invention of tradition,' c. 1820–1977." Pp. 101–64 in Eric Hobsbawm and Terence Ranger, eds., *The Invention of Tradition*. Cambridge: Cambridge University Press.

Cantor, Muriel G., and Joel M. Cantor. 1986. "Audience composition and television content: the mass audience revisited." Pp. 214–25 in Sandra J. Ball-Rokeach and Muriel G. Cantor, eds., *Media, Audience, and Social Structure.* Beverly Hills, Ca.: Sage.

Cantor, Norman F. 1988. *Twentieth-Century Culture: Modernism to Deconstruction.* New York: Peter Lang.

Carlson, James M. 1985. *Prime-Time Law Enforcement: Crime Show Viewing and Attitudes Toward the Criminal Justice System.* New York: Praeger.

Carter, Stephen. 1993. *The Culture of Disbelief: How American Law and Politics Trivialize Religious Devotion.* New York: Basic.

Centre for Contemporary Cultural Studies. 1980. *Culture, Media, Language.* London: Hutchinson.

Certeau, Michel de. 1984 (1980). *The Practice of Everyday Life.* Berkeley, Ca.: University of California Press.

Chakrabarty, Dipesh. 1992. "Postcoloniality and the artifice of history: who speaks for the 'Indian' pasts?" *Representations* 37: 1–26.

—— 2000. *Provincializing Europe: Postcolonial Thought and Historical Difference.* Princeton, N.J.: Princeton University Press.

Chodorow, Nancy. 1978. *The Reproduction of Mothering: Psychoanalysis and the Reproduction of Gender.* Berkeley, Ca.: University of California Press.

Christopherson, Richard W. 1974. "Making art with machines: photography's institutional inadequacies." *Urban Life and Culture* 3: 3–34.

Clark, T.J. 2002. "Modernism, postmodernism, and steam." *October* 100: 154–74.

Clifford, James. 1986. "Introduction: partial truths." Pp. 1–26 in James Clifford and George Marcus, eds., *Writing Cultures: The Poetics and Politics of Ethnography, Literature, and Art.* Berkeley, Ca.: University of California Press.

Cohen, Albert. 1955. *Delinquent Boys.* Glencoe, Il.: Free Press.

Collins, Patricia Hill. 2000. *Black Feminist Thought: Knowledge, Consciousness, and the Politics of Empowerment*, 2nd ed. New York: Routledge.

Collins, Randall. 1979. *The Credential Society.* New York: Academic Press.

—— 1986. *Weberian Sociological Theory.* New York: Cambridge University Press.

—— 1989. "Sociology: proscience or antiscience?" *American Sociological Review* 54: 124–39.

—— 1997. "An Asian route to capitalism: religious economy and the origins of self-transforming growth in Japan." *American Sociological Review* 62: 843–65.

Connolly, Paul. 1997. "Racism and postmodernism: towards a theory of practice." Pp. 65–80 in David Owen, ed., *Sociology after Postmodernism.* London: Sage.

Cooley, Charles Horton, Robert Angell, and Lowell J. Carr. 1933. *Introductory Sociology.* New York: Scribner's.

Cooper, Frederick. 1994. "Conflict and connection: rethinking colonial African history." *American Historical Review* 99: 1516–45.

—— 1996. *Decolonization and African Society: The Labor Question in French and British Africa.* Cambridge: Cambridge University Press.

—— 2001. "What is the concept of globalization good for?: An African historian's perspective." *African Affairs* 100: 189–213.

Cooper, Frederick, and Ann Laura Stoler, eds. 1997. *Tensions of Empire: Colonial Cultures in a Bourgeois World.* Berkeley, Ca.: University of California Press.

Corrigan, Philip, and Derek Sayer. 1985. *The Great Arch: English State Formation as Cultural Revolution.* Oxford: Blackwell.

Coser, Lewis A., Charles Kadushin, and Walter Powell. 1982. *Books: The Culture and Commerce of Book Publishing.* New York: Basic.

Cowan, Ruth. 1976. "The 'industrial revolution' in the home: household technology and social change in the twentieth century," *Technology and Culture* 26: 1–23.

Craik, Jennifer. 1994. *The Face of Fashion: Cultural Studies in Fashion.* London: Routledge.

Crane, Diana. 1976. "The reward system in art, science, and religion." Pp. 57–72 in Richard A. Peterson, ed., *The Production of Culture.* Beverly Hills, Ca.: Sage Publications.

—— 1987. *The Transformation of the Avant-Garde: The New York Art World, 1940–1985.* Chicago: University of Chicago Press.

—— 2000. *Fashion and Its Social Agendas: Class, Gender, and Identity in Clothing.* Chicago: University of Chicago Press.

Croteau, David, and William Hoynes. 2001. *The Business of Media: Corporate Media and the Public Interest.* Thousand Oaks, Ca.: Pine Forge Press.

—— 2003. *Media Society: Industries, Images, and Audiences.* Thousand Oaks, Ca.: Pine Forge Press.

Darnovsky, Marcy, Barbara Epstein, and Richard Flacks. 1995. *Cultural Politics and Social Movements.* Philadelphia: Temple University Press.

Darnton, Robert. 1984. *The Great Cat Massacre and Other Episodes in French Cultural History.* New York: Basic.

Davidman, Lynn. 1991. *Tradition in a Rootless World.* Berkeley, Ca.: University of California Press.

Davis, Belinda. 1996. "Food scarcity and the empowerment of the female consumer in World War I Berlin." Pp. 287–310 in V. de Grazia 1996.

Davis, Clark. 2000. *Company Men: White-Collar Life and Corporate Cultures in Los Angeles, 1892–1941.* Baltimore, Md.: Johns Hopkins University Press.

Davis, Fred. 1992. *Fashion, Culture, and Identity.* Chicago: University of Chicago Press.

Davis, Natalie Zemon. 1983. *The Return of Martin Guerre.* Cambridge, Ma.: Harvard University Press.

—— 1988. "On the Lame." *American Historical Review* 93: 572–603.

D'Emilio, John, and Estelle B. Freedman. 1997. *Intimate Matters: A History of Sexuality in America*, 2nd ed. Chicago: University of Chicago Press.

Dayan, Daniel, and Elihu Katz. 1988. "Articulating consensus: the ritual and rhetoric of media events." Pp. 161–86 in J.C. Alexander 1988.

de Grazia, Edward. 1991. *Girls Lean Back Everywhere: The Law of Obscenity and the Assault on Genius.* New York: Random House.

de Grazia, Victoria, ed. 1996. *The Sex of Things.* Berkeley, Ca.: University of California Press.

Demers, David P. 1999. *Global Media: Menace or Messiah?* Cresskill, N.J.: Hampton Press.

Der Derian, James. 2001. "9.11: before, after, and in between." http://www.ssrc.org/sept11/essays/der—derian.htm.

DeVault, Marjorie. 1990. "Novel readings: the social organization of interpretation." *American Journal of Sociology* 95: 887–921.

deYoung, Mary. 1998. "Another look at moral panics: the case of satanic daycare centers." *Deviant Behavior* 19: 257–78.

DiMaggio, Paul. 1987. "Nonprofit Organizations in the Production and Distribution of Culture." Pp. 195–220 in Walter Powell, ed., *The Nonprofit Sector.* New Haven, Ct.: Yale University Press.

DiMaggio, Paul, and Michael Useem. 1978. "Social class and arts consumption." *Theory and Society* 5: 141–61.

DiMaggio, Paul, Wendy Cage, Lynn Robinson, and Brian Steensland. 2001. "The role of religion in public conflict over the arts in the Philadelphia area, 1965–1977." Pp. 103–37 in Arthurs and Wallach 2001.

Doane, Janice, and Devon Hodges. 1987. *Nostalgia and Sexual Difference: The Resistance to Contemporary Feminism.* New York: Methuen.

Docker, John. 1994. *Postmodernism and Popular Culture: A Cultural History.* Cambridge: Cambridge University Press.

Dollard, John. 1957 (1937). *Caste and Class in a Southern Town.* New York: Doubleday.

Douglas, Ann. 1977. *The Feminization of American Culture.* New York: Knopf.

Douglas, Mary Tew. 1966. *Purity and Danger.* London: Routledge & Kegan Paul.

—— 1973. *Natural Symbols: Explorations in Cosmology.* New York: Vintage.

—— ed. 1982. *Essays in the Sociology of Perception.* Boston, Ma.: Routledge & Kegan Paul.

Dubin, Steven C. 1987. *Bureaucratizing the Muse: Public Funds and the Cultural Worker.* Chicago: University of Chicago Press.

—— 1992. *Arresting Images: Impolitic Art and Uncivil Actions.* London: Routledge.

Duby, Georges. 1968 (1962). *Rural Economy and Country Life in the Medieval West.* Columbia, S.C.: University of South Carolina Press.

Duncan, Hugh Dalziel. 1968. *Symbols in Society.* New York: Oxford University Press.

Duneier, Mitchell. 1999. *Sidewalk.* New York: Farrar, Straus & Giroux.

Durkheim, Emile. 1951. *Suicide.* Glencoe, Il.: Free Press.

—— 1964 (1893). *The Division of Labor in Society.* New York: Free Press.

—— 1989 (1925). *Readings from Emile Durkheim*, Kenneth Thompson, ed. New York: Routledge.

—— 1995 (1915). *The Elementary Forms of Religious Life.*, translated with an introduction by Karen E. Fields. New York: Free Press.

Eagleton, Terry. 1983. *Literary Theory.* New York: Blackwell.

Eisenstein, Elizabeth. 1979. *The Printing Press as an Agent of Change: Communications and Cultural Transformations in Early-Modern Europe*, 2 vols. New York: Cambridge University Press.

Elazar, Daniel J. 1998. *Constituting Globalization: The Postmodern Revival of Confederal Arrangements.* Lanham, Md.: Rowman & Littlefield.

Elias, Norbert. 1978. *What is Sociology.* London: Hutchison.

—— 1982. *The Civilizing Process*, vol. 1. New York: Pantheon.

Eliasoph, Nina. 1998 *Avoiding Politics: How Americans Produce Apathy in Everyday Life.* Cambridge: Cambridge University Press.

Elphicke, Conan. 2001. "Lollywood Babylon." *Sight and Sound* 11 (4): 8–9.

Emirbayer, Mustafa. 1997. "Manifesto for a relational sociology." *American Journal of Sociology* 103: 281–317.

Erickson, Bonnie. 1996. "Culture, class, and connections." *American Journal of Sociology* 102: 217–51.

Evans-Pritchard, E.E. 1974. *Nuer Religion.* New York. Oxford University Press.

Ewen, Stuart. 1976. *Captains of Consciousness: Advertising and the Social Roots of the Consumer Culture.* New York: McGraw-Hill.

Faith, Nicholas. 1987. *Sold: The Revolution in the Art Market.* London: Hodder & Stoughton.

Falasca-Zamponi, Simonetta. 1997. *Fascist Spectacle: The Aesthetics of Power in Mussolini's Italy.* Berkeley, Ca.: University of California Press.

Filer, Randall K. 1986. "The starving artists – myth or reality? Earnings of artists in the United States." *Journal of Political Economy* 94: 56–75.

Fine, Gary Alan. 1979. "Small groups and culture creation." *American Sociological Review* 44: 733–45.

—— 1987. *With the Boys: Little League Baseball and Preadolescent Culture.* Chicago: University of Chicago Press.

Fine, Gary Alan, and Sherryl Kleinman. 1979. "Rethinking subculture: an interactionist analysis." *American Journal of Sociology* 85: 1–20.

Finlay, Robert. 1988. "The refashioning of Martin Guerre." *American Historical Review* 93: 553–71.

Fish, Stanley. 2002. "Postmodern warfare: the ignorance of our warrior intellectuals." *Harpers* (July): 33–40.

Fiske, John. 1987. *Television Culture.* London: Methuen.

Flax, Jane. 1989. *Thinking Fragments: Psychoanalysis, Feminism, and Postmodernism in the Contemporary West.* Berkeley, Ca.: University of California Press.

Foucault, Michel. 1965. *Madness and Civilization: A History of Insanity in the Age of Reason.* New York: Pantheon.

—— 1975. *The Birth of the Clinic: An Archeology of Medical Perception.* New York: Vintage.

—— 1978–86. *The History of Sexuality*, vols. I–III. New York: Pantheon.

—— 1979 (1975). *Discipline and Punish: The Birth of the Prison.* New York: Vintage.

Fowler, Bridget. 1997. *Pierre Bourdieu and Cultural Theory: Critical Investigations.* London: Sage.

Fox, Richard Wightman, and Jackson Lears. 1983. *The Culture of Consumption: Critical Essays in American History, 1880–1980.* New York: Pantheon Books.

Fradenburg, Louise, and Carla Freccero, eds. 1996. *Premodern Sexualities.* London: Routledge.

Freeman, Carla. 2000. *High Tech and High Heels in the Global Economy.* Durham, N.C.: Duke University Press.

Freud, Sigmund. 1962 (1930). *Civilization and Its Discontents.* New York: Norton.

—— 1990. *Freud on Women: A Reader.* Elizabeth Young-Bruehl, ed. New York: Norton.

Friedland, Roger, and John Mohr, eds. 2003. *Matters of Culture: Cultural Sociology in Practice.* Cambridge: Cambridge University Press.

Friedman, Debra, and Doug McAdam. 1992. "Collective identity and activism: networks, choices, and the life of a social movement." Pp. 156–72 in Aldon Morris and Carol Meuller, eds., *Frontiers of Social Movement Theory.* New Haven, Ct.: Yale University Press.

Fritz, Noah J., and David L. Altheide. 1987. "The mass media and the social construction of the missing children problem." *Sociological Quarterly* 28: 473–92.

Gadamer, Hans Georg. 1975. *Truth and Method.* New York: Seabury Press.

Gamson, Joshua. 1998. *Freaks Talk Back: Tabloid Talk Shows and Sexual Nonconformity.* Chicago: University of Chicago Press.

Gamson, William. 1992. *Talking Politics.* New York: Cambridge University Press.

Gans, Herbert. 1962. *The Urban Villagers: Group and Class in the Life of Italian-Americans.* New York: Free Press.

—— 1967. *The Levittowners: Ways of Life and Politics in a New Suburban Community.* New York: Random House.

—— 1974. *Popular Culture and High Culture.* New York: Basic.

—— 1979. *Deciding What's News: A Study of CBS Evening News, NBC Nightly News,* Newsweek, *and* Time. New York: Random House.

Gardner, Helen. 1959. *Art Through the Ages*, 4th ed. New York: Harcourt Brace.

Gartman, David. 2000. "Why modern architecture emerged in Europe, not America: the new class and the aesthetics of technocracy." *Theory, Culture & Society* 17(5): 75–96.

Gavey, Nicola, and Virginia Gow. 2001. "'Cry wolf', cried the wolf: constructing the issue of false rape allegations in New Zealand media texts." *Feminism and Psychology* 11: 341–60.

Geertz, Clifford. 1973. *The Interpretation of Cultures.* New York: Basic.

—— 1983. *Local Knowledge: Further Essays in Interpretive Anthropology.* New York: Basic.

Gerbner, George, Larry Gross, Michael Morgan, and Nancy Signorielli. 1980. "The 'mainstreaming' of America, violence profile no. 11." *Journal of Communication* 30: 10–29.

Gerke, Solvay. 2000. "Global lifestyles under local conditions: the new Indonesian middle class." Pp. 135–58 in Beng-Huat 2000b.

Gilligan, Carol. 1982. *In a Different Voice: Psychological Theory and Women's Development.* Cambridge, Ma.: Harvard University Press.

Gilmore, Samuel. 1987. "Coordination and convention: the organization of the concert world." *Symbolic Interaction* 10: 209–28.

—— 1990. "Art worlds: developing the interactionist approach to social organization." Pp. 148–78 in Becker and McCall 1990.

Gilroy, Paul. 1991 (1987). *There Ain't No Black in the Union Jack.* Chicago: University of Chicago Press.

Ginsberg, Benjamin. 1986. *The Captive Public: How Mass Opinion Promotes State Power.* New York: Basic.

Ginsberg, Faye. 1990. *Contested Lives.* Berkeley, Ca.: University of California Press.

Gitlin, Todd. 1980. *The Whole World is Watching: Mass Media and the Making and Unmaking of the New Left.* Berkeley, Ca.: University of California Press.

—— ed. 1986. *Watching Television.* New York: Pantheon.

—— 1988. "Hip deep in post-modernism." *New York Times Book Review* (November 6): 1, 35–36.

Gladwell, Malcolm. 1997. "The coolhunt." *New Yorker* (March 17): 78–88.

Glassner, Barry. 1990. "Fit for postmodern selfhood." Pp. 215–43 in Becker and McCall 1990.

Goad, Jim. 1997. *The Redneck Manifesto: How Hillbillies, Hicks, and White Trash Became America's Scapegoats.* New York: Simon & Schuster.

Goffman, Erving. 1951. "Symbols of class status." *British Journal of Sociology* 2: 294–304.

—— 1959. *The Presentation of Self in Everyday Life.* Garden City, N.Y.: Doubleday.

—— 1961. *Asylums.* Garden City, N.Y.: Anchor.

—— 1968. *Interaction Ritual: Essays on Face-to-Face Behavior.* Garden City, N.Y.: Anchor Books.

—— 1971. *Relations in Public.* New York: Basic.

—— 1974. *Frame Analysis.* Cambridge, Ma.: Harvard University Press.

—— 1979. *Gender Advertisements.* New York: Harper & Row.

Goldberg, Edward L. 1983. *Patterns in Late Medici Art Patronage.* Princeton, N.J.: Princeton University Press.

Goldman, Robert. 1984. "Legitimation ads, part I." *Knowledge and Society: Studies in the Sociology of Culture Past and Present* 5: 243–67.

Goldstone, Jack A. 2000. "The rise of the West – or not? A revision to socio-economic history." *Sociological Theory* 18: 175–94.

Goodman, Barak, and Rachel Dretzin, producers. 2001. "Merchants of Cool," program #1911 (February 27). Transcript: http://www.pbs.org/wgbh/pages/frontline/shows/cool/etc/script.html.

Goodwin, Jeff, James M. Jasper, and Francesca Polletta, eds. 2001.*Passionate Politics: Emotions and Social Movements.* Chicago: University of Chicago Press.

Goody, Jack. 1977. *The Domestication of the Savage Mind.* New York: Cambridge University Press.

Gottdiener, M. 1985. "Hegemony and mass culture: a semiotic approach." *American Journal of Sociology* 90: 979–1,001.

—— 2001. *The Theming of America: American Dreams, Media Fantasies, and Themed Environments*, 2nd ed. Boulder, Co.: Westview.

Graber, Doris A. 1984. *Processing the News: How People Tame the Information Tide.* New York: Longman.

Graburn, Nelson H.H. 1967. "The Eskimo and commercial art." *Transaction* 4: 28–33.

—— 1976. *Ethnic and Tourist Arts: Culture Expressions From the Fourth World.* Berkeley, Ca.: University of California Press.

Grahn, Judy. 1984. *Another Mother Tongue.* Boston, Ma.: Beacon Press.

Gramsci, Antonio. 1971. *Selections from the Prison Notebooks of Antonio Gramsci.* New York: International Publishers.

Granovetter, Mark S. 1974. *Getting a Job: A Study of Contacts and Careers.* Cambridge, Ma.: Harvard University Press.

Gresham, Jewell Handy, and Margaret B. Wilkerson, eds. 1989. *Scapegoating the Black Family: Myths, Realities, A Program for Action*, special issue. *The Nation* 249 (July 24–31).

Griffith, Marie. 1997. *God's Daughters: Evangelical Women and the Power of Submission.* Berkeley, Ca.: University of California Press.

Grigsby, Mary. 2003. *Buying Time and Getting By: The Voluntary Simplicity Movement.* Albany, N.Y.: State University of New York Press.

Grimes, Kimberly. 1998. *Crossing Borders.* Tucson: University of Arizona Press.

Grindstaff, Laura. 2000. "(In defense of) Cultural Studies at UC Davis." *Culture* (newsletter of the Culture Section of the American Sociological Association) 14 (2): 9–11.

—— 2002. *The Money Shot: Trash, Class, and the Making of TV Talk Shows.* Chicago: University of Chicago Press.

Griswold, Wendy. 1981. "American character and the American novel: an expansion of reflection theory in the sociology of literature." *American Journal of Sociology* 86: 740–65.

—— 1986. *Renaissance Revivals: City Comedy and Revenge Tragedy in the London Theater, 1576–1980.* Chicago: University of Chicago Press.

—— 1987a. "A methodological framework for the study of culture." *Sociological Methodology* 17: 1–35.

—— 1987b. "The fabrication of meaning: literary interpretation in the United States, Great Britain, and the West Indies." *American Journal of Sociology* 92: 1,077–118.

—— 2000. *Bearing Witness: Readers, Writers, and the Novel in Nigeria.* Princeton, N.J.: Princeton University Press.

Gross, Larry, ed. 1995. *On the Margins of Art Worlds.* Boulder, Co.: Westview Press.

Grossberg, Lawrence. 1997. *Bringing it all Back Home: Essays on Cultural Studies.* Durham, N.C.: Duke University Press.

Grossberg, Lawrence, Cary Nelson, and Paula Treichler, eds. 1992. *Cultural Studies.* New York: Routledge.

Guerrilla Girls. 1998. *The Guerrilla Girls' Bedside Companion to the History of Western Art.* London: Penguin.

Guillén, Mauro F. 2001. "Is globalization civilizing, destructive or feeble? A critique of five key debates in the social science literature." *Annual Review of Sociology* 27: 235–60.

Habermas, Jürgen. 1987. *The Theory of Communicative Action, Vol. II: Lifeworld and System: A Critique of Functionalist Reason.* Boston, Ma.: Beacon Press.

Hagaman, Dianne. 1996. *How I Learned Not to be a Photojournalist.* Lexington: University Press of Kentucky.

Halberstam, Judith. 1998. *Female Masculinity.* Durham, N.C.: Duke University Press.

—— 2001. "The transgender gaze in *Boys Don't Cry.*" *Screen* 42: 294–8.

Hall, John R. 1978. *The Ways Out: Utopian Communal Groups in an Age of Babylon.* Boston, Ma.: Routledge & Kegan Paul.

—— 1987. *Gone From the Promised Land: Jonestown in American Cultural History.* New Brunswick, N.J.: Transaction.

—— 1988. "Social organization and pathways of commitment: types of communal groups, rational choice theory, and the Kanter thesis." *American Sociological Review* 53: 679–92.

—— 1992. "The capital(s) of culture: a non-holistic theory of status situations, class, gender, and ethnicity." Pp. 257–85 in Lamont and Fournier 1992.

—— ed. 1997. *Reworking Class.* Ithaca, N.Y.: Cornell University Press.

—— 1999. *Cultures of Inquiry: From Epistemology to Discourse in Sociohistorical Research.* Cambridge: Cambridge University Press.

—— 2003. "Cultural history is dead: (long live the Hydra)." Pp. 151–67 in Gerald Delanty and Engin Isin, eds., *Handbook of Historical Sociology.* London: Sage.

Hall, John R., and Mary Jo Neitz. 1993. *Culture: Sociological Perspectives.* Englewood Cliffs, N.J.: Prentice-Hall.

Hall, Peter, and Dee Spencer-Hall. 1982. "The social conditions of the negotiated order." *Urban Life* 11: 328–49.

Hall, Stuart. 1977. "Culture, media, and the ideological effect." Pp. 315–48 in James Curran, Michael Gurevitch, and Janet Woollacott, eds., *Mass Communication and Society.* London: Edward Arnold.

Halle, David. 1993. *Inside Culture: Art and Class in the American Home.* Chicago: University of Chicago Press.

—— 2001. "The controversy over the show *Sensation* at the Brooklyn Museum, 1999–2000." Pp. 139–87 in Arthurs and Wallach 2001.

Halter, Marilyn. 2000. *Shopping for Identity: The Marketing of Ethnicity.* New York: Schocken.

Hannigan, John. 1998. *Fantasy City: Pleasure and Profit in the Postmodern Metropolis.* London: Routledge.

Haraway, Donna. 1985. "A manifesto for cyborgs: science, technology, and socialist feminism in the 1980s." *Socialist Review* 85 (2): 64–107.

Hardt, Michael, and Antonio Negri. 2000. *Empire.* Cambridge, Ma.: Harvard University Press.

Harper, Douglas. 1987. *Working Knowledge: Skill and Community in a Small Shop.* Chicago: University of Chicago Press.

Harrington, Michael. 1962. *The Other America.* New York: Macmillan.

Harris, Marvin. 1979. *Cultural Materialism.* New York: Random House.

Harris, Neil. 2001. "Reluctant alliance: American art, American religion." Pp. 1–30 in Arthurs and Wallach 2001.

Hartsock, Nancy. 1983. *Money, Sex, and Power: Toward a Feminist Historical Materialism.* New York: Longman.

Hatfield, Elaine, and Susan Sprecher. 1986. *Mirror, Mirror: The Importance of Looks in Everyday Life.* Albany, N.Y.: State University of New York Press.

Hauser, Arnold. 1982 (1974). *The Sociology of Art.* Chicago: University of Chicago Press.

Hebdige, Dick. 1979. *Subculture.* London: Methuen.

Hechter, Michael. 1978. "Group formation and the cultural division of labor." *American Journal of Sociology* 84: 293–318.

Heilman, Samuel. 1981. "Constructing orthodoxy." Pp. 141–57 in Thomas Robbins and Dick Anthony, eds., *In Gods We Trust: New Patterns of Religious Pluralism in America.* New Brunswick, N.J.: Transaction.

Herdt, Gilbert, ed. 1994. *Third Sex, Third Gender: Beyond Sexual Dimorphism in Culture and History.* New York: Zone Books.

Herman, Edward S., and Noam Chomsky. 1988. *Manufacturing Consent.* New York: Pantheon.

Hirsch, Paul. 1972. "Processing fads and fashions: an organization-set analysis of the cultural industry." *American Journal of Sociology* 77: 639–59.

Hobsbawm, Eric. 1983. "Introduction: inventing traditions." Pp. 1–14 in Eric Hobsbawm and Terence Ranger, eds., *The Invention of Tradition.* Cambridge: Cambridge University Press.

Hochschild, Arlie Russell. 1983. *The Managed Heart: Commercialization of Human Feeling.* Berkeley, Ca.: University of California Press.

Hodge, Robert, and David Tripp. 1986. *Children and Television: A Semiotic Approach.* Cambridge: Polity Press.

Holub, Robert C. 1984. *Reception Theory: A Critical Introduction.* New York: Methuen.

hooks, bell, and Cornell West. 1991. *Breaking Bread: Insurgent Black Intellectual Life.* Boston, Ma.: South End Press.

Horkheimer, Max, and Theodor W. Adorno. 1982 (1944). *Dialectic of Enlightenment.* New York: Continuum.

Horney, Karen. 1967. *Feminine Psychology.* New York: Norton.

Hunt, Darnell. 1997. *Screening the Los Angeles "Riots": Race, Seeing, and Resistance.* New York: Cambridge University Press.

Hunt, Lynn. 1984. *Politics, Culture, and Class in the French Revolution.* Berkeley, Ca.: University of California Press.

—— 1992. *The Family Romance of the French Revolution.* Berkeley, Ca.: University of California Press.

Hunter, James Davison. 1991. *Culture Wars.* New York: Basic.

Huntington, Samuel P. 1996. *The Clash of Civilizations and the Remaking of World Order.* New York: Simon & Schuster.

Hurtado, Albert L. 1999. *Intimate Frontiers: Sex, Gender, and Culture in Old California.* Albuquerque: University of New Mexico Press.

Huyssen, Andreas. 1986. *After the Great Divide: Modernism, Mass Culture, Postmodernism.* Bloomington: Indiana University Press.

Ikegami, Eiko. 1995. *The Taming of the Samurai: Honorific Individualism and the Making of Modern Japan.* Cambridge, Ma.: Harvard University Press.

Jacobs, Janet. 2002. *Hidden Heritage: The Legacy of the Crypto-Jews.* Berkeley, Ca.: University of California Press.

Jacobs, Jerry. 1984. *The Mall: An Attempted Escape from Everyday Life.* Prospect Heights, Il.: Waveland.

Jameson, Fredric. 1991. *Postmodernism or, the Cultural Logic of Late Capitalism.* Durham, N.C.: Duke University Press.

Jameson, Fredric, and Masao Miyoshi, eds. 1998. *The Cultures of Globalization.* Durham, N.C.: Duke University Press.

Jasper, James M. 1997. *The Art of Moral Protest.* Chicago: University of Chicago Press.

Jay, Martin. 1973. *The Dialectical Imagination: A History of the Frankfurt School and the Institute of Social Research, 1923–1958.* Boston, Ma.: Little Brown.

—— 1993. *Downcast Eyes: The Denigration of Vision in Twentieth-Century French Thought.* Berkeley, Ca.: University of California Press.

Jeffords, Susan, and Lauren Rabinovitz, eds. 1994. *Seeing Through the Media: The Persian Gulf War.* New Brunswick, N.J.: Rutgers University Press.

Jencks, Charles A. 1981. *The Language of Post-Modern Architecture*, 3rd ed. London: Academy.

Jenkins, J. Craig, and Craig M. Eckert. 1986. "Channeling black insurgency: elite patronage and professional social movement organizations in the development of the black movement." *American Sociological Review* 51: 812–29.

Jenkins, Philip. 1992. *Intimate Enemies: Moral Panics in Contemporary Great Britain.* New York: Aldine de Gruyter.

Johnson, Richard. 1986–7. "What is cultural studies anyway?" *Social Text* 16 (winter): 38–80.

Johnston, Hank, and Bert Klandermans, eds., 1995. *Social Movements and Culture.* Minneapolis, Mn.: University of Minnesota Press.

Johnston, Hank, Enrique Larana, and Joseph Gusfield. 1994. "Identities, grievances and new social movements. Pp. 3–35 in Larana *et al.* 1994.

Jones, Mark, with Paul Craddock and Nicolas Barker, eds. 1990. *Fake?: The Art of Deception.* Berkeley, Ca.: University of California Press.

Kane, Anne. 1997. "Theorizing meaning construction in social movements: symbolic structures and interpretation during the Irish Land War, 1879–1882." *Sociological Theory* 15: 249–76.

Kang, David C. 1995. "South Korean and Taiwanese development and the new institutional economics." *International Organization* 49: 555–87.

Kauffman, Bette J. 1995. " 'Woman artist': Between myth and stereotype." Pp. 95–120 in Gross 1995.

Kealy, Edward R. 1979. "From craft to art: the case of sound mixers and popular music." *Sociology of Work and Occupations* 6: 3–29.

Kellner, Douglas. 2002. "Theorizing globalization." *Sociological Theory* 20: 285–305.

Kendall, Gavin, and Gary Wickham. 2001 *Understanding Culture: Cultural Studies, Order, Ordering.* London: Sage.

Kertzer, David. 1988. *Ritual, Politics, and Power.* New Haven, Ct.: Yale University Press.

Khalil, Samir. 1991. *The Monument: Art, Vulgarity, and Responsibility in Iraq.* London: Deutsch.

Kim, Seung-Kuk. 2000. "Changing lifestyles and consumption patterns of the South Korean middle class and new generations." Pp. 61–81 in Beng-Huat 2000b.

Kirby, E.T. 1975. *Ur-Drama: The Origins of Theater.* New York: New York University Press.

Klein, Melanie. 1984. *The Writings of Melanie Klein.* New York: Free Press.

Koshar, Rudy. 2002. *Histories of Leisure.* New York: Berg.

Kroeber, Alfred, and Talcott Parsons. 1958. "The concepts of culture and of social system." *American Sociological Review* 23: 582–3.

Kubler, George. 1962. *The Shape of Time: Remarks on the History of Things.* New Haven, Ct.: Yale University Press.

Kumar, Amitava. 2000. *Passport Photos.* Berkeley, Ca.: University of California Press.

Kumar, Krishan. 1978. *Prophecy and Progress: The Sociology of Industrial and Post-Industrial Society.* New York: Penguin.

—— 1995. *From Post-Industrial to Post-Modern Society: New Theories of the Contemporary World.* Oxford: Blackwell.

Kuper, Adam. 1988. *The Invention of Primitive Society: Transformations of an Illusion.* London: Routledge.

Kuritz, Paul. 1988. *The Making of Theater History.* Englewood Cliffs, N.J.: Prentice-Hall.

Kyle, David. 2000. *Transnational Peasants: Migrations, Networks, and Ethnicity in Andean Ecuador.* Baltimore, Md.: Johns Hopkins University Press.

Lachman, Richard. 1988. "Graffiti as career and ideology." *American Journal of Sociology* 94: 229–50.

Laing, R.D. 1967. *The Politics of Experience.* New York: Pantheon.

Lamont, Michèle. 1992. *Money, Morals, and Manners: The Culture of the French and the American Upper-Middle Class.* Chicago: University of Chicago Press.

—— ed. 1999. *The Cultural Territories of Race.* Chicago: University of Chicago Press.

—— 2000. *The Dignity of Working Men: Morality and the Boundaries of Race, Class, and Immigration.* Cambridge, Ma.: Harvard University Press.

Lamont, Michèle, and Marcel Fournier, eds. 1992. *Cultivating Differences: Symbolic Boundaries and the Making of Inequality.* Chicago: University of Chicago Press.

Lamont, Michèle, and Laurent Thévenot. 2000. *Rethinking Comparative Sociology: Repertoires of Evaluation in France and the United States.* Cambridge: Cambridge University Press.

Lamphere, Louise, Helena Ragoné, and Patricia Zavella. 1997. *Situated Lives: Gender and Culture in Everyday Life.* London: Routledge.

Lang, Gladys Engle, and Kurt Lang. 1988. "Recognition and renown: the survival of artistic reputation." *American Journal of Sociology* 98: 79–109.

Larana, Enrique, Hank Johnston, and Joseph Gusfield, eds. 1994. *New Social Movements: From Ideology to Identity.* Philadelphia: Temple University Press.

Lareau, Annette. 2003. *Inside Families: The Importance of Social Class in Children's Daily Lives.* Berkeley, Ca.: University of California Press.

Larose, Serge. 1977. "The Meaning of Africa in Haitian Vodu." Pp. 85–116 in Ioan Lewis, ed., *Symbols and Sentiments: Cross Cultural Studies in Symbolism.* London: Academic Press.

Larson, Magali Sarfatti. 1993. *Behind the Postmodern Façade: Architectural Change in Late Twentieth-Century America.* Berkeley, Ca.: University of California Press.

Lasch, Christopher. 1979. *The Culture of Narcissism: American Life in an Age of Diminishing Expectations.* New York: Norton.

—— 1984. *The Minimal Self: Psychic Survival in Troubled Times.* New York: Norton.

Latour, Bruno. 1993. *We Have Never Been Modern.* Cambridge, Ma.: Harvard University Press.

Leacock, Eleanor B., ed. 1971. *The Culture of Poverty: A Critique.* New York: Simon & Schuster.

Lears, Jackson. 1983. "From salvation to self-realization: advertising and the therapeutic roots of the consumer culture, 1889–1930." Pp. 2–38 in Fox and Lears 1983.

Lechner, Frank. 1990. "Fundamentalism revisited." Pp. 77–97 in Thomas Robbins and Dick Anthony, eds., *In Gods We Trust: New Patterns of Religious Pluralism in America*, 2nd ed. New Brunswick, N.J.: Transaction.

Leidner, Robin. 1993. *Fast Food, Fast Talk: Service Work and the Routinization of Everyday Life.* Berkeley, Ca.: University of California Press.

Leiss, William, Stephen Kline, and Sut Jhally. 1988. *Social Communication in Advertising.* New York: Routledge.

Leuthold, Steven. 1995 "Native American art and artists in visual arts documentaries from 1973 to 1991." Pp. 265–81 in Gross 1995.

Lévi-Strauss, Claude. 1966 (1962). *The Savage Mind.* Chicago: University of Chicago Press.

Lewin, Ellen. 1998. *Recognizing Ourselves: Ceremonies of Gay and Lesbian Commitment.* New York: Columbia University Press.

Lewis, David. 1969. *Convention.* Cambridge, Ma.: Harvard University Press.

Lewis, Hylan. 1967. *Tally's Corner.* Boston, Ma.: Little, Brown.

Lewis, Oscar. 1959. *Five Families: Mexican Case Studies in the Culture of Poverty.* New York: Basic.

Liebert, Robert M., and Joyce Sprafkin. 1988. *The Early Window: Effects of Television on Children and Youth*, 3rd ed. New York: Permagon.

Lieberson, Stanley. 2000. *A Matter of Taste: How Names, Fashions, and Culture Change.* New Haven, Ct.: Yale University Press.

Liebes, Tamar, and Elihu Katz. 1993. *The Export of Meaning: Cross-Cultural Readings of Dallas.* Oxford: Oxford University Press.

Lincoln, C. Eric, and Lawrence H. Mamiya. 1990. *The Black Church in the Afro-American Experience.* Durham, N.C.: Duke University Press.

Long, Elizabeth. 1985. *The American Dream and the Popular Novel.* Boston, Ma.: Routledge & Kegan Paul.

—— ed. 1997. *From Sociology to Cultural Studies.* Oxford: Blackwell.

Lorber, Judith. 1994. *Paradoxes of Gender.* New Haven, Ct.: Yale University Press.

Luhmann, Niklas. 1982. *The Differentiation of Society.* New York: Columbia University Press.

Lurie, Alison. 1981. *The Language of Clothes.* New York: Random House.

Lynd, Robert S., and Helen Lynd. 1929. *Middletown.* New York: Harcourt, Brace.

Lyotard, Jean-François. 1984 (1979). *The Postmodern Condition: A Report on Knowledge.* Minneapolis, Mn.: University of Minnesota Press.

McClelland, David. 1961. *The Achieving Society.* Princeton, N.J.: Van Nostrand.

McCracken, Grant. 1988. *Culture and Consumption: New Approaches to the Symbolic Character of Consumer Goods and Activities.* Bloomington: Indiana University Press.

McDannell, Colleen. 1995. *Material Christianity: Religion and Popular Culture in America.* New Haven, Ct.: Yale University Press.

McDowell, Linda. 1997. *Capital Culture: Gender at Work in the City.* Oxford: Blackwell.

MacIntyre, Alasdair C. 1984. *After Virtue: A study in Moral Theory*, 2nd ed. Notre Dame, In.: University of Notre Dame Press.

Maclean, Marie. 1988. *Narrative as Performance: The Baudelairean Experiment.* New York: Routledge.

McLuhan, Marshall. 1964. *Understanding Media.* New York: McGraw-Hill.

Mahoney, Eileen. 1989. "American empire and global communication." Pp. 37–50 in Angus and Jhally 1989.

Mallon, Florencia E. 1994. "The promise and dilemma of subaltern studies: perspectives from Latin American history." *American Historical Review* 99: 1,491–515.

Mannheim, Karl. 1937. *Ideology and Utopia.* New York: Harcourt, Brace & World.

Manoff, Robert K., and Michael Schudson, eds. 1986. *Reading the News.* New York: Pantheon.

Marcus, George. 1986. "Contemporary problems of ethnography in the modern world system." Pp. 165–92 in James Clifford and George Marcus, eds., *Writing Cultures: The Poetics and Politics of Ethnography, Literature, and Art.* Berkeley, Ca.: University of California Press.

Marcuse, Herbert. 1962 (1955). *Eros and Civilization: A Philosophical Inquiry into Freud.* New York: Vintage.

Martin, Randy. 2001. "The renewal of the cultural in sociology." Pp. 63–78 in T. Miller 2001.

Martorella, Rosanne. 1990. *Corporate Art.* New Brunswick, N.J.: Rutgers University Press.

Marx, Karl. 1978 (1843). "On the Jewish question." Pp. 26–52 in Robert C. Tucker, ed., *The Marx-Engels Reader.* New York: W.W. Norton.

Maxwell, Richard. 2001. "'Political economy within cultural studies." Pp. 116–38 in T. Miller 2001.

Mead, George Herbert. 1934. *Mind, Self, and Society.* Chicago: University of Chicago Press.

Meiselas, Susan. 1976. *Carnival Strippers.* New York: Farrar, Straus & Giroux.

Melucci, Alberto. 1985. "The symbolic challenge of contemporary social movements." *Social Research* 52: 789–816.

Merton, Robert. 1957. *Social Theory and Social Structure.* New York: Free Press.

Meyrowitz, Joshua. 1985. *No Sense of Place: The Impact of Electronic Media on Social Behavior.* New York: Oxford University Press.

Miller, Mark Crispin, ed. 1990. *Seeing through Movies.* New York: Pantheon.

Miller, Michael B. 1981. *The Bon Marché.* Princeton, N.J.: Princeton University Press.

Miller, Toby, ed. 2001. *A Companion to Cultural Studies.* Oxford: Blackwell.

Mills, C. Wright. 1959. *The Sociological Imagination.* New York: Oxford University Press.

Milner, Murray, Jr. 1994. *Status and Sacredness: A General Theory of Status Relations and an Analysis of Indian Culture.* Oxford: Oxford University Press.

Mitchell, W.J.T. 1994. *Picture Theory: Essays on Verbal and Visual Representation.* Chicago: University of Chicago Press.

Monteiro, Mark. 1997. "Him/her: discourses of masculinity in a Brazilian magazine, 1969–1972." *Antropologia* http://www.artnet.com.br/~marko/him.html.

Mowlana, Hamid, George Gerbner, and Herbert Schiller, eds. 1992. *Triumph of the Image: The Media's War in the Persian Gulf.* Boulder, Co.: Westview Press.

Muggleton, David. 2000. *Inside Subculture: The Postmodern Meaning of Style.* Oxford: Berg.

Mukerji, Chandra. 1983. *From Graven Images: Patterns of Modern Materialism.* New York: Columbia University Press.

—— 1997. *Territorial Ambitions and the Gardens of Versailles.* Cambridge: Cambridge University Press.

Mukerji, Chandra, and Michael Schudson, eds. 1991. *Rethinking Popular Culture: Contemporary Perspectives in Cultural Studies.* Berkeley, Ca.: University of California Press.

Mulhern, Francis. 2000. *Culture/Metaculture.* London: Routledge.

Mullaney, Steven. 1988. *The Place of the Stage: License, Play, and Power in Renaissance England.* Chicago: University of Chicago Press.

Myerhoff, Barbara G. 1978. *Number Our Days.* New York: Dutton.

Neitz, Mary Jo. 1987. *Charisma and Community: A Study of Religious Commitment Within the Charismatic Renewal.* New Brunswick, N.J.: Transaction.

—— 1994. "Quasi-religions and cultural movements." *Religion and the Social Order* 4: 127–49.

—— 2002. "Walking between the worlds: permeable boundaries, ambiguous identities." Pp. 33–46 in James V. Spickard, J. Shawn Landres, and Meredith McGuire, eds., *Personal Knowledge and Beyond: Reshaping the Ethnography of Religion.* New York: New York University Press.

Nochlin, Linda. 1971. "Why have there been no great women artists?" Pp. 1–34 in Thomas B. Hess and Elizabeth C. Baker, eds., *Art and Sexual Politics: Women's Liberation, Women Artists, and Art History.* New York: Macmillan.

Nolan, James. 1998. *The Therapeutic State: Justifying Government at the Century's End.* New York: New York University Press.

Nora, Pierre. 1989. "Between memory and history: les lieux de mémoire." *Representations* 26: 13–25.

Norris, Christopher. 1990. "Lost in the funhouse: Baudrillard and the politics of postmodernism." Pp. 119–53 in Roy Boyne and Ali Rattansi, eds., *Postmodernism and Society.* Basingstoke, U.K.: Macmillan.

Norris, Pippa, and David Sanders. (1998). "Does balance matter? Experiments in TV news." Paper presented at the annual meeting of the American Political Science Association, Boston, Ma. http://ksghome.harvard.edu/~.pnorris.shorenstein.ksg/acrobat/balance.pdf.

Numrich, Paul David. 1996. *Old Wisdom in the New World: Americanization in Two Immigrant Theravada Buddhist Temples.* Knoxville, Tn.: University of Tennessee Press.

O'Brien, Mary. 1981. *The Politics of Reproduction.* Boston, Ma.: Routledge & Kegan Paul.

O'Connell, Michael. 1999. "Is Irish public opinion towards crime distorted by media bias?" *European Journal of Communication* 14: 191–212.

Offe, Claus. 1985. "New social movements: challenging the boundaries of institutional politics." *Social Research* 52: 817–68.

Olick, Jeffery K. 1999. "Collective memory: the two cultures." *Sociological Theory* 17: 333–48.

Omi, Michael, and Howard Winant. 1994. *Racial Formation in the United States: From the 1960s to the 1990s.* New York: Routledge.

Ortega y Gasset, Jose. 1932. *The Revolt of the Masses.* New York: Norton.

Ortner, Sherry. 1989. *High Religion.* Princeton, N.J.: Princeton University Press.

—— 2001. *Life and Death on Mt. Everest: Sherpas and Himalayan Mountaineering.* Princeton, N.J.. Princeton University Press.

Orwell, George. 1933. *Down and Out in Paris and London.* New York: Harper.

Padgett, John. 1992 "The alchemist of contingency theory." *American Journal of Sociology* 97: 1,462–70.

Parenti, Michael. 1986. *Inventing Reality: The Politics of the Mass Media.* New York: St. Martin's Press.

Pareto, Vilfredo. 1966. *Sociological Writings.* New York: Praeger.

Park, Robert, and Ernest W. Burgess. 1921. *Introduction to the Science of Sociology.* Chicago: University of Chicago Press.

Parsons, Talcott. 1951. *The Social System.* New York: Free Press.

Parsons, Talcott, and Edward A. Shils, eds. 1951. *Toward a General Theory of Action.* Cambridge, Ma.: Harvard University Press.

Peiss, Kathy. 1986. *Cheap Amusements: Working Women and Leisure in Turn-of-the-Century New York.* Philadelphia: Temple University Press.

Peterson, Richard A. 1976. "The production of culture: a prolegomenon." Pp. 7–22 in Richard A. Peterson, ed., *The Production of Culture.* Beverly Hills, Ca.: Sage.

—— 1978. "The production of cultural change: the case of country music." *Social Research* 45: 292–314.

—— ed. 1997a. Special issue, "Changing representation of status through taste displays." *Poetics* 25: 71–193.

—— 1997b. *Creating Country Music: Fabricating Authenticity*: Chicago: University of Chicago Press.

Peterson, Richard A., and Roger M. Kern. 1996. "Changing highbrow taste: from snob to omnivore." *American Sociological Review* 61: 900–7.

Peterson, Richard A., and Albert Simkus. 1992. "How musical tastes mark occupational status groups." Pp. 152–86 in Lamont and Fournier 1992.

Phillips, David P., and Kenneth A. Bollen. 1985. "Same time, last year: selective data dredging for negative findings." *American Sociological Review* 50: 364–71.

Pidduck, Julianne. 2001. "Risk and queer spectatorship." *Screen* 42: 97–102.

Pillsbury, Edmund P. 1971. *Florence and the Arts: Five Centuries of Patronage.* Cleveland, Ia.: Cleveland Museum of Art.

Polatnick, M. Rivka. 1983. "Why men don't rear children: a power analysis." Pp. 21–40 in Joyce Trebilcot, ed. *Mothering: Essays in Feminist Theory.* Totowa, N.J.: Rowman & Allanheld.

Polletta, Francesca. 1998. "'It was like fever…': narrative and identity in social protest." *Social Problems* 45: 137–59.

Polletta, Francesca, and James M. Jasper. 2001. "Collective identity and social movements." *Annual Review of Sociology* 27: 283–305.

Pomeranz, Kenneth. 2000. *The Great Divergence: Europe, China, and the Making of the Modern World Economy.* Princeton, N.J.: Princeton University Press.

Popkin, Samuel. 1979. *The Rational Peasant: The Political Economy of Rural Society in Vietnam.* Berkeley, Ca.: University of California Press.

Prakash, Gyan. 1994. "Subaltern studies as postcolonial criticism." *American Historical Review* 99: 1,475–90.

Press, Andrea. 1991. *Women Watching Television.* Philadelphia: University of Philadelphia Press.

Press, Andrea, and Elizabeth Cole. 1999. *Speaking of Abortion: Television and Authority in the Lives of Women.* Chicago: University of Chicago Press.

Pritchard, David. 1986. "Homicide and bargained justice: the agenda-setting effect of crime news on prosecutors." *Public Opinion Quarterly* 50: 143–59.

Protess, David L., Donna R. Leff, Stephen C. Brooks, and Margaret T. Cordon. 1985. "Uncovering rape: the watchdog press and the limits of agenda setting." *Public Opinion Quarterly* 49: 19–37.

Puri, Jyoti. 1999. *Women, Body, Desire in Post-colonial India.* London: Routledge.

Radway, Janice. 1984. *Reading the Romance: Women, Patriarchy, and Popular Literature.* Chapel Hill, N.C.: University of North Carolina Press.

Randolph, Vance. 1976. *Pissing in the Snow, and Other Ozark Folktales.* Urbana, Il.: University of Illinois Press.

Rawvision.com. 2002. "Nek Chand – the untutored genius who built a paradise." http://www.rawvision.com/nekchand/nekchand.html.

Redfield, Robert. 1940. "The folk society and culture." *American Journal of Sociology* 45: 731–42.

—— 1956. *Peasant Society and Culture.* Chicago: University of Chicago Press.

Reed, Rita. 1997. *Growing Up Gay: The Sorrows and Joys of Lesbian and Gay Adolescence.* New York: W.W. Norton.

Reich, Wilhelm. 1960. *Selected Writings.* New York: Farrar, Straus & Giroux.

Reitman, Ben L. 1988 (circa 1930). *Boxcar Bertha: An Autobiography*, as told to Dr. Ben L. Reitman. New York: Amok Press.

Rieff, Philip. 1966. *The Triumph of the Therapeutic.* New York: Harper & Row.

—— 1991. *The Feeling Intellect.* Chicago: University of Chicago Press.

Riesman, David, Nathan Glazer, and Reuel Denney. 1953 (1950). *The Lonely Crowd: A Study of the Changing American Character.* New York: Doubleday.

Robnett, Belinda. 1997. *How Long? How Long?: African-American Woman in the Struggle for Civil Rights.* New York: Oxford University Press.

Rosen, Ruth. 1986. "Search for yesterday." Pp. 42–67 in Gitlin 1986.

Rosenberg, Roy 2001. "Infinite Justice?" Salon.com.

Rosenblum, Barbara. 1978a. *Photographers at Work: A Sociology of Photographic Styles.* New York: Holmes & Meier.

—— 1978b. "Style as Social Process." *American Sociological Review* 43: 422–38.

Rostow, Walt W. 1960. *The Stages of Economic Growth: A Non-Communist Manifesto.* New York: Cambridge University Press.

Roth, Guenther. 1976. "History and sociology in the work of Max Weber." *British Journal of Sociology* 27: 306–18.

—— 1987. "Rationalization in Max Weber's developmental history." Pp. 75–91 in Scott Lash and Sam Whimster, eds., *Max Weber, Rationality, and Modernity.* London: Allen & Unwin.

Rubenstein, Richard L. 1978. *The Cunning of History: The Holocaust and the American Future.* New York: Harper.

Ruddick, Sara. 1989. *Maternal Thinking: Toward a Politics of Peace.* Boston, Ma.: Beacon Press.

Rudofsky, Bernard. 1964. *Architecture Without Architects: A Short Introduction to Non-Pedigreed Architecture.* Garden City, N.Y.: Doubleday.

Rueschemeyer, Marilyn. 1993. "State patronage in the German Democratic Republic: artistic and political change in a state socialist society." Pp. 209–3 in Balfe 1993.

Rushing, Andrea Benton. 1988. "Hair-raising." *Feminist Studies* 14: 325–36.

Sahlins, Marshall D. 1976. *Culture and Practical Reason.* Chicago: University of Chicago Press.

—— 1985. *Islands of History.* Chicago: University of Chicago Press.

—— 1994. "Cosmologies of capitalism: the trans-Pacific sector of 'the world system'." Pp. 412–55 in Nicholas B. Dirks, Geoff Eley, and Sherry B. Ortner, eds., *Culture/Power/History.* Princeton, N.J.: Princeton University Press.

—— 1995. *How "Natives" Think: About Captain Cook, for Example.* Chicago. University of Chicago Press.

Said, Edward. 1994 (1978). *Orientalism.* New York. Vintage.

Sanders, Clinton. 1988. "Marks of mischief: becoming and being tattooed." *Journal of Contemporary Ethnography* 16: 395–432.

Sandler, Kathe. 1993. *A Question of Color* (video). San Francisco: California Newsreel.

Sarlo, Beatriz. 2001. *Scenes from Postmodern Life.* Jon Beasley-Murray, trans. Minneapolis, Mn.: University of Minnesota Press.

Sassen, Saskia. 1998. *Globalization and its Discontents.* New York: New Press.

Scheff, Thomas. 1966. *Being Mentally Ill: A Social Theory.* Chicago: Aldine.

Scheler, Max. 1961 (1915). *Ressentiment.* New York: Free Press.

Schluchter, Wolfgang. 1989. *Rationalism, Religion, and Domination.* Berkeley, Ca.: University of California Press.

Schneider, Jane. 1978. "Peacocks and penguins: the political economy of European cloth and colors." *American Ethnologist* 5: 413–47.

Schudson, Michael. 1978. *Discovering the News: A Social History of American Newspapers.* New York: Basic.

—— 1984. *Advertising, the Uneasy Persuasion: Its Dubious Impact on American Society.* New York: Basic.

Schutz, Alfred. 1967 (1932). *The Phenomenology of the Social World.* Evanston, Il.: Northwestern University Press.

—— 1970. *Reflections on the Problem of Relevance.* New Haven, Ct.: Yale University Press.

Schwartz, Barry. 1987. *George Washington: The Making of an American Symbol.* New York : Free Press.

Seay, Albert. 1965. *Music in the Medieval World.* Englewood Cliffs, N.J.: Prentice-Hall.

Sedgewick, Eve. 1990. *Epistemology of the Closet.* Berkeley, Ca.: University of California Press.

Seeley, John R., R. Alexander Sim, and Elizabeth W. Loosley. 1956. *Crestwood Heights: A Study of the Culture of Suburban Life.* New York.: Basic Books.

Shibutani, Tomatsu. 1955. "Reference groups as perspectives." *American Journal of Sociology* 60: 562–9.

Shils, Edward. 1967. "Mass society and its culture." Pp. 1–27 in Norman Jacobs, ed., *Culture for the Millions?* Boston, Ma.: Beacon.

Simmel, Georg. 1950. *The Sociology of Georg Simmel.* New York: Free Press.

—— 1984 (1911). "Female Culture." Pp. 65–101 in Guy Oakes, ed., *Georg Simmel: On Women, Sexuality, and Love.* New Haven, Ct.: Yale University Press.

Singal, David Joseph. 1987. "Toward a definition of American modernism." *American Quarterly* 39: 7–26.

Skelton, Tracey, and Tim Allen, eds. 1999. *Culture and Global Change.* London: Routledge.

Sklar, Kathryn Kish. 1973. *Catharine Beecher: A Study in American Domesticity.* New Haven, Ct.: Yale University Press.

Skocpol, Theda. 1979. *States and Social Revolutions.* New York: Cambridge University Press.

Smith, Anthony. 1991. *The Age of Behemoths: The Globalization of Mass Media Firms.* New York: Priority Press.

Smith, Philip, ed. 1998. *The New American Cultural Sociology.* Cambridge: Cambridge University Press.

Smith-Rosenberg, Carroll. 1975. "The female world of love and ritual: relations between women in nineteenth-century America." *Signs* 1: 1–29.

Snow, David E., Burke Rochford, Jr., Steven Worden, and Robert Benford. 1986. "Frame alignment and mobilization." *American Sociological Review* 51: 454–81.

Sombart, Werner. 1976 (1906). *Why Is There No Socialism in the United States?* London: Macmillan.

Somers, Margaret. 1997. "Narrativity, narrative identity, and social action: rethinking English working-class formation." Pp. 73–105 in J.R. Hall 1997.

Somers, Margaret, and Gloria Gibson. 1994. "Reclaiming the epistemological 'Other': narrative and the social constitution of identity." Pp. 37–99 in Calhoun 1994a.

Spillman, Lyn. 1997. *Nation and Commemoration: Creating National Identities in the United States and Australia.* Cambridge: Cambridge University Press.

—— ed. 2002. *Cultural Sociology.* Oxford: Blackwell.

Spivak, Gayatri Chakravorty. 1988. "Can the subaltern speak?" Pp. 299–307 in Cary Nelson and Lawrence Grossberg, eds., *Marxism and the Interpretation of Culture.* Urbana, Il: University of Illinois Press.

Srinivas, Tulasi. 2002. "'A tryst with destiny': the Indian case of cultural globalization." Pp. 89–116 in Berger and Huntington 2002.

Stack, Steven. 1987. "Celebrities and suicide: a taxonomy and analysis." *American Sociological Review* 52: 401–12.

Stange, Maren. 1989. *Symbols of Ideal Life: Social Documentary Photography in America 1890–1950.* Cambridge: Cambridge University Press.

Stevenson, Nick. 1997. "Globalization, national cultures, and cultural citizenship." *Sociological Quarterly* 38: 41–66.

Stevenson, Robert L., and Donald L. Shaw, eds. 1984. *Foreign News and the New World Information Order.* Ames, Ia.: Iowa State University Press.

Stimson, Blake. 2001. "Andy Warhol's red beard." *Art Bulletin* 83 (3): 527–47.

Stokes, Gale. 2001. "The fate of human societies: a review of recent macro-histories." *American Historical Review* 106: 508–25.

Stoler, Ann Laura. 1997. "Sexual affronts and racial frontiers: European identities and the cultural politics of exclusion in colonial Southeast Asia." Pp. 198–237 in Cooper and Stoler 1997.

Storey, John. 1999. *Cultural Consumption and Everyday Life.* London: Arnold.

Strasser, Susan. 1982. *Never Done: A History of American Housework.* New York: Pantheon.

Strauss, Anselm. 1978. "A social world perspective." *Studies in Symbolic Interaction* 1: 119–28.

Sturken, Marita. 1997. *Tangled Memories: The Vietnam War, the Aids Epidemic and the Politics of Remembering.* Berkeley, Ca.: University of California Press.

Sullivan, Zohreh. 1998. "Eluding the Feminist, Overthrowing the modern? Transformations in twentieth century Iran." Pp. 215–42 in Lila Abu-Lughod 1998.

Swartz, David. 1997. *Culture and Power: The Sociology of Pierre Bourdieu.* Chicago: University of Chicago Press.

Swidler, Ann. 1980. "Love and adulthood in American culture." Pp. 120–47 in Neil Smelser and Erik H. Erikson, eds., *Themes of Love and Work in Adulthood.* Cambridge, Ma.: Harvard University Press.

—— 1986. "Culture in action: symbols and strategies." *American Sociological Review* 51: 273–86.

Szasz, Thomas. 1987. *Insanity: The Idea and its Consequences.* New York: Wiley.

Szelényi, Iván, and Szonja Szelényi. 1995. "Circulation or reproduction of elites during the postcommunist transformation of Eastern Europe: introduction." *Theory and Society* 24: 615–38.

Taub, Richard. 1969. *Bureaucrats under Stress: Administrators and Administration in an Indian State.* Berkeley, Ca.: University of California Press.

Thompson, E.P. 1963. *The Making of the English Working Class.* New York: Pantheon.

Thompson, James. 1967. *Organizations in Action.* New York: McGraw-Hill.

Thompson, John B. 1994. "Social theory and the media." Pp. 27–49 in David Crowley and David Mitchell, eds., *Communication Theory Today.* Stanford, Ca.: Stanford University Press.

—— 1995. *The Media and Modernity: A Social Theory of the Media.* Cambridge: Polity.

Thompson, Robert F. 1959. *Safari of One* (sound recording). New York: Spanish Music Center.

Thorbeck, Susanne. 1994. *Gender and Slum Culture in Urban Asia.* London: Zed.

Thrift, Nigel. 1999. "Capitalism's cultural turn." Pp. 135–61 in Larry Ray and Andrew Sayer, eds., *Culture and Economy after the Cultural Turn.* London: Sage.

Thrisk, Joan. 1978. *Economic Policy and Projects: The Development of a Consumer Society in Early Modern England.* Oxford: Clarendon Press.

Tocqueville, Alexis de. 1945. *Democracy in America*, Phillips Bradley, ed. New York: Vintage.

Touraine, Alain. 1981. *The Voice and the Eye.* New York: Cambridge University Press.

—— 1985. "An introduction to the study of social movements." *Social Research* 52: 749–87.

Trevor-Roper, Hugh. 1976. *Princes and Artists: Patronage and Ideology at Four Hapsburg Courts, 1517–1633.* New York: Harper & Row.

—— 1983. "The invention of tradition: the highland tradition of Scotland." Pp. 15–42 in Eric Hobsbawm and Terence Ranger, eds., *The Invention of Tradition.* Cambridge: Cambridge University Press.

Trinh T. Minh-ha. 1989. *Woman, Native, Other: Writing Postcoloniality and Feminism.* Bloomington: Indiana University Press.

—— 1991. *When the Moon Waxes Red: Representation, Gender, and Cultural Politics.* New York: Routledge.

Tronto, Joan. 1987. "Beyond gender difference to a theory of care." *Signs* 12: 644–63.

Tsing, Anna Lowenhaupt. 1993. *In the Realm of the Diamond Queen: Marginality in an Out-of-the-Way Place.* Princeton, N.J.: Princeton University Press.

Tuchman, Gaye. 1974. *The TV Establishment: Programming for Power and Profit.* Englewood Cliffs, N.J.: Prentice-Hall.

Turner, Victor. 1967. *The Forest of Symbols: Aspects of Ndembu Ritual.* Ithaca, N.Y.: Cornell University Press.

Turow, Joseph. 1997. *Breaking Up America: Advertisers and the New Media World.* Chicago: University of Chicago Press.

Tydeman, William. 1978. *The Theater in the Middle Ages: Western European Stage Conditions, c. 800–1576.* New York: Cambridge University Press.

Tylor, Edward B. 1871. *Primitive Culture.* London: J. Murray.

Tyrell, Heather. 1999. "Bollywood versus Hollywood: battle of the dream factories." Pp. 260–73 in Skelton and Allen 1999.

U.S. Census Bureau. 1975. *Historical Statistics of the United States, Colonial Times to 1970.* Washington, D.C.: U.S. Government Printing Office.

—— 1983. *1980 U.S. Census, Vol. A, Chapter C: General Social and Economic Characteristics of the Population.* Washington, D.C.: U.S. Government Printing Office.

—— 1996. *Statistical Abstract of the United States.* Washington, D.C.: U.S. Government Printing Office.

van Ham, Peter. 2001. *European Integration and the Postmodern Condition.* London: Routledge.

Veblen, Thorstein. 1965 (1899). *The Theory of the Leisure Class.* New York: A.M. Kelley.

Venturi, Robert, Denise Scott Brown, and Steven Izenour. 1977. *Learning from Las Vegas.* Cambridge, Ma.: MIT Press.

Vinitzky-Seroussi, Vered. 2002. "Commemorating a difficult past: Yitzhak Rabin's memorials." *American Sociological Review* 67: 30–51.

Wagner, Peter. 1994. *A Sociology of Modernity: Liberty and Discipline.* London: Routledge.

Wagner-Pacifici, Robin, and Barry Schwartz. 1991. "The Vietnam Veterans Memorial: commemorating a difficult past." *American Journal of Sociology* 97: 376–420.

Walkowitz, Judith R. 1992. *City of Dreadful Delight.* London: Virago Press.

Wallerstein, Immanuel. 1974. *The Modern World-System: Capitalist Agriculture and the Origins of the European World-Economy in the Sixteenth Century.* New York: Academic Press.

—— 1979. *The Capitalist World-Economy: Essays.* New York: Cambridge University Press.

Warner, Michael, ed., 1993. *Fear of a Queer Planet: Queer Politics and Social Theory.* Minneapolis, Mn.: University of Minnesota Press.

Warner, R. Stephen. 1988. *New Wine in old Wineskins: Evangelicals and Liberals in a Small-town Church.* Berkeley, Ca.: University of California Press.

Wasilewski, Jacek, and Wnuk-Lipinski, Edmund. 1995. "Poland: winding road from the communist to the post-Solidarity elite." *Theory and Society* 24: 669–96.

Weber, Max. 1946. *From Max Weber: Essays in Sociology*, Hans H. Gerth and C. Wright Mills, eds. New York: Oxford University Press.

—— 1958a (1905). *The Protestant Ethic and the Spirit of Capitalism.* New York: Scribner's.

—— 1958b. *The Rational and Social Foundations of Music.* Carbondale, Il.: Southern Illinois University Press.

—— 1978 (1922). *Economy and Society: An Outline of Interpretive Sociology*, Guenther Roth and Claus Wittich, eds. Berkeley, Ca.: University of California Press.

—— 1981 (1923). *General Economic History.* New Brunswick, N.J.: Transaction.

Webster, Frank. 2001. "Sociology, cultural studies, and disciplinary boundaries." Pp. 79–100 in T. Miller 2001.

Webster, Murry, Jr., and James E. Driskell, Jr. 1983. "Beauty as status." *American Journal of Sociology* 89: 140–65.

Weinbaum, Batya, and Amy Bridges. 1978. "The other side of the paycheck." Pp. 190–205 in Zillah R. Eisenstein, ed., *Capitalist Patriarchy and the Case for Socialist Feminism.* New York: Monthly Review Press.

Weiss, Gerald. 1973. "Shamanism and priesthood in light of the Campa Ayahuasca ceremony." Pp. 40–7 in Michael J. Harner, *Hallucinogens and Shamanism.* New York: Oxford University Press.

Wiley, Norbert. 1994. "The politics of identity in American history." Pp. 131–49 in Calhoun 1994a.

Williams, Christine L. 1989. *Gender Differences at Work: Women and Men in Nontraditional Occupations.* Berkeley, Ca.: University of California Press.

Williams, Raymond. 1982. *The Sociology of Culture.* New York: Schocken.

Williams, Rhys, and Robert Benford. 2000. "Two faces of collective action frames: a theoretical consideration." *Current Perspectives in Social Theory* 20: 127–51.

Williams, Rosalind. 1982. *Dream Worlds: Consumption in Late 19th Century France.* Berkeley, Ca.: University California Press.

Willis, Paul. 1977. *Learning to Labor.* New York: Columbia University Press.

—— 1990. *Common Culture.* Boulder, Co.: Westview Press.

Wilson, William J. 1980. *The Declining Significance of Race: Blacks and Changing American Institutions.* Chicago: University of Chicago Press.

Wittag, Monique. 1992. *The Straight Mind.* Boston, Ma.: Beacon Press.

Wolfe, Eric. 1982. *Europe and the People without History.* Berkeley, Ca.: University of California Press.

Wolff, Janet. 1981. *The Social Production of Art.* New York: New York University Press.

—— 1983. *Aesthetics and the Sociology of Art.* London: Allen & Unwin.

—— 1987. "The ideology of autonomous art." Pp. 1–12 in Richard Leppert and Susan McClary, eds., *Music and Society: The Politics of Composition, Performance and Reception.* New York: Cambridge University Press.

Wong, R. Bin. 1997. *China Transformed: Historical Change and the Limits of European Experience.* Ithaca, N.Y.: Cornell University Press.

Woodard, Michael D. 1988. "Class, Regionality, and Leisure among Urban Black Americans." *Journal of Leisure Research* 20: 87–105.

Wright, Eric Olin. 1985. *Classes.* London: New Left.

Wu Hung. 1991. "Tiananmen Square: a political history of monuments." *Representations* 35: 84–117.

Wuthnow, Robert. 1987. *Meaning and Moral Order: Explorations in Cultural Analysis.* Berkeley, Ca.: University of California Press.

—— 1989. *Communities of Discourse: Ideology and Social Structure in the Reformation, the Enlightenment, and European Socialism.* Cambridge, Ma.: Harvard University Press.

—— 1991. *Acts of Compassion.* Princeton, N.J.: Princeton University Press.

Yoshimi, Shunya. 2000. " 'Consuming 'America': from symbol to system." Pp. 202–24 in Beng-Huat 2000b.

Yudice, George. 1998. "The globalization of culture and the new civil society." Pp. 353–79 in Alvarez *et al.* 1998.

Zainul Abiden, Nurazimah. 2002. *Towards Enlightenment: The Changing Cultural Practices of the Malays in Singapore from 1970 to 2000.* M.A. thesis. Columbia, Mo.: Department of Sociology, University of Missouri, Columbia.

Zaret, David. 2000. *Origins of Public Culture: Printing, Petitions, and the Public Sphere in Early-Modern England.* Princeton, N.J.: Princeton University Press.

Zaretsky, Eli. 1994. "Identity theory, identity politics: psychoanalysis, marxism, poststructuralism." Pp. 198–215 in Calhoun 1994a.

Zelizar, Barbie. 1995. Reading the past against the grain: the shape of memory studies." *Critical Studies in Mass Communication* 12: 214–39.

Zelizer, Viviana. 1989. "The Social Meaning of Money: Special Monies." *American Journal of Sociology* 95: 342–77.

Zerubavel, Eviatar. 1991. *The Fine Line: Making Distinctions in Everyday Life.* New York: Free Press.

Zolberg, Vera L. 1990. *Constructing a Sociology of the Arts.* Cambridge: Cambridge University Press.

—— 1993. "Remaking nations: public culture and postcolonial discourse." Pp. 234–50 in Balfe 1993.

Zolberg, Vera L., and Joni Maya Cherbo, eds. 1997 *Outsider Art: Contesting Boundaries in Contemporary Culture.* Cambridge: Cambridge University Press.

Zukin, Sharon. 1991. *Landscapes of Power: From Detroit to Disney World.* Berkeley, Ca.: University of California Press.

Index

Note: Page numbers in *italics* refer to illustrations (or their captions)